ALEXANDER GRAHAM BELL

Alexander Graham Bell

A Life

JAMES MACKAY

John Wiley & Sons, Inc.

New York • Chichester • Weinheim • Brisbane • Singapore • Toronto

For Evelyn Glennie

This book is printed on acid-free paper. ⊗

Copyright © 1997 by James Mackay. All rights reserved
First published in the United States by John Wiley & Sons, Inc.
Published simultaneously in Canada

First published in Great Britain in 1997 as *Sounds Out of Silence: A Life of Alexander Graham Bell* by Mainstream Publishing Company (Edinburgh) Ltd.

This publication is designed to provide accurate and authoritative information in regard to the subject matter covered. It is sold with the understanding that the publisher is not engaged in rendering professional services. If professional advice or other expert assistance is required, the services of a competent professional person should be sought.

Library of Congress Cataloging-in-Publication Data:
Mackay, James A. (James Alexander)
    Alexander Graham Bell : a life / James Mackay.
      p.   cm.
    Includes index.
    ISBN 0-471-24045-1 (cloth : alk. paper)
    1. Bell, Alexander Graham, 1847–1922. 2. Inventors—United
States—Biography I. Title.
TK6143.B4M26   1998
621.385′092
[B]—DC21   97-34231

Printed in the United States of America

10 9 8 7 6 5 4 3 2 1

Contents

Introduction

The seventy-five years of Alexander Graham Bell's life were arguably the most momentous for the progress of mankind. Certainly in the field of communications this was true. In 1847, the year of his birth, railways and the telegraph were still in their infancy; by 1922, the year of his death, public broadcasting had become a reality and already fellow Scotsman John Logie Baird had invented television. In between, man had conquered the air, and less than sixteen years after the first faltering flight, men would cross the Atlantic by aeroplane, and even fly from England to Australia. Radio, television, and even aviation to some extent, depend on the transmission and reception of sounds. The repercussions of this extend infinitely, from hearing aids and diagnostic probes to metal detectors and computers. Sound is all around us in many different forms and coming to us from all directions, so much so that we take it all for granted. Cheap postage, introduced only six years before Bell's birth, revolutionised communications and human relationships; today the telephone is doing the same thing, but in ways and extents which would not have been imaginable even a few years ago. 'It's good to talk,' say British Telecom, and we are encouraged to use the phone more than ever, at home, at work, even driving our cars or walking down the street. The telephone, in fact, has taken over our lives, whether we realise it or not.

There is a story that Bell grew to loathe his own invention, and that on one occasion, when being importuned by a salesman engaged on what must have been an early form of telemarketing, he ripped the instrument from the wall and hurled it across the room in anger and disgust. The story is apocryphal but it symbolises the love-hate relationship we have with the telephone. It can, and often does, ring at an inopportune moment, and there can be few people who have not cursed it at one time or another; but it is impossible to imagine a world without its convenience and comfort. It is an indispensable tool of buying and selling; it is the lifeline of the fire, police and ambulance services and, through organisations like the

Samaritans, it has saved many lives from suicide. The telephone has even revolutionised the way we live and, increasingly, the way we work, making it possible to work and conduct business from the comfort of one's own home. Above all, the telephone has shrunk the world itself, keeping far-flung families and friends in close touch in a far more meaningful way than any other form of communication could ever hope to do. And now video-phone, the seeing telephone, is a reality; within a few years, no doubt, it will be as commonplace as the mobile phone is today.

The gallows and butter-stamp telephones of the 1870s seem outlandish and unbelievably crude when compared with the sleek, streamlined models of the present day, but the amazing thing is that they would still work reasonably well if connected to the modern network. Of course, great refinements and improvements have been wrought in the telephone over the intervening years, but the fundamental principle is still the same.

What is even more remarkable is that the technology that made the telephone possible had been in existence for many years before Bell was even born: Hans Oersted discovered electromagnetism in 1820, and Michael Faraday induction in 1831, while Charles Wheatstone invented the electric telegraph in 1837. The make-and-break principle by which the dots and dashes of the Morse code were transmitted telegraphically led Charles Boursel in France (1854) and Philipp Reis in Germany (1861) to attempt the electrical transmission of speech. So long as scientists approached the problem by this avenue they were doomed to failure. Bell's great contribution to the art of communication was his concept of an undulatory or wave-shaped current which varied in intensity precisely as the air varies in density during the production of sound.

The extraordinary thing is that some of the best scientific minds for two generations had wrestled with the problem but the solution continued to elude them. Yet this young man, still in his twenties, who admitted that he knew very little about electricity, would succeed where others had failed. It could be argued that had he known more about electricity he, too, would have never invented the telephone. But what Alexander Graham Bell possessed were some special skills and expertise. He was the son and grandson of men who each made a valuable contribution to the science of speech. Grandfather Alexander Bell was a shoemaker turned actor and self-taught elocutionist who devised methods of curing or mitigating stammering, stuttering, lisps and other speech impediments. Father Alexander Melville Bell would take his father's pioneer work further, by codifying all the sounds the human voice could produce and inventing Visible Speech as a means of describing sounds visually. And young Alexander Graham Bell would see in Visible Speech a medium through which the congenitally deaf could be made to understand what speech was, and thus free them from the shackles of their deafness.

This, in fact, was his life's work, first, last and foremost. He did not set out to invent the telephone, but he would be the right man, in the right place, at the right time. Had he not been teaching deaf Mabel Hubbard to speak, and had not her father, Gardiner Hubbard, been deeply interested in telegraphy, the telephone might not have been invented when it was. As it happens, the invention depended indirectly on yet another casual factor. Bell was an accomplished pianist, and one evening he entertained the Hubbards. Then he showed them a party trick: he sang a note into the piano, and the instrument responded by sounding the same note back. Furthermore, he added that a tuned instrument would also respond to a telegraphic impulse of the same frequency. What this meant was that Alec had stumbled upon the principle of sending a number of messages simultaneously over a single tele-graph wire. At a time when telegrams could only be sent one at a time, in one direction, this was a startling claim. The Stearns duplex and later the Edison quadriplex systems would permit two and then four messages to be transmitted simultaneously, but what Bell proposed would revolutionise telegraphy and, by making it much cheaper, would have an enormous impact on the communications and commercial development of the United States.

And it was while attempting to perfect the harmonic telegraph that Aleck Bell and his assistant Tom Watson got sidetracked into the trans-mission of the human voice, where Bell's knowledge of acoustics and the physiology of the human ear would prove invaluable. The telephone patent granted to Bell shortly after his twenty-ninth birthday would eventually prove to be the most valuable single patent ever issued.

If a large part of this book is taken up with the trials and tribulations that preceded the triumph of the telephone in 1876 it should not be assumed that the remaining forty-six years of Bell's life were a long, slow anticlimax. He would go on inventing till the day he died; indeed, at that time, he was working on a project for the distillation of sea water in a device small enough to be fitted to lifeboats. It is singularly appropriate that the problem which was exercising his mind in July 1922, shortly before his death, should have been for the benefit of shipwreck survivors. All his life, he had been motivated by a strong desire to help other people less fortunate than himself. Along the way, he also invented the photophone and transformed Edison's imperfect phonograph into the graphophone which paved the way for Berliner's gramophone.

The death of both his baby sons through breathing difficulties impelled him to invent the vacuum jacket, forerunner of the iron lung, while his work on sonics led him to invent the telephonic probe; if it failed to save the life of President Garfield after an assassin's bullet struck him down, it would go on to save the lives of thousands on the battlefield, before the advent of X-rays.

No more than a quirk of fate robbed him of inventing the first heavier-than-air flying machine, though he would have the consolation of immeasurably improving the stability and safety of aircraft. Similarly, his tetrahedral space frame, originally devised for aircraft construction, would later be used in all forms of architecture and structural engineering. In his sixties he was actively engaged in the development of hydrofoils which have in more recent times revolutionised seaborne communications. Perhaps he lacked the single-mindedness of his great rival Edison in carrying invention to a successful commercial conclusion to the same extent, but his papers and notebooks reveal an astonishing range of ideas, many of them a generation or more ahead of their time.

Apart from his inventions, Bell was a great man of science rather than a scientist, although he made a notable contribution to our understanding of the laws of heredity and for several years worked on the principles of eugenics. Infinitely more practical, however, were the ways in which he used his wealth to fund or subsidise many projects, including the periodical *Science*, and putting the fledgling National Geographic Society on its feet. His father-in-law Gardiner Hubbard was its co-founder and first president and Bell himself would succeed him in that office. In time both his son-in-law Gilbert Grosvenor and grandson Melville Bell Grosvenor would give a lifetime of service to this great universal institution. It is particularly fitting that the Society should be the repository of the vast Alexander Graham Bell archives.

But it is for his work on behalf of the deaf that Bell's name deserves to live on. From 21 May 1868 in South Kensington when he taught two little girls, Lotty and Minna, a dozen sounds in the space of an hour, till a month before his death when he was lecturing to the Clarke School, Bell crusaded for the welfare and education of the deaf. Above all, he fought long and hard to liberate the deaf from their silent prison, teaching them to speak and lip-read. It seems hard to grasp the apathy towards his aims and methods and the hostility directed against Bell personally from others who also had the welfare of the deaf at heart, but who contented themselves with sign language and argued against his oral methods. Bell founded the Volta Bureau and the American Association for the Promotion of the Teaching of Speech to the Deaf. These bodies later amalgamated and in 1956 acknowledged their indebtedness to their founder when the name was changed to the Alexander Graham Bell Association for the Deaf, now the world's leading body in this field. The spread of articulation among the deaf, now the norm rather than the rare exception, is his enduring legacy.

Thomas Alva Edison, born in the same year as Bell, summed up the achievement of his rival and friend when he spoke of his 'world-famed invention [which] annihilated time and space, and brought the human family in closer touch'. He was speaking, of course, about the telephone, but doubtless he also had in mind Bell's great humanitarian contribution. Edison, who had once dismissed Bell and his associates as 'a bunch of pirates', would live to eat those words. Increasingly hard of hearing in later life, Edison would become a member of the advisory council of the AAPTSD and help to carry on his late friend's great work.

Immensely famous in his own lifetime and fêted the world over, Bell has the rare distinction of being a household name everywhere, three-quarters of a century after his death. So long as people continue to use the telephone, or the congenitally deaf experience the miracle of conversing like hearing people, the name of Alexander Graham Bell will surely live on.

I must confess that although I was familiar with Bell's role in pioneering the telephone, I was quite unaware of his work in phonetics, acoustics and the education of the deaf, nor did I know of his contribution to the development of aviation, far less his other inventions, or his long-running experiments in sheep-breeding – until 1986 when I visited Baddeck in Nova Scotia and was spellbound by the exhibits in the Alexander Graham Bell National Historical Park and Museum. There and then, I resolved that one day I would produce my own tribute to this truly great man. This biography, in fact, signals the 150th anniversary of his birth.

Over the intervening period, frequent visits to Canada and the United States have given me further opportunities to pursue his remarkable history, while travels all over Britain have enabled me to add considerably to Bell's early life, as well as the momentous year which was part prolonged honeymoon and part promotion of his invention.

My thanks are due to a great many people on both sides of the Atlantic for making this book possible. First of all, I must thank Dr Alan Marchbank of the National Library of Scotland, whose own visit to Beinn Bhreagh reinforced my resolve to write this book. J.W. Stephen, superintendent of the Bell Museum at Baddeck, and his staff afforded me every help with the many different aspects of Bell's life there. Although Bell was an American citizen, and so proud of the fact that he had this put on his tombstone, it is worth remembering that for almost four decades (more than half his lifetime) Bell spent the greater part of each year in his beloved Nova Scotia, and that was where he died in August 1922. I am also indebted to J. Brian Studier, curator of the Bell Homestead in Brantford, Ontario, and Miss E.M.L. Geraghty, historian of Bell Canada, Montreal. My old friend Greg Gatenby in Toronto furnished details on Bell's Canadian period as well as helping in other ways. I must also give special thanks to Mary and Ian MacMillan of Toronto who took my wife and me to Brantford in October 1995. By an amazing coincidence, their son Michael has produced a television film about Bell under the title of *The Sound and the Silence*. I hasten to add that my title for this book was settled three years ago, long before I had seen or heard of this film. Perhaps this is another case of 'great minds thinking alike', but it uncannily parallels the story of the telephone itself, on which a number of inventors were working more or less simultaneously, though quite independently of each other. I hope that this Canadian production will get the screening it merits in the British Isles, perhaps in connection with the sesquicentennial celebrations in 1997.

In the United States the staff of the Alexander Graham Bell Association for the Deaf in Washington provided me with background information on the history of articulation in general, as well as Bell's unique contribution to the subject. In the same city, the staff of the National Geographic Society permitted me to study the vast archives of the Bell Room. Bell is the biographer's dream – and nightmare for, conscious of his place in history, he meticulously preserved every scrap of paper, dating and exhaustively documenting all his researches, experiments and inventions, so that the task of working through this mass of material would be well-nigh impossible. The task of producing the authorised biography of Alexander Graham Bell was outlined by Mabel Hubbard Bell in 1922, soon after his death and shortly before her own untimely end, but forty years elapsed before this monumental task was entrusted to Robert V. Bruce. His book *Alexander Graham Bell and the Conquest of Solitude*, published in 1973, must stand as *the* definitive biography. Immensely detailed and especially valuable for the insights into Bell's work on the harmonic telegraph and telephone, it is a very hard act to follow. What I have attempted here is more of an overview of a long and immensely fruitful life, but along the way I have uncovered a great many details, large and small, especially in regard to Bell's life in Scotland and England.

Nearer home, I have had a great deal of assistance from the staff at Post Office Archives, British Telecom Archives and Historical Information Centre, the British Telecom Museum, the Science Museum, the British Library, Westminster Reference Library, the National Library of Scotland, Dundee District Library, Edinburgh City Library, Glasgow University Library and the Mitchell Library, Glasgow. The staff of Elgin's public library ferreted out details of Bell's time as a teacher at Weston House and helped me to track down the Bells' honeymoon cottage at Covesea, while the staff of the Greenock library provided interesting material on Bell's school for the deaf which he founded there in 1878. Others who have helped with this project in some way include Bruce Allen of Glasgow, Ian Robertson of Toronto and Victor Gregg of Bell South in Atlanta, Georgia. Last, but not least, I must thank my sister Eleanor and her husband, Dr Gordon S. Harris, who helped me with research into the Bell family in St Andrews.

James Mackay, Glasgow, January 1997

1

Edinburgh
1847–62

A boy's will is the wind's will,
And the thoughts of youth are long, lost thoughts.
                              Longfellow, *My Lost Youth*

Edinburgh's *Scotsman* newspaper of 6 March 1847 contained two announcements which were singularly apposite. One was a news item about the imminent arrival of the telegraph: 'When the lines of communication are once fully established, a question asked in London will be received and answered by a person in Edinburgh or Inverness, in little more time than the words could be written on paper.' The other was a brief note intimating that Eliza, wife of Alexander Melville Bell, had been safely delivered of a son on 3 March, the boy taking his father's first name.

The Bell family hailed from Fife, at least seven generations of the menfolk having worked as shoemakers in the ancient university town of St Andrews.[1] James Bell, born in 1726, dabbled in burgh politics and eventually became a bailie, but his chief claim to fame was his close association with Alexander Wilson and John Baine. Wilson is regarded as the father of Scottish typefounding, while Baine had the distinction of casting the first dollar signs at his type-foundry in Philadelphia in 1797. Alexander Bell, grandson of Bailie Bell and son of David Bell and Isabella Swan, was born on 3 March 1790, served his apprenticeship as a shoemaker under his father and continued in that trade till his marriage, on 4 April 1814, to Elizabeth Colvill, a lady seven years his senior.

Elizabeth had pretensions, despite the somewhat dubious circumstances of her birth. She was born at Dairsie, Fife, in 1783 but her birth was never recorded in the parish register, perhaps because her parents, Andrew Colvill and Euphan Smith, did not actually get married till 23 July the following year.[2] Andrew Colvill, born at Leuchars in March 1756, was a medical man in general practice at Gauldry and when he was not

13

ministering to the sick of that village he was making bagpipes and waging a long, fruitless legal battle on rather specious grounds for succession to the title and estates of Lord Colville of Culross. Bloodied but unbowed by lengthy litigation, the old man remained active into his nineties and died at Gauldry on 12 January 1851 in his ninety-fifth year. The manner in which the young cobbler of St Andrews met and wooed Miss Colvill has not been recorded, but the marriage resulted eventually in a radical change of direction for the groom. Alexander Bell did not give up his last and go on the boards, as previous biographers have alleged, but increasingly he became involved in the theatre.

By 1817 he was appearing regularly on the Dundee stage in comic roles and playing Scotch characters, and in January 1818 he was attracting favourable notices in the role of Andrew Fairservice in *Rob Roy* during its first Edinburgh production. The Bells were still domiciled in St Andrews at this time, and it was here that their son David was born on 12 May 1817,[3] followed by Alexander Melville on 1 March 1819. During that year the Bells moved to Edinburgh, renting a flat at 7 St Patrick's Square, where their third child, a daughter named Elizabeth Samuel Bell, was baptised on 20 August 1822. Alexander Bell was listed in the Edinburgh directory as a boot and shoemaker, which contradicts the school of thought which held that his chief occupation was the stage and that he and his wife augmented his precarious income by running a tavern. By Whitsun 1823, however, the Bells were on the move again. Another legend has it that Edinburgh failed to appreciate Alexander's histrionic talents and the promised stage career never developed beyond the occasional bystander in crowd scenes and what he later described as 'the responsible and honourable situation of Prompter'. In fact, Alexander, in the theatrical seasons of 1819–22, had been a valued member of the company at the Theatre Royal under the actor-manager William Murray, a man whose connection with the Bell family was to have scandalous repercussions a few years later.

Back in St Andrews once more, Alexander had not given up on his yearnings to become something more than a cobbler. His stint as a prompter and player of minor roles had trained his voice. He had learned the importance of breathing correctly and mastered the skills of voice projection. These talents, coupled with a commanding presence and a rich, resonant voice, encouraged him to set himself up as a teacher of elocution. He obtained an appointment with the Grammar School as English master, and augmented his teacher's salary by giving occasional readings in the town hall. His self-taught skills as an elocutionist brought him to the attention of Professor Duncan of the university, and in the academic session of 1825–26 Bell was given the use of a lecture room in St Mary's College where he conducted a course of lessons in speech.

Armed with a letter of introduction from Professor Duncan, Alexander Bell moved to Dundee in 1826 to work full time in elocution. During the day he conducted classes and in the evenings gave individual tuition to the wives and children of well-to-do merchants and businessmen. It was during this period that he began to develop an interest in the problems of speech impediment, particularly stammering. Achieving a measure of success with stammerers enhanced his standing in the town, and for a time the Bells prospered. They rented a substantial house in fashionable Tay Street, adjoining the house occupied by their old friend William Murray who was now rector of Dundee Academy. Within a year or two, however, certainly by the spring of 1829, forty-six-year-old Elizabeth had embarked on a reckless affair with Murray, her scandalous conduct exacerbated by the fact (as it emerged later) that sexual intercourse was deemed to have taken place on 18 April, 'the fast-day preceding the dispensation of the Lord's Supper'. Apparently Mrs Bell was in the habit of knocking through the adjoining wall to her lover, to let him know that Alexander had gone out for the evening to teach his private pupils. This was Murray's cue to come next door, while Elizabeth bribed her servant with money and fine clothing to keep quiet.

It seems that the whole of Dundee knew what was going on – all, that is, except the cuckold himself. Late in December 1829, temporarily laid low by some unspecified malady which may have been no more than seasonal over-indulgence, Alexander entrusted Elizabeth with the manuscript of a textbook on speech which he wished to deliver to an Edinburgh publisher. Normally she lodged with friends when visiting the capital but on this occasion the errant wife had an ideal opportunity to meet her lover far from the prying eyes of Dundee. Travelling in separate coaches, they booked in at a hotel of questionable reputation. There was an element of farce when they discovered that their rooms, far from adjoining, were at either end of the corridor. Later, the boot-boy would testify to having witnessed Mrs Bell and her paramour tiptoeing along the corridor in the dead of night, while the chambermaid caught them together in compromising circumstances. Worse still, they were recognised by an acquaintance from Dundee. Inevitably word of the affair got back to Alexander, and by the time Elizabeth returned home he had worked himself into a towering rage. She tried to bluff her way out and stoutly denied any impropriety. Terrified at her husband's new-found fury, she tried to send a letter to Murray by James Stewart, guard of the Tally-ho coach, to warn him. Stewart was to look out for Murray on the coach from Edinburgh to Dundee, but on its journey to the capital the Tally-ho tried to make up lost time and passed the Dundee-bound coach without stopping. On his return to Dundee the following day Stewart thought the simplest solution would be to return the letter to the Bell household, and thus it fell into Alexander's hands. The incriminating words left him in no doubt as to his wife's infidelity. There was a dramatic scene, followed by the woman in a state of near-total breakdown beseeching her servant, Lizzie Baird, to procure her some poison so that she might end her life. Lizzie sensibly refused, and so divorce rather than suicide brought this sorry episode to a messy and extremely expensive conclusion, in July 1831.

To complicate matters, Lizzie Baird, compearing before the Kirk Session of Dundee St Mary's on 22 December 1830 to answer a charge of fornication that was self-evident from the size of her belly, blurted out that the father of the child in her womb was her employer, Alexander Bell, a charge which he strenuously refuted. Both Lizzie (who had been castigated by the Kirk elders as 'a thoroughly bad woman') and Alexander Bell were ordered to appear before the Session on 5 January 1831, but neither presented themselves. By that time Lizzie had returned in disgrace to her parental home in Monifieth where, on 1 April, she gave birth to a daughter whom she named Isabella. No father's name was entered in the parish register so the case against Alexander Bell remains not proven. Five years later, however, Lizzie recovered her respectability by marrying James Mitchell at Dundee.[4]

In July 1833, William Lindsay, Provost of Dundee, gave Alexander a testimonial which stated that 'Mr Bell's private character has been irreproachable'. This character reference may have been a desperate last-ditch attempt to salvage his reputation; for the effect of the divorce, conducted in the savagely recriminatory fashion of the time and compounded by Miss Baird's revelations concerning her unwanted pregnancy, was to alienate Bell's clients who removed their children from his classes. Apart from the loss of earnings Alexander found that his work suffered in general, while legal fees amounting to hundreds of pounds rapidly eroded his savings. By 1832 his annual income was reduced to less than forty pounds, and he was forced to sell off his furniture to pay his rent and move into much more modest accommodation in Union Street. In desperation he sued William Murray for £2,000 damages, but his case, tried in the Court of Session in Edinburgh the following December, was weakened by a fine legal technicality over the admissibility of the intercepted letter as evidence of 'criminal correspondence'. In the end he was obliged to accept a settlement of only £300, which was as much as Murray (who had now lost his lucrative position at the Academy) could afford. With this meagre sum Alexander could at least settle his debts and leave Dundee for ever.[5]

At the break-up of the marriage Elizabeth Bell returned to her native village, taking eleven-year-old Elizabeth with her. For many years she kept house for her widowed father, but after his death in 1851 she moved to Cupar, Fife, where she died on 29 December 1856, in her seventy-fourth year.[6]

Melville, aged fourteen in 1833, stayed with his father, and moved with him to London. The eldest, David, was then sixteen, and although his movements at this time are not known, it seems probable that he, too, accompanied his father to the capital. In a letter of 13 September 1837 from London to his mother, living at Gauldry, David wrote, 'You will be anxious to know if I have given up the Stage. Most likely I will once again tempt the angry main.' From this tantalisingly brief comment it may be deduced that he had spent some part of the intervening years at sea, before following in his father's footsteps and entering the theatre. He went on to say that he was confident of ultimate success 'either as a teacher or an actor', though he dismissed the stage 'from its uncertainty and bad name'. Indeed, shortly after writing this letter, David went to County Durham to take up an appointment at an academy as a teacher of English and elocution.

Early in 1834 Alexander Bell had travelled south to London, settling eventually in Norton Street, around the corner from Portland Place in the fashionable West End. A handbill of 3 December that year implies that he was well established by that date as an expert in

> Elocution and Impediments of Speech. Mr Bell . . . attends Pupils for all departments of Public Speaking. Stammering and other Impediments of Speech, completely and permanently removed. Schools attended on advantageous terms.

Here, also, his long-projected book on speech finally saw the light of day, under the title of *The Practical Elocutionist*. The book, published late in 1834, marked a radical departure in several respects. An ingenious system of symbols helped the reader to visualise speech, and the way in which words should be grouped or emphasised. Its most important feature was the section dealing with stammering which stressed the importance of breath control (with useful insights into the mechanism of the vocal organs) and the mental state of the stammerer – an early recognition of the psychological aspects of the disorder. Two years later he followed this seminal work with *Stammering and other Impediments of Speech* and in 1837 an edition of the New Testament annotated with the symbols as an aid to proper reading. The London *Morning Advertiser* of 5 April 1838 contained a glowing account of one of his public readings, and referred to him as 'the celebrated Professor of Elocution'.

Thus, within five years of the disastrous breakdown of his marriage, Alexander Bell had recovered. His rehabilitation was completed by his second marriage, on 15 April 1834, to Sarah Pain, the widow of a publisher. The second Mrs Bell was a homely soul; but what she lacked in beauty she made up for in other ways, giving her husband the comfort and dependability which he had lacked first time around.

By 1837 both sons were off his hands. In his letter of that autumn to his mother, David had commented on Melville's recent visit to her having worked wonders: 'at least his good looks obtained him several compliments. He had much need of some fresh air after his long confinement.' This referred to a dreary stint as a draper's assistant, working long hours for a pittance, as a result of which the boy's health had suffered. The benefits of the bracing North Sea air at Gauldry encouraged Alexander to send his younger son farther afield in search of health, and in 1838 he was packed off to St John's, Newfoundland, where he lodged with a family friend.

To pay for his board and lodging, Melville took a job as clerk in a shipping office. In a letter to his mother and sister dated 23 September 1838, he wrote that his employer was 'exceedingly kind' and that he got up early twice or thrice weekly to row in the harbour for an hour, 'the finest exercise in the world'. In the exhilarating climate of Newfoundland, Melville was fully restored to health. A watercolour portrait, painted by his fiancée five years later, shows delicate features but there is a strength of character tinged with boyish humour in the lustrous dark eyes. During his sojourn in Newfoundland, Melville became involved in the successful campaign to secure shorter hours and better working conditions for his fellow clerks and shop assistants, as well as organising a class for students of Shakespeare and directing amateur theatricals. Significantly, he also won acclaim for treating stammerers by the Bell system, and on his departure in February 1842 grateful clients joined with his many friends to give him a public dinner and a testimonial to his 'kind and gentlemanly traits'. Ever afterwards he would look back on his three and a half years in the New World with nostalgia.

When twenty-three-year-old Melville returned to London in the spring of 1842 he was more than ready to join his father in his work. Within three months he was taking classes in elocution up to three hours a day. Not content merely to follow his father slavishly, he set about a systematic study of all previously published literature on speech defects and the anatomy and physiology of the vocal organs. He soon discovered that the textbooks in both fields were sadly lacking, and so determined to remedy this. Meanwhile, David Bell was married and settled in Dublin and likewise engaged in teaching elocution. To his boyhood friend George Davis, Melville wrote on 5 July of his own plans: 'I intend to *get married* as soon as I can meet with a young lady to please me.'

In October 1843 Melville paid what was intended as only a brief visit to

Edinburgh where he renewed the acquaintanceship of a young man whom he had met on the ship the previous year. Through this friend he was introduced to an Englishwoman, Eliza Grace Symonds, a painter of miniature portraits who lived with her widowed mother at 33 Dundas Street. Almost fifty years later Melville would record his first impressions of his future wife, in a memoir for his grandchildren:

> It was not exactly a case of love at first sight, but it was a case of *struck* at first sight. I found the lady very pretty, slim, and delicate-looking, and with the sweetest expression I think I ever saw. But she was deaf, and could only hear me with the help of an ear-tube. My sympathy was deeply excited. But she was so cheerful under her affliction that sympathy soon turned to admiration.

Melville was twenty-four, Eliza a day past her thirty-fourth birthday, when they met.[7] This lively, handsome, personable, charming and accomplished young man would be the best birthday present she ever received – and probably the least expected, for there is no evidence of any previous romantic attachment in her life. Melville's impression of Eliza was subjective to say the least. Her portraits show a rather gaunt, beaky profile, the nose long and thin, the chin too pointed, the cheeks too hollow, for anyone who was not madly in love with her to describe her as pretty. With her hair drawn back severely and coiled at the sides, and dressed in unrelieved black, Eliza must have presented a rather forbidding aspect which her deafness and shyness only heightened. The eldest of a family of four, she had had an unhappy childhood; her father Samuel, who had risen from the lower deck to become a surgeon in the Royal Navy, had died in 1818 when she was nine. Her remarkable mother Mary, indomitable and ruthlessly self-sufficient, had somehow raised three sons for the Royal Navy and the colonial service. Eliza, handicapped by her deafness, was intelligent, widely read and cultivated. Above all, she had a placid, equable nature and a sweet temper which immediately endeared her to Melville. She and her mother had apparently come to Edinburgh about 1840, taking lodgings at 59 Castle Street and moving in 1842 to 47 Castle Street before settling in Dundas Street the following year. Miss Symonds was listed in the directories of the period, initially as a teacher of drawing but latterly as a miniature painter.[8]

The young man who had returned to Edinburgh only on a flying visit would actually live there for twenty-two years. Soon he and Eliza were exchanging confidences. Deaf she might be, but Eliza seems to have been amazingly receptive and responsive to Melville's dreams for the future. At the immediate, practical level, however, he asked her advice on where he could find lodgings. Eliza told him that there were vacant rooms in the house where she and her mother resided, so he rented them. Six months later he proposed marriage, and on 19 July 1844 they were wed.

Considering their differences in age, background, temperament and outlook, their marriage was a remarkably happy one, lasting until Eliza's death in January 1897. She was pious and much given to reading her Bible; Melville was a sceptic, but they very soon came to terms with each other's views. Early in their courtship Eliza let it be known that she heartily detested his tobacco habit. 'Yet,' wrote Melville, 'she came not only to tolerate the offensive thing, but to sit by the hour with book or needle in my smoke-laden study; and sometimes even to light my cigar, by taking the first puff.' Melville concluded his affectionate memoir of his late wife, 'She was so kind, so gentle, so loving that during the fifty-two years of our companionship, I never saw a frown on her sweet face.'

The young couple moved into rooms at 15 St Andrew Street, their landlord, William P. Kennedy, occupying the ground floor where he had a stationery and publishing business. Melville lost no time in setting himself up, hiring a classroom at 36 George Street and advertising that he was ready 'to attend pupils in Edinburgh for the perfect adjustment of the articulation in all cases of defective or impeded utterance'. He stated that the system of cure had been practised by his father for upwards of ten years in London, and he himself had numerous testimonials from satisfied customers in all parts of England, Scotland and Ireland:

> The system is purely scientific, and is certain in its results. There can be no relapse: the principles ensure progressive and permanent improvement.
>
> Among Mr A.M. Bell's recent cures in Edinburgh, is a case which was of THIRTY YEARS' STANDING. The gentleman who was the victim of this very severe impediment had been, at different times previously, under several persons who professed to cure, but failed to benefit him. *He now enjoys fluency of utterance.*
>
> Lisping, Burring, Nasal Intonation, and all minor defects of speech, speedily and completely corrected.
>
> The terms depend on the nature of the case, and the circumstances of the pupil; in all cases they are moderate.
>
> Private instruction in Elocution, the Art of Speech, Gesticulation and all Departments of Oratory.
>
> To Professional Speakers and others, who experience Pulmonary Uneasiness, or Articulative Difficulty in Reading or Speaking, Mr Bell can guarantee perfect relief, in a short course of Private Lessons. Distinct Articulation, the Correction of Provincialisms in Speech, Improvement and Modulation of the Voice, Systematic respiration, and the acquirement of a

neat and efficacious system of Gesture, are the certain results of Mr Bell's System.[9]

Melville followed his father into print early in 1845, when he published a modest pamphlet entitled *The Art of Reading*. At the end he included an advertisement announcing that 'Mr Bell undertakes the perfect and permanent eradication of Stammering, of however long standing, and however convulsive its paroxysms'. Sales of the pamphlet brought a modest return, but set 'Professor' Bell on the road to success. Soon the remarkable trio of Alexander in London, David in Dublin and Melville in Edinburgh were in a fair way to revolutionising the science of elocution. It was hard getting started, but from modest beginnings Melville gradually built up his practice while Eliza carried on with her miniature painting and ran a frugal household. 'We were not accustomed to luxuries, and therefore did not miss them.' By the beginning of 1845 they had saved enough to be able to move to more salubrious surroundings, taking a first-floor flat at 16 South Charlotte Street at an annual rental of £22 8s.

It was here, on 13 May that year, that Eliza gave birth to the first of her three children, Melville James. Unusually, for the period, the baby was not named after his father's father. Instead he was given his father's middle name and also named after Eliza's eldest brother James. The breach of etiquette was mended two years later when Eliza brought forth her second son, named simply Alexander after his paternal grandfather.

Superficially, Charlotte Square has not changed much since it was laid out two centuries ago; the douce little octagonal park which occupies its centre is still framed by the elegant façades designed by Robert Adam, dominated on the west side by the lofty pillared portico of St George's Church, and affording a splendid view on the east along still fashionable George Street to the Melville Monument in St Andrew's Square. But the houses are now offices and even the church has become West Register House; where the Bells and other solid burghers of the West End once worshipped there is now the repository of Scotland's archives. The south side of the square may lack the resplendent charm of the north, its buildings being generally more modest in scale; but it does have a major historic landmark, the house in which Alexander Bell was born.[10] Access to the Bell apartment was through an unpretentious doorway, unlike the impressively arched and fanlighted entrance of the house next door and those on the north and south sides of the square, but the interior was commodious, with lofty ceilings and well-proportioned windows. Between her second and third pregnancies Eliza and her family moved to a much larger flat at 13 Hope Street on the south-west corner of the square, with windows fronting on to the square itself. Here, on 20 September 1848, Eliza gave birth to her third son, christened Edward Charles after Eliza's other brothers, both now rising rapidly through the ranks of the New South Wales bureaucracy.

This flat was Aleck's home from his second to his seventh year, though he had little recollection of it when he penned his family memoirs. A miniature by Eliza, painted when Aleck was about five, shows a solemn little boy with light brown hair, penetrating dark eyes, a lofty forehead and a long nose, a feature inherited from his mother.

Aleck's earliest memories were unpleasant, but perhaps that is why they remained in his mind.[11] The first was of a family outing to Ferry Hill, when he strayed into a field of wheat standing taller than himself. He sat quietly in the centre 'trying hard to hear the wheat grow' but all he heard was the quiet soughing and the drowsy hum of insects. Suddenly he was stricken with panic, lost and all alone, and struggled blindly to find his way out. Presently he lay down exhausted and cried himself to sleep. Later he was roused by the sound of his father's voice crying his name. Running towards the sound he emerged from the wheat straight into the reassuring arms of his father.

Some time later he was confined to bed with scarlet fever, in those days a deadly disease. In his delirium he looked up and saw the hooded figure of a woman standing silently at the foot of the bed, the eyes in her shadowy face fixed upon him. Young as he was, it occurred to him that the apparition might be nothing but a figment of his fevered imagination, so slowly, gingerly, he crept out of bed and approached the silent figure with trepidation – only to discover that the ghost was nothing more than his mother's hooded cloak draped over the bed-post. Thus reassured, he snuggled down in bed again, but the figure continued to haunt him. Eventually he mustered the strength and courage to get out again and remove the cloak from the bed-post. But even after he laid it down on the counterpane it continued to terrorise him and in the end he gave way to his fear and screamed for help.

Another early memory is of coming across some writing paper and a pencil in the compendium of a family guest. Though he did not yet know his alphabet he was seized by the desire to write a letter, just as grown-ups did, and he duly folded it, placed it in an envelope, scribbled the name and address, and affixed a penny stamp which he filched from the compendium. So far so good, but his undoing came when he handed the letter to the servant-girl to post for him. She took one look at the childish scribble and began laughing loudly. At that moment Melville Bell bellowed to him from a nearby room. Aleck snatched back the letter and hid it behind his back as he answered the parental summons. It was at this precise moment that he was first conscious of right and wrong.

Melville, sensing his son's unease, soon discovered the epistle and laughed, as the servant had done, but pointedly asked Aleck where he had got the stamp. Now Aleck realised his misdemeanour and stuttered that his mother had given it to him. 'Ask your mother to come here,' said Melville, but Aleck darted off and hid behind the massive wardrobe in the guest-room. From there he heard the hunt for him ranging all over the house. Through a chink he watched with bated breath as his parents frantically searched in cupboards and under the bed but to no avail. Eventually they went away. Hours ticked by, mealtimes came and went, and day passed into night. Melville, now afraid that the boy had somehow got out of the house, stood in the hallway shouting in his powerful voice, 'Aleck, come out and I will forgive you.' This yielded no result, so the search was resumed, more thoroughly than before, and this time the tiny fugitive was discovered cowering behind the wardrobe. The terrified boy clearly expected retribution – and he got it. A thrashing was duly administered in Papa's study, a painful incident seared into Aleck's memory for the rest of his life.

There was one characteristic which marked out the Bells from their contemporaries and rivals in the field of speech improving. While Thomas Braidwood and his nephew Joseph Watson sought by every means to shroud their work in elocution with an air of mystery, Alexander Bell had from the outset believed in making the principles of his work in curing speech defects plain, and communicating them to the world at large. This admirable policy was pursued by his two sons, and explains the readiness with which Melville laboured to put his ideas and methods in print. A clear thinker, he also had the ability to express himself as lucidly in print as in the spoken word. In his *Principles of Elocution* he defined elocution simply as 'the effective expression of thought and sentiment by speech, intonation and gesture'. He was at pains to stress that what he was setting forth was a series of principles, but not rigid rules:

> Elocutionary exercise is popularly supposed to consist of merely Recitation, and the fallacy is kept up both in schools and colleges . . . This is a miserable trifling with an art of importance, and art that embraces the whole SCIENCE OF SPEECH.

This was enunciated in his 312-page book, *A New Elucidation of the Principles of Speech and Elocution*, which was published at six shillings and sixpence in 1849 by his former landlord William Kennedy. But this was not the end of Melville's work, merely a beginning. Having set out his principles in print, he reviewed them and realised that there were enormous gaps in the understanding of human speech and how it was created. Melville himself was blessed with one of the finest voices of his generation, remarkable for its purity, flexibility, precision and resonance. He used it effectively not only in the classroom but also on the lecture platform, giving readings from Shakespeare and Dickens in Edinburgh, Glasgow and other Scottish towns and cities. At an early stage in his career Melville recognised the importance of training the ear; one must recognise a tone to be able to reproduce it exactly. He also laid emphasis on intellectual and emotional understanding as a prerequisite of mechanical skill in speech. Speech training, he argued, should be not for show but for the art and business of living. In his writings he distilled the quintessence of the elocutionary movement since its beginnings in the middle of the eighteenth century, and summed up the best thoughts of others in the field. This seminal work, however, was no more than a foretaste of what was to come. In this book he looked forward to a time when it should be possible 'to reconstruct our alphabet, and furnish it with invariable marks for every appreciable variety of vocal and articulate sound . . . with a natural analogy and consistency which would explain to the eye their organic relations'.

This aim had been the fantasy of elocutionists for almost a century, and to attain it would cost Melville Bell a further fifteen years of intensive labour and thought. Slowly and systematically he collected and tabulated all the oral sounds he came across, until existing letters and diphthongs ran out. Then he devised fresh symbols to aid his memory. Gradually, as relations between the elements of speech fell into place, he revised his symbols to take note of these relations. Along the way he developed a shorthand system which, though in many respects superior, could not overturn the Pitman system, and he continued with his practical work on elocution which resulted in *The Standard Elocutionist*. The preface indicates that his brother David assisted in its compilation. A concise introduction encapsulating all his theories on elocution was followed by a lengthy anthology of literary pieces systematically arranged for elocutionary practice. This book was a steady seller for almost half a century; no fewer than 168 printings had appeared in Britain by 1892, while over a quarter of a million copies were sold in the United States alone. Naïvely, Melville had sold his rights to his publisher and thus recouped little monetary benefit, but the book enhanced his reputation enormously. It broadened Melville's popularity on the lecture circuit and, in turn, brought him more and more influential pupils, including educationists, ministers of religion, rising politicians and the children of the aristocracy. More importantly, his work was recognised at an academic level when he was appointed to lecture on a regular basis at the University of Edinburgh. With the status and security conferred by this position, Melville was enabled, in the autumn of 1853, to purchase the house at 13 South Charlotte Street, the second house down from the south-east corner of the square and facing Aleck's birthplace. The new house was what six-year-old Aleck would ever afterwards regard as his Edinburgh home.[12]

Melville let out the ground and first floors, to a dentist named Robert Watt and an English cabinetmaker named George Brown, together with their families, servants and lodgers, while he and his family occupied the second and top floors, comprising ten large, well-appointed rooms. The second floor had a guest-room, Melville's study and the main sitting-room, while the nursery was at the rear of the top floor, with sloping ceilings under the roof. At the front, with a bow-fronted dormer window, was the boudoir occupied by Aleck's English grandmother, Mrs Symonds, whose savings had helped Melville to buy the house. If he craned his neck, Aleck could gaze from Granny Symonds' window on to the Pentland Hills to the south and to the Firth of Forth with the grey-blue hills of Fife beyond.

Melville Bell had received his early education at home from his talented father. Similarly, Melly, Aleck and Ted were tutored in the cosy domestic atmosphere, though Melville seems to have had little direct hand in their instruction. Most, if not all, of this devolved on Eliza who imbued her sons deeply with her own piety 'at least until I reached years of discretion', Aleck would later note wryly. In the custom of the period, attendance at St George's was regular and rigorous. While the boys looked up the hymns and texts for Eliza to read along, Melville took down the minister's sermons in his own shorthand, so that he could read them back to his wife afterwards. Eliza habitually used a clumsy ear trumpet, but Aleck alone mastered the technique of conversing with her without such mechanical contrivance. He would speak in a low, well-modulated voice close to her forehead and, remarkably, she heard him with reasonable clarity.

She taught the boys not only the customary range of subjects but also to draw and paint, to play the piano and to communicate with her by means of the English two-handed sign language. Although all three sons acquired an excellent grounding in academic subjects by this home tuition, differing skills and aptitudes produced varying results. Aleck excelled as a caricaturist, but lacked the patience and discipline to produce good paintings. On the other hand, Ted was the best draughtsman and emulated Eliza's skill with pencil and brush. Remarkably, for someone so hard of hearing, Eliza was a beautiful pianist, able to hear every note and subtlety of tone by resting the bell of her ear trumpet on the sounding board. It was said that she played Scottish melodies so expressively that listeners could almost hear the words. Both Melly and Ted would become competent pianists, but Aleck surpassed them, being able to sight-read music with great ease. Music dominated his adolescence; it would flood his mind in the still of the night, disturbing his sleep and leaving him with a hungover feeling the following morning. Fragments of tunes would torment him for days on end until he had got them out of his system. Eliza would call these bouts Aleck's 'musical fever'.[13]

The boy undoubtedly had a rare gift for music, and Eliza was determined that he should develop it to the fullest. Perhaps he might become a concert pianist. To that end she secured the services of Auguste Benoit Bertini. Though not so famous as his celebrated brother Henri Jerome (both born in London of French émigré parents), Auguste, who had settled in Edinburgh, was noted for his composition of chamber music and piano studies, and was a popular figure on the concert platform with his performances of Chopin and Liszt as well as his own compositions. For a time Aleck was swept up in the heady romanticism of the period, and under Bertini's expert tuition made spectacular progress; but Bertini died suddenly, and somehow the magic evaporated. Other, more mundane, aspects of education now loomed larger.

In 1857 Aleck and Ted followed Melly into James Maclaren's Academy at 11 Hamilton Place, a school located unobtrusively in a plain terraced house. The rather nondescript exterior belied the fact that this was something of a powerhouse in teaching, for Maclaren was one of those reforming educationists far ahead of his time. Maclaren himself was a close friend of Melville Bell who shared his views, and Maclaren's sons James and William were coeval with the Bell brothers. This was a very happy period in Aleck's life, and the transition from instruction at his mother's knee was made painlessly at the age of ten. In the course of the following year he also took the first major decision of his life. About this time a young man named Alexander Graham, a former pupil of Melville's in Newfoundland, came to Edinburgh and lodged with the family. Aleck hero-worshipped this youth, to the extent that when it came to his eleventh birthday party, on 3 March 1858, he let it be known that what he wanted most of all as a birthday present was a new name. Both of his brothers had two Christian names, and plain Alexander Bell was not good enough. Melville sagely conceded the point and when he rose to toast the birthday boy at dinner that evening he named him as 'Alexander Graham Bell'.[14]

One of Aleck's closest boyhood friends was Ben Herdman, barely a year younger, who had been sent to Melville for the eradication of stammering. Ben's father John was a corn merchant and proprietor of Sunbury House and Bell's Mill (no connection), a flour mill located nearby in Dean Village by the Water of Leith. The mill and the picturesequely wooded ravine of the river became Aleck's favourite haunts where he could escape from the growing pressures of city life. John and Mina Herdman had eight children, ranging in age from Helen, twenty-five in 1861, to baby Mina. The first four were grown up by the time Aleck met Ben. There was a five-year gap between James and Ben who was the eldest of the younger children. He and his sisters Margaret and Annie would, for a couple of years, be Aleck's constant companions.

Melville and Eliza themselves were rustics at heart, and in 1858 they purchased a pleasant two-storey stucco house on the outskirts of Edinburgh at Trinity, an area near the fishing village of Newhaven which was then coming into fashion as a holiday resort. In the 1850s speculative builders from the nearby city began throwing up holiday homes that rejoiced in such names as Grecian Cottage, Gothic Cottage, Mayville, Woodville and Rose Villa. The Bells' home from home had a more literary flavour, being known as Milton Cottage. Here, only two miles north-east of the city centre, were windswept sandy beaches, open fields and winding country lanes to be explored on long summer rambles. The house itself was something of an oddity, with an impressive brick tower affording magnificent views across the Firth from its battlemented roof, but its chief attraction was a stone pulpit standing in the garden where the boys endlessly practised their oratory. For more than a decade, the Bells would spend their weekends at Trinity, a welcome escape from the daily grind of city life. At Charlotte Square the boys were invariably turned out like little gentlemen, in stiff Eton collars and high-crowned silk hats; but at Trinity they ran wild in the scruffiest of old clothes. Not surprisingly, Aleck in old age would look back on the liberal régime at Milton Cottage with the fondest of memories, recollecting that it was 'my real home in childhood'.

Melville let his hair down, and joined his sons in their capers. Besides them were James and William Maclaren, Ben, Margaret and Annie Herdman, and Aleck's cousins, Elizabeth, Mary and Louisa Symonds, the three lively daughters of James White Symonds who had retired from the navy, settled in Edinburgh and married Elizabeth Bell, Melville's sister. James, the retired naval officer, gave lessons in navigation to aspiring mariners at his home in Gardner's Crescent which became another of Aleck's favourite haunts.

This network of close friends and relatives formed one great big extended family. Aleck had inherited his mother's diffidence and serious-ness, and his ertswhile playmates would later recall him as thoughtful, restrained and shy; but he gradually responded to the rough and tumble of the other children and became (superficially, at any rate) outgoing and extrovert. This was an era of home entertainment and everyone was encouraged to develop his or her talents for the benefit of the others. While Melville and Eliza would play duets on the flute and piano, Ted had a fine tenor voice and Melly had extraordinary gifts for impersonation and legerdemain, which he often combined in outrageous practical jokes. Melly also had a talent for the comic monologue, but Aleck's chief party piece (when he was not playing the piano) was an imaginary bee-chase, matching the buzz of the insect with a balletic mime that reduced his audience to helpless laughter.

Aleck, it is clear, could rise to the occasion; but he seems to have been rather overwhelmed by the larger-than-life ebullience of his father and elder brother. One of Melville's obsessions around this period was photography, still in its infancy, and the earliest portrait now extant of Aleck (other than miniatures painted by Eliza) is a photograph taken in 1858 at Milton Cottage. Given the time exposure required, it is hardly surprising that the picture shows a very solemn boy, his inward-slanting brows knitted in perplexity, puzzlement or suspicion (though he may only have been squinting with the sun in his eyes). His aquiline nose, thin, straight upper lip and unassertive chin suggested to an earlier biographer intensity and introspection, with the look of a quick, alert, somewhat delicate boy.[15] Another photograph, taken at Trinity a few months later, shows a robust, more assertive figure, the features suggesting vigour and self-assurance. Annie Herdman later described Aleck in his early teens as 'tall and handsome, with long, black hair, which he had a trick of always throwing back'. Aleck and his brothers, from their Symonds inheritance, could not be described as handsome by conventional criteria, but those who knew them personally all attest to their powerful attractiveness arising from strength of personality and character.

Essentially the teenage Aleck was a loner, delighting in escaping from the noisy camaraderie. 'In boyhood,' he wrote to his future wife eighteen years later, 'I have spent many happy hours lying among the heather on the Scottish hills – breathing in the scenery around me with a quiet delight that is even now pleasant for me to remember.' And his cousin Mary Symonds would recall many years later (in 1908) how one of Aleck's favourite haunts was Corstorphine Hill. Here, on the grassy knoll known as Rest-and-be-thankful, he would lie back on a summer's day watching the seagulls soaring and gliding, and he would endlessly ponder on the mysteries of flight.

Aleck also went through youthful phases of collecting. For a time botany was a consuming interest and he collected specimens of flowers and grasses during his rambles, not only in the environs of Edinburgh but from his grandfather and uncle in London and Dublin. Melville, however, insisted that each specimen had to be properly mounted and annotated with its full scientific name; but the struggles with the Latin polysyllables 'spoiled the whole thing for me'. Aleck could concentrate enormous energy and persistence on a project that captured his imagination, but he saw little purpose in memorising jaw-breaking Latin names, and so dropped botany. Instead, birds' eggs caught his interest and this subject got his undivided attention. Characteristically, he was not content merely to amass specimens of blown eggs, but puzzled over the incubation of eggs and the hatching process. When he placed the egg of one species in the nest of another to see what happened, he was mortified when the fledgling, in cuckoo fashion, ejected its smaller fellows from the nest.

Thereafter he concentrated on animals. Milton Cottage acquired a veritable menagerie of cats, dogs, mice, rabbits and guinea pigs, and there was even a tank for toads, frogs and newts. To Melly and Ted cats and dogs, even rabbits, were pets; but to Aleck they were objects of scientific study. He drew the line at killing in the interests of science, but when he came across a dead creature he would dissect it and study its anatomy minutely. One of the rooms at the top of the house in Charlotte Street became Aleck's study and laboratory, and here he founded a Society for the Promotion of Fine Arts among Boys, enrolling his brothers and classmates. Each member was a professor, Aleck being designated Professor of Anatomy. In the course of a lecture before this group of youthful savants, Aleck dramatically thrust a knife into the belly of a dead piglet. The gas trapped in the intestines escaped with a loud groan, whereupon the meeting broke up in disorder as the boys, led by 'Professor' Bell, stampeded out of the room and careered headlong downstairs.

Melville's enthusiasm for photography rubbed off on his sons, all of whom not only learned the tricks of taking a good picture, but mastered the technical aspects. Melville taught them to coat the glass plates with collodion, dipping them in a bath of silver nitrate. In the family dark-room Aleck and his brothers perfected the art of developing and printing. This, at least, was one hobby that would remain with him all his life.

Aleck was about eleven or twelve when he devised his first practical invention. He and Ben Herdman had been playing rowdily around the flour mill when Ben's father called them into his office and in exasperation said, 'Why don't you do something useful?' When Aleck asked what he had in mind, John Herdman picked up a handful of grain and remarked, 'If you could only take the husks off this wheat you would be of some help.' Aleck took the suggestion to heart and began experimenting with a nail brush. This worked well enough at removing the husks, but the problem was how to convert this laborious manual task to a mechanical process. At the mill there was a machine containing rotating paddles, used for some other purpose. Aleck reasoned that if the interior were lined with brushes the paddles might force the grain against it so that the husks were shucked off. Eventually he put his ideas into practice and found that it worked amazingly well. Aleck's dehusking machine was put into operation and worked efficiently for a number of years. 'So far as I remember,' wrote Aleck many years later, 'Mr Herdman's injunction to do something useful was my first incentive to invention, and the method of cleaning wheat the first fruit.'[16]

Annie Herdman also recalled that her brother and Aleck went through a phase where they were always trying to invent things, though she doubted whether they were successful. Perhaps with the benefit of hindsight, however, she commented that Aleck's interest in the transmission of sound was kindled by the vibration of wires in a field fence. It is impossible to verify this, though significantly Aleck himself made no mention of it in his reminiscences. Yet an interest in the transmission of sound may have suggested itself to him through observing the working of his mother's ear trumpet.

In October 1858, at the beginning of the winter term, Aleck and Ted were enrolled at the Royal High School of Edinburgh, whither Melly had proceeded a couple of years earlier. Thirty years previously, the High School had been translated from the Old Town to a commanding position on the flank of Calton Hill. Today, this impressive building in the best classical style of the 1830s has been converted for use as a parliament building, against the time when Scotland might once more have a say in its own affairs. No less an authority than Robert Louis Stevenson, in his *Edinburgh: Picturesque Notes*, extolled the merits of this building, chiefly on account of the magnificent views it offered of all Edinburgh's best landmarks and scenery.

Aleck has left us only tantalising glimpses of his time at the High School. To Gilbert Grosvenor he wrote in 1906 describing an incident where his Christian upbringing was sorely tested. When one of his classmates slapped his face in the playground, Aleck calmly offered the other cheek, and got a hearty slap there too. Having run out of cheeks, Aleck proffered a fist and the two boys went at it hammer and tongs until separated by a master. After that, Aleck had no more fights on his own account, though sometimes he stepped in to protect Ted from playground bullies.

The four years which Aleck spent at the High School marked a transition in educational methods and recreations. When he first attended the school boys still habitually went around with a *clackan* strapped to their wrist, a wooden bat for playing hails or shinty that could also be pressed into service as a weapon should the need arise. But by the summer of 1860 the High School boys were granted permission 'to play at cricket in Holyrood Park', and football along the rules of Rugby School followed soon afterwards.

The curriculum was still organised on traditional lines, with English, mathematics, history, geography, Latin and the rudiments of science for all. Pupils were divided into Classics and Moderns, the former studying Greek while the latter concentrated on chemistry, physics and natural history at a more advanced level. Surprisingly, in view of his subsequent career, Aleck opted for the classical course (or probably was obliged by Melville to take it). It is not surprising, therefore, to discover that Aleck was an indifferent pupil according to his form master James Donaldson, a brilliant educator who went on to become Rector of the High School before ending as Principal of St Andrews University.[17] Not even Donaldson, who had an uncanny talent for motivating the dullest schoolboy, seems to have roused Aleck. He coasted along, usually somewhere about the middle of the class, and exhibiting none of those traits of genius one usually associates with men whose inventions change the world. To be sure, Aleck read fluently enough and appeared to have the family aptitude for recitation, but apart from a minor talent for doggerel rhyme he did not distinguish himself in any way. One of his few surviving juvenile pieces was inspired by the relief of Lucknow at the end of the Sepoy Mutiny in India:

> Victoria, Queen Victoria,
> She rules a mighty band,
> Who'll stand by her for ever,
> To guard their Native Land.[18]

Melly, predictably, took first prize for recitation in 1858, a special award for reading and recitation in 1860, and second prize in French pronunciation in 1862,[19] but regarding Aleck and Ted the High School prize lists remain totally silent. Aleck ran swiftly over his schooldays in his reminiscences: 'I passed through the whole curriculum of the Royal High School, from the lowest to the highest class, and graduated, but by no means with honours, when I was about fourteen years of age.'[20] In fact, he left school in the summer of 1862, at the age of fifteen, having completed the first four forms only.

2

Out in the World

1862–70

The noblest prospect which a Scotchman ever sees is the high road that
leads him to England.

Samuel Johnson, 6 July 1763

In London, Grandfather Bell's career over a period of almost thirty years
had had its ups and downs. When Melville had returned from Newfoundland in 1842, Alexander had built up a respectable clientele at his residence
in Norton Street, but had ambitions to bring elocution to the masses. He
even got as far as announcing a project of 'National and Simultaneous
Eloquence' in which it was hoped that upwards of five hundred pupils
would take part. But like so many of his grand ideas, it never had any hope
of succeeding, and when Melville let it be known that he intended
remaining in Edinburgh his father had to soldier on, preferring to deal with
stammerers on an individual basis. Gradually he worked up a lucrative
business in elocution, training ministers of religion and would-be public
speakers and charging up to a hundred guineas for a three-month course.
At a time when that sum represented the annual salary of many clerks and
most skilled manual workers, it would not have taken many pupils to give
Alexander and Sarah Bell a very comfortable living. By 1849, indeed, they
had moved to a more prestigious address in Bond Street, but later that year
Alexander faced yet another of those reversals of fortune that periodically
beset him. In desperation he applied for a position at King's College, even
importuning his sons into furnishing glowing testimonials; but nothing
came of it and, in straitened circumstances for some inexplicable reason, he
was forced to vacate his Bond Street premises. He considered moving back
to Scotland, but Melville came to the rescue and lent his father sufficient
funds to tide him over.

Alexander and Sarah rented an elegant eleven-room house at 18
Harrington Square near Regents Park. This part of London's fashionable

West End was then in course of development and Alexander was obviously delighted with the move when he wrote to Melville on 26 May 1850: 'The house is new, elegantly ornamented, and, certainly, *most* delightfully situated.' It was a handsome four-storey terraced house with a twin-pillared portico and tall windows opening on to a wrought-iron balcony that overlooked a private park. Rental and rates came to about two pounds a week, but now that he was teaching again (and renting out several rooms to suitable lodgers), Alexander felt secure once more.

Here he and Sarah passed an idyllic decade, which ended in her death in March 1860. Now, at the age of seventy, Alexander was on his own again. He still had his work, of course, and if that were not enough there were lectures and literary pursuits. He retained his bearing and magisterial presence in old age. A photograph of him about this period shows finely chiselled features, penetrating, sagacious eyes and a lofty forehead crowned by a magnificent mop of curly white hair. One can easily imagine audiences spellbound as he lectured on 'Parliament and the Social Order' or 'Humbug', or gave his series of 'Morning Shakespearian Readings'.[1] Professor Bell (it was never more than a self-assumed courtesy title) regularly coached the young ladies who came to Cavendish College in Wimpole Street to give their speech and manners a polish, and despite the failure to secure a permanent position at King's College, there was occasional university teaching as well.

Alexander also had literary ambitions. Like his sons and grandsons (and probably most of the literate population of the period) he fancied himself as a poet. Never a man to do anything by halves, in 1846 he produced a masterpiece of epic proportions entitled *The Tongue, a Poem in Two Parts*. In 1,232 lines of blank verse he celebrated the former glories of elocution and mourned the decline of the art of speaking. The following year, however, he returned to his old love, the stage, by writing a five-act play entitled *The Bride*. In the opening scene the valet Allplace comments:

> How much I have improved the manners of this family . . . Polishing a prosy lawyer into a tolerable baronet is a task to break a man's back . . . I was taken into this family for the sake of example. The entire establishment, including Sir Cicero himself, was confoundedly vulgar.

Alexander sent a copy of this play to his son David in Dublin and many years later David's son Chichester showed it to his closest friend, George Bernard Shaw, on whom, despite its shortcomings, it evidently made a considerable impression. He shamelessly borrowed Allplace as the prototype of his Professor Henry Higgins whom he launched before the world in 1913 in *Pygmalion*. It was probably no coincidence that Shaw placed Higgins's laboratory in the very street where Alexander Bell had taught the young ladies of Cavendish College, but lest his debt to the pioneers of phonetics be overlooked Shaw provided the text of his play with a lengthy preface touching on a subject which was ever dear to his heart, and to which a large part of his considerable fortune would ultimately be devoted, the reform of the English alphabet:

> The English have no respect for their language, and will not teach their children to speak it. They cannot spell it because they have nothing to spell it with but an old foreign alphabet of which only the consonants – and not all of them – have any agreed speech value. Consequently no man can teach himself what it should sound like from reading it . . . The reformer we need most today is an energetic phonetic enthusiast: that is why I have made such a one the hero of a popular play.
>
> There have been heroes of that kind crying in the wilderness for many years past. When I became interested in the subject towards the end of the eighteen-seventies, the illustrious Alexander Melville Bell, the inventor of Visible Speech, had emigrated to Canada, where his son invented the telephone . . .[2]

It is ironic that Melville and Aleck should be thus remembered, while Alexander was forgotten.

For more than a year Alexander lived alone, but kept in close touch with Melville by post. As the latter confided his worries about young Aleck, the old man perceived that the boy was being overwhelmed by his father and elder brother. Clearly he needed the space to develop his own personality and at last Alexander came up with the perfect solution: send the boy to London. Aleck would have his education rounded off and would provide company for his lonely old grandfather. Melville readily assented and in October 1862 Aleck boarded the train south, a moment that was 'the turning point of my whole career'.[3]

In best *Pygmalion* fashion, Grandfather Bell peremptorily condemned Aleck's provincial clothing and took him immediately to Savile Row to be accoutred in the latest London fashions. The gauche Edinburgh schoolboy emerged as a dapper young gentleman, elegantly arrayed and finished off with a silk topper, the finest kid gloves and a gold-topped cane. Gone was the freedom of Milton Cottage; seven days a week he was expected to turn out like a fashion plate, his only recreation a sedate promenade round the handkerchief-sized lawn of Harrington Square. Anything remotely suggesting running, jumping or other strenuous exercise was definitely *outré*. This might have been a stifling period for the adolescent Aleck, but life in the metropolis had its compensations. At home he had been completely dependent on his father doling out pocket money in small amounts and making his son account for every penny of it, but in London Aleck had a regular remittance from Melville, and Grandfather Bell gave him an entirely free hand in its expenditure. Essentially the old man treated the boy as an equal, and Aleck appreciated this. 'We became companions and friends,' he wrote simply, many years later.

Alexander dedicated himself to grooming and polishing his grandson and pursued this course singlemindedly. Together they read through the plays of Shakespeare and Aleck was set to learn all the great soliloquies from the histories and tragedies. Contemporary novels were frowned upon; Aleck's time would be better spent in concentrating on the best works of English literature to improve his mind. Above all, Grandfather Bell succeeded in motivating his young charge as neither Melville nor James Donaldson had hitherto been able to. Something of the old man's ideas of humanism and social justice also rubbed off on Aleck at this time. Alexander, who had started life as a humble shoemaker and had raised himself by his own efforts, extolled the merits of education as the means of developing natural ability and materially improving the lot of the poorest and most deprived in society. The criminal classes were, with very few exceptions, 'the neglected portion of the community . . . our brethren, God's creatures . . . the products of man's neglect, and not innate vicious-ness'. By the same argument he despised the antiquated and outmoded class structure of Britain, and in particular the system of hereditary titles. A free thinker in politics and religion, he abhorred dogma and orthodoxy in any shape or form. If education was the key to the ideal meritocracy which he craved, then speech was the key to communication that was vital to all educative processes.

In March 1863 Aleck celebrated his sixteenth birthday. From his father he received an additional half-sovereign and a letter:

> God bless you, my dear boy, and may you ever be as happy as I have tried to make you during your past life! We miss you sadly when we assemble by the fireside at the cottage, but we are reconciled to your absence by the fact that you are good to grandpapa and have been a great comfort to him in his illness, and also that you are making good progress in your studies. You will have cause of thankfulness all your life that you had the benefit of such a training as my father has lovingly afforded you.

During the preceding winter Alexander had gone down with a heavy cold which, exacerbated by winter fogs and damp cold weather, deepened into a severe bronchial infection. The old man's stamina was sorely tested but, thanks to the devoted nursing of his housekeeper, he pulled through.

Increasingly, however, he would have to rely on others, and such responsibility was too much for his teenage grandson. In the early summer of 1863 Melville journeyed to London to see how his father was keeping, but mainly to reclaim his son. Even he was gratified by the startling transformation. Physically Aleck had shot up and filled out, but the change lay more in attitude and outlook. In place of the awkward, clumsy, diffident schoolboy was an elegant young man of poise and self-assurance. 'From this time forth, my intimates were men rather than boys, and I came to be looked upon as older than I really was . . . The year with my grandfather converted me from a boy somewhat prematurely into a man.'[4]

One of the purposes of Melville's visit was to consult Charles Wheatstone (1802–75). A maker of musical instruments, Wheatstone had been intrigued by the sounding boards of harpsichords and pianos which led him to enquire into the mysteries of vibrations and acoustics. Despite his almost pathological shyness he had been appointed Professor of Experimental Philosophy at King's College, London, at the young age of thirty-two, and about the same year determined the speed of electrical discharge in conductors by means of a revolving mirror, a piece of research that was to have enormous repercussions. The great velocity of electrical transmission suggested the possibility of utilising it for sending messages, and in 1837 Wheatstone patented the electric telegraph. A polymath, he was fascinated by cryptography and deciphered a number of manuscripts in the British Museum before inventing a decoding machine. Among his many inventions were the concertina, the stereoscope and the kaleidophone, a device which made visible the movements of a sounding body. He was a prolific researcher into all manner of physical phenomena and wrote papers on the human eye, the physiology of vision, binocular vision and colour, though his most important discoveries were in the field of electricity. In 1868, on the perfection of the automatic telegraph, he was knighted for his services to science and died in 1875.

At the age of nineteen Wheatstone had mystified and entertained visitors to his father's music shop with the enchanted lyre, a contrivance in which tuned metal rods were sounded by vibrations transmitted over a distance by means of a solid conductor. The *Repository of Music* (1822) prophesied that it would eventually be feasible to broadcast operas from the King's Theatre all over the city, adding, 'Perhaps words of speech may be susceptible of the same means of propagation.' Ten years later Wheatstone was convinced that some day a means of articulating speech electrically would be invented.

What particularly interested Melville Bell, however, was Wheatstone's improved version of a device originally invented in the eighteenth century by Baron De Kempelen for mechanically reproducing human speech. In the 1820s Wheatstone had wrestled with the problem and had eventually produced a crude speaking machine. Years later Joseph Faber had demonstrated a more advanced model at the Egyptian Hall in London and this induced Melville to suggest to Wheatstone that he return to the problem. In the summer of 1863 the Bells, father and son, were favoured by a demonstration by Wheatstone of his old machine. Aleck listened spellbound as the inventor blew into a tube and heard the apparatus 'pronounce, in a very mechanical manner, a few simple words and sentences'. Generously Wheatstone lent Melville a copy of De Kempelen's treatise, including detailed diagrams of his machine.

In Edinburgh, to his dismay, Aleck found that he had reverted to schoolboy status, subject to parental discipline and control. Even Melly, two years his senior, was chafing at his father's restrictions, despite the fact that, since December 1862, he had been making his mark as a public reader in Edinburgh and the surrounding towns. Before restiveness erupted into rebellion, Melville channeled his sons' energies into a challenging project, their own improved version of the speaking machine. Hitherto Melly had tended to treat his kid brother with condescension, but now he found an ally and collaborator. Working on the problem of replicating speech by mechanical means brought the brothers much closer together.

Together they avidly studied De Kempelen's treatise, then discussed the problem and worked out a division of labour. Aleck would concentrate on the tongue, lips, palate and mouth while Melly worked on the lungs, throat and larynx. The larynx proved a stumbling block – there was no adequate diagram or description in any existing textbooks on anatomy. With the greatest reluctance the brothers decided to sacrifice their pet cat in the interests of advancing knowledge. In due course they took the cat to a medical student of Melly's acquaintance to put it to sleep painlessly. The deed was to be done in the greenhouse at Milton Cottage. In speechless horror the boys watched as the student funnelled nitric acid down the hapless animal's gullet. The cat let out a pitiful scream and raced round the greenhouse in frenzied agony. With great difficulty they managed to catch the poor beast and restrain it long enough for their friend to cut an artery and terminate its suffering. The memory of that awful afternoon remained with Aleck to the end of his days, and never again would he indulge in vivisection. In the end, Aleck obtained a lamb's larynx from the local butcher.[5]

From impressions taken from a human skull Aleck made gutta–percha replicas of jaws, teeth, pharynx and nasal cavities, though Melville suggested a simple resonance chamber for the latter and talked his exuberant son out of giving the apparatus a face and wig, though they compromised over rubber lips and cheeks. The trickiest part was the tongue and soft palate, which Aleck contrived from ingeniously carved pieces of wood, hinged and articulated, covered with rubber sheeting padded with cotton. The tongue consisted of six sections, each capable of being raised or lowered separately to simulate the precise position required for each sound. Eventually the machine was assembled and ready for trial. Melly breathed life into it, through a tinplate tube, while Aleck manipulated the lips, palate and tongue to produce weird, disembodied sounds, a cross between Donald Duck and the high-pitched squawking of a Punch and Judy show. By trial and error, they learned to produce the sounds of some consonants. Not surprisingly, the first successful word to come out of the machine was 'Mama!', the most basic and universal human sound which a baby makes by instinctively opening and closing the lips while sustaining the basic vowel sound 'ah'. When one of the tenants downstairs came up to see 'what can be the matter with that baby', Melly and Aleck knew that they had a success on their hands.

Constructing the machine had been a great diversion, but it was no mere plaything. Along the way, the Bell brothers had learned a great deal about the organs of speech and the physiology of the human voice. To be sure, there was as much error as there was trial, but Melville kept them at it by encouragement, thought-provoking argument and penetrating questions. The most important lesson this exercise taught them was to face up to failure fairly and squarely and redouble their efforts.

This project occupied the months of June and July but as it drew to a conclusion the old restlessness resurfaced. Fired by his father's tales of Newfoundland, Aleck decided to run away to sea. He had got as far as packing a small valise and checking out the feasibility of stowing away aboard one of the ships in the docks at Leith, when he suddenly abandoned the idea. Instead, he would apply for a job suitable to his talents. At that period boarding-schools and academies relied heavily on pupil-teachers, young people scarcely older than their students and without formal educational qualifications. Scanning the advertisements in *The Scotsman*, Aleck came across a notice by Weston House, a school for the board and education of young gentlemen at Elgin, which was seeking pupil-teachers. Aleck applied for the position of teacher of piano while Melly applied for the vacancy as teacher of English and recitation. Both boys named their father Professor Bell as a referee. As luck would have it, the school's principal, James Skinner, had been one of Melville's elocution students and thus word of his sons' intentions came to him. Realising that the time had come for the young men to strike out on their own, Melville offered them a deal. If Melly would agree to enrol at Edinburgh University during the coming academic year, Aleck could go to Weston House; but after one year they would have to change places.

The boys consented to these terms, and thus it was that, in August 1863,

Aleck took up his appointment at Weston House, as teacher of music and elocution. As it happened, several of the senior pupils were actually older than Aleck, but his London polish and maturity conveyed the impression of a young man in his twenties. The work of transforming the boy into the man, begun the previous year by his grandfather, was completed at Elgin where Aleck took to his new duties with cheerful enthusiasm and also entered into the hectic social activities of the northern county town. There were hills and moors to explore, endless beaches and excellent swimming at nearby Covesea, and excursions along country lanes and spectacular cliffs. During the university mid-term holiday Melly came north to check out the school and give public readings at the Elgin Mechanics' Institute. According to the *Elgin Courant* of 6 November, Mr Bell's performance as Young Lochinvar failed to move 'the large and fashionable audience' but a week later the paper reported that his repertoire of comic monologues was widely acclaimed.

It was Aleck's turn to come under the scrutiny of the local newspaper at the conclusion of the school session the following summer when the pupils were subjected to their annual examination, a grand public affair, the examination hall gaily decorated with bunting and flowers, and the fond parents seated in the auditorium. The *Courant* of 24 June reported that the pupils read 'in measured tones with tasteful modulation, bringing out the sense of the author'. Similarly, in reciting poetry, there was a marked absence of mouthing and 'unnatural gesticulation', but 'the placing of emphasis on the really emphatic passages and words. The pronunciation was accurate to a remarkable degree, the very youngest boys being apparently grounded in the proper sound of the vowels, and giving every one of them its full effect.' Their teacher was identifed as 'the son of Mr Melville Bell, professor of Elocution in the University of Edinburgh'.

While Aleck was making his first mark in public, Uncle David in Dublin was enthusiastically espousing the cause of Irish nationalism. A year or two later he would make a tremendous impression on one of his pupils at the Wesleyan Connexional School. 'He was by far the most majestic and imposing-looking man that ever lived on this or any other planet,' wrote George Bernard Shaw,[6] recalling the man who taught him to appreciate the English language. David's undoing was his involvement with the Fenian Brotherhood, a forerunner of Sinn Fein and the IRA, which sent him on a fundraising tour of the United States in the autumn of 1864. On his return to Dublin, he was arrested on a charge of sedition and spent a year in Mountjoy Prison. From his cell he wrote to his brother on 1 October 1865: 'I must bear it; still, however, looking forward to the proud watchwords – Ireland! Independence! No Saxon government, no base, bloody, and brutal whiggery, no Juggernaut of Palmerstonian policy shall depress my spirits.' Significantly, he concluded that the United States of America was the place where democracy had found its greatest flowering. 'Even as a boy I looked to the *stars and stripes*, and now, with a life's experience, I believe that the *United States* is in many respects the best.'

Over the winter of 1863–64, Melville rapidly reached the goal which had eluded him and other students of phonetics for so many years. Since 1854 the world's leading experts in this field had been striving, so far without success, to evolve a foolproof alphabet which would truly represent the full range of sounds of which the human voice was capable. Devising a system which could reduce to written form the sounds made in the various European languages was difficult enough, but when it came to Oriental tongues, especially Chinese with its rising and falling tones, the problem entered another dimension altogether. Hitherto, scientists had tried to group sounds and analyse the manner in which they were produced, but Melville Bell tackled the problem by concentrating on the vocal organs themselves and testing the sounds emitted when the position of these organs was varied. Blessed with an uncanny ear which could detect the subtlest nuance in sound, Melville tried again and again to classify these sounds in some written form. After many false starts and disappointments, it suddenly struck him, early in 1864, that there were four basic classes of vowels rather than three as had hitherto been believed. The revelation came to him in a blinding flash one evening, a quantum leap which set him feverishly on the right track at long last.

In Melville's new alphabet all consonants were represented by a horse-shoe shape (the tongue), facing upwards, downwards or to left or right according to the part of the tongue used. All vowels had a vertical line representing the breath aperture. Melville identified a new class of sounds which he termed 'glides', midway between vowels and consonants, and gave them distinctive symbols also. The basic symbols could be endlessly modified by various subsidiary marks to denote specific vocal positions. Finally, a group of small symbols signified tones and inflections as well as sucking, clicking or trilling effects. By permutations and combinations of these symbols, Melville found that he could reduce to visual form absolutely every sound. Even noises such as a sneeze, a wheezing cough, or rasping, grunting and growling could be faithfully reproduced by this method.

Melville christened his invention Visible Speech. At one stroke he had transformed phonetics and philology into an exact science and opened up the way to global communication in a manner which had never been contemplated before. The efficacy and value of the system seemed self-evident, but Melville had to convince a sceptical public and get massive financial backing from the government. For a start he taught the system to his three sons. Aleck, confronted with his father's startling discovery on his return from Elgin that summer, mastered it in five gruelling weeks. Linguists and philologists from all over the British Isles and even farther afield flocked to Edinburgh and subjected the system to the most searching examination. They would pronounce a word which Melville would immediately write in Visible Speech on a piece of paper. Someone would take the paper to another room and hand it to Melly or Aleck, and presently one or other would come into the presence of the sceptic and repeat the word precisely. The boys were tested in American Indian languages as well as Arabic, Hindi, Farsi, Urdu and obscure dialects of European tongues, and passed with flying colours. Melville would not divulge the mechanics of his system while he was hoping to enlist government support, but these demonstrations were extensively reported in both local and national newspapers.

Sadly, the authorities were lukewarm, and Melville was faced with considerable expense in publishing his Visible Speech, which of course entailed special typefaces, training for compositors and teachers, and promotional costs. It was time to call in the interest-free loan made to his father years before. Alexander responded to Melville's importuning with bad grace. Sending the cash, he wrote: 'I *could* say much in reply to your *swaggering* note, but I forbear.' But the old man was mollified two months later on receipt of the first proofs from the printer, and begged for a score of copies. 'If the system is as advertised, your invention will certainly be esteemed as one of the wonders of this wonderful age.' In August, when Melly went to Elgin to take up his teaching appointment, Melville journeyed south with Aleck and Ted to launch Visible Speech in the capital, using Harrington Square as his base.

Headway was slow at first, but when Alexander John Ellis, then widely regarded as the greatest philologist of the period, was converted, Visible Speech at long last caught on. Ellis, a Falstaffian eccentric whose quaint, slovenly appearance and roly-poly girth belied his tireless energy, industry and integrity, had himself evolved a universal alphabet with ninety-four symbols. He was naturally sceptical on hearing that the Bell system got by with only thirty-four symbols, and argued that it could not possibly articulate every human sound. In a letter to the *Morning Star* he politely said as much, but kept an open mind when Melville invited him to Harrington Square for a private demonstration. Later he would describe the event in a further letter to the newspaper:

> I gave Mr Melville Bell a most heterogeneous collection of sounds, such as
> Latin pronounced in the Etonian and Italian fashions, and according to a

purposely rather eccentric theoretical fancy; various provincial and affected English and German utterances . . . Cockneyisms mixed up with Arabic sounds, and so forth, including some sounds not amenable to any known alphabet. Young Mr [Aleck] Bell came in, took the paper and slowly echoed my very words. Accent, tone, drawl, quantity, all were reproduced with remarkable fidelity, with an accuracy for which I was totally unprepared.[7]

With such endorsement, and the enthusiastic approval of Charles Wheatstone, Melville and Aleck called on Lord Palmerston, but the prime minister failed to grasp the importance of the discovery. On their way from Downing Street back to Harrington Square, Melville paused to buy a copy of the *Illustrated London News*; it was some consolation to read therein: 'We cannot pretend even to guess at the horizons opened up by such an alphabet in the training of the deaf, the dumb, and the blind.' Nor, indeed, could Aleck, though within a decade he would be extending the uses of Visible Speech in ways undreamed of.

Melville himself made a singularly prophetic statement in the preface to the 1863 edition of his *New Elucidation of the Principles of Speech*. Referring to the 'wonderful mechanical adaptation of optical principles' which had developed from the science of vision he commented, 'Might not an analogous result attend the philosophical investigation of the faculty of speech, and acoustic and articulative principles be developed, which would lead to mechanical inventions no less wonderful and useful than those in optics?'

Attempts to win an audience with Queen Victoria fell on deaf ears. Melville's petition was batted around Whitehall from one government department to another, but by October it was clear that he was getting nowhere. Swallowing their disappointment at the insensitivity of officialdom, the Bells packed their bags and returned to Edinburgh in time for Aleck to enrol at the university for the autumn term. Dutifully, he attended Professor Blackie's Greek class and Professor Sellar's Latin course, but increasingly his studies were interrupted by Melville who needed him as his assistant in demonstrating Visible Speech at lectures and public meetings all over Scotland.

On St George's Day, 23 April 1865, Alexander Bell died. Melville decided, for practical rather than sentimental reasons, that the family's work in elocution and phonetics could best be continued in London and promptly made arrangements to move there with Eliza and their two younger sons. Melly, now twenty, was left to hold the fort in Edinburgh. The move was largely dictated by Melville's desire to press on with the task of establishing Visible Speech, and by June the family was installed in

Alexander's house in Harrington Square. The following month Melville, assisted by Aleck and Ted, gave an impressive demonstration of the Bell system before the Ethnological Society, as a curtain-raiser to a series of articles on Visible Speech published in *The Phonetic Journal*. Melville was now coming under increasing pressure to divulge the secrets of his system, but he remained obdurate, refusing to publish details so long as he had even the faintest hope of government support.

In September 1865 Aleck returned to Weston House in Elgin. The eighteen-year-old was now promoted to assistant-master, with an appropriate increase in salary. Melly, stricken down by some unspecified ailment, rejoined his family in London, whence his father wrote jocularly to Aleck on 22 September with a list of commandments which ranged from 'Don't lie down heated on the ground' to 'Don't go psalm-singing in a choir', but ending on a more serious note with 'Don't hate London – for home's sake – if you can't love it; don't gloom at my doubts, and don't doubt the constant affections of your fond father.' Aleck's father need not have worried on the last score; rather touchingly, about this time, the boy took to signing his name 'A.G. Melville Bell'.

Despite this, Aleck was discovering a mind of his own, and in making his own independent study of phonetics he was not afraid to challenge his father, or even disagree heartily with him when the occasion arose. Aleck's independence was asserted in the matter of certain vowel sounds which, when whispered in a certain order, appeared to Melville to form a rising musical scale. When he tried this out on Aleck, however, the whispered vowels seemed to form a descending scale. For some time Melville and Aleck disagreed on the matter, but in the end Aleck concluded that each of the vowels was made up of two pitches, one rising in sequence, the other falling.

At Weston House, Aleck shared a bedroom with another assistant-master who was often mightily puzzled by the eccentric behaviour of his room-mate. On one occasion he awoke to find Aleck making faces at the looking-glass and snapping a finger against his throat. On being asked what he was doing, Aleck explained that he was trying to determine the respective pitches of his mouth and throat cavities in various vocal positions. None the wiser, the room-mate fell soundly asleep.

An Indian summer turned dramatically into violent winter, with some of the heaviest November rain on record, resulting in severe flooding from the Moray Firth to Deeside. That stormy month ended with winds of hurricane strength.[8] Unable to get out and about for his customary rambles, Aleck whiled away his leisure time in his top-floor bedroom, pondering problems of phonetics. The results of these lengthy cogitations were distilled into a report sent to Melville shortly before Christmas 1865, headed rather self-consciously *The Result of some Experiments in Connection with Visible Speech made in Elgin in November 1865.* The dispute over rising and falling vowel sounds had niggled. 'I have experimented again, and I find the general results of my former trial correct – and now I *see the reason*.' He likened the vocal cavities to bottles. When you blew a sound from an open bottle, the pitch was higher as the bottle was more nearly filled, or as the neck of the bottle narrowed. Similarly, in vocal sounds the pitch was varied according to the position of the vocal cavity or the constriction of the breath aperture. What was important, however, was Aleck's conclusion that the tongue acted as a bottleneck between two cavities, as if they were bottles, each with its own pitch. He could distinguish these pitches by tapping successively against his throat and in front of his mouth.

Aleck had also discovered a method of determining the exact pitch of certain vowels. He would sound a tuning-fork – or 'pitchfork' as he called it – before his open mouth, while moving his tongue through the positions of the vowel scale. One of the positions would make the fork sound loudly because of resonance. The pitch of the vowel made in that position would be precisely that of the fork. He could imagine a number of experiments along this line. 'If only I could get a box of pitchforks!!!' he exclaimed. Over Christmas Aleck was in London and Melville presented him with the required tuning-forks, commenting very encouragingly on the experiments so far. Back in Elgin for the spring term of 1866, however, Aleck found that his duties now included teaching part-time at Miss Gregory's Academy for Young Ladies, so the experiments could not proceed at the same pace as before.

As the spring term drew to a close, Aleck began thinking of the future. He wanted to settle in Glasgow where there was a great, and largely unfilled, demand for elocutionists. Besides, that city would give him every opportunity to study for the external examinations of London University. Melville, however, insisted that Aleck return to London for full-time study at University College before setting up on his own account in Glasgow. Melville worried that Aleck would seriously endanger his health by trying to combine an exacting course of studies with the grinding business of earning a living. Eliza had written to her wayward son on 8 February 1866, after Aleck had locked horns with his father yet again: 'I think you should implicitly surrender yourself to Papa's judgement in this matter'. In further letters, written in March, Eliza sighed with exasperation: 'What I would not give if I could only get at you!' Aleck's health was suffering from the frustrations of adolescence as much as from overwork and the *ennui* of Elgin. 'Keep off pickles,' warned Eliza solicitously. 'Try a little beer, and explain to Mr Skinner that we approve it . . . Try bathing your eyes with cold water . . .' When Aleck continued to complain of low spirits and being thoroughly out of sorts Eliza diagnosed liverishness. 'Its symptoms are lassitude, faintness, a lowering of the spirits, and a disposition to take a disheartening view of passing events. Under such circumstances one is incapable very often of forming a correct judgement.' She accompanied this letter with a large bottle of Dr Collis-Brown's patent mixture. 'In future when you feel a beginning of these symptoms, take a dose of Chlorodyne, and if not better next day, take another. A third will be seldom necessary.'

Gradually, as the better weather returned, Aleck's sense of well-being improved, but no amount of beer or Chlorodyne cured his desire for independence. At nineteen, he was tormented by other feelings which he did not understand, and for which his scientific training had not prepared him. In the senior class at Miss Gregory's Academy was a bewitching, dark-eyed creature just turned sixteen named Anna Daun. Aleck was smitten by her, and he fondly imagined that his feelings were reciprocated; but the rigid conventions of Victorian Britain, not to mention the puritanical atmosphere of a small Scottish county town, stifled these feelings before they could be evoked. Timid and utterly inexperienced in the ways of women, Aleck could only admire the object of his affections at a distance, but he did succeed, through a mutual friend, in getting hold of a daguerreotype of the young lady. Forty years later he screwed up the courage to write to Mrs Acklone as she then was, when both he and she were grandparents, and admitted that he had treasured her photograph all those years and had often thought of her.[9]

As if making up for the fierceness of winter, the spring of 1866 was unusually mild and sunny. In this halcyon period Aleck recovered his equilibrium by going off for long rambles into the countryside. The Vale of St Andrew became his favourite haunt, and here he discovered a tolerable substitute for Corstorphine in the pine-clad slopes of Heldon Hill overlooking the splendid ruins of Pluscarden Priory, where he could escape from the drudgery of schoolteaching. Aleck was on the brink of manhood, brimming over with ideas but frustrated as he tried to put them into practical realisation. An undated letter from Ted to Aleck about this time is very revealing, referring as it does to 'your wish to do something great, also the extreme poverty of thrilling ideas which you manifest in most of your prose and dramatic works'. What these literary efforts were, we have no means of telling, for Aleck appears to have destroyed this juvenilia; but in March 1866 he wrote at length to Alexander Ellis, sending him an account of his theory of vowel tones. It is significant that Aleck should have confided in a rival phoneticist rather than in his own father at this crucial period.

Ellis replied at the end of that month, coming straight to the point. 'I find you are exactly repeating Helmholtz's experiments for determining the musical tones of the vowels.' One can only imagine Aleck's chagrin on learning that his fixed-pitch theory of vowel tones had, in fact, been elaborated in Hermann von Helmholtz's book on acoustics, published in an English edition in 1862 under the title of *Sensations of Tone*. It was little consolation for Aleck to reflect that, at the age of nineteen, he had independently worked out a theory which had engaged one of the sharpest intellects of Europe over many years. Ironically, by 1866 Helmholtz (who had previously discovered the three primary colours and invented the ophthalmoscope) had already moved on from optics and acoustics to electromagnetism and was about to suggest to one of his brighter students, Heinrich Hertz, that he should investigate the existence of electromagnetic waves which would lead eventually to radio.

Ellis was aware of Helmholtz's current investigations and generously passed this information on to young Aleck. By means of electromagnets Helmholtz had kept several tuning-forks at once in continuous vibration. He could adjust the loudness of each fork, and by this means had succeeded in synthesising vowel sounds. 'If you read German I shall be very happy to lend you Helmholtz's book, which I can send by post,' added Ellis. Unable to read German, Aleck had to curb his impatience until his return to London for the Easter holidays. On the last day of the spring term Aleck's contract came to an end, and much to his surprise, he found himself on the receiving end of a presentation at Miss Gregory's, made by Anna Daun no less. For once, his poise and articulate manner deserted him, and he found himself blushing, tongue-tied and overcome with emotion as Anna made a very pretty speech and handed him a writing-case. Writing to Anna forty years later he confided, 'This was the first present of the kind I had ever received and I was very proud of it.'

In Edinburgh at this time Melly was settling down in South Charlotte Street, giving elocution lessons and curing speech impediments. Family correspondence makes fleeting, if tantalising, references to an apparatus which Melly had invented and satisfactorily demonstrated before two interested parties, but nothing came of it, and what its purpose was remains unknown to posterity. By way of light relief, Melly hired the Edinburgh Music Hall and advertised the imminent arrival of the celebrated Russian conjurer, the Great Loblinski. Melly, suitably disguised with a false beard and fake accent, hoodwinked a capacity audience.

In London Melville was now filling his late father's shoes, teaching part-time at University College and giving private lessons to, among others, Robert Wiedemann Barrett Browning, who had been born to his poet-parents at Florence in 1849 and was anxious to eliminate the heavy Italian accent with which he spoke English. Meanwhile Melville, assisted by Ted, persevered with Visible Speech, undaunted by the pusillanimity of the Treasury, the Department of Education, the Foreign Office and the Home Office among whom his project ricocheted endlessly. All the while, members of the phonetic and philological fraternity continued to press Melville hard for the key to his alphabet. By June 1866 his fame had spread as far as the United States, and that summer he had a visit from the distinguished American philologist Samuel Haldeman to whom Ellis had written with a fair critique of the system. Haldeman would later use Visible Speech effectively in systematising the American Indian languages. The following month an American periodical reprinted an article on Visible Speech from *MacMillan's Magazine* and prefaced it with a brief account of Melville Bell, asking rhetorically:

> How could a man who probably does not make any pretensions to learning have found what famous scholars had sought in vain? He found it because he happened to take the way to the place where it was, while the learned men were misled by their learning to seek for it where it was not.[10]

It was quite coincidental that this magazine was published in Boston, Massachusetts, a city with which Aleck Bell would later be closely associated for several years. The editor's remark, indeed, was uncannily prophetic of Aleck's future.

Back in London in the summer of 1866 Aleck lost no time in visiting Alexander Ellis and pestering him about the Helmholtz machine. This apparatus had three elements: a device to keep tuning-forks in constant vibration by means of an intermittent current; a device to generate such a current; and a device to regulate the loudness of each fork. The current was passed through the arms of a tuning-fork at the end of which a platinum wire barely touched the surface of a cup of mercury, thus making and breaking the current as the arms vibrated. To keep the fork vibrating continually, the intermittent current was also passed through the coils of an electromagnet, placed in such a way that its magnetic impulses reinforced the vibrations of the fork. This process was repeated for eight other magnets and tuning-forks. These forks were tuned in such a way that the magnetic force coincided with each natural vibration of the lowest-tuned fork, every other vibration of the next fork, every third of the next, and so on. Each successive fork was thus less strongly reinforced in its natural vibration. The loudness of each fork could be independently adjusted by means of a resonator, a cardboard tube closed at both ends but with a small hole at the end next to the fork. Each resonator, resembling a miniature organ pipe, was of exactly the correct length to amplify its fork's vibration by resonance. With the lowest fork sounding loudly and the others more or less softly Helmholtz produced a composite sound that bore an uncanny similarity to a vowel.

Aleck and Ellis endlessly discussed Helmholtz's work, the older man translating the technical passages of the book in an attempt to make sense of the complex diagrams of the machine. Unfortunately neither Ellis nor Aleck knew much about electricity, with the result that Aleck formed the erroneous impression that the machine *transmitted* vowel sounds instead of merely generating them. Sometimes, however, a little ignorance can be extremely beneficial; based on a false premise, Aleck reasoned that if electricity could be made to transmit vowels over wires, then it could also send consonants, musical notes, indeed any sounds whatsoever, including the full range of human speech. It was an exceedingly exciting prospect, one that would henceforth haunt Aleck waking and sleeping and eventually become a magnificent obsession, although his motive in learning all he could about electricity was primarily to harness this force to the science of speech.

He had hardly spent his summer vacation in idleness, but with the onset of autumn Aleck's thoughts returned once more to the matter of earning a living. He had now gone off the notion of settling in Glasgow; instead, he was induced by Melville to take a teaching position at Somerset College in the elegant Georgian city of Bath. This was Melville's idea of a compromise: Glasgow was much too far away, but Bath, barely a hundred miles west of London, was far enough from the metropolis for the boy to spread his wings without constant parental pressure. In Bath, Aleck found a softer, gentler, smaller version of Edinburgh. There was much in the sandstone terraces to remind him of the Scottish capital's New Town district, but the climate was kinder.

The college was located in one of the tall houses of the Royal Circus, grander than its Edinburgh namesake. The college was a crammer that prepared the sons of gentlemen for entrance to the universities or the military colleges at Sandhurst and Woolwich. Like the Royal High School of Edinburgh, the college placed emphasis on the classics and mathematics, but scored heavily in having fewer than a hundred students on the roll, with a very high ratio of teachers to pupils. Aleck lived in lodgings, at first several blocks from the college but from January 1867 in a convenient boarding-house on Bennett Street close by. In the depths of winter Aleck took up skating with great enthusiasm. Later he would enjoy rowing on the Avon, getting a different perspective of the city from the river as he glided under Pulteney Bridge and admired the elegant shops designed by Robert Adam.

During his time in Bath Aleck pursued his own studies singlemindedly.

From his conversations with Ellis he was suddenly aware of the deficiencies in his education. Greek and Latin were all very well, but modern languages were a closed book, so he pursued French so avidly that by the spring of that year he himself was conducting an evening class in that subject. It is not recorded what his landlady thought, but Aleck soon transformed his bed-sitting-room into a study-cum-laboratory, with an impressive array of bottles, zinc and copper plates and a carboy of acid, with which he proceeded to make a series of electrical wet-cell batteries. From his bed-room window he strung copper wires along the eaves of two houses, to terminate at the window of a friend in Mrs Prankerd's boarding-house, where the college students lived and Aleck took his meals. Soon he and his colleague were exchanging telegraphic messages from house to house, using Wheatstone instruments.

The year in Bath should have been a very happy and fulfilling one for Aleck, but it was marred by a terrible personal tragedy which left an indelible mark on him. Ted, at six foot four, was now the tallest of the Bells, but Eliza worried that he had grown too fast for his constitution. He had planned to follow in his brothers' footsteps, with a stint at Weston House, but on the eve of his departure in the autumn of 1866 he was struck down by tuberculosis, a dread disease for which there was then no cure. By Christmas he was bedridden, and by the following February he was so weak that he could only sit up for an hour at a time. Something of Eliza's mounting anxiety for her youngest son showed in the letter she wrote to Aleck at the time of his twentieth birthday that March. Despite Mrs Prankerd's kindly attentiveness, Aleck had succumbed to seasonal colds and bouts of indigestion. Eliza wrote solicitously, sending a mercurial compound for his biliousness and exhorting him to take his Chlorodyne regularly. Ted, however, was now too weak to send his own birthday greetings. Aleck got over his seasonal ailments, despite the length of an unusually cold and wet winter that stretched beyond Easter. Back in London for the holidays, he was appalled at the deterioration in his brother's condition. It was with a very heavy heart that Aleck returned to the college for the summer term. A few weeks later he noted painfully in his 'Scribbler's Diary':

> Edward died this morning at ten minutes to four o'clock. He was only 18 years and 8 months old. He literally 'fell asleep' – he died without consciousness and without pain, while he was asleep. So may I die! AGB.[11]

Ted's death was a severe blow. Shortly after his youngest son was laid to rest in Highgate Cemetery alongside Grandfather Bell, Melville abandoned his attempts to gain government support for Visible Speech. With dogged determination, however, he later decided that the time had come to reveal his system to the world, and though it cost him dearly he spared no expense in the casting of the special typefaces used to print it. *Visible Speech* appeared later that year, with the poignant dedication:

> To the Memory of Edward Charles Bell, one of the first proficients in 'Visible Speech' whose ability in demonstrating the linguistic applications of the system excited the admiration of all who heard him; but whose life of highest promise was cut off in his nineteenth year.

Soon afterwards Melly announced his engagement to Caroline Margaret Ottaway whom he had met in London. On receipt of this news Aleck wrote to his parents on 9 June: 'I only wish I *were as fortunate as Melly is!!!*' In this letter he complained of 'nasty headaches, in fact the only idea I can form of this past week is *one immense headache*'. He could not determine whether this malaise was psychological or purely physical. Coming to the latter conclusion, he promised to take 'plenty of Porter or Portwine every day, as a kind of medicinal course'. There was a two-day delay before Alec finished this letter, but Eliza and Melville must have been reassured by the postscript: 'I feel decidedly the benefit of a rest – Headache vanished – Health capital – but appetite ALARMING (owing to a small pull on the river before breakfast).'

At the beginning of July the College term came to an end and Aleck returned to London. In the aftermath of Ted's death, there was no question of going to Glasgow, or anywhere else. Aleck settled in at Harrington Square and let his mother fuss over him. This ministration was short-lived, for Eliza and Melville had already made plans to travel north to Edinburgh, leaving Aleck to his own devices. During their absence Aleck kept himself gainfully employed in the company of a native seaman from Natal who taught him his own strange language. Aleck was absorbed in the task of translating Zulu clicks into Visible Speech which, in due course, would occupy the last page of the book, with a credit to 'the Author's Son (A.G.B.)'.

The Zulu sailor was not Aleck's sole companion that summer. He renewed his acquaintance with James Murray, one of Melville's Edinburgh pupils who had settled in London as a bank clerk. Murray, ten years Aleck's senior, had recently lost his wife and baby and Aleck played a vital role in hauling the grief-stricken young man out of the depths of depression. Later that summer Aleck was best man at Murray's second marriage, to Adah Agnes Ruthven of Kendal in Westmorland.[12] Intrigued by Aleck's work on transcribing the Zulu language, Murray's interest in philology was kindled, and he was recruited by Melville into the Philological Society, eventually taking over the society's ambitious project of a definitive English dictionary.

By the time of his death forty-eight years later, he had led this mammoth undertaking, like a philological Moses, to the brink of realisation as the monumental *Oxford English Dictionary*. He was personally responsible for about half the dictionary, covering the letters A–D, H–K, O, P and T, and along the way he (who had had no formal higher education) acquired a clutch of honorary degrees and (in 1908) a knighthood.[13]

Another constant companion of this period, nearer Aleck's own age, was Adam Scott. He had been orphaned as a little boy and then raised by a maiden aunt who had abused him cruelly. The circumstances in which Adam met Aleck are not recorded, but he would later recall that the house in Harrington Square was 'the nearest approach to a home that I ever then knew'.[14] He was inordinately fond of walking and induced Aleck to join him in long rambles round the London streets in the early hours of the morning, though Aleck, who had acquired Melville's bad habit of working to the wee small hours and then sleeping late, sometimes failed to keep the assignation. Scott recollected, 'We several times arranged to meet at half past six in the morning at King's Cross for a stroll before breakfast, but he never turned up, and it always ended in my going round to Harrington Square, and finding him dead asleep in his bedroom.'[15]

Professional acquaintances rather than friends included his father's colleagues. After Alexander Ellis, the profoundest influence on Aleck came from Dr Frederick James Furnivall (1825–1910), a pioneer Christian Socialist and founder of the Working Men's College, a tireless promoter of early English literature and best remembered today as editor of Chaucer's *Canterbury Tales*. A long-time secretary of the Philological Society, he contributed a ton and a half of papers to Murray's dictionary. A lifelong oarsman, he also encouraged Aleck's enthusiasm for rowing, though his chief contribution to the sport was to introduce races for sculling eights on the Thames in 1886.[16]

Then there was Henry Sweet, two years older than Aleck, who became a surrogate Melly. He had had a brilliant academic education at King's College, Balliol and Heidelberg, and by the time Aleck met him he had already published his first books, an Anglo-Saxon reader and *A Short Historical English Grammar*, both in 1866. The eccentric, irascible yet lovable Sweet was a mercurial genius, for whom the University of Oxford created a Readership in Phonetics in 1901, and it was shortly after Sweet's death in 1912 that Shaw created the character of Henry Higgins in affectionate memory of him.

Another amateur philologist was Louis Lucien Bonaparte, the son of Lucien Bonaparte, elder brother of Napoleon. By a strange quirk of fate Prince Lucien, as he was known, was born at Thorngrove, Worcestershire, in January 1813 (after his father and mother were captured by the British at

Malta, *en route* to America). He spent his youth in England and never visited France till the revolution of 1848 brought his cousin to power. Napoleon III later made him a senator and prince of the Empire but he continued to reside mainly in London. His chief contribution to philology was his monumental study of the Basque language, and he died childless at his London home in 1891. Aleck remembered accompanying Melville to dine with Prince Lucien and being served by three waiters who whipped away his plate every time he let his knife or fork rest on it – upwards of twenty times in the course of the meal!

Aleck adopted a stray Skye terrier whom he named Trouve and trained it to growl on cue. By manipulating the animal's mouth and throat, Aleck taught it to articulate the sounds 'ow, ah, ooh, ga, ma, ma' which, strung together, produced a tolerable imitation of 'How are you, Grandmama?' In later years, when Aleck's reputation in another field was universal, the myth would grow that he had taught his dog to converse with him, but Trouve never progressed beyond this basic greeting.

In the spring of 1868 Susanna Hull, a former student of Melville's, contacted her old teacher. She ran a private school for deaf children in South Kensington and had recently come across a reference to Visible Speech in some magazine which had speculated that it might become useful in teaching deaf people to speak. As a direct result, Melville challenged Aleck to have a go. On 21 May that year, he was introduced to 'two remarkably intelligent, happy-looking girls' named Lotty and Minna, aged six and eight. Both had lost their hearing as a result of illness and consequently had never developed vocal powers beyond babyhood. Aleck began by drawing a face in profile on the blackboard, the side cut away to reveal the various parts of the tongue and the glottis. By gestures and sign language he pointed out the parts of the tongue and related them to the basic symbols in Visible Speech. Within a matter of minutes he had got the little girls pointing out the parts of their mouths corresponding to each of the symbols; by the time the lesson was over Lotty and Minna had learned a dozen sounds.

Later they were joined by Kate and Nelly, 'lovable little children, each about eight years of age'. Nelly had been mistaught previously and now had the added burden of unlearning all she knew in order to start again. Slowly and with infinite patience, Aleck worked with the four little girls. By the end of the fifth lesson they had mastered all the consonants and some of the vowels, sufficient for Aleck to teach them many words in common use. Aleck's greatest reward was to learn from Miss Hull that little Kate had gone home at the end of that lesson and astonished her parents by saying clearly, 'I love you, Mama, I love you, Mama.'

There was a continuing ambivalence about Aleck's relationship with his own parents. At twenty-one he was a grown man, yet still treated by both Melville and Eliza as though he were a child. To an old boyhood friend, the Revd Tom Henderson, Melville would write on 18 November 1869 (when Aleck was in his twenty-third year) that his son, in many respects, was 'a perfect baby . . . and needs to be told when to wrap up in going out, when to change boots or wet clothes, etc. etc.' This may, in fact, have arisen from the 'absent-minded professor' syndrome; for Aleck was by that time more and more absorbed in work and study and had little time for such mundane matters as food and clothing. In June 1868 he passed the entrance examination and matriculated as a student at London University and that autumn embarked on a full-time course of study. Two or three years older than the average, he seems to have had little to do with his fellow students, but applied himself wholeheartedly and singlemindedly to his course work, while continuing to assist his father and work on his own pet project in teaching deaf children the rudiments of speech. This last was exciting and gave Aleck the exhilaration of navigating uncharted waters.

There was great family rejoicing when Melly came south from Edinburgh and married Caroline, or Carrie as she was known, at St Pancras Old Church on 30 September 1867,[17] Aleck once again acting as best man. The young couple immediately set off for Edinburgh, with the briefest of honeymoons *en route*. By contrast, Melville was meeting with considerable disappointment. In August 1867 *Visible Speech: the Science of Universal Alphabets* had appeared. At best, philologists greeted it with qualified acclaim but lost no time in picking holes in Bell's system. It was far in advance of any alphabetical system hitherto devised, but its publication was enough to stimulate phoneticians to improve upon it. Visible Speech fell between the two stools of the professional philologist and the layman. While the basic concept was simple, the permutations and combinations of symbols capable of denoting fifty-two consonants, thirty-six vowels and twelve diphthongs known to the speech of all mankind was far too complicated for ordinary people to grasp. In a bid to popularise the system Melville rushed out a sixteen-page pamphlet the following year, optimistically entitled *English Visible Speech for the Million*. Melville hoped that this would prove effective in teaching illiterate adults to read and write, or to assist foreigners in learning English, but it seems that there was very little demand for this publication and today it is something of a rarity.

Brother David, back on the American lecture circuit after his spell in prison, persuaded Melville to accompany him on a tour of the United States, to publicise his work and recoup the outlay on its publication. Melville needed little persuasion, and late in July 1868 the brothers set sail. Their first view of New York was at dawn on 2 August as the ship glided past Staten Island — 'a perfect picture of landscape loveliness'. Melville was captivated by New York, its parks superior to any in London and Wallack's Theatre second only to the Opéra in Paris for comfort and elegance.

Melville's arrival in America came hard on the heels of a lengthy and highly critical review of Visible Speech in the *North American Review*, written by William D. Whitney, Professor of Sanskrit at Yale. A generally sour review was tempered only slightly with the conclusion that, whatever its faults, Visible Speech would stimulate renewed interest in phonetics and that perhaps some day a truly useful international alphabet might emerge. In spite of (or perhaps because of) Whitney's strictures, Melville got an enthusiastic reception from Harvard whose president, Thomas Hill, had learned Visible Speech from a thorough perusal of the book. Hill arranged a reception for Melville, at which he had the opportunity to explain his system in detail to a gathering of savants and literati in Cambridge, Massachusetts. Among the gentlemen present on that auspicious occasion was a Cambridge lawyer named Gardiner Greene Hubbard who had established a school for the deaf and dumb at Northampton in the western part of the state. A chance remark by Melville, that his son Aleck was making great strides with teaching deaf children to speak, excited Hubbard's interest. Melville later gave Hubbard Aleck's reports on his work at Miss Hull's school to read. Hubbard's motives in setting up the Northampton school were not entirely altruistic; his little daugher Mabel had been deaf from infancy, and an overwhelming desire to help her had been the driving force behind his public spirit.

Thomas Hill and his colleagues were very impressed by Melville and as a result he was invited to give six guest lectures at the Lowell Institute that autumn. In the interim, Melville and David travelled north to Ontario, meeting Aleck's chosen namesake Alexander Graham and his young wife, and being touched on discovering that Tom Henderson had named his daughter Eliza Bell after Melville's wife. Wherever they travelled in Ontario they found old friends from their youth, thriving in their adopted land. Melville could not get over how *young* they all looked – not a day older than when they had left Scotland. Eliza, writing to her husband on 16 September 1868, commented shrewdly, 'I shall not be at all surprised if you are smitten with a desire to settle there. It must be a glorious country!'

Melville and David reached Chicago ('a most wonderful place, its build-ings magnificent, grand in proportions and palatial in solidity') in the midst of the presidential campaign, were intoxicated by the welter of street-corner oratory, and beat a hasty retreat back to Canada. From Paris, Ontario, Melville wrote glowingly to Eliza on 16 September suggesting that her brother James could live like a prince on his naval pension in a country like this. On 14 October Eliza responded: 'I doubt if James would have the nerve to emigrate. I think in his place *I* should prove the better man of the two, for I would not hesitate.' And so it turned out. While James Symonds was content to live out the remainder of his life in Edinburgh, the families of both David and Melville Bell would eventually settle in North America. In October Melville was back in Boston to deliver his course of lectures. They were very well received and, more importantly, produced six hundred dollars which yielded a modest profit on the entire trip. 'The lectures have been quite a hit,' wrote Melville to his wife in November, unconsciously using an Americanism which he had just picked up, 'and I have no doubt of their leading to plenty of work when we return together.' Already he had made up his mind to return to the United States with Eliza and Aleck. After one of his lectures he met the principal of the Boston School for Deaf-Mutes, Sarah Fuller, who would later have an important bearing on the course of his career.

Melville arrived back in London in December 1868 to find that his son had shed those childish traits of which he had been so concerned. He expressed himself 'delighted to find that Aleck is justifying my hopes in him . . .. Not one man in ten thousand, of his years, could occupy his present position with credit! I am proud of him.' More probably, he saw Aleck with new eyes, perceiving at last that Aleck was, indeed, a grown man who had willingly shouldered responsibility for the business of elocution during his father's prolonged absence. To be sure, the old restlessness was still in evidence. That autumn Aleck had been fired with enthusiasm for the volunteer movement (the Victorian equivalent of the Territorial Army) by Adam Scott, newly returned from manoeuvres in Scotland, but it was a passing phase. More importantly, Alexander Ellis had sent Aleck proof sheets of his forthcoming book *On Early English Pronunciation* and readily accepted the young man's corrections and criticisms of the section dealing with Visible Speech.

Most important of all, in August 1868 Aleck resumed his teaching course at Miss Hull's school in Kensington. The modest success with the four little girls in the previous session had been magnified as news of his teaching methods spread. Of course there were setbacks, and periods when Aleck felt that he was making little headway with his small pupils; but then there were compensations and minor achievements as when Minna, who was the most backward of the original quartet, suddenly broke through the barrier of silence in October. That month, Aleck embarked on the classes in anatomy and physiology at London University. Soon he was attending hospitals, observing surgical operations and going round the wards with the doctors. His medical studies left little space for his work with deaf children but somehow Aleck made time. Reluctantly he was persuaded to accompany his mother and aged grandmother to Dover for several days before the term began at Miss Hull's school. The rambles along the cliff-tops exerted him physically but left him to his thoughts. Less congenial were the social activities, leading Aleck to confess to his father later, 'Rather sorry I went. Was introduced to people I would not care to recognise if I went there again.'[18]

Probably the most maturing factor that momentous year was Aleck's meeting with Marie Eccleston. Until now, this woman has been something of an enigma. Previous biographers such as Bruce dismiss her as 'a buxom lady, some years older than himself. Wherever and whenever they may have met, by the summer of 1868 Marie was writing Aleck long letters.'[19] In fact Marie, who hailed from Wigan in Lancashire, was three months Aleck's junior.[20] By late September this postal courtship had reached the point at which Marie was promising to visit London shortly. Eliza, writing to Melville in America, gloomily predicted that Aleck would soon know his fate. Without having met the girl, Eliza was convinced that 'she would need to marry somebody with a purse and I doubt if she could sit down contentedly to home duties – without extra excitement'. Yet, when Eliza eventually met Marie in mid-November, she was captivated by her, though doubtful of her son's ability to woo her successfully:

> I suppose it will cost him something to bring his courage up to the point
> . . . I shall be sorry if he loves in vain – for he will not find many like Marie
> in strength of character . . . Our young folks got home *late* in a pouring rain.
> I have not been able to ascertain particulars – but A is *hopeful*.[21]

Hopes of an early engagement were dashed, when Marie went off just after Christmas to become a pupil-teacher in a German school. The affair resumed its epistolary character; such letters from Marie as have survived indicate the rather desultory nature of their relationship. In an undated letter of 1869 to Aleck's mother, Marie commented, 'I am glad to hear Aleck is deep in study, else I should have begun to think it was out of sight, out of mind as far as I am concerned, or that I had *unwittingly* offended him.'

After the success of his American tour, Melville was now feeling un-settled. The failure of Visible Speech to win widespread acceptance in Britain underscored this malaise. In 1869 he went on to develop a shorthand system on Visible Speech lines. The *Shorthand Writers' Journal* thought it clear, aesthetically pleasing and correct in analysing sounds but not fast or flowing enough to displace Pitman's well-established system. Moreover, Melville's lectures no longer drew the crowds as formerly. He was fifty that year and obviously afflicted with what has since become fashionably known as a mid-life crisis. It was in a perplexed mood of mixed emotions that he finally took the decision to emigrate. Flattering notices of his Boston lectures and adulatory letters from American admirers, as much as Tom Henderson's constant extolling of the virtues of the Ontario climate, all combined to harden Melville's resolve. But in the course of the ensuing months other events occurred to make this momentous move inevitable.

Meanwhile Melly and his bride had settled in Melville's Edinburgh house. Carrie was attractive, energetic and resourceful, the ideal wife and helpmeet. Their union was blessed on 8 August 1868 by a son, christened Edward in memory of Melly's late brother. Eliza travelled to Edinburgh to see her first grandchild and wrote exuberantly to Melville: 'He has very *fine* eyes . . . and looks so hard at one sometimes.' A photograph of baby Ted taken a few months later showed 'a determined little fellow, with his large eyes and clenched fists'. Determination, however, was not enough. The toddler soon contracted some mysterious ailment, Carrie was worn out with worry and the fatigue of constant care, and Melly's joking references to 'the little nuisance' abruptly ended. In February 1870 baby Ted finally succumbed.

It was a tragedy that would hasten Melly's own untimely end. During the winter of 1868–69 he had written to his parents complaining of coughs and headaches brought on by the thick fogs to which Auld Reekie was prone, as well as biliousness and sundry other ailments that often sapped his strength. Early in 1869 Melly was so ill, in fact, that Aleck was temporarily despatched to Edinburgh to take over his elocution classes. After little Ted's death, Melly's illness emerged as a full-blown case of pulmonary tuberculosis, that scourge that had already robbed Eliza of her youngest son. Melly wrote a poignant letter to Aleck on 1 April that year:

> I *do* wish you would give me a line now and then . . . Is it that your scientific attainments are so much further advanced than mine that you can take no interest in the little I can say on such subjects?
>
> As for your fighting shy of me, because I sometimes make fun of such of your ideas as strike me as ridiculous, it is absurd to give such a reason, and I suspect that this is the foundation of all I complain of.
>
> Write soon like a good chap.

Before Aleck could respond, the Bell household in London was galvanised by a telegram from Carrie. Melly was now desperately ill and she besought her brother-in-law to come to Edinburgh and take over Melly's professional engagements as well as help her with domestic matters. Aleck abandoned his studies and a day or two later took the train north. In Charlotte Street he found his brother wan and emaciated from the consumption, but still lucid. It seemed vital to get Melly away from the damp, polluted atmosphere of the city, and Aleck promptly arranged for his brother and Carrie to make the long, tiring journey to London by one of the new-fangled sleeping cars, while he remained in Edinburgh to take charge of Melly's affairs. At Harrington Square Melly was confined to bed and went into a rapid decline. He died on 28 May 1870 and was interred in Highgate Cemetery beside his grandfather and brother.

Melly's death, though not unexpected, devastated Aleck. He could never recall this tragedy without feeling immense pain. For a time he flirted with spiritualism in the vain hope of communicating with his dead brother. His parents, alarmed at the impact of Melly's death on their remaining son, were now more determined than ever to emigrate to a climate that would be more conducive to health. Immediately after Melly's funeral, Melville broached the subject, recalling how his own health had been restored when he had gone to Newfoundland thirty years earlier. Aleck's reaction was not at all favourable. He was now of an age when he should be free of his parents at long last. He fondly imagined a time when he would have a wife of his own, and a career independent of his overpowering father. But filial devotion was deeply ingrained, and he could not bear to contemplate letting his parents go off to the New World without him.

Many years later he recalled his inner turmoil, when he went off for a late-night stroll round the quietened London streets to wrestle with his conscience and find a solution to the dilemma. He was torn between the ambition to carve out his own career with the woman he loved at his side, and a profound sense of obligation towards his parents. In the end he returned to Harrington Square in the early hours, surprised to see the lamp still burning in Melville's study. Indoors, he found his mother and father seated on the sofa, tightly clutching hands and looking at him anxiously. Suddenly, the sense of their loneliness overwhelmed him and undid his resolution to break free.

A few days later he went back to Edinburgh to wind up Melly's affairs for good and arrange the sale of his father's property. From Charlotte Street, on 5 June, he wrote despairingly:

> The dream that you know I have cherished for so long has *perished* with poor Melly. It is gone and for ever. If you exult at this please have the heart not to let me know it. I do not wish to have it referred to again. Do not think me ungrateful because I have been unhappy at home for the last two years. I have *now* no other wish than to be near you, Mama and Carrie, and I put myself unreservedly into your hands to do with me whatever you think for the best.
>
> I am, dear Papa, your affectionate and *only* son, Aleck.

What exactly was the dream which he had cherished can only be a matter of speculation: a medical degree, marriage to Marie and an independent career, with the opportunity to make a name for himself? Now his studies at London University had been abruptly terminated, he wrote Marie a letter of resigned farewell and enclosed two recent photographs of himself on which he had placed expressions of passion and tenderness, in Visible Speech shorthand. On 2 July she replied coolly, saying that she had forgotten the shorthand he had taught her, and endorsing his plans – rather too heartily for Aleck's liking. Her parting shot contained sound advice which reflected on Aleck's personality and forebodings:

> Don't grieve about your examinations, &c. – all the degrees in the world would not make up for ill-health . . . Make a name for yourself away. Don't get absorbed in yourself – mix freely with your fellows – it is one of your great failings . . . You see in all this arrangement your father is only *letting* out the love he has borne towards you your life long, tho' when sarcasm has made you feel thoroughly hurt, you half doubted he had it for you. As to your mother, she is so gentle you *experienced* hers . . . How I shall miss you all! . . . I scarcely expect you will return, England would be too *slow* for you after America. Even your father caught the 'go-ahead' infection the short time he was there.

As it was Aleck who had made it plain that his plans did not now include marriage, it seems rather unreasonable that he should subsequently have regarded Marie's letter as a rejection. In June 1875, in a letter to his parents, he touched on this matter, referring to it as 'the *one sore subject of my life*'. This intriguing letter revealed that the soreness was induced mainly by Melville: 'Ever since Papa's unintended conduct in the matter of Marie Eccleston made me feel so bitterly . . . it has almost been impossible for me to approach him confidentially.' This passing allusion was nowhere explained and Melville's conduct towards Marie, real or imagined, remains an enigma to this day. In the same letter, however, Aleck soberly came to the conclusion:

> I had created an ideal which had no existence. Still I believe that I should have learned to love her had I not awakened to the conviction that she cared nothing for me – that she merely wished to give me sufficient encouragement to keep me – in case no other came forward.

After the Bells went to Canada, Marie married a banker named McBurney with whom she eventually emigrated to Australia.

While Aleck was in Edinburgh dealing with Melly's last pupil (an Australian with a bad lisp), settling accounts and selling the family piano and Melly's conjuring kit, Melville was disposing of his household effects by public auction. In mid-July Melville, Eliza and their widowed daughter-in-law moved into a boarding-house where they were joined, in due course, by Aleck. Early on the morning of 21 July 1870 Adam Scott and Trouve, the Skye terrier, turned out to watch the emigrants' departure. More than half a century later Scott would vividly recall their leave-taking. The little dog seemed perplexed and stood quietly, almost sadly, as each of them petted him in turn. Even when the emigrant party entered the carriage he made no attempt to follow them. 'As the train moved off, Trouve looked fixedly at the familiar faces in the carriage windows, and his eyes followed till they disappeared to the view, then he stood staring at vacancy.'[22]

3

Teaching the Deaf
1870–73

My mother's deafness is very trifling, you see, just nothing at all. By only raising my voice, and saying everything two or three times over, she is sure to hear.

Miss Bates in *Emma* by Jane Austen

Two days before the family left London, Aleck purchased a small notebook whose cover he self-consciously annotated *Thought Book of A. Graham Bell July 19th 1870*. This first commonplace book helped him to while away the tedium of the ocean crossing from Liverpool. Aleck's introspectiveness comes across very clearly in the pages wherein he recalled the salient incidents of his past life and philosophised in a manner that revealed lingering resentment over the manner in which he felt his life had so far been directed: 'A man's *own* judgement should be the final appeal in all that *relates to himself*. Many men . . . do this or that *because some one else* has thought it right.' There followed a brief account of the arrival at Quebec on the morning of 1 August, the bustle of the dockside and the frantic transfer of baggage and personal effects to a Palace steamer for the journey up the St Lawrence to Montreal, whence the Bells journeyed overland to Paris, Ontario, and the manse of Tom Henderson where they lodged while prospecting properties in the nearby town of Brantford. On 6 August Melville purchased for $2,600 (then about £500) a roomy, two-storey clapboard house with assorted outbuildings and ten and a half acres of land at Tutela Heights, four miles west of the town. The house, painted white with a black trim, stood well back from the main road, with a belt of tall trees and well-established shrubbery providing a good screen. There were four bedrooms upstairs, while the ground floor was dominated by a long parlour and a spacious sitting-room whose french windows gave on to a front porch and trim lawns. There was also a study for Melville, a dining-room, large country kitchen and bathroom. On one side of the house stood a glazed conservatory with a workroom at the rear. When the laboratory equipment amassed by Melville and Aleck arrived later that autumn, it was found that precious bottles and instruments were smashed beyond repair. This did not dent Melville's sense of euphoria and replacements were soon procured from Toronto. Beyond the house and separate from it were the stables, carriage shed, henhouse, pigsty and icehouse. Water was drawn from a deep well, but rainwater was also collected in cisterns. The orchard was well stocked with apple, pear, plum and peach trees, and the Bells had arrived in nice time to reap an excellent harvest. The ground ran back to a lofty promontory around the base of which wound the Grand River on its way to Lake Erie. From the edge of this escarpment Aleck would get a clear view of the precipitous peninsula known locally as the Eagle's Nest and, in the distance, the spires and smokestacks of Brantford, then a town of some 13,000 people.

To the south the land dropped sharply to the plains of Bow Park, the thousand-acre estate of George Brown. Like Aleck, he had been born in Edinburgh and educated at the Royal High School. A year older than Melville, he was regarded as the father of Canadian journalism, the proprietor of the influential *Toronto Globe*. As a leading Liberal politician, Brown had been the indefatigable champion of the federation of the British colonies in North America. Ironically, when this was achieved in 1867, he had lost his seat in parliament and never stood for re-election. Though he later entered the senate, he turned down a knighthood twice and refused the lieutenant-governorship of Ontario.

Aleck, cosseted by his mother who fretted that her son might have contracted tuberculosis, would often sit among the birches at the edge of the bluff, in a deckchair piled high with pillows and rugs, and idle away the Indian summer with his books. In later years he would often claim that he had come to Canada a dying man, but by early October he was 'jolting over an *awful* road' on his way to a reservation to record Indian words for Visible Speech, and a week later he was out in the orchard with the others, 'picking apples as fast as we can'.[1]

Meanwhile Melville was back in Boston, delivering a second course of lectures at the Lowell Institute and drawing larger crowds than before. Again he met Sarah Fuller who earnestly told him that she was very keen to apply Visible Speech to the teaching of deaf-mutes at her school in Boston. Melville told her that, having laboured long and hard to perfect the system, he had no desire to spend the rest of his days teaching it, but he casually mentioned this encounter in a letter home, and drew an immediate response from Aleck that 'I should not personally object to teaching Visible Speech in some well-known Institution if you would get an appointment – even if it was not remunerative'.[2] Melville assented and made suitable enquiries, as a result of which Aleck was offered a month's appointment at the Boston School for Deaf-Mutes (later the Horace Mann School), to be followed by a similar stint at the Clarke School for the Deaf in Northampton. Several months elapsed before the first of these appointments was confirmed on 15 March 1871, with an offer of $500 from the Revd Dexter King, founder and chief proponent of the Boston School.

On 5 April Aleck stepped out of the train in Boston to find the city bathed in the warmth of a fine spring afternoon. He strode briskly from the station to his lodgings on Beacon Hill, taking in the sights and sounds as he crossed the Common. At 2 Bulfinch Place he was greeted effusively by his landlady, Miss Fisher. Later his patron called round and undertook to give the young teacher a guided tour of the city on foot. Dexter King was tall and spare, with fine patrician features and a dignified mien mellowed by kindliness. The following morning was a sacramental fast-day in the tradition of the Pilgrim Fathers but Boston was in holiday mood as people from the outlying suburbs flocked into the city for the religious services. What impressed Aleck most of all was the splendid brick and sandstone public library on Boylston Street, founded in 1852 and at that time the largest free library in the United States, and the neo-classical buildings of the Boston (later Massachusetts) Institute of Technology, standing on recently reclaimed land at Back Bay. That very evening Professor Edward C. Pickering, a pioneer in the electrical transmission of sound, was to deliver a lecture on acoustical theory.

Within hours of his arrival Aleck got straight to the heart of the matter. That afternoon he called on Professor Lewis Monroe, a warm admirer of his father's work, and in minutes the conversation centred on the science of sound. Monroe could give Aleck new insights into the experiments of Helmholtz and the Irish scientist John Tyndall and lent the young man Tyndall's latest treatise on the subject. Aleck electrified Monroe with his grasp of human sound production, especially his research into whispered vowels, and both he and his wife were entertained by Aleck's demonstration of larynx tapping.

The following day King took him to the State House to witness democracy in action. Aleck was most impressed by a negro congressman speaking out against the Ku Klux Klan's campaign of terror and intimidation in the South. The colour question was brought home dramatically when Aleck attended a performance that evening of a play entitled *The Octoroon*. Highlight of that momentous day, however, was the discovery that the Institute had a complete set of Helmholtz apparatus, and Aleck wrote home excitedly that Monroe was going to repeat Helmholtz's experiments with him shortly.

Experiments in acoustics were relegated to second place when Aleck reported for duty at the School for Deaf-Mutes, and was immediately struck by the spectacle of some thirty boys and girls who, in the midst of a noisy, bustling city, were cocooned in total silence. He was immediately captivated by Sarah Fuller: 'I never saw *Love, Goodness* and *Firmness* so blended in one face before.' Aleck repeated the technique he had evolved at Miss Hull's school, drawing a human profile on the blackboard and then stripping it down to the essential parts which produced speech, and reducing them to the simple pictograms of Visible Speech. Within thirty minutes he had even the smallest children identifying the four classes of symbols. The staff were 'thunderstruck', the children delighted, and Miss Fuller was agreeably surprised that progress should be so swift and dramatic. Aleck next assessed each child individually and concluded a hectic lesson with an experiment involving the older pupils.

Within two or three days, progress by the Bell method had been so rapid that a meeting of school governors and parents was hastily convened for Aleck to put his pupils through their paces. The *Boston Journal* reported the meeting in glowing terms and Aleck proudly sent a cutting with a letter of 16 April to his parents.

The initial breakthrough had been spectacular, but it would be followed by weeks of hard, grinding toil with numerous setbacks, as progress to the next stage was painfully and dishearteningly slow. Aleck's letters home reveal a sense of anticlimax after the initial euphoria had worn off, mingled with worries that he was letting down his pupils and their parents who had put so much faith in him as a miracle worker.

The first major setback came when Aleck started up an evening class for deaf men. All went well at first, but on the third evening he pushed his students too far. '*I made a mistake,*' he wrote home. The attempt was 'a most *ignominious failure*'. The men knew what to do, but not how to do it, and the class dissolved into utter chaos with each man babbling away in 'the most lamentable *squeaks* imaginable'. Worse still, the class broke up in great despondency and only three men turned up the following evening. It was a salutary lesson for Aleck to curb his enthusiasm and adjust his pace to the abilities of the slowest pupils. Undaunted, he decided simply to write on the blackboard, in Visible Speech, the actual sounds produced, no matter what gibberish appeared at first, so that the men could *see* what sounds they were making. Thus, slowly but inexorably, they groped their way towards perfection. In the end Aleck triumphed, but he soon learned that there was no short-cut to success. Henceforth the core of his teaching methods would be to build up the confidence of each pupil slowly, step by step.

By 23 May Aleck was telling his parents that he was now so busy that he was being forced, reluctantly, to turn work down. All the time he was proceeding by trial and error and constantly exploring new ways and means of conveying sound to his pupils. He experimented with a toy balloon, arguing that if held tightly to the body it would vibrate in sympathy with street noises and thus warn a deaf child of traffic; but he soon found that the balloon picked up street noises indiscriminately, and that a child was less likely to be confused by picking up the rumble of traffic and hoofbeats through the soles of its feet.

Sarah Fuller lodged with her married sister Mrs Jordan and her three little daughters, to whom Aleck soon became 'Uncle Allie'. The Jordan home was at Lower Newton Falls in the outer suburbs and beyond lay open countryside where Aleck would go for long rambles in the spring sunshine. His work gave him a new-found zest for life and the combination of wholesome food and hearty exercise soon built him up. Already he was planning ahead; after the summer holidays he would return to Boston, his ambition being to establish a training college for deaf-mute teachers. Lewis Dudley, a trustee of the Clarke School for the Deaf in Northampton, was urging him to go there when his contract in Boston expired, but Aleck felt that he must return to Brantford first. There was a moment of the old indecisiveness, exacerbated by some thoughtless remark of Melville's in a letter, perhaps pouring cold water on the training college project. This triggered off a bout of 'nervous insomnia'. Night after night Aleck tossed and turned, sleep eluding him as he agonised over his ambitions and worried about the imminent school examination on 21 June. In the end, the public display at the end of term was a triumph, the superintendent of Boston Schools pronouncing the results 'more than satisfactory, they are wonderful!' and forecasting that the Bell method 'must speedily revolutionise the teaching in all articulating deaf-mute schools'. The ritual examination over, pupils and teachers poured out of the building to pose on the steps for a group photograph. The tall, gaunt figure of Dexter King appears on the left of the top step, already showing the marks of the illness that would strike him down a few weeks later. On the right of the top step stood a tall, intense young man, now sporting a full beard.

Before returning to Canada, Aleck travelled west to Northampton for a meeting with Lewis Dudley and Harriet Rogers, principal of the Clarke School. The following day Dudley accompanied Aleck to Hartford, Connecticut, for a discussion with the principal of the American Asylum for Deaf-Mutes. On 24 June he took the train north, to spend an idyllic summer at Brantford. Aleck thrived on farmwork, interspersed by long rambles, fishing, shooting, swimming, boating and riding. Melville had erected a little summer-house on the edge of the bluff and this became Aleck's favourite retreat where he could indulge in reverie while taking in the wide sweep of the river valley and the sprawling town beyond. Before he knew it, September was upon him and it was time to return to Boston, his spirit renewed, his body refreshed.

Dexter King's death ended the guarantee of employment at the Boston School, but Aleck determined to return to that city regardless. 'I go to Boston in *faith*,' he wrote to Sarah Fuller in August, asking her to place an advertisement for him 'at *once* in what you consider the most influential paper in Boston'. When he arrived back in September 1871, however, the advertisement yielded only four pupils; but Lewis Dudley sent his daughter Theresa from Northampton and her hundred-dollar fee, paid up front, covered most of Aleck's board and lodging expenses to Christmas. Hitherto Aleck had dealt with children and adults whose deafness was caused by illness or accident; Theresa was his first experience of congenital deafness. She was a girl of seventeen who had never heard a human voice. Despite four years at the Clarke School, her speech was slurred and hideously distorted, lacking voice control and unintelligible to all but her nearest and dearest.

Apart from his letters to his parents, often full of news of progress (or lack of it) with Theresa, Aleck kept a systematic diary of his work on this special pupil which documents, inch by agonising inch, the struggle to get this girl to comprehend and finally to triumph over her handicap. After two months of daily two-hour sessions, Theresa had made sufficient headway for Aleck to put her through her paces before Boston's leading educators. On 1 December Aleck wrote home triumphantly, 'I cannot describe to you the effect produced . . . I believe this experiment constitutes an epoch in the History of the Education of the Deaf and Dumb'. To prove the point, he attached clippings from the *Boston Transcript* of 29 November and later sent a fuller report from the *Boston Advertiser* of 6 December, full of admiration and wonder at the young Scotsman's achievements.

Aleck continued to preach the gospel of Visible Speech, giving a teacher from Clarke a crash course in it and writing an article on the subject which was published in the *American Annals of the Deaf and Dumb* the following January. Later he would mail over a hundred and fifty offprints of the article to enquirers from schools all over Canada and the United States. In December he gave a lecture on Visible Speech to the American Social Science Association and this was transcribed in a popular periodical. In the course of this lecture Aleck dropped a casual remark which was to have immense repercussions a few years later. He said he envisaged a system of using code numbers for Visible Speech symbols so that 'a telegraphic dispatch may be sent through any country without translation, and in the very words and sounds of the original message'.

When Melville urged him to embark on a nationwide tour, lecturing on Visible Speech to deaf-mute institutions everywhere, Aleck politely demurred. He was now more set than ever on establishing a teacher-training college in Boston, planning to open it on 1 March 1872 as an appropriate birthday present for Melville, the inventor of Visible Speech. In this way, he argued, he could propagate Visible Speech more readily and easily. The scheme would put him 'in such a position, that, if I still contemplated such a thing, I could be married', although Aleck did not actually have anyone in mind. Back in Brantford over the winter, however, he locked horns with Melville over the best method of promoting Visible Speech, and the stress of these family rows induced a recurrence of the bilious attacks and violent headaches. Melville's dogged refusal effectively scuppered Aleck's plans; in the end, he decided to honour his commitments to Northampton and Hartford and put back the proposed college project until the autumn of 1872. Once his mind was made up and his plans seemed settled, the headaches miraculously disappeared.

Over the winter of 1871–72 Theresa Dudley boarded with the Bell family at Tutela Heights so that Aleck could continue uninterrupted with the work he had begun in Boston. During this period he kept Sarah Fuller informed of progress, and these letters, together with Aleck's case notebook, provide a valuable insight into the evolution of his working methods. Always the empiricist, Aleck was quick to respond to even the most trivial or accidental variations and see their potential for helping his pupil. Early in March he took Theresa back to Northampton and embarked on the long-promised teaching course at Clarke School on Round Hill. As winter gave way to spring, he took long solitary walks through the hills and the Connecticut Valley, marvelling at the breathtaking beauty of the landscape. Afraid that Visible Speech was taking over his life, by way of diversion he worked up a passion for geology and went out rock hunting.

By now Visible Speech was attracting serious attention in influential newspapers and magazines, and the work of young Mr Bell was extolled in the popular press. The Japanese commissioner of education, no less, arrived one day with a couple of professors from Amherst and examined the feasibility of applying Visible Speech to Japanese education in general. Aleck parted with the last offprint of his article. On 8 April the president of the Clarke School returned to Northampton at the conclusion of a two-year tour of European articulation schools, and that same day Aleck gave him and the board of governors a demonstration of his pupils' progress. In this manner he met Gardiner Greene Hubbard for the first time.

The son of a Massachusetts supreme court judge who could trace his American ancestry back almost to the Pilgrim Fathers, Hubbard was born in 1822 and named after his mother's father, Gardiner Greene, who had migrated from Ireland with a considerable fortune which increased enormously after he settled in Boston. His estate occupied much of what is now downtown Boston, including Pemberton Hill, the location of Miss

Fuller's school. Hubbard graduated from Dartmouth in 1841, studied law for a year before entering a prestigious Boston legal firm, and eventually became one of the city's most prominent businessmen and entrepreneurs. He organised the first streetcar system anywhere in the United States outside New York and promoted the Cambridge Water Company and the Cambridge Gas Light Company. By the 1860s he had a controlling interest in three of the most lucrative public utilities in the greater Boston area, quite apart from maintaining a busy law practice in which he specialised in patent cases. As far back as 1850 he had acquired an interest in telegraphy and kept abreast of technical developments in the field of communications.

Ironically, the greatest problem in communications existed in his own home. The tragic loss of his only son as a baby in 1847 may have instinctively drawn Hubbard to the young Scotsman; the son he never had a chance to know would have been the same age as Aleck. But Hubbard had four surviving daughters and the second of these, Mabel, born on 25 November 1857, had been struck down by scarlet fever at the age of five and robbed of her hearing. At that age, whatever speech she had had soon reverted to unintelligible sounds. Frantically Hubbard had sought out teachers and the proprietors of deaf schools, but they were unanimous in their advice. It was futile trying to teach the little girl to speak; instead, she should concentrate on learning the sign language devised by the Abbé de l'Epée in the mid-eighteenth century and used the world over. To be sure, Thomas Braidwood of Edinburgh had devised a method of teaching deaf-mutes to lip-read and to speak, after a fashion, but he jealously guarded his technique. Besides, it was infinitely easier to teach children sign language than to persevere with the oral method which called for a high degree of intelligence and perseverance on the part of the pupil. The American pioneer of education for the deaf and dumb was Thomas Gallaudet of Hartford; in 1817 he founded the American Asylum for the Education and Instruction of the Deaf and Dumb and thither successive generations of the aurally handicapped had come from every part of New England to learn how to communicate through their fingers.

Hubbard refused to be fobbed off with sign language and continued his hopeless quest for a teacher who favoured the oral method. In Samuel Gridley Howe he eventually found a staunch ally. Howe had seen this method used in Germany in the 1840s and had tried to open an articulation school in Massachusetts but without success. In the end he channelled his energies into helping the blind and was the principal of the Perkins Institution for the Blind in South Boston where he attained a measure of fame for his work with Laura Bridgman, a girl who was both blind and deaf. In 1864, in his capacity as chairman of the Massachusetts Board of State Charities, Howe (at Hubbard's instigation) launched an attack on the American Asylum's methods. Simultaneously Hubbard used his formidable legal and business connections in a bid to get the state to fund a school applying the oral method. Ironically, in light of subsequent events, the most prominent among Hubbard's opponents at that time was none other than Lewis Dudley whose daughter Theresa, then aged ten, was a pupil at Hartford.

Gardiner and Gertrude Hubbard clung to the fact that little Mabel could still utter a few intelligible words and refused to give way. With infinite patience they continued trying to communicate orally with Mabel, a bright, lively child. In the summer of 1865 they hired Mary True, daughter of a Maine clergyman, as governess. By a combination of endless perseverance and tender loving care, Mary succeeded in enlarging Mabel's vocabulary as well as developing her general education. Many years later Mabel would recall her remarkable governess with great affection: 'She was my teacher for three years and my friend for all time.' Significantly, Mary gave the little girl an excellent grounding in reading and writing so that by the age of nine Mabel was expressing her thoughts fluently on paper. Later that year, she was examined by a public school inspector in Cambridge who was agreeably surprised to discover that Mabel easily read his lips, though they had never met before, and understood him without difficulty. In January 1867 she was trotted out before a committee of the Massachusetts legislature and put through her paces. The pert little girl utterly charmed her august audience, overturned their scepticism and made an immediate and highly emotional convert of Lewis Dudley himself.

A few months later Hubbard and Howe scored another success when they publicised the work then being done by Harriet Rogers at a private school in Chelmsford. They persuaded wealthy businessman John Clarke of Northampton to put up the generous sum of $50,000 to endow the deaf school which later bore his name. The school got the enthusiastic backing of the state legislature and opened in October 1867 as the Clarke Institution for Deaf-Mutes. The oral method was used exclusively and Harriet Rogers was appointed principal, with Gardiner Hubbard as president and Lewis Dudley an energetic and committed trustee.

The twenty-five-year-old raven-haired Scot and the lean, rangy Yankee businessman made an oddly assorted couple. Aleck's youthful exuberance and impetuous enthusiasm sometimes clashed with the older man's businesslike hard-headedness in the ensuing years, but on first meeting they instinctively took to each other. If Hubbard was occasionally brusque and invariably assertive, he fortunately lacked Melville's gift for sarcasm which had so often put Aleck down. When it came to the education of the deaf, though, Aleck and Hubbard were in total accord. Indeed, Aleck had staunchly championed the oral method against Melville's misgivings, arguing that lip-reading helped to bridge the gaps in what could be seen of vocal action. Interestingly, both Aleck and Hubbard had a long-running fascination with telegraphy, though this shared interest did not emerge till some time later.

After making a considerable impact on the Clarke School in Northampton, Aleck went on to Hartford on 1 May 1872, to launch an assault on the great bastion of sign language; but by the time he got to the American Asylum he found that the old opposition to lip-reading had vanished and he was welcomed with open arms. Resisting the temptation to play the piano which he found in his hotel bedroom, Aleck went off immediately to the Asylum where the assembled pupils were put through the great public demonstration they had mounted as part of the May Day celebrations.

This was to be Aleck's workplace for the next two hectic months. During that period he worked with a class of ten congenital deaf-mutes and gave vocal exercises and instruction in Visible Speech to the entire school of 250 pupils, realising an old dream of simultaneous training to a large number. Every morning the school would assemble for mass exercises, described graphically in a contemporary journal. The pupils would stand up and stretch their arms back and forward to expand their lungs:

> Then, in a low tone and all together, they say what may sound like i i i i i i, as long as Mr Bell wishes. He moves his hand, with thumb and forefinger close together, slowly from left to right, for this, and spreads out his fingers quickly when he wants them to stop. Then he begins again but with his thumb and forefinger wide apart, and such a roar comes up as makes the floor tremble, the windows rattle, and the hall resound again. With these simple motions . . . he has the whole two hundred and fifty voices, from deep bass to shrill treble, under sufficient control to make them roar in concert or die away softly . . . The pupils like it. It is a new sensation to most of them . . . People stop on the street to listen, and stare at the windows. The noise may be heard a quarter of a mile off.[3]

The same magazine also reported that Aleck made a neat speech in sign language, which all the pupils understood. The report concluded that Mr Bell had 'won the friendship of everybody by his kindness, cheerfulness, and earnestness'. His letters show abundant evidence of the compassion he felt for the deaf-mute children he encountered. He was deeply affected by the death of a boy from dropsy of the lungs. 'When he was dying, he did not *want to go home*. His friends, he said, could not *understand* him and he was happier in the Asylum.' In Northampton he had witnessed the tragic spectacle of a four-year-old girl whose parents, unable to comprehend her handicap, let her run wild and uncontrolled. In the frustration of her silent world, the child was given to violent rages and tantrums. 'The little thing gives one a most painful idea of what an uneducated deaf-mute may be,' wrote Aleck sadly.

At the end of June 1872 he returned to Tutela Heights, being greeted by the sad news that Grandmother Symonds, left behind in Edinburgh, had just died at the age of eighty-four. Eliza, on the other hand, had never looked so well. Melville no longer poured cold water on Aleck's ambition to establish a teacher-training college in Boston. To Sarah Fuller, Aleck confided that 'since he sees that I am determined to make the experiment, he will put no obstacles in the way and will assist me as much as possible'.[4] Melville had resumed academic work, giving lectures in elocution at Queen's College in Kingston, Ontario, interspersed with speaking engagements in London, Toronto, Montreal and other Canadian cities where he was often joined by his brother David who had also settled permanently in Canada by this time, with a house in Brantford itself. Melville also returned to literary endeavour, working on a book which would eventually see the light of day in 1879 as *On Teaching Reading in Public Schools* and destined to become the standard textbook in Canada and the United States until the end of the century.

In July 1872 Aleck's article on Visible Speech was published in the influential magazine *Old and New*, and the following month he received an invitation to the annual convention, at Flint, Michigan, of the principals of the American deaf schools. He delivered a paper on speech – 'a mere motion of the air', he described it – lucidly explaining that the sounds of the human voice were made up of a series of undulations, of which the frequency determined pitch, the amplitude governed loudness, and the shape determined the quality or timbre. The paper was duly reprinted in *Silent World* on 1 September.

Now the National Deaf-Mute College in Washington invited him to teach Visible Speech there, holding out the possibility of a year-long contract. Aleck was sorely tempted. In the nation's capital he might be able to persuade Congress to give Visible Speech the financial support that had been so long denied; but any hopes he had on that score were soon dashed by the president of the college. Aleck wrote to Sarah Fuller on 23 August, concluding that while Washington might be the political centre of the country, Boston was its intellectual centre. There, he confided, he would make his mark.

At the end of September 1872 Aleck returned to Boston and rented two rooms at 35 West Newton Street, a tall freestone house at the corner of Washington Street opposite Blackstone Square. Aleck's rooms were on the ground floor and consisted of a sitting-room carpeted in green and black, chairs upholstered in green and a marble-topped table. A door gave on to the room in which Aleck held classes. Its black walnut furniture included a sofa which opened out at night to form a bed. This modest suite was to be Aleck's first permanent home in the United States.

During that winter he had about a dozen pupils. Theresa Dudley came in October and stayed till the end of the year. The oldest student was Jeannie Lippitt, aged twenty-one; like Mabel Hubbard, this daughter of a wealthy Rhode Island manufacturer had lost her hearing as a result of scarlet fever. Aleck was disappointed that Mabel herself, recently returned from two years in Germany, did not enrol in his class at this time.

On the other hand, Aleck derived a great sense of achievement with his youngest pupil, five-year-old George Sanders. His father Thomas was the scion of an old Salem family, a horse-breeder who had returned from Vermont to his birthplace to develop a prosperous leather business at Haverhill. George, his first-born, was deaf from birth. He was too young to attend Sarah Fuller's school but she had recommended Aleck instead. So, about the same time as his teacher, little George, accompanied by his nurse, moved into rooms in the same house. From the outset Aleck was taken with his little charge. On 19 November he wrote home, saying, 'Little George progressing splendidly, a loving and lovable little fellow . . . Expect great results with him if I can have him with me for two or three years.'

4

The Musical Telegraph
1872–74

A solid man of Boston,

A comfortable man, with dividends.

Longfellow, *New England Tragedies*

Boston's population had grown dramatically in the aftermath of the Civil War and by 1870 had passed the quarter-million mark. Ever since the infant community had purchased the Common from Blaxton in 1634, this open ground had been preserved, though by the time Aleck Bell arrived on the scene it had long ceased to be the communal pasturage of the townsmen's cows. Many of the buildings in its vicinity dated from the early eighteenth century and maintained the air of turbulent colonial times. Outside the Old State House, seat of royal government (and arguably the oldest public building in the United States), the bloody fracas known to posterity as the Boston Massacre had taken place in March 1770. The New State House on Beacon Hill, seat of the state legislature, was eighty years old by the time Aleck came to Boston; though its splendid dome was as yet incomplete and would not be gilded until 1874, it was nevertheless the most imposing building in a city noted for the magnificence of its architecture.

Aleck's comment about Boston being the intellectual capital of America was true enough. Just beyond the city limits, in Cambridge, was Harvard, most venerable and prestigious of American universities, but Boston and its environs boasted Boston University, with its numerous colleges and specialised schools, as well as Radcliffe College for Women, the Massachusetts Institute of Technology, Boston Jesuit College, Tufts College at Medford and Wellesley College. It boasted the oldest public school in America, established in 1635, while the Grammar School in Roxbury was barely ten years younger. In addition to its world-famous public library, Boston had the library of the Athenaeum which included the books that had once belonged to George Washington. Both the Boston Society of

Natural History and the American Academy of Arts and Sciences possessed large specialised libraries in the city. In theatres and concert halls Boston was almost as well endowed as it was in churches, still predominantly Congregational though embracing all major denominations. Boston was the literary and cultural powerhouse of the United States; America's chief essayists, poets, historians, philosophers and novelists lived in and around the city. Emerson, Hawthorne, Bancroft, Prescott, Motley, Parkman, Thoreau, Mark Twain, Whittier, Longfellow, Holmes, Lowell, Richard Dana and Thomas Bailey Aldrich were among the great men of letters who were more or less contemporary, and at the height of their fame in the third quarter of the nineteenth century.

Aleck was not long settled at West Newton Street when the greatest calamity to hit Boston took place. On Saturday, 9 November 1872, Aleck had gone off into the countryside for a long hike. Heading home that evening he was struck by the angry glow in the sky over the city and on returning to his lodgings he discovered that a large part of the commercial district was ablaze. The fire had erupted in a workshop but spread rapidly through the wooden houses and buildings, gathering the fearful momentum of a fire-storm which left over sixty-seven acres of the city in smouldering ashes. Despite the strenuous exertions of the day, Aleck paced the streets that night, spellbound by the appalling spectacle in which eight hundred buildings were destroyed and fourteen people lost their lives. The following morning he dashed off an eye-witness account and mailed it to the *Toronto Globe*, but George Brown never published it, and Aleck never retained a copy so it has vanished without trace.

Property, real and personal, estimated at $75,000,000 was destroyed in a matter of hours. Mercifully, the conflagration was confined to the commercial district and little in the way of private housing was destroyed. Boston made a quick recovery and a new district soon rose from the ashes of the old, designed and built in more permanent materials, with streets straightened and widened. As one New York reporter observed, the fire had left untouched the best treasures of Boston. 'Her grand capital of culture and character, science and skill, humanity and religion, is beyond the reach of the flames.' So far as Aleck was concerned, 'science and skill' were the key words. The city's position as the cradle of the nation's scientific expertise was unassailable. It was the centre of instrument-making and the home of many inventors, scientists and engineers, the technocrats who were in the process of transforming an agricultural country into the world's most highly industrialised nation.

Although primarily drawn to Boston for intellectual reasons, Aleck could not have made a better choice.

★

Adam Scott, Aleck's confidant in London, vividly remembered how his friend had 'tried his hand at an electric piano' though with little success. While playing the family piano, Aleck had noticed the phenomenon of sympathetic vibration. In particular, he observed that by depressing the pedal which lifted the felt dampers off the strings and then singing into the piano, he could sound the wire that matched the pitch of his voice, the others remaining silent. Aleck also noticed that one piano would echo a chord struck on another instrument close by – at Harrington Square all three public rooms contained a piano. This curious effect gave him the idea of an 'electric piano' with an electromagnet rigged under each string, all linked in a circuit with tuning-forks as in the Helmholtz apparatus. The vibratory current from a tuning-fork would produce magnetic impulses of that frequency in all the electromagnets, but only the piano string tuned to the fork would sound, by the principle of resonance or sympathetic vibration. This remained no more than a theory, Aleck being unable to construct so elaborate a device. He argued, however, that several tuning-forks might be made to transmit impulses simultaneously over a single wire; the jumble of vibrations would be sensed electromagnetically by each piano string, but the string would only respond to that frequency in the mixture with which it happened to be in tune. The principle of sympathetic vibration would unscramble the mingled frequencies. From this it was but a short step to envisage a number of messages in Morse code transmitted simultaneously over a single wire at different pitches.

This was the genesis of the multiple telegraph to which Aleck returned in seriousness during his second winter in Boston. By an amazing coincidence the same idea had occurred to a young American, only three weeks older than Aleck, who had spent more than three years working on it in a corner of the workshop of Charles Williams in Court Street, Boston. By the summer of 1869 Thomas Alva Edison had filed his first patents (for an electric vote recorder and a stock ticker) but trouble with his financial backers had left him on the verge of bankruptcy, and he had then gone to New York to make a fresh start. Aleck differed fundamentally from Edison in his approach to the problem of sending several telegraph messages at once over a single wire by adopting the harmonic approach, like a chord composed of several notes which could be played on a piano at the same time. What rekindled his interest in the problem was a brief report in the *Boston Transcript* of 18 October 1872 of the annual meeting of the Western Union Telegraph which mentioned that the company had acquired the 'duplex telegraph' of Joseph B. Stearns, a client of the Williams workshop. This device, by means of a secondary parallel circuit, enabled messages to be sent and received simultaneously over the same line.

In the same month, Aleck attended the Lowell Lectures on light and heat, given by John Tyndall (1820–93), the Irish-born natural philosopher. Largely self-taught, he had a genius for making difficult concepts clear. He was also blessed with an attractive personality and a natural devotion to science. His immensely successful lecture tour of America in 1872–73 netted him several thousand pounds, all of which he handed over to a trust for the benefit of American science, an act of lavish generosity which bespeaks a noble nature. Aleck was spellbound by Tyndall's magnetic personality, but it was Tyndall's remarks, in the course of the final lecture, concerning his undulatory theory of light propagation, that galvanised the young elocutionist. The notion that light and sound travelled in 'waves' would eventually be at the core of Aleck's greatest achievement.

In addition to Tyndall's lectures, Aleck attended the free public lectures on geology, zoology and mechanics at the Massachusetts Institute of Technology. A talk on experimental mechanics was given by Charles Cross, assistant to the Institute's Professor Edward Pickering, who had worked on a device for the electrical transmission of sound. Like the Helmholtz experiments, a vibrating tuning-fork made and broke a battery-powered circuit whose current passed through an electromagnet attached near the tinplate bottom of an open box. The intermittent force of the magnet vibrated the tinplate sheet like a diaphragm, resulting in a loud tone of the same pitch as the tuning-fork. It never occurred to Pickering to try to transmit anything to his tinplate receiver other than the tone of a tuning-fork, and it remained no more than an electromagnetic curiosity. The Pickering device was demonstrated so briefly that Cross could not later recollect having done so, nor could Aleck recall the incident, which shows that it had only a fleeting impact on him. Yet Pickering's experiment was a portent of what was just around the corner, if scientists had been able to grasp its true significance.

Indeed, it would be true to say that all the technology needed to produce the telephone was in place by 1872; all it required was someone to put it together. In October 1872 Aleck was still primarily absorbed in teaching the deaf to speak, but inside this gauche, diffident, serious young man of twenty-five was a scientist struggling to get out. Significantly, Aleck first seriously addressed the question of transmitting vibrations purely as a means of helping lip-readers to distinguish between the letters P and B. On 10 November Melville wrote from Brantford, answering a previous letter from Aleck which has not survived, brusquely telling his son that he would be wasting his time in trying to make an instrument for this purpose. Undeterred by Melville's blunt scepticism, Aleck revived his earlier idea of the musical telegraph. First of all, however, he would have to recreate the Helmholtz device in order to produce a sustained intermittent current of precise frequency. Would it really sound a fork of one pitch and leave the rest silent? Achieving this primary goal would absorb much time and effort over the ensuing year.

On his teaching salary Aleck had barely enough for his board and lodging and certainly could not afford the services of a patent lawyer or a skilled mechanic. Besides, as a British subject, he was unsure of his position should he wish to take out an American patent anyway. He would have to make his own equipment and conduct his experiments in secret. The only outside help he sought at this stage was that of a cabinetmaker who made him a table with a lockable cover. Slowly and painstakingly, by trial and error, Aleck built his own apparatus, even undertaking the extremely tedious task of winding the coils of his electromagnets. One of the few intimate friends who were allowed an inkling of what he was up to was Percival Richards who lived in the adjoining house. Aleck took his meals with Richards and his wife and the other man was induced to take part in Aleck's experiments with telegraphy, just as he had done at Bath. Wires were rigged up from Aleck's lodgings to the Richards apartment so that they could send and receive messages by Morse code. Richards had an interest in electricity and sometimes sat with his young friend far into the night, giving advice, encouragement and sympathy by turns as the experiments continued.

Replicating the Helmholtz effect proved to be very much more difficult than Aleck had anticipated, and the current-breaking tuning-fork refused to keep on vibrating. No amount of tinkering with the device seemed to overcome this defect, and there were times when Aleck was on the point of abandoning the quest in black despair. Inevitably, all this extra-mural activity took its toll. In December Eliza wrote anxiously, 'We are grieved but not surprised at your being unwell. You undertake too much . . . We will talk of your invention, my dear boy, when you are at home . . . I want you not to think about it just now.'

Aleck locked his table and packed up for the Christmas vacation. Back in Brantford there was 'one continued round of parties' to distract him, but rest and relaxation, interspersed with strenuous exercise in the bracing cold atmosphere, proved just the tonic he needed. In January 1873 he returned to Boston, restored in health and armed with some equipment made to his specifications by the Brantford blacksmith. This equipment made adjustments easier and more precise, and Aleck experimented with alcohol to coat the mercury and postpone the oxidation which tended to cut off the current. The intermittent current lasted longer; he was getting there, but not quite yet.

Meanwhile, progress in teaching deaf children was likewise slow and bedevilled by setbacks that undermined Aleck's confidence in himself. The situation was eased by April when Abby Locke came from Buffalo as a pupil-teacher, but nervous attacks, biliousness and 'horrid debilitating headaches' developed again as the time approached when he would deliver a lecture on Visible Speech in the training of deaf-mutes before the Massachusetts Medical Society in June. As it happened, he need not have agonised over his performance. On 4 June 1873 he wrote exultantly to Melville, 'This has been a glorious day for Visible Speech. I did as you suggested and spoke entirely impromptu – and words came all right'. He had addressed an audience of more than a thousand medical men who, at the conclusion, had given him 'a most gratifying reception' and 'fairly besieged' him with questions about deaf patients. But, within days, the old mood of self-doubt and despair assailed him once more. On 22 June he wrote home complaining of the 'dreary monotony' of his existence. He was plagued by headaches and homesickness and at night sleep evaded him as he tossed and turned and could not get the sounds of tuning-forks out of his head. When the Boston School Committee approved a teaching grant that would have extended Aleck's sojourn for a further month, Melville wrote anxiously on 5 July urging him to turn it down. 'I value your health above all things . . . I prescribe a steam-boat trip on the upper lakes'. In mid-July Aleck took a telegraphic farewell of Percival Richards and set off for Brantford once more.

In the summer of 1873 Aleck took his father's advice and, accompanied by young George Coats, scion of the Paisley cotton-thread family,[1] he set off on a leisurely steamer trip through Lake Superior and back by Lake Huron. In letters to Sarah Fuller and his parents, Aleck described in racy terms the raw, frontier mining villages he visited. 'Superb' was his favourite adjective, applied to scenery and game-fishing alike. He and George slept with loaded revolvers under their pillows. They camped out in the hills for a week and wished they could stay a month. Early in August Aleck came back to Tutela Heights, his health and strength renewed. He was met by Uncle David, who had come from Dublin for the summer with his wife Ellen and son Charles. Subsequently little George Sanders and his nurse took lodgings nearby and resumed tuition.

It was not until late September that Aleck returned to the United States. This time he would take up an appointment as professor at the fledgling Boston University. Founded as recently as 1869 with the largest single endowment up to that time – $1,700,000 worth of downtown business property from the estate of the fish merchant Isaac Rich – the new university was very hard hit by the disastrous fire of 1872 and the rash of insurance company failures that came in its wake. But the university had the brash exuberance of its extreme youth and an irrepressible 'can-do' spirit. In 1869 it had opened its doors to students regardless of their sex – the first American university to admit women. Three years later it had established faculties of law, science and medicine and, in spite of the severe setbacks of the fire, it added a college of liberal arts in 1873, including an experimental School of Oratory. Although he possessed no academic qualifications, Aleck was offered the professorship of vocal physiology and elocution by Lewis Monroe, dean of the School of Oratory. His duties would be light, a mere five hours a week in formal lecturing, at the rate of five dollars an hour, plus the free use of a classroom where he could teach his private pupils.

Aleck's new home was located in Salem, a coastal town some fifteen miles north-east of Boston, in Essex county. Here, in Essex Street, Mrs George Sanders, grandmother of wee Georgie, provided Aleck with free rooms and board in return for instructing the boy. The Sanders mansion was a huge, rambling clapboard house, painted a dazzling white with contrasting green shutters, that dated from the reign of Queen Anne. Its trim lawns were fringed with venerable elms, in the full glory of their fall colouring when Aleck arrived on the evening of 1 October in nice time to join the Sanders family for supper. His bedroom was on the top floor, with sloping ceilings and a large dormer window that opened on to a railed walkway from which, in Salem's maritime heyday, earlier generations of merchants had anxiously scanned the horizon for the sails of their ships returning from the Indies laden with the rich cargoes of silks and spices on which the Sanders fortune was based. Aleck's horsehair furniture was stored in the Sanders barn out back, while his precious apparatus and locked table were set up in the commodious basement.

Aleck fitted in easily with the Sanders establishment. His easy-going, lively temperament, good looks, warm, resonant voice, musical accomplishments and Scottish charm soon endeared him to the family. When old Mrs Sanders that first evening testily denounced the university for admitting women students, Aleck was obliged to defend its policy. 'I come out strongly for the plaintiff in the action Woman vs. Man, because Mrs Sanders *will* take the other side,' he wrote home the day after his arrival.

Aleck's chief accomplishment in the Sanders home that winter was to teach Georgie to read. He cut some pictures out of magazines and pasted them on the left-hand pages of a notebook. On the facing pages he made up short, simple stories describing each picture, and set questions on things in the picture, designed to extend Georgie's reading ability as well as stimulate his imagination. There were eighteen picture-stories altogether. Aleck marked the fingers of one of the little boy's white gloves with the letters of the alphabet and taught him to communicate by finger spelling.

During his stay at Salem, Aleck was a very late riser; after brunch he would play with Georgie, endlessly patient with the boy and disguising tuition in the form of word-picture games. Then he would walk to the station and take the commuter train into Boston to attend to his classes at 18 Beacon Street, lecturing on Mondays and conducting practical work on Wednesdays. Seven students turned up for the inaugural lecture; within a few weeks the class had increased to twenty. In the late afternoon he would return to Salem, to be greeted invariably by Georgie waiting expectantly at the window for news of the big city. Aleck would tell the eager boy about the sights and the people, mimicking shopkeepers and organ-grinders and dramatising the most trivial of incidents for Georgie's entertainment and edification. Thus he developed the boy's imagination and brought before him an exciting world that was otherwise silent to him.

Aleck's slender salary was boosted by private teaching. Abby Locke returned from Buffalo to teach pupils under Aleck's supervision, dividing the fees with him. There were three private pupils that autumn, a stammerer named Aldrich from Rhode Island and two deaf-mutes from Massachusetts named Brookes and Hubbard. Mabel, daughter of Gardiner Hubbard, was a pretty teenager, not yet sixteen, recently returned from Germany with a proficiency in reading and writing that language, but her speech was little improved. She was then lodging with her older cousin Mary Blatchford in Cambridge. Twenty years later she recorded her memory of first meeting the brilliant young professor. She recalled walking up Beacon Hill to the university with Mary True, reading the lips of her erstwhile teacher who was singing Aleck's praises, and thinking he must be some sort of crank. At length they entered the building, went up to the first floor and found themselves in a gloomy room painted dark green, with a solitary window overlooking the Old Granary cemetery. First impressions were decidedly unfavourable:

> When Bell came in, I did not like him. He was tall and dark, with jet black hair and eyes, but dressed badly and carelessly in an old-fashioned suit of black broadcloth, making his hair look shiny, and altogether, to one accustomed to the dainty neatness of Harvard students, he seemed hardly a gentleman.[2]

Mabel's antipathy soon vanished when this strange, slovenly young man began speaking. There was an earnest frankness, an engaging intensity, about him that brought her round. Perhaps he had something after all. If only he could really improve her speech she might indeed marry a rich man and keep up a position in society. At first, Mabel was taught by Abby Locke, with Aleck intervening only every other week or so. In Mabel's mind, teaching was not a profession for gentlemen in the real sense; yet, as time passed, she came under his spell. 'He was so quick, so enthusiastic, so compelling, I had whether I would or no to follow all he said and tax my brains to respond as he desired.' Soon she came to look forward to Professor Bell's lessons and was disappointed if only Abby turned up. Mabel had intended merely to give the Bell system a brief trial, but by mid-November she was writing enthusiastically to her mother in New York:

> Mr Bell said today my voice was naturally *sweet* . . . He continues pleased with me. He said today he could make me do everything he chose . . . I enjoy my lessons very much and am glad you want me to stay. Everyone says it would be such a pity to go away just as I am really trying to improve.[3]

And on 25 November, just after her sixteenth birthday, Mabel again wrote to her mother: 'I am getting along very well with Prof. Bell, interest continues unabated. I went yesterday in a driving rain and was the only scholar who came.' By mid-December, Professor Bell was telling her that he had never had such a bright, responsive pupil who had made such rapid progress. A month later she was reporting that the professor continued to compliment her, 'but I am much dissatisfied with myself. The days are slipping away so fast and hug them as I may they slip out and never come back.' Heavy rain and gale-force winds gave way to blizzards and Arctic temperatures at the beginning of February, yet Mabel, muffled up against the intense cold, battled through the snow to Beacon Hill. Anyone, far less Mrs Hubbard, who perused Mabel's letters of this period might have read between the lines:

> Both Miss Locke and Mr Bell were surprised to see me, but I did not want to lose a lesson when each costs so much, but Mr Bell said he would not charge for the times I could not come . . . Mr Bell lost [missed] his train and when I was going out . . . took me back to the cars. We had a grand time running downhill through the deep snow and in face of snowflakes that were very nearly hailstones, they hurt my face so much . . . I would have been almost sorry to get to the apothecary's, but I was quite out of breath, besides my waterproof and veil were flying about me and it was all I could do to hold them on . . . If it is pleasanter tomorrow I will go, otherwise not, for Mr Bell almost forbid [*sic*] me to go in and I'm afraid he will take it into his head that he must go back with me again.[4]

Soon it was spring again and as the days lengthened Mabel's speech continued to improve, though not as rapidly as she would have wished. She began a new notebook on 1 June and on the first page Aleck wrote a characteristically forthright comment: 'I think nearly the *whole* peculiarity of your utterance arises from defective positions of the throat, and from the lack of *diaphragm* action.' Below he sketched a diagram of vocal action. 'If you look into my mouth you will see that I have *two uvulas*. Now you may watch my soft palate while I move it up and down.' Touchingly, he concluded, 'Your voice has a beautiful quality.' Mabel, who would never hear her own voice, was dazzled by the compliment.

Although Aleck became more and more preoccupied by this particular pupil, he continued to have a very full and hectic workload. In addition to lengthy sessions at Salem with George Sanders, Aleck conscientiously carried out his academic duties. At the same time, he was waging a campaign to win wider recognition for Visible Speech, although he privately conceded that, were it not for Melville's sensitivity, he would have made radical changes in the system, including its name. Publicly, however, he stood firmly behind his father. In December he visited the Clarke School in Northampton and preached the gospel of Visible Speech with renewed fervour, as a result of which he called a convention of Visible Speech teachers at Worcester the following month. Sixty teachers took part in the seminar, out of which arose *The Visible Speech Pioneer*, a manuscript periodical to which a number of teachers contributed papers on their work and experiences of the system. These handwritten documents circulated among the various schools for the deaf and dumb and were extensively serialised in the newspapers of Worcester and Boston. Dean Monroe gave this project his wholehearted backing and made instruction in Visible Speech obligatory in the School of Oratory.

Aleck worked tirelessly in promoting Visible Speech, editing the periodical, lecturing to the School of Oratory, and even trying to interest the trustees of the Perkins Institution in a Braille version of Visible Speech. He was invited to address various bodies on the subject. At the Thursday Evening Club at the beginning of March he lectured to 'the cream of Boston's intellectual men . . . of course it was a grand success'. The following month he addressed an audience of four hundred at MIT's Society of Arts and Sciences, 'the finest minds in Boston'. This lecture brought Aleck 'into contact with the *scientific minds* of the *city*' and resulted immediately in 'free access to the Institute of Technology – and permission to experiment with Helmholtz' apparatus and with Scott and Koenig's Phonautograph and Revolving Mirror Apparatus'.[5]

During the winter of 1873–74 Aleck continued to work far into the night in the basement of the Sanders home on his experiments with the musical telegraph. As he felt, more and more, as if he were on the verge of a breakthrough, his obsessiveness with secrecy reached the brink of paranoia. Every night, he carefully tidied away his apparatus and locked the cover of his table as a precaution against 'the hands and eyes of curious domestics',[6] though what the household servants would have made of the tangle of wires is anyone's guess. By mid-December he had succeeded in producing a current-interruptor, or 'rheotome' which would keep going for an appreciable time. He tinkered with spring-steel strips and platinum wires and devised a variable tuning-fork. This idea came to him from J. Baile's *The Wonders of Electricity* which he found in the Boston Public Library. The work of the French physicist, in an English translation published only the previous year, included the thought-provoking remark, 'Some years hence, for all we know, we may be able to transmit the vocal message itself with the very inflection, tone and accent of the speaker.'

The squeaks and bleeps of the electric telegraph produced the dots and dashes of the Morse code by the operator depressing a key that completed the circuit. What Baile suggested was an *acoustic* telegraph in which a sound would vibrate a thin metal plate, making and breaking an electrical circuit. The intermittent current, by activating an electromagnet, would make another metal disc vibrate with the same pitch (like Pickering's tin-box receiver). Baile pointed out that this device transmitted only pitch, not amplitude, and therefore speech was impossible:

> A series of vibrating plates, answering to the strings of a harp, has been arranged, each of which vibrates when struck by a particular sound, and sends off electricity to create at the end of the line the same vibrations in a corresponding plate, or, in other words, to produce the same sound.

But Baile, metaphorically, had struck a chord, immediately reminding Aleck of his old trick of singing into a piano and hearing the strings echo back. This idea would lead him, a year later, to the basic concept of the telephone.

For the time being, however, the musical telegraph took priority. In the autumn of 1873 he built two steel-reed rheotome transmitters of different pitch in parallel with each other and in series with two receivers consisting of steel reeds projecting over electromagnets. Each receiver was tuned to a particular transmitter, and when a signal was sent, it sounded in the corresponding receiver, the other (though subjected to the same current) remaining silent except for a slight tremor. When Aleck tried the second transmitter, nothing happened. Neither receiver reed sounded, though he could feel both trembling silently. Undeterred, he diagnosed the fault as improper tuning and laboriously dismantled the receiver, redesigning it to produce finer tuning. During this process he put his ear against the unresponsive reed while both transmitters were sounding. What he heard, but failed to recognise, was the first faint call of the telephone receiver. Like the human voice, it was a compound sound, a blend of both transmitter pitches. The pressure of Aleck's ear had damped the reed's natural vibration and made it, like a diaphragm, the faint but faithful mimic of whatever frequencies bore upon it.

But what Aleck sought at that moment was a harmonic receiver rejecting all but its own frequency, so he ignored the weak whisper in his ear; though, good scientist that he was, he automatically noted the phenomenon. Realising that it sounded the pitch of whatever transmitter was in operation, he reasoned that if a reed did not respond properly to a distant transmitter, he could 'hear' the transmitter's pitch by damping the receiver reed with his ear. He could pluck the receiver reed with his finger to determine its own natural pitch, then he could adjust the setting of the receiver until the two pitches coincided. In due course this process of ear-pressing and reed-plucking became automatic.

By 6 December 1873 Aleck concluded that the basic principle of his invention had been proved experimentally. This should have been a time for rest and relaxation and, indeed, Aleck entered into the Thanksgiving spirit by attending a lavish banquet hosted by the Saltonstall family, followed by almost two weeks of dances, dinners and parties. Aleck, burning the candle at both ends, suffered the consequences. Mabel turned up for a lesson shortly before Christmas to find her professor miserable and out of sorts after four days in bed with a prolonged attack of his old biliousness and blinding headaches. 'He has his machine running beautifully,' she told her mother, 'but it will kill him if he is not careful.' Aleck gave up smoking for some time, then decided that the occasional cigar would be beneficial. Old Mrs Sanders, ever-solicitous for her lodger, made up an evil-smelling mixture of camphor and chloroform which relieved tension when rubbed into his neck.

There remained seemingly insurmountable problems in refining his invention. When he tried to improve or correct flaws in the system, he inadvertently created new problems. It took him some time to reach the conclusion that using a conventional telegraph circuit would not suit his purpose. Instead, he would place each transmitter on a separate local circuit, which would not be connected to the main line at all, but instead would *induce* a current in it. Presently fresh snags cropped up. A receiver reed on the main line would feel an electromagnetic impulse both when the vibrating transmitter reed made a contact and when it broke one. So it would vibrate at twice the transmitter frequency, which meant that it would have to be tuned an octave higher to respond efficiently. When the main-line current reversed direction the electromagnet of the receiver reversed its polarity, producing a 'push and pull' effect which, if not evenly spaced, would put the receiver reed off its stride. Baffled by this complex web of problems Aleck, like his classical namesake, cut the Gordian knot. He would have to devise an entirely new transmitter.

Why not use a receiver as transmitter? This was a truly inspired thought. If a polarised receiver reed were mechanically vibrated, its motion would induce a fluctuating current in the coil of its electromagnet. Such a current would be *continuous* rather than intermittent. Sent through the coil of another receiver, it would presumably make that receiver's reed vibrate precisely as the first was doing. This would do away with both transmitter batteries and the cumbersome current interrupters with their unreliable mercury cups. In theory a vibrating reed might make another reed vibrate audibly, though Aleck doubted whether the human ear would be able to detect it. He dismissed the possibility out of hand, and did not even spare the few minutes needed to connect two of the receivers he already possessed. Had he done so, he might have arrived at the telephone many gruelling months earlier.

Aleck concentrated instead on making an intermittent battery-powered current with makes and breaks evenly spaced. He sketched a diagram of a device using rotating cylinders and induction coils. Satisfied that this device would work, he tried to patent his make-and-break harmonic telegraph. At this embryonic stage it was possible for an inventor to file a caveat, stating the concept and his intention of developing it. This gave the inventor security and breathing space in which to make his idea a practicable reality. Aleck, as a British subject, was told that this procedure was barred to aliens. He could make an application for a patent, but while the deposit of working models was no longer a legal requirement, for all practical purposes the United States Patent Office still insisted upon them. Aleck felt that his apparatus was too crude and amateurish for this purpose and he found himself in a frustrating position: if he hired a mechanic with the required electrical skills the idea might leak out. In any case, he could not afford such expertise, far less the costs of legal and patent fees.

Seeking a way out of the impasse, he wrote in January 1874 to the Chief Superintendent of Telegraphs at the British Post Office in London. In due course he received a rather pompous stock reply from Richard Spellman Culley:

> If you will submit your invention it will be considered, on the understanding, however, that the department is not bound to secrecy in the matter, nor to indemnify you for any loss or expense you may incur in the futherance of your object, and that in the event of your method of telegraphy appearing to be both original and useful, all questions of remuneration shall rest entirely with the Postmaster General.[7]

In mitigation, Culley was a very sick man by that time. Had his assistant, William Preece, dealt with the matter, the outcome might have been very different. Preece had the vision and the imagination that Culley lacked. Twenty years later he would be the first to appreciate the genius of Marconi. As it was, Aleck was outraged, taking this as a personal affront. The rebuff from the British government had the effect of turning him away, for the time being, from his experiments. Instead, in the early months of 1874, he concentrated on his university lectures, his private pupils and the campaign to disseminate Visible Speech. Then, on 3 March, he celebrated his twenty-seventh birthday and was touched when Mrs Sanders presented him with a set of gold cuff-links and 'A STUDY!! . . . a special room for me to carry on my experiments in'.[8] His apparatus and lockable table were brought up from the basement and installed in his new laboratory. Immediately he resumed work, testing out paper theories and circuit diagrams which he had worked on over Christmas and the New Year, and almost immediately verified 'a supposition (the only part of the theory that I felt shaky about) that one battery could keep two tuning-forks going at different frequencies'.

It will be recalled that Aleck met Charles Cross in March, and the following month, after Aleck's lecture at MIT on speech training for deaf-mutes, Cross offered him the use of the Institute's equipment and laboratories. That very Wednesday afternoon in mid-April Aleck went to the Institute to make some experiments, not in telegraphy but in acoustics. He was intrigued by a device called the Phonautograph, invented by a Frenchman named Leon Scott and recently improved by one of Cross's students, Charles Morey. If one spoke or sang into the mouth of a wooden cone, the sound vibrated a membrane stretched over the tip which activated a wooden rod with a bristle at the free end against a piece of smoked glass, leaving a mark that varied according to the sound made.

Another device, the Manometric Flame, responded more precisely to sound vibrations but made no record of them. It had been invented by another Frenchman, Rudolph Koenig, and involved a membrane diaphragm stretched over a hole in a gas pipe. A speaking tube, just like Eliza's ear trumpet, bore the sound of the voice to the diaphragm whose vibrations made the gas pressure fluctuate and thus varied the shape of a gas flame. The format of the flame was reflected from four mirrors mounted on the circumference of a revolving wheel, producing a broad band of light with a distinctive pattern for each sound. This was an exciting prospect for Aleck who wrote to his parents, 'If we can find the definite shape due to each sound, what an assistance in teaching the deaf and dumb!' The teacher could show pupils what a sound looked like in the manometric flame and then help them experiment until they reproduced it. 'In any future publication concerning Visible Speech, pictures of the vibrations due to each sound could be given, and thus the sounds be identified through all eternity.'

Linking the two French inventions, Aleck reasoned that if it were possible to cut a phonautograph tracing through the wall of a cylindrical shell, and an air nozzle with a long, thin opening were held across the sinuous slit as the cylinder revolved, a 'pencil of air' would be blown through which, in tracing the phonautograph line, might reproduce the original sound. If, instead of the pencil of air, Aleck had considered a stylus, and a groove in place of a slit, he might have anticipated Edison's phonograph by three years; but at that time Aleck was set on producing a visual aid to teaching the deaf to speak, and thus became bogged down in problems of trying to reconcile the phonautograph tracings with the manometric flame patterns. Although this line of enquiry ultimately led nowhere, Aleck's experiments were taken seriously, and he was invited to address the audience during Cross's own lecture on the phonautograph and manometric flame.

Up to this point, Aleck had had no contact with Cross's superior, Professor Pickering, regarded as Boston's (and therefore America's) foremost authority on acoustics. Their paths almost crossed when Edward Pickering, who had a mild speech impediment, was urged by a friend to consult Professor Bell about it; but Pickering saw nothing untoward in his inability to roll his Rs and ignored the advice. Consequently Pickering's tin-box receiver was not brought to Aleck's attention. Instead, Aleck collaborated with Cross in acoustic experiments involving a liquid-column gauge sensitive to sound waves. Aleck also pursued another line by renewing his acquaintanceship with Dr Clarence J. Blake, a Boston ear specialist who had made a study of sound transmission while working as a postgraduate in Vienna. Blake proved to be an invaluable ally, giving Aleck an excellent grounding in the mechanics of the human ear. This began a year-long period of close collaboration which Blake would recall forty years later as 'one of the joyous scientific experiences of a lifetime'.[9] Blake procured the temporal bones from the ears of two medical cadavers, including the eardrums and the chains of tiny bones of auriculation, and the two men began experiments to replicate the effect of sound on the human ear. At the same time Aleck was working on an ambitious treatise on lip-reading for his *Visible Speech Pioneer*. Although this paper was never completed, he sent a draft of it to his parents, provoking Eliza to ask wistfully, 'Do you think I could learn [lip-reading] so late in the day?' Sadly, for Eliza, now sixty-five, it was too late.

On 6 May 1874 Mabel Hubbard wrote to her mother, commenting anxiously that Professor Bell was 'again quite sick from overwork'. Despite this, Aleck was pushing himself relentlessly, spurred on by encouraging signs that Visible Speech was proving of immense value in teaching certain categories of the deaf and dumb – 'the semimute, the semideaf and the more intelligent and determined of the congenitally deaf'. Aleck was particularly heartened by the remarks of Edward Miner Gallaudet, the brilliant but sharp-tongued son of the pioneering teacher of the deaf, Thomas Gallaudet, who visited the Clarke School and prophesied success for the system. On the other hand, one of Aleck's Hartford teachers reported that, after a two-year trial, the drill bored or discouraged many pupils. Classroom use of the system ran up against wide differences in pupils' aptitudes and progress in it. Furthermore, reported the leading American journal on the subject:

> The labor of teaching is greater and more wearing than teaching by signs. No one who has not seen it can appreciate it . . . Great patience and enthusiasm are necessary, besides the ability to distinguish sounds accurately, and to translate them into the symbols of Visible Speech, and also a knowledge of vocal physiology.[10]

This was a serious setback. The second Convention of Articulation Teachers of the Deaf and Dumb, held at Worcester on 13 June 1874, would be the last for more than ten years. On this occasion, however, Aleck was elected president and his swan-song was a demonstration of the phonautograph and manometric flame equipment borrowed from MIT.

By an amazing coincidence, that very same day, several hundred miles south in Washington, Elisha Gray gave a demonstration of his Washbasin Receiver. Born at Barnesville, Ohio, in August 1835, Gray had worked as a carpenter and mechanic while studying physics in his leisure time, before going to Oberlin College where he taught for some years. In 1867 he patented a telegraphic switch and annunciator and began experimenting with the transmission of 'electro-tones' and musical tones by wire. He moved to Chicago and formed a partnership for the manufacture of electrical and telegraphic equipment which, in 1872, became the Western Electric Company. In the winter of 1866–67 he had experimented with telegraphic relays, connecting a vibrating rheotome to a primary induction coil and a polarised relay to a secondary coil. Thus, independently of Aleck Bell, Gray was working on a telegraphic instrument capable of transmitting melodies, but as Western Electric expanded he became bogged down with managerial responsibilities and research took a back seat. About February 1874, however, his interest was revived when his nephew got hold of the apparatus and connected it to the taps of the bathtub. Holding a vibrating rheotome in one hand, the boy ran his other hand along the zinc lining of the bathtub to produce a peculiar whining sound. Gray tried this for himself and found that, the harder he rubbed the bath, the louder the noise became. In the ensuing weeks the Musical Bathtub inspired Gray to explore its possibilities, using a much smaller and more practical receptacle as receiver, with a metal diaphragm vibrated by an electromagnet, like Pickering's tin-box receiver. By May 1874 Gray had perfected the Washbasin Receiver and a transmitter with eight keys of different pitches so that a simple melody could be sounded.

A fundamental difference between Gray's apparatus and Aleck's was that the Gray receivers would respond to any frequency, whereas the Bell device was designed to respond selectively. Gray's receivers therefore pointed towards the telephone, whereas Aleck's, at that time, turned towards multiple telegraphy. The only snag was that Gray's transmitters could only produce fixed sounds; they were quite incapable of transmitting multiple signals, far less human speech. Gray's invention, in effect, was a dead-end.

Gray's experiment was only one of many conducted in the course of the nineteenth century whereby scientists groped towards their goal, often without realising what that goal was. As far back as 1837, Charles Page of Salem had stumbled upon the fact that an electromagnet expands slightly when magnetised and contracts similarly when demagnetised. In this way an intermittent current makes it vibrate and produce a sound of the same frequency – what Page had termed 'galvanic music'. Charles Boursel in France (1854) and Philipp Reis in Germany (1861) had attempted the electrical transmission of speech by the make-and-break principle of telegraphy but had failed. To this day, Reis, not Aleck Bell, is regarded in Germany as the inventor of the telephone (indeed, he coined the name *Telephon* for his instrument) although it fell far short of the device invented by the Scot.

Reis succeeded in producing a machine which would pick up and transmit the pitches of sounds, using a membrane diaphragm with a platinum contact point in its centre that made and broke a battery-powered current, but this intermittent current did not vary in strength to correspond with the volume of the circuit-breaking sound. As it could not reproduce amplitudes or degrees of loudness, the Reis instrument could never have transmitted the subtle and extremely complex mixture of frequencies and amplitudes that constitute the sounds of the human voice. It could simulate the rhythms and pitches of speech, producing a stream of gibberish suggestive of speech, but no more than that. Reis himself was aware of the shortcomings of his invention and never patented it, regarding it as nothing more than a scientific experiment without practical application.

This should not be confused with Elisha Gray's Telephone, the name which he bestowed on his instrument for producing 'music by telegraph' which was described at great length in the *New York Times* of 10 July 1874. By means of this device, 'anyone at the receiving end can distinctly hear, without the aid of electromagnetism, the tune or air which is being played 500 or 1,000 miles away'. All that was required by way of a receiver was 'anything that is sonorous so long as it is in some degree a conductor of electricity', citing, for example, 'a tin hoop, with foil paper heads stretched over it . . . a nickel five-cent piece, or an old oyster can'. An official of the Western Union Telegraphic Company predicted that 'in time the operators will transmit the sound of their own voices over the wires'.

Fortunately, Aleck did not read this report, or the transcripts published at length in the *Boston Morning Advertiser* of 11 July and the *Boston Morning Journal* two days later; on 10 July he had left Boston for his summer vacation in Canada. Until he died, he was blissfully unaware of how perilously close he had come to being beaten to the goal. Gray had not yet stumbled across the harmonic multiple telegraph concept but it would only have been a matter of time. The statement that a transmitted tone could be received 'without the aid of electromagnetism' would have seemed to imply that Bell's receiver was both obvious and outmoded, and would probably have induced Aleck to give up the quest.

In August, Gray left Washington and headed north on the first stage of a journey that would take him to Europe to file patents on his invention. In Boston a patent lawyer tried to get him an interview with Pickering but he, too, was out of town on his summer vacation. The lawyer may, indeed, have been the individual who sent Dr Clarence Blake a press-cutting about Gray's musical telegraph. As a result, Blake wrote to Gray, telling him of the phonautograph experiments by Bell and himself and offering to exchange information about their respective researches. The letter arrived too late, and did not catch up with Gray in Europe until September.

On 20 August 1874 the *Hartford Courant* reported the closing session of the annual convention of the American Association for the Advancement of Science which was being held in that city. Buried in the lengthy proceedings was a brief item:

> A curious and striking invention, called a 'telephone', the effect of which is to telegraph musical sound, and even tunes, through any length of wire, has been made, it is said, by Mr Elisha Gray, of Chicago . . . Mr Gray hopes one day to be able to transmit the sound of the human voice also by telegraph . . . but towards this curious result nothing seems to have been done.

Neither the newspaper nor the American Association could have known that, only a few weeks earlier, Professor Bell, still unaware of Gray's telephone, had already figured out how to do what Gray could only dream of doing.

5

The Birth of the Telephone
1874–75

I am become as sounding brass, or a tinkling cymbal
St Paul, 1st Corinthians, xiii, 1

Arriving back at Tutela Heights on 11 July 1874, there was a certain restlessness about Aleck; the old country pursuits soon palled and he spent days on end daydreaming in the little summer-house on the edge of the escarpment. Melville and Eliza were concerned for their son, who seemed old beyond his years. He was preoccupied by his invention and the problems of perfecting it, but – he would hardly admit this to himself – thoughts of Mabel Hubbard kept obtruding themselves. Hastily he put them from his mind. She was more than ten years younger; no great age difference between adults perhaps, but Aleck was twenty-seven and Mabel only sixteen and still a child in the eyes of the law and society. Apart from the age difference, she was deaf, and oddly enough he agonised over his parents' reaction to this handicap, despite the fact that Eliza herself suffered impaired hearing.

He had hardly arrived in Brantford, however, when he set off for Bellville, about a hundred miles north-east of Toronto, to attend the annual convention of American Instructors of the Deaf and Dumb. Aleck gave a paper concerning the difficulties for lip-readers in distinguishing between B and P, and suggesting a solution: 'If some simple apparatus could be contrived to bring the vibrations of the speaker's voice to the hand of the lip-reader, one half of the ambiguities of lip-reading would disappear, and the awkwardness would be avoided of having the lip-reader place his hand upon the speaker's chest or throat'.[1]

On 21 July he returned to Brantford and soon settled into his contemplative routine. A cryptic note in Melville's diary of 26 July indicates what was on Aleck's mind at the time: 'New Motor (hopeful). Electric speech (?)'. The 'new motor' was an idea of Aleck's to harness the energy released by the expansion and contraction of electromagnets when magnetised and demagnetised. If a large number of electromagnets were immersed in some confined fluid and subjected to an intermittent current, he thought that the fluctuating pressure created by expansion and contraction might be utilised to drive a piston. As late as 1878 he was still toying with this impractical notion. But if he had always been hard-headed enough to reject the impractical, he might never have persevered with the idea of 'electric speech'. During his reveries, drawing inspiration from the panoramic scenery, he kept returning to the concept of a vibrating, magnetised reed inducing a fluctuating current in an electromagnetic coil. Somewhere in this idea there was a practical method of transmitting speech if he could but perceive it.

These daydreams were punctuated by frenetic bursts of activity in his workshop behind the conservatory. Through Clarence Blake, he obtained a human ear which he connected to a speaking tube, with a slender stalk of hay attached to one of the bones. The free end of the stalk vibrated against a piece of smoked glass, producing a pattern when he spoke into the tube. This was an advance on Scott's phonautograph. Aleck noted excitedly that the sound waves acting on the tiny membrane of the eardrum could move relatively heavy bones. This led him to speculate that sound waves themselves might be strong enough to generate an appreciable current. Echoing piano strings and Baile's reference to vibrating harp strings recurred in his thoughts. One day late in July – perhaps on the very day that Melville made that laconic entry in his diary – the chaos of unrelated ideas and thoughts suddenly unravelled.

Broadly, Aleck speculated that if one spoke or sang into Baile's series of tuned vibrating plates, as into a piano, the plates or reeds would, if there were a fine enough gradation of pitches among them, echo the speech. Further, he postulated, if instead of Baile's or Reis's battery-powered intermittent currents, each vibrating polarised reed induced a continuous fluctuating current, then the amplitude of the current as well as the frequency would be exactly proportioned for each. The resultant of all these currents could be transmitted through a single point, as in the case of the phonautograph stylus. At the other end of the line an electromagnet would transform the resultant current into pulses or undulations of magnetic force. The force, acting on another array of tuned reeds, would reproduce the original sound. Thus speech would travel great distances with the rapidity of light itself. Aleck's first thought to test this theory was what he termed his harp apparatus, but he lacked the expertise and resources to make such a device at that time. Doubting that this apparatus would be practicable, he switched tack again and concentrated his inventive mind on the multiple telegraph. It was not until he was back in Boston that winter and discussed the idea with the electrical mechanic Moses Farmer that Aleck realised that it was feasible. On 23 November he wrote to his parents from Boston clearly setting out the fundamental principles of the telephone as if for the first time. Brantford's claim as the birthplace of the telephone, in late July 1874, however, is perfectly valid, based on the sketch of the harp apparatus made at that time, and the entry in Melville's diary, though it was not set out in detail till four months later. Strangely enough, Aleck himself was maddeningly vague about the chronology of his invention, and in his testimony much later concerning patent litigation he was uncertain whether he had discussed the 'harp apparatus' at Brantford or not.[2] The debate is largely academic anyway, for the letter of 23 November 1874, clearly setting out the concept, anticipated the earliest rival claim by twelve months.

What is more puzzling is why Aleck that momentous summer should have been thinking along the lines of an array of tuned reeds, like the teeth of a metal comb, rather than the diaphragm transmitter and receiver eventually adopted. This is all the more surprising because he was fully conversant with diaphragms and had worked with them for some time previously. The first specific reference to a diaphragm in his plan for 'electric speech' dates from late October, following his return to Boston. In retrospect this simple device may seem to be very obvious. Both Pickering and Gray had used diaphragms in their receivers (though Aleck was unaware of this fact). Instead, Aleck, by virtue of his training to recognise the sounds of speech as compounds of tone, was influenced by Helmholtz, not to mention the echoing piano strings and Baile's vibrating plates. Gray's expertise was more limited and so he was not sidetracked as Aleck was; while Pickering had a formidable knowledge of acoustics, and the training to select data and phenomena which would suit his purpose. At this stage Aleck's knowledge probably fell between the two. Nevertheless, he probably spoke the truth when he maintained, many years later, that if he had known more about electricity he would never have conceived the principle of the telephone.

Although he continually mulled over these problems, endlessly seeking a way of realising them in practice, Aleck was mainly preoccupied with more mundane matters. In September 1874 he returned to the Sanders home at Salem and noted approvingly the changes in little Georgie, now more outgoing and self-confident as his speech improved. Aleck placed an advertisement in the daily newspaper and garnered a modest number of private pupils which boosted his professorial fees. Though Eliza implored him to save his hard-won cash and not 'dissipate it in mere experiments', her son resumed those late-night sessions in his study-cum-laboratory. Blake suggested that Aleck should collaborate with him on a paper on their research into the phonautograph and Cross importuned him to review the summer's findings; but then external events took a hand and acoustics gave way to telegraphy.

That autumn the Hubbards returned to Cambridge after a prolonged sojourn in New York, and Aleck was invited to their home on Brattle Street. This was a more modern, and certainly more luxurious, homestead than the Sanders mansion, screened from the main road by firs and copper beeches that bordered the five acres of grounds. The house itself was approached by a winding driveway flanked by broad lawns and formal flower beds. In an autobiographical note, written in October 1922, Mabel described Aleck's first visit to her home exactly forty-eight years earlier, on 22 October 1874. He had trudged up the long driveway, mounted the veranda steps and been admitted rather diffidently. His keen eye took in the opulence of the hallway, with its mahogany balustrades and three flights of stairs leading to the upper floors. He was ushered into the drawing-room, with its rich red velvet wallpaper, crimson damask curtains and heavy gilt valances. The circumstances of the visit are not recorded, though it may be supposed that he had been invited by Gardiner Hubbard. At any rate, he was asked to stay for tea, and afterwards played the piano for the delectation of Mrs Hubbard who was an aficionado of classical music.

Having entertained the family with a small selection from his vast repertoire, Aleck stopped suddenly and asked his host if he was aware that a piano would repeat a note sung into it. He then proceeded to give a demonstration, leading to a discussion of the phenomenon of a tuned instrument responding to a telegraphic impulse of the same frequency. Hubbard asked what value there was in that and Aleck explained that by this means several messages might be transmitted over a single wire. Hubbard, with his longstanding interest in telegraphy, was immediately intrigued and excited and pressed the young professor for further details. Afterwards, Hubbard explained the import of Aleck's words to his wife. Aleck, writing home the following day, stated that 'When she raised some objection to one point, he answered it himself saying Don't you see there is only one *air* and so there need be but one *wire!*'

Unbeknown to Aleck, Gardiner Hubbard was at that very moment desperately searching for a practical method of multiple telegraphy, his ambition being to beat the near-monopoly of Western Union and undercut them by offering cheap-rate telegrams. Multiple telegraphy, therefore, was the key to the problem. He was aware of the fact that in Britain the telegraph companies had been taken over by the government in 1869 and operated by the Post Office since January 1870. He was an ardent campaigner for a similar system in the United States. He did not wish to have the existing companies nationalised, but felt that the Postal Telegraph

Company, by offering half-price telegrams to the general public, would either drive them out of business or force them to cut their own rates. He felt so passionately about this that he had expended considerable money and energy in trying to promote a bill in Congress to this effect, and had now reached the point at which he was contemplating selling his property in Cambridge to finance the venture. By the end of 1874 Hubbard was hocked to the eyeballs, and his wife was increasingly alarmed at the extent of his indebtedness to her father. Western Union placed their faith in the Stearns duplex system, to which they had acquired the rights. This permitted the transmission of two telegrams simultaneously. In 1874 the company purchased the rights to Edison's quadruplex system which immediately doubled output. William Orton, president of Western Union, smugly believed that telegraphy had advanced as far as humanly possible. Now, here was this young man, Mabel's teacher no less, calmly telling Hubbard that he could beat Edison's new system five or six times over. Hubbard could scarcely believe his ears.

Back at Essex Street that evening Aleck regaled the Sanders family with his afternoon's doings. Thomas Sanders, Georgie's father, was immediately apprehensive. A prominent businessman himself, he was acutely aware of Hubbard's financial difficulties and hinted that Aleck had been less than discreet in blurting out as much as he had. Sanders implored him to file a patent on his invention immediately. Aleck had found that he needed to submit a working model to the Patent Office in Washington, but was constrained by lack of cash, so in the end he offered Sanders a half share in the venture if he would put up the necessary money. Aleck's anxieties were not allayed when he received a letter from Clarence Blake the very same day, casually mentioning that he had received a letter from Elisha Gray from the Royal Institute in London where he had been experimenting in telegraphing vocal sounds, 'which you will be glad to see', added Blake ingenuously. In fact, Gray had said nothing of the kind; it was Blake who had read more into the letter than it actually imparted. Gray had merely stated that he had been conducting experiments in London with the help of John Tyndall and would be interested in exchanging views and data on acoustics. When Aleck called at Blake's office on 23 October he would not peruse Gray's letter, lest he be accused later of having stolen Gray's ideas. Consequently he went off without settling his mind on the matter. To Blake, however, Aleck confided that he had his own ideas on vocal telegraphy and made some crude sketches of the membrane transmitters which he now proposed to use in addition to the harp apparatus. Fortunately, Blake preserved these rough notes, settling for all time the earliest date on which the principles of the Bell telephone were enunciated publicly.

Meanwhile, Gardiner Hubbard was losing no time in making discreet enquiries at the Patent Office regarding any rival scientists working on the harmonic telegraph. Having ascertained that the field was clear for the moment, Hubbard offered to fund Aleck's experiments for a share of the patent rights. Aleck, worried about Gray and flattered by Hubbard's interest in him (and perhaps subconsciously seeking a means of getting closer to Mabel), readily assented, so long as Thomas Sanders was agreeable. Sanders, perceiving Hubbard's entrepreneurial talents, had no objection; and so the three men agreed to a tripartite partnership, Hubbard and Sanders putting up the money and Aleck the inventions.

This was a major breakthrough for the budding inventor, but at the same time his work as a teacher of the deaf and dumb was also making dramatic progress. More pupils than ever were coming forward and the Medical Society of Massachusetts was showing considerable interest in his ear experiments. Aleck decided to take the plunge and become an American citizen, a matter attended to with far less formality in the 1870s than it would be today. This hurdle surmounted, Aleck was able to file a caveat. He could see light at the end of the tunnel and wrote jubilantly to his parents on 30 October: 'I feel as if I may yet TAKE OFF SOME HUSKS!!!', alluding to his first boyhood invention. He was careful not to let Melville feel out of it, adding, 'Should I be able to make any money out of the idea, we shall have Visible Speech put before the world in a more permanent form than at present.'

Melville's characteristically forthright response was that Aleck was biting off more than he could chew. 'Your wisest course would be to sell your plans to Messrs Sanders and Hubbard . . . You can't work out the scheme without neglecting your other business . . . Take what you can get at once.' Fortunately Aleck ignored this well-meant advice. At the same time he was being pushed by Hubbard who urged him to take a skilled assistant. Aleck refused, and his pride likewise made him reluctant to ask his partners for money. He told Hubbard firmly that he had his priorities, and his lectures at Boston University, his teacher-training course, his private pupils and little Georgie Sanders all took precedence over multiple telegraphy. Hubbard was put out, frustrated and impatient by turns, but Aleck refused to change his mind. He would confine his experiments to weekends and late nights.

Early in November, Gardiner Hubbard travelled to Washington to check more closely on rival caveats and patents in the telegraphic field. There he ran into William Orton who touched briefly on Elisha Gray's tone-transmitting apparatus as 'very curious' but seemed blissfully unaware of the implications for multiple telegraphy. Nevertheless, Aleck's patent lawyer, Joseph Adams, putting out feelers to the lawyer acting for Gray, reported

CLOCKWISE FROM TOP LEFT: *Alexander Melville Bell, 1868; Eliza Grace Bell; Alec's grandfather, Alexander Bell; an advertisement for Melville's work*

ABOVE: *Alec in Elgin and* (RIGHT) *in London, 1862;* BELOW: *Weston House School, Elgin*

[Pronounce the Nos.]	[Names.]	[Name the Objects.]		[Name the Objects.]	
1.					
2.					
3.					
4.					
5.					
6.					
7.					
8.					

[EXERCISE.]

One by one.
Two or three.
Four at once.
Five o'clock.
Half-past six.
Seven-thirty.
Eight to nine.
Ten or twelve.
Twice two, four.
Twice three, six.
Four and four, eight.
Nine and two, eleven.
Twice or thrice.

Two, a couple.
Twelve, a dozen.
Twenty, a score.
A book-case.
A few books.
New book shelves.
A silver watch.
A gold watch.
The watch-key.
A good saw.
Cap and feather.
Tongs and shovel.
Sugar-tongs.

A hunting whip.
A table lamp.
A bunch of onions.
Corns and bunions.
A ship's boat.
A sailing boat.
Cart and horse.
A round tent.
Bows of house.
A dog-kennel.
A little monkey.
A pretty cage.
A green canary.

A page from Melville's book, Visible Speech

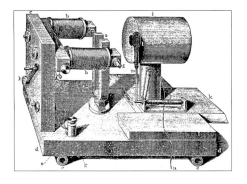

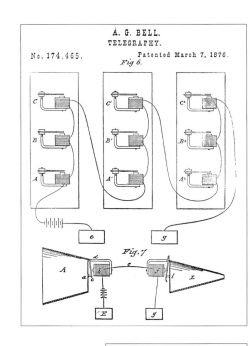

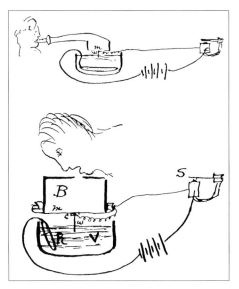

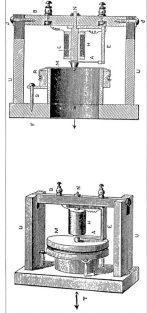

CLOCKWISE FROM TOP LEFT: *Helmholtz's tuning-fork sounder; a page from Bell's patent on 'Improvement in Telegraphy' showing the tuned reeds of a harmonic multiple telegraph and a magneto-electric telephone; the first membrane diaphragm telephone, June 1875; harmonic telegraph instruments; and sketches from the inventor's notebook, March 1876*

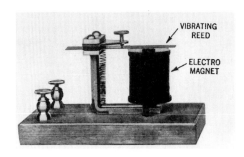

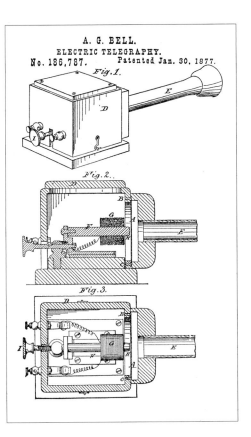

A. G. BELL.
ELECTRIC TELEGRAPHY.
No. 186,787. Patented Jan. 30, 1877.

Fig.1.

Fig.2.

Fig.3.

CLOCKWISE FROM TOP LEFT: *a page from Bell's second basic telephone patent, January 1877; the 'gallows' telephone; an experimental model, February 1877; and diagrams from the Centennial Exhibition*

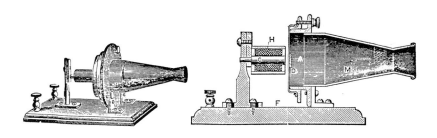

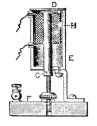

The Bell family at Tutela Heights, c.1880 (Melville is on the right)

The Bell homestead at 94 Tutela Heights Road, Brantford, Ontario, where the telephone was conceived, 26 July 1874

LIST OF SUBSCRIBERS.

New Haven District Telephone Company.

OFFICE 219 CHAPEL STREET.

February 21, 1878.

Residences.	*Stores, Factories, &c.*
Rev. JOHN E. TODD.	O. A. DORMAN.
J. B. CARRINGTON.	STONE & CHIDSEY.
H. B. BIGELOW.	NEW HAVEN FLOUR CO. State St.
C. W. SCRANTON.	" " " " Cong. ave.
GEORGE W. COY.	" " " " Grand St.
G. L. FERRIS.	" " " Fair Haven.
H. P. FROST.	ENGLISH & MERSICK.
M. F. TYLER.	NEW HAVEN FOLDING CHAIR CO.
I. H. BROMLEY.	H. HOOKER & CO.
GEO. E. THOMPSON.	W. A. ENSIGN & SON.
WALTER LEWIS.	H. B. BIGELOW & CO.
	C. COWLES & CO.
Physicians.	C. S. MERSICK & CO.
DR. E. L. R. THOMPSON.	SPENCER & MATTHEWS.
DR. A. E. WINCHELL.	PAUL ROESSLER.
DR. C. S. THOMSON, Fair Haven.	E. S. WHEELER & CO.
	ROLLING MILL CO.
Dentists.	APOTHECARIES HALL.
DR. E. S. GAYLORD.	E. A. GESSNER.
DR. R. F. BURWELL.	AMERICAN TEA CO.
Miscellaneous.	*Meat & Fish Markets.*
REGISTER PUBLISHING CO.	W. H. HITCHINGS, City Market.
POLICE OFFICE.	GEO. E. LUM, " "
POST OFFICE.	A. FOOTE & CO.
MERCANTILE CLUB.	STRONG, HART & CO.
QUINNIPIAC CLUB.	
F. V. McDONALD, Yale News.	*Hack and Boarding Stables.*
SMEDLEY BROS. & CO.	CRUTTENDEN & CARTER.
M. F. TYLER, Law Chambers.	BARKER & RANSOM.

Office open from 6 A. M. to 2 A. M.

After March 1st. this Office will be open all night.

*The first telephone directory and (RIGHT)
an early telephone switchboard, c.1885*

Alec in 1880 (© British Telecommunications plc, 1985)

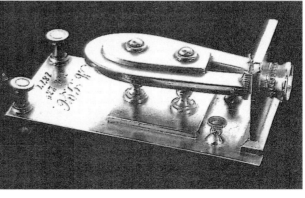

CLOCKWISE FROM TOP LEFT:
*Mabel Gardiner Hubbard, Alec's
wife; Mabel at the age of six;
Alec's father-in-law Gardiner
Hubbard; the silver replica of the
first telephone, given by Alec to
Mabel*

Alec with Helen Keller and Annie Sullivan, July 1894;
RIGHT: *George Sanders*

LEFT: *Alec communicates with Charlie Crane, a blind and deaf Canadian boy;* BELOW: *this children's glove with letters of the alphabet written on it was used by Alec as an aid in the teaching of the deaf;* BOTTOM: *Boston School for the Deaf; top row (left) shows Dexter King and (far right) Alec Bell; fourth row (second from left) is Sarah Fuller and (far right) Mary True*

Mabel and Alec with their daughters Elsie and Daisy, 1885

Alec and Mabel boating at Beinn Bhreagh

Alec with his grandchildren

The house at Beinn Bhreagh

Alec (far right) flying a tetrahedral kite, 1900

Inaugurating the Tetrahedral Tower, Beinn Bhreagh

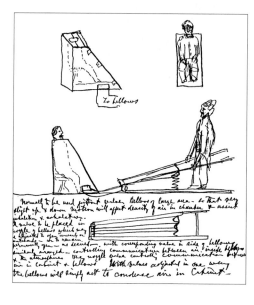

When Alec's new-born son died from respiratory problems, he invented a 'vacuum jacket', forerunner of the iron lung, which might have saved his son

The HD-1, 16 July 1912

The Alexander Graham Bell Museum contains relics of his aeronautical experiments

Commemorating the telephone:
LEFT: *Alec speaks to Tom Watson on the inter-continental link-up, 1915;*
BELOW: *silver crown coin from the Isle of Man;*
BOTTOM: *stamp marking the hundredth anniversary of Alec's invention*

100TH ANNIVERSARY OF ALEXANDER GRAHAM BELL

$3

Telephone in 1976

GRENADA GRENADINES

back that Aleck should redouble his efforts. In the second week of November Aleck worked day and night on the project and finally submitted his caveat papers on 14 November. On the same day *The Commonwealth*, a Boston paper, reprinted the *New York Times* article of the previous July on Gray's invention. Aleck's attention was drawn to the article, reprinted word for word, which said that Gray had got the idea 'about two months ago'. Thinking that Gray had only thought of it in September, Aleck was jubilant; but he was soon brought back down to earth by Hubbard who wrote from Washington pointing out that Gray had applied for a patent on his musical telegraph as early as August.

Anticipating legal problems, Hubbard insisted that Aleck produce a signed and dated document describing each stage of his experiments in detail. Aleck himself persuaded Percival Richards to put on paper a record of the experiments at West Newton Street as far back as early 1873. Anthony Pollok, Hubbard's lawyer in Washington, got Aleck to withdraw his caveat, as Gray had already applied for a patent covering at least one aspect of the harmonic telegraph. A caveat at this late stage would not have protected Aleck but merely alerted Gray to what was afoot. It was better to wait until Aleck was ready to apply for a full patent, which would have the effect of negating Gray's application so long as Aleck could produce proof of priority in conception. Facing the fact that he desperately needed skilled assistance, Aleck now turned to Moses Farmer who seconded one of his best assistants, George Hamilton, to translate Aleck's rough sketches into working machines. Professor Joseph Lovering of Harvard was also enlisted to check Aleck's theories. Aleck even tested his telephone theory on Farmer and reported home:

> To my delight he said the theory was *all right* but that the difficulties of practically working the idea were such that it would take years to solve the problem practically. He advised me to publish the idea in the *Philosophical Magazine* after I had protected my telegraphic scheme.[3]

Charles Cross concurred, considering that the currents generated by the human voice would not be strong enough to make such a device workable. As a result, Aleck put the telephone to the back of his mind and focused all his energy on the multiple telegraph. In the same letter to his parents Aleck voiced his fears:

> It is a neck and neck race between Mr Gray and myself who shall complete our apparatus first. He has the advantage over me in being a practical electrician – but I have reason to believe that I am better acquainted with the phenomena of sound than he is . . . The very opposition seems to nerve

me to work. I feel that I shall be seriously ill should I fail in this now I am so thoroughly wrought up.

The following day he wrote again, reporting that Hamilton had finished a battery-operated instrument which worked perfectly. On 26 November, Aleck's third letter home in four days informed Melville of 'a most extraordinary discovery'. Grasping a vibrating receiver armature to damp it, Aleck discovered that the tone continued. When he removed the armature altogether he heard the sound coming directly from the iron core of the electromagnet. This pointed him in the direction of an entirely new kind of receiver. The following day he stumbled on the fact that an empty coil without a core would emit a sound of the same pitch as the transmitter. Cross, however, was quick to point out that Joseph Henry had already discovered the vibrating electromagnetic core, though not the effect on an empty coil. Furthermore, Cross stated that Reis had used this effect in his instrument of 1861.

Deflated by these revelations, Aleck also despaired of overcoming niggling little practical problems that continually cropped up. Oxidation of the circuit-breaking contact, due to sparking, might be overcome by a condenser, but other matters were not so readily put right. The transmitter pitch varied with circuit length and battery strength, entailing wearying experiments and adjustments; but Hamilton was unable to transform Aleck's diagrams for an induced-current circuit into practical reality, while the bar magnets on a revolving cylinder did not yield an oscillating current with the frequency expected. For the time being, therefore, Aleck concentrated on direct-current circuits for the patent application.

Inevitably anxieties over these problems induced sleeplessness and in the daytime he conducted his classes like a zombie. Then, on the morning of 1 December, he got out of bed and immediately collapsed. Several days in bed and a very reluctant reduction of night work restored his physical equilibrium though his mind was as restless and hyperactive as ever. By 14 December he was charging off in other directions, hearing sounds from the bar-magnet cylinder and making a miniature organ using vox humana reeds as tuned transmitters. With this device he sent tunes from the Sanders barn to the house; by pressing his ear to a single receiver reed, he could even hear chords, but the air-vibrated organ reeds could not be tuned as readily as the electrically vibrated steel reeds. Faced with the dilemma of keeping up with his teaching commitments, balanced against the urge to get ahead of Gray, Aleck considered staying on at Boston over the Christmas holidays, but on the spur of the moment he packed up and went off to Brantford, arriving as the family were recovering from their Christmas dinner. Melville's diary records how his son was brimming over with news of his latest experiments. 'Al's experiments described' (26 December); 'long talk on multipl teleg and speech trans. Al sanguine' (27 December); 'talking half the night motor and telephone' (29 December). By 2 January 1875 Aleck was back in Boston, immediately thrust into teaching at the university and devising a series of charts for teachers of Visible Speech as well as investigating ways and means of reducing the typesetting costs of printing the exercises.

Not only did these extraneous duties delay work on the telegraph, but Aleck now lost the services of George Hamilton who had gone to Newport, Rhode Island, to assist Moses Farmer there in his work for the United States Naval Torpedo Station. In desperation Aleck turned to Charles Williams for help. Williams, it will be remembered, ran an electrical workshop at 109 Court Street, where many ambitious mechanics and aspiring inventors congregated. In July 1872 Williams took on as assistant an eighteen-year-old named Thomas Augustus Watson, son of a livery stable foreman in Salem. Tom Watson was a natural; within two years he had emerged as one of the ablest of the two dozen workmen employed by Williams to manufacture all kinds of electrical gadgets from call bells to telegraph instruments. He had continued to study in his spare time and had the breadth of intellect which made him ideal for the work that would immortalise him. By mid-1874 he had been taken off the routine assembly-line and promoted to custom work, advising and helping budding inventors to convert their ideas into working models. It was in this capacity that Watson first encountered the man who would change his life for ever:

> He was a tall, slender, quick-motioned young man with a pale face, black side-whiskers and drooping moustache, big nose and high, sloping forehead crowned with bushy jet-black hair. It was Alexander Graham Bell, a young professor in Boston University.[4]

At that time Aleck was having an instrument made through Farmer and Hamilton and it was actually a grave breach of etiquette for him to go direct to the Williams employee who was working on the device at Farmer's behest, but this was not untypical of Aleck, headstrong and impetuous and always impatient to cut corners to get a job done. When Farmer and Hamilton left Boston, however, Aleck remembered the bright young mechanic who had bent the rules to help him out in a hurry, and promptly approached him. At that point this assignment was no more than any other job which Watson was carrying out on behalf of the firm's clients, but over the ensuing weeks he came to know the young professor much more intimately, and the experience had a tremendous impact. 'No finer influence ever came into my life,' he wrote fifty years on. Watson was impressed as much by Aleck's impeccable British table manners as by 'his punctilious courtesy to every one, his expressive speech, his clear, crisp articulation', all of which were a revelation. He talked knowledgeably of music and literature and introduced the younger man to the great scientific works of the period.

Watson's first assignment was to make a brass cylinder as a prelude to the latest round of Aleck's experiments to produce a rotating current-interrupter. When this failed, Aleck concentrated on steel-spring rheotomes, of which Watson fashioned several in a new pattern simplifying the operation. Now Aleck could see a glimmer of light at the end of the tunnel. The next setback came from an unexpected quarter. Late in January he received a letter from Joseph Adams who had handled the caveat which was sub-sequently withdrawn. Adams, who was privy to a great deal of Aleck's experiments, now wondered whether he was free 'to act in the interest of other parties in matters involving the same subject'. Aleck, in alarm, sent a telegram to Gardiner Hubbard on 26 January, complaining of this 'dishonourable and blackmailing letter'. Hubbard subsequently replied saying that he would find some way of preventing Adams acting for anyone else in the same line, but this did little, if anything, to allay Aleck's fears. He planned to travel south to Washington on 12 February, but his schedule was delayed, partly by a technical problem and partly because he had another idea. The hitch arose because the model transmitters stopped vibrating after a few minutes. This problem was solved only after Aleck worked till four in the morning to come up with a simple but ingenious solution, of running a piece of platinum wire through a tiny hole in the reed. Commenting on this hiccup, he wrote home, 'I trust you may never know the agony I endured all night and yesterday.'

The brilliant idea which also hit him suddenly was the 'vibratory circuit breaker' which would adapt his multiple telegraph to an autograph device capable of printing out the dots and dashes of the Morse code on strips of paper. By this method Aleck reasoned that up to thirty needles could operate simultaneously to create closely spaced parallel broken lines on a sheet of paper. These lines would reproduce writing, even pictures, when viewed through a fine grid. If the original image were written or drawn on special paper, using special ink which would close a contact where marked, and break contact where blank, it could be pulled along under contact points connected to thirty transmitters. In existing autograph devices a single receiver stylus had to cross the sheet a number of times. 'The new attachment will render it possible to reproduce a long message almost instantaneously by a single turn of a cylinder,' he wrote confidently to his parents on 12 February.

A week later Aleck, accompanied by Thomas Sanders, boarded the overnight train for Washington and arrived there on the evening of 20 February. The following day was spent in unpacking the apparatus at Gardiner Hubbard's town-house and preparing it for demonstration. Even then, Aleck was almost in hysterics when he could not procure workable battery cells from the only electrician in the capital, and his old paranoia surfaced when the electrician's messenger 'came right into the parlor and stared about, to see what kind of instruments I had got'. Hubbard then dropped the bombshell that William Orton of Western Union would be calling round in about thirty minutes to see the instruments. As Aleck told his parents, 'The Western Union is probably the largest corporate body that has ever existed. It controls more miles of telegraph wire than there *are in the whole of Europe!*'. Aleck laboured frenetically to produce makeshift battery cells from slop-basins, sawn-off carbon rods and substitute acids, and finally got the apparatus to work 'just half a minute' before Orton arrived. Fortunately the demonstration was an unqualified success; the instruments had never performed so well. Orton had intended popping round for a few minutes but actually tarried for more than an hour. He had to leave Washington that night, but he urged Aleck to come to New York where he could demonstrate his invention on Western Union's network.

While it was improbable that Elisha Gray had nobbled Washington's one and only electrician, Aleck had much to fear from his rival, who, in January, had renewed patent applications for his animal-tissue tone transmitter and a vibratory musical telegraph. The first was of no concern to Aleck, but the second was very close to his own concept, apart from the fact that it used a single Reis-type electromagnetic sounding-box receiver rather than a number of tuned reeds, and relied on the traditional make-and-break principle rather than on the continual vibration of the transmitting keys.

On the other hand, it may have been no mere coincidence that Gray (who had not thought of a harmonic multiple telegraph till the spring of 1874, fully three years after Aleck) should make a formal application for a patent on the basic harmonic multiple telegraph on 23 February – three days after Aleck's arrival. It is a matter for speculation whether Joseph Adams tipped off Gray's patent lawyer in a bid to forestall the Scotsman. At any rate, it was not until 25 February that Aleck filed his patent. Consequently Anthony Pollok and Marcellus Bailey, the patent lawyers hired by Gardiner Hubbard, were doubtful whether Aleck would succeed in his application. What clinched it, so far as they were concerned, was the vibratory circuit breaker, which had been an afterthought. A stroke of luck intervened when it transpired that one of the Patent Office examiners was a deaf-mute who knew Aleck and could vouch for his character. On 5 March Aleck wrote home hopefully, reporting on a chance meeting in Pollok's office that day with Zenas F. Wilber, the Patent Office examiner who had been assigned the task of handling Aleck's patent applications. 'I had a long interview with him in which I explained everything, and I can't help thinking that he must have been convinced of my independent conception of the whole thing.'

Acting on advice from the patent lawyers, Aleck applied for three patents: on the harmonic telegraph using direct current with a return wire instead of grounding; on the harmonic telegraph using induced currents on a single wire without grounding; and on the vibratory circuit breaker with its corollary of an autograph telegraph. The last-named was granted on 6 April, and Aleck exulted in the knowledge that this was the key to the entire system, without which Gray could do little of commercial value. But the other two were deemed to interfere with Gray's applications and also with one filed on 3 March by Paul La Cour of Copenhagen. Nevertheless, as none of the interfering applications had been granted, the matter hinged not on dates of filing but on priority of conception. While these portentous matters were pending, Aleck, with Sanders and Hubbard, drew up a document on 27 February agreeing to equal shares in Aleck's telegraphic inventions, including 'any further improvements he may make in perfecting said inventions'. In the event of the inventions proving valuable, a company was to be formed to control the patents, each partner getting a third of the stock. This extremely simple agreement originated what eventually became the largest single business enterprise in world history.

Two days later Aleck had an interview with the director of the Smithsonian Institution. Born at Albany in 1797 of Scottish parents, Joseph Henry had become professor of Natural Philosophy at Princeton in 1832 and secretary of the Smithsonian in 1846; he had been at the helm of that scientific institution for longer than Aleck had lived. Apart from setting up the United States Weather Bureau, his greatest achievement had been the establishment of the first great agency for the free dissemination of science and an international system for the exchange of scientific publications which flourishes to this day. As chairman of the Lighthouse Board since 1871, Henry had turned in old age to a study of fog signals, and this had revived a much earlier interest in sound and acoustics in general. President of the National Academy of Sciences and the leading light in both the Philosophical Society of Washington and the American Association for the Advancement of Science, he was unanimously regarded as America's foremost physicist. Joseph Henry was a man of varied culture, of large breadth and liberality of views, of generous impulses, of great gentleness and courtesy of manner, kindly good humour, combined with firmness of purpose, tireless energy and vast organisational abilities. As a young man he had experimented with electromagnetism, and his electromagnet of 1829 was the practical basis for every dynamo and electric motor devised since then. What Wheatstone and Faraday were to England, Henry was to America. He produced the first electric telegraph in 1831 and four years later discovered the principle of grounding or earthing as a return conductor. He invented the first electric motor in 1831 and self-induction the following year. He elucidated the principles of the electric transformer and stumbled across radio waves as early as 1842.

One can imagine Aleck's trepidation on being ushered into the presence of such a great man. Though now in his late seventies, Henry was as vigorous and alert as a man half his age. He had anticipated Aleck's discovery of sound from an electromagnet core, so Aleck told the old man of his other experiments to ascertain which were new and which previously known. Henry listened impassively until Aleck mentioned sound from the empty coil. This had, in fact, been discovered by a French scientist in the 1860s but Henry had forgotten this and thought that it was a fresh discovery. He offered to repeat the experiment and publish the results through the Smithsonian, giving the young man full credit, of course. Aleck was flattered with this response. Henry was even quite ready to accompany Aleck back to Hubbard's house there and then, despite a heavy cold, his advanced years and the bitterness of the weather, but Aleck promised to bring his apparatus to the Smithsonian the following day. On the conclusion of this demonstration, Aleck was emboldened to consult Henry about his theory of transmitting the human voice by means of his harp apparatus. The old scientist responded favourably, declaring it 'the germ of a great invention'. Later he showed Aleck the actual Reis membrane transmitter in the Smithsonian collection but dismissed it as unsuitable for speech.

As Henry did not rule out Aleck's theory, the young man asked him, 'What would you advise me to do; publish it and let others work it out, or attempt to solve the problem for myself?' Henry had bitter memories of the fame and fortune he had thrown away by letting Samuel Morse work out the commercial application of the telegraph, so he had no hesitation in urging the young man to keep the idea to himself. When Aleck confessed that he lacked the necessary electrical knowledge, Henry riposted gruffly, 'Get it!' Excitedly Aleck reported to Brantford on 18 March:

> I cannot tell you how much these two words have encouraged me. I live in an atmosphere of discouragement for scientific pursuits. Good Mrs Sanders is unfortunately one of the *cui bono* people, and is too much in the habit of looking at the dark side of things. Such a chimerical idea as telegraphing *vocal sounds* would indeed to *most minds* seem scarcely feasible enough to spend time in working over. I believe, however, that it is feasible, and that I have got the clue to the solution of the problem.

On the way back to Boston Aleck lingered in New York long enough to demonstrate his multiple telegraph on one of Western Union's wires. A few weeks later he returned to New York for a lengthy discussion with Orton and his chief engineer George Prescott, who was most impressed by the Bell instruments. 'By a happy chance,' Aleck reported home, 'they are much more perfect than I thought at first.' Even using much weaker electromagnets, the signals came through clearly over a distance of two hundred miles. Aleck was asked to come back that afternoon, when Prescott would test the instruments with much more powerful electromagnets. On his return, however, Aleck was dismayed to learn that his instruments were not ready. Moreover, to his consternation, he was informed by Orton that Elisha Gray had just been in to see him. Orton sang the praises of Gray as an 'ingenious workman' with 'good apparatus' which made Bell's look crude by comparison. Though Orton bragged that Western Union was a great power whose influence could make 'the weaker party the stronger', he added a sting in the tail: 'Inventors are apt to overestimate the value of their work,' he concluded dismissively.

As Aleck got up to leave, Orton asked casually, 'By the bye, is Mr Gardiner G. Hubbard interested in this matter with you?'

'Yes,' Aleck replied.

'The Western Union will never take up a scheme which will benefit Mr Hubbard,' said Orton with finality.

Orton, 'perfectly gentlemanly and polite in his manner', drove Aleck back to his hotel and promised to accord him full facilities at Western Union to test his instruments. But he reiterated that Hubbard had done too much to injure the company for it to aid any scheme in which he had an interest. Hubbard happened to be in New York that evening and when Aleck gave him the doleful news, he generously offered to withdraw from the project, but Aleck would not hear of it. Hubbard's sound advice was for Aleck to stay a day longer, retrieve his instruments from Western Union, and take them across the street to that company's great rival, the Atlantic and Pacific Telegraph Company.

Shrewdly, Hubbard reckoned that the merest hint of Aleck flirting with the opposition would bring Orton into line. Unbeknown to Aleck, in fact, he had no sooner left Western Union than Orton and Prescott had retested his instruments with more powerful electromagnets and were forced to admit that the Bell system was far superior to anything that Gray could come up with. The following day Orton shifted his position: while his company would not help *develop* any scheme for Hubbard's benefit, no such proviso attached to the purchase of a product once it had attained perfection. Of course, if Mr Bell chose to go to their rivals, Western Union would back Gray to the hilt. Orton hastily admitted that he had no such arrangement with Elisha Gray as yet, and had no immediate thought to make one.[5]

It is not surprising that Aleck came back to Boston 'thoroughly worn out'. His doctor, concerned for Aleck's mental and physical health, prescribed immediate rest followed by a drastic cut-back in work. Reluctantly, Aleck cancelled his lucrative private tuition but continued his university classes and, of course, Georgie's lessons; but henceforward telegraphy would consume him more and more. It was a painful decision, both on moral and financial grounds, especially the latter. By June Aleck was reduced to borrowing money off Tom Watson (whose weekly wages of $13.25 were about half what Aleck earned at the university). Scots pride, and Aleck's growing fondness for Mabel, prevented him from admitting his predicament to Gardiner Hubbard, far less appealing to him for help. Perhaps Dean Monroe sensed the dire straits in which his young professor found himself, for in June he tactfully paid Aleck in advance for the following year's lectures. Without this timely assistance, Aleck later confessed, 'I would not have been able to get along at all.'

Now he was able to redouble his efforts, relieved of money worries. That spring he concentrated on multiple and autograph telegraphy, spurred on by Orton's arrogant dismissal of the Hubbard Bill the previous year, which he had publicly attacked because the existing system of autograph telegraphy was too slow. Now that Aleck promised a system ten times as fast, Hubbard was desperate to make Orton eat his words. Hard-headed Yankee that he was, Hubbard regarded the autograph telegraph as the real money-spinner; and, besides, of all Aleck's inventions it was the one that was quite unassailable by anything that Elisha Gray could so far come up with.

Having achieved the initial breakthrough, Aleck found himself running out of steam when it came to the fine tuning and the ironing-out of minor problems. Some of the snags were not so small, and his heart sank when he discovered that he had been far too optimistic in imagining that thirty simultaneous needles could work quite well. He soon found that, even operating with no more than six receivers, there were problems in eliminating interference from the various frequencies; and devising transmitter pitches which would yield the least interference was proving a major headache. By late May he admitted to his parents that his lack of experience in electricity was 'a great drawback', although he took some crumb of comfort from the fact that 'Morse conquered his electrical difficulties although he was only a painter, and I don't intend to give in either till all is completed'.

He had to discipline himself strictly to stick to the matter in hand, even when the notion of telephony beckoned him so seductively. At the

Williams workshop one evening, after a particularly disheartening day, Aleck broached the subject with his assistant. 'Watson, if I can get a mechanism which will make a current of electricity vary in its intensity, as the air varies in density when a sound is passing through it, I can telegraph any sound, even the sound of speech.' He went on to describe the 'harp apparatus', giving Watson the impression that the instrument he had in mind would be the size of a piano. Perhaps Joseph Henry's misgivings about a diaphragm transmitter continued to govern Aleck's ideas. Taking this a step further, Aleck wrote to Gardiner Hubbard on 4 May saying that he had come up with an idea for overcoming 'the feebleness of the induced currents', the supposed practical objection to his 'electric speech' project:

> I have read somewhere that the resistance offered by a wire . . . is affected by the *tension of the wire*. If this is so, a *continuous current of electricity* passed through a vibrating wire should meet with a varying resistance, and hence a pulsatory action should be induced in the current . . . [corresponding] in *amplitude*, as well as in rate of movement, to the vibrations of the string . . . Thus the *timbre* of a sound could be transmitted . . . and the strength of the current can be increased *ad libitum* without destroying the *relative intensities of the vibrations*.

This letter is of the utmost importance, as it established Aleck's priority of conception concerning variable resistance, the fundamental principle of the modern telephone.

Aleck was so excited at this prospect that he could hardly wait to test the theory. The following day he and Watson rigged wires from Aleck's study in Salem to the neighbouring music room of Manuel Fenellosa, a Spaniard who had come to America four decades earlier with a travelling orchestra, married into one of Salem's leading families, and settled down as a teacher of music. The strings on Fenellosa's piano were mounted on a steel frame but Aleck chose a string as close to the transmitter frequency as possible and listened while Watson, in the study next door, sent an intermittent current through it. Aleck heard the faint whine of the transmitter, but could not determine whether it came from the piano string or directly through the air. Then he sent a steady current through the circuit and listened to a receiver in the study while Watson plucked the piano wire. Again he was unsure whether the faint sound had been transmitted electrically. Aleck put down the failure of this experiment to the metal frame of the piano and resolved to try again, when time permitted, using a wire stretched across a membrane.

This blind alley sent Aleck back to the autograph telegraph and by 24 May he could report cautiously to Hubbard that 'I think I have at last mastered the Autograph; at least, I see clearly one or two sources of difficulty . . . and I hope in a few days to have some good results to show.' The same day, he wrote to Brantford on the subject that was now dearest to his heart: 'I think that the transmission of the human voice is much more nearly at hand than I had supposed.'

Summer came to Boston early that year, and by the beginning of June the city was oppressively hot. The attic workshop at 109 Court Street felt like an oven. Aleck had sweated with mounting frustration over the maddening problem of getting his transmitter pitches into the most jarring dissonance he could create, a matter which must have given the consummate musician in him one of his worst headaches. Over and over again he wrestled with the problem that had baffled him all day. He was using three transmitters and three correspondingly tuned receivers in one room, connected in series to three receivers in the adjoining room. Aleck pressed a key that sent one transmitter's tone through the circuit, and the proper receiver in both rooms sounded correctly. He sent another frequency through the circuit and again the appropriate receivers sounded; but when he tried the third, Watson's receiver failed to respond. Aleck called out to Watson to try adjusting the free end of the reed above the electromagnetic pole. As he waited for his assistant to try this, Aleck sat and stared at the receiver coupled to the refractory instrument next door.

Suddenly, as if miraculously, the reed began vibrating, apparently of its own accord, with no transmitter current in the circuit. On a hunch, Aleck bounded next door to see what Watson was actually doing. 'Keep plucking the reed!' he barked, then ran back to his own room to see the miracle repeated. Now, excitedly, Aleck silenced the whining transmitters and recoupled the circuit, confined to the three receivers in his room and the three next door. Watson commenced plucking his receiver reeds one by one; and one by one the corresponding reeds in Aleck's room not only vibrated but sounded. To anyone else coming upon this scene, Aleck's antics would have been irrational and inexplicable; but no music of the spheres could ever have sounded more sweetly to his ears than the ping of those plucked reeds.

Aleck immediately realised the significance of what was happening. The plucked reeds were inducing the undulatory current he had postulated almost a year previously. That incredibly weak current, exciting the electromagnets in his room, made their reeds vibrate in exactly the same manner, vibrating with sufficient strength to produce audible sounds. It occurred to Aleck that he had overemphasised the degree of vibration required to make a sound. The merest disturbance, it seemed, would suffice!

While Watson continued to pluck the reed, Aleck pressed his ear against one of his own reeds not attuned to it, damping that reed's natural vibration. Hoping against hope, he was elated to hear a faint sound, the pitch not of his reed but of Watson's. Furthermore, he heard its *timbre*. He heard faintly but faithfully exactly what Watson was hearing next door. And, as Aleck appreciated, what he heard was nothing more, and nothing less, than harmonics as complex and variable as, dared he hope, human speech.

At that precise moment, on the sultry evening of 2 June 1875, the telephone was born.

6

The Transmission of Speech
1875–76

'Tis a lesson you should heed,

   Try, try again.

If at first you don't succeed,

   Try, try again.

William Edward Hickson

All else was driven from his mind. Aleck now devoted every minute of his time to the transmission of speech. Disregarding the oppressive humidity, he and Tom Watson laboured long and hard and far into the cooler nights to perfect the mechanism. At this juncture Aleck jettisoned the harp apparatus and concentrated on diaphragms. Hastily he outlined his idea on a scrap of paper which Tom pored over during a midnight train-ride back home to Salem, and a couple of days later the young mechanic produced the first practical instrument. The membrane of the diaphragm was much too fine and the armature far too heavy, with the result that the latter tore the former when transmission was attempted. Had Watson not made these understandable but fundamental errors, the practical realisation of the telephone might have come much sooner; but Aleck was sufficiently discouraged by this failure to delay further experimentation for four crucial weeks.

Meanwhile Gardiner Hubbard was becoming more and more anxious concerning the multiple telegraph and urged Aleck to concentrate on the main business in hand. On 19 June he wrote to his youthful partner:

When I was at your work shop the other day and saw your new arrangements, I was almost convinced that it was of more value than the autography but further reflection brings me back to the autograph as the 'Ne plus ultra'.[1]

Hubbard seems to have been referring to the earliest diaphragm instruments. His gentle hint did the trick, and Aleck abandoned the telephone for several weeks while he and Watson renewed their efforts to increase the strength of induced undulatory currents, with a view to bringing the autograph telegraph to a practical result. Nevertheless, always at the back of Aleck's mind was his cherished goal. On 30 June he wrote to his parents:

> At last a means has been found which will render possible the transmission . . . of the human voice. By tomorrow afternoon I will have ready an instrument modeled after the human ear, by means of which I hope tomorrow (but I must confess with fear and partial distrust) to transmit a vocal sound . . . I am like a man in a fog who is sure of his latitude and longitude. I know that I am close to the land for which I am bound and when the fog lifts I shall see it right before me.[2]

The following day Aleck and Tom tested the original transmitter, now fitted with a thicker membrane and a lighter armature, connecting it with a reed receiver on another floor as previously. When Aleck sang into the transmitter, his assistant heard the tune on the receiver. 'Grand telegraphic discovery today', he wrote jubilantly to Sarah Fuller that afternoon, 'Transmitted *vocal sounds* for the first time . . . With some further modifications I hope we may be enabled to distinguish . . . the timbre of the sound. Should this be so, conversation *viva voce* by telegraph will be a *fait accompli*.'

Once more, Aleck was on the brink of a major breakthrough; once again, however, he was brought up short by Gardiner Hubbard who wrote to him on 2 July. Not grasping the significance of Aleck's latest discovery, he dismissed it merely as something Elisha Gray had already achieved. This, combined with a quirk of fate that afternoon, deflected Aleck from telephony for eight months. Aleck sang and recited into his transmitter, bringing to bear all his skills as an elocutionist. Tom came charging upstairs and burst in excitedly to report that he had heard Aleck's voice plainly: 'I could almost make out what you said!' Aleck went downstairs to listen while Watson spoke into the transmitter, but he was disappointed to hear only a stream of unintelligible, distorted sounds. To be sure, the din and clangour of the workshop where the receiver was fitted was hardly conducive to good reception. There was certainly nothing wrong with Aleck's hearing; more probably Tom Watson's enunciation was not of the clearest. At any rate Aleck heard enough to confirm him in the belief that the human voice could be transmitted; but clearly a great deal more would be required in fine tuning and modifications before the invention had any practical application. Ironically, identical instruments tested in more ideal conditions a few years later managed to transmit speech perfectly. But for the moment Aleck was baffled; it would not be until the following March, when his patent was granted, that he would resume work on the telephone in all seriousness.

Aleck's health was suffering again. Exhausted both physically and mentally by his prodigious efforts, he was forced to cut back on his journeys from Salem to Boston and concentrate on the autograph telegraph. By the end of July the theoretical system was perfected. On the practical side, however, there had been many setbacks over the previous months. Early in June Watson fell ill; by the time Tom had got over this illness, Aleck himself was embroiled in an emotional crisis with the Hubbards.

Ever since his return from Washington in March, Aleck had been frequenting the Hubbard mansion several times a week. Ostensibly these visits had been to keep Gardiner abreast of developments as well as to continue with Mabel's speech therapy. Some years later she would recall that 'Our lessons continued irregularly, but they were no longer confined to articulation, indeed they never had been. Aleck used to give me information of the most miscellaneous kind and we often got into political discussions.' Until midsummer Aleck was Mabel's teacher, no more, no less; but when he discovered that she was planning to leave Cambridge for Nantucket off Cape Cod for several months, he was suddenly assailed by pangs of he knew not what. He was in an emotional turmoil when he wrote to Mrs Hubbard on 24 June confessing that he was in deep trouble. 'I have discovered that my interest in my dear pupil . . . has ripened into a far deeper feeling . . . I have learned to love her.' He was uncertain how Mabel's parents would react to this revelation; indeed, he had no way of telling how Mabel herself felt. Naïvely, he concluded, 'I promise beforehand to abide by your decision.'

Gardiner Hubbard responded robustly, telling Aleck bluntly that Mabel, at seventeen, was too young even to be told of Aleck's feelings. She must have time to develop and mature, and know herself before having to make any momentous decisions. Interestingly, the Hubbards believed Aleck to be a great deal older than his twenty-eight years. Had he been clean-shaven, the truth might have been more readily apparent. Mrs Hubbard handled the delicate situation more gently, asking Aleck to hide his feelings for a year. Gardiner wished that a two-year ban had been imposed, though he grudgingly admitted that he liked Aleck a lot.

In a close-knit family it was impossible to conceal Aleck's confession. Mabel's sister Roberta and cousin Mary Blatchford were evidently apprised of his feelings for they inveigled Aleck and Mabel into the garden that balmy moonlit evening and then ran off, leaving the couple alone. Mabel's hand rested on his arm, and Aleck found it impossible to hide his feelings any longer. Presently Roberta and Mary returned with a bunch of flowers and proceeded to play the game of 'He loves me, he loves me not', peeling off the petals one by one. Aleck's flower came out 'Love' and Mabel innocently asked him what he was thinking. He blushed and, for once, could not get the words out. The mischievous pair laughed and gave him a knowing look before they ran off giggling. Mabel chased after them, with Aleck, flustered and strangely out of breath, bringing up the rear. His heart was pounding furiously as he sat at Mabel's feet on the veranda with her family.[3]

Conversation was inconsequential and desultory, and Aleck struggled to keep up the small talk, concealing his deep despair with lighthearted sallies. Inwardly, he was indulging in an agony of introspection. He was awkward and ungainly, slovenly and careless of his appearance. In sum, he was not the sort of man who could ever attract such a vivacious young girl. Suddenly he found himself asking her, 'If you could choose a husband what should you wish him to be like?' He was so confused at having blurted it out that he could not recall what her response was, but she seems to have brushed it aside with some quip which brought an uneasy laugh from the others, and left poor Aleck more confused than ever. In a letter to Brantford, written on 30 June, Aleck tried to put his jumbled thoughts into some rational order. Apart from her deafness, he assured his parents, Mabel was the sort of girl they would be proud of. She was beautiful, accomplished, well born, and more affectionate by nature than anyone he had ever known before. They were to tell no one, not even his sister-in-law Carrie (who had recently remarried) or Uncle David (who had now settled in Brantford), with one exception: 'I should like *Marie Eccleston* to know,' he added cryptically.[4]

On the very day that Watson heard Aleck's voice over the wire for the first time, Mabel, with her sister Roberta and cousin Mary, left for Nantucket. The anguish and longing for Mabel's company did nothing to improve Aleck's mental equilibrium as July drew to a close. By the end of the month he found himself telling her parents that he could not conceal his feelings for her any longer. He threatened to follow her to Nantucket immediately – unless they forbade it. Tactfully, Gardiner persuaded him to wait until Mabel returned to Cambridge. In Nantucket cousin Mary (who disapproved of Aleck) took it upon herself to tell Mabel exactly what she thought. Mabel's reaction to this well-intentioned meddling was to write to her mother about 2 August:

> I think I am old enough now to have a right to know if he spoke about it to you or Papa. I know I am not much of a woman yet, but I feel very very much what this is to have as it were, my whole future life in my hands . . .

Oh Mamma, it comes to me more and more that I am a woman such as I did not know before I was. I felt and feel so much of a child still . . . Of course it cannot be, however clever and smart Mr Bell may be; and however much honored I should be by being his wife I never could love him or even like him thoroughly . . . Oh it is such a grand thing to be a woman, a thinking, feeling, and acting woman . . . But is it strange I don't feel at all as if I had won a man's love. Even if Mr Bell does ask me, I shall not feel as if he did it through love . . . You need not write about my accepting or declining this offer if it should be made . . . I would do anything rather than that . . . I feel so misty and befogged . . . Help me please.[5]

Mrs Hubbard immediately called in Aleck and read out parts of Mabel's tortured and confused letter. The following day he called at the Hubbard mansion on his way to the station where he intended catching a train for Nantucket; but he confessed that the anxiety of it all had made him physically ill, and it took little persuasion on the part of the Hubbards to change his mind and convince him to remain in Salem. Mrs Sanders was genuinely concerned for him on his return home that night. He was like a man demented, and she was afraid that he had lost his reason through overwork. In fact, she contemplated summoning a physician with a strait-jacket to have the madman carted off to the asylum, when Aleck calmed down and, in a voice cracking with emotion, poured out his heart to her.[6] Later that evening, in the relative tranquillity of the Sanders' homestead, Aleck, having regained his composure, wrote to Mabel's parents:

The letter which was read to me yesterday was not the production of a girl – but of a true noble-hearted woman – and she should be treated as such. I shall show my respect for her by going to Nantucket whether she will see me there or not . . . I shall not ask permission from you now – but shall merely go.[7]

On the way, however, he again called in on the Hubbards. By now they were struck by his earnestness and passion and won over by his obvious sincerity. Aleck told them that, whatever happened, he would respect Mabel's wishes. If she did not want to see him when he arrived, he would abide by that. But go he must, as he felt it would be best for Mabel's peace of mind as well as his own health, and he would do right as he saw it, regardless of the opinions of others. Later he recorded in his journal that, at the end of the interview, 'both Mr and Mrs Hubbard said that they liked the way I acted about it'.[8]

Aleck reached Nantucket on the evening of 7 August and checked in at the Ocean House. Although exhausted by the journey and worn down by anxiety, he was so strung out that he could not sleep. The following day a violent thunderstorm raged over the island preventing Aleck from going out of doors. He whiled away the afternoon on a letter to Mabel, recounting events and reviewing the situation at great length. He began with a simple declaration: 'I have loved you with a passionate attachment that you cannot understand, and that is to myself new and incomprehensible. I wished to tell you of my wish to make you my wife – if you would let me try to win your love.'

He told her of his promise to keep silent, but added: 'It did not occur to me to measure the breadth and depth of my affection so as to consider whether it was *possible* for me wholly to conceal it. My pride told me I could do it.' Then, when Mabel's letter to her mother had revealed her distrust of him (as Mrs Hubbard had interpreted it without reading the relevant passage to him), 'I was so distressed as to be ill.'[9]

He summarised what had transpired between him and her parents:

> It is for *you* to say whether you will see me or not. You do not know – you cannot guess – how much I love you . . . I want you to know me better before you dislike me . . . Tell me frankly all that there is in me that you dislike and that I can alter . . . I wish to amend my life for you.

On the morning of 9 August, the storm having abated, Aleck plucked up the courage to pay a call at the Hubbard summer residence. At the door, however, Aleck was confronted by a hostile Mary Blatchford who told him, in no uncertain manner, that Mabel would not see him. Somewhat to Mary's surprise, Aleck gave way immediately and did not try to argue with her. Perhaps his courage had deserted him at the last moment; in any case, he felt that the long letter would be more effective than any face-to-face encounter.[10] Later that day he travelled back to Salem, from where he wrote to Mabel again the following morning, in more measured terms:

> Now that I have done my best to show you what I am – I am contented – and can wait . . . I shall not trouble you any more until the original year is out. And then if you still think of me as you do just now, I shall try to be happy in my *work*. If I may not be any nearer or dearer – believe me at all events,
> Your sincere *friend*, A. Graham Bell.[11]

Five days later, Mabel replied with becoming dignity:

> Thank you very much for the honorable and generous way in which you treated me. Indeed you have both my respect and esteem. I shall be glad to

see you in Cambridge and become better acquainted with you . . .
Gratefully, your friend, Mabel G. Hubbard.[12]

In the meantime, Mrs Hubbard herself had gone to Nantucket to visit her daughter. On her return to Cambridge she invited Aleck over on 17 August for 'a delightful and encouraging evening' as he noted in his diary. He was agreeably surprised to be told that Mabel was afraid that her letter had not been written 'warmly enough'.[13]

It appeared that Mabel was worried lest Eliza and Melville Bell would not like her, and she conveyed, via her mother, that she would make them like her. Eliza's reservations concerning the girl were based on the affliction they had in common. When Aleck had confessed how he felt about Mabel, Eliza had written back early in July: 'You are of course the best judge, but if she is a congenital deaf-mute, I should have great fears for your children.' This unfortunate remark enraged Aleck who did not write a word to his parents for almost six weeks as a result; but on 18 August he wrote to them at length, barely concealing his resentment. He had long been grieved that there was 'so little confidence and sympathy' between him and his father and he had hoped that the news would bring them closer together. But, he complained, only his mother had deigned to reply, and that in a dismissive manner:

> Should this also be received with the same shameful neglect as my last, I feel that there is danger of a complete alienation of my affections from home.
> Your loving son Aleck.[14]

Hurt and bewildered at this, Eliza replied on 23 August. She was at pains to explain that, naturally, she had been writing for his father as well, that the apparent curtness of her comment had arisen merely in the hope of further details about Mabel, and hastening to point out that being deaf herself, yet happily married, she could scarcely condemn Aleck for marrying a deaf girl. To this heart-wringing letter Eliza added a postscript a week later:

> We are the victims of your own excited imagination . . . There are not so many of us left that we can afford to take up unreasonable offence against each other . . . I can only excuse you by thinking that your mind must be unhinged by close and prolonged application to Telegraphic work.[15]

Aleck's response to this pathetic letter was immediate. On 31 August he wrote to his father:

Please forgive me for my harsh allusions to you and do not think I do not love you. You do not know how much trouble I have passed through – and how ill I have been . . . Do not think badly of me. I know you love me dearly and I have longed to feel that I could talk to you as freely as I wish without fear of ridicule.[16]

Shortly afterwards he packed his bags and set off for Brantford. Before he left Boston, however, he pressed his advantage with the Hubbards. On 24 August he had written to them:

I feel myself still *hampered* by promises that I should not have made . . . I must be *free* to do whatever I think right and best – quite irrespective of your wishes – or those of other people . . . When I am sure of her affection I wish to be engaged to her. When I am in a position to offer a *home* I wish to marry her – whether it is in two years or two months! If you do not like my conduct in the matter . . . you can deny me the house – and I can *wait*.[17]

To his pleasant surprise, he received an immediate, and unexpected, response, in the form of a note from Mrs Hubbard who invited him to call: 'I give you back your promise, entirely, unreservedly. I believe your love for my Mabel to be unselfish and noble. I trust you perfectly. If you can win her love I shall feel happy in my darling's happiness.'[18]

The following day, 26 August, was the happiest of Aleck's life, as he wrote jubilantly that night in the special journal which he had opened to record his courtship. Earlier in the evening he and Mabel at last talked freely and alone. She did not love him, but she did not dislike him, and that would suffice for the moment. He concluded triumphantly: 'Shall not record any more here. I feel that I have at last got to the end of my troubles – and whatever happens I may now safely write: FINIS!'[19]

Aleck's letter to his father crossed with one from Melville, written on 31 August:

Come home and rest. We shall conclude that 'blood ill-tempered vexeth you' . . . You will find no change in our affection and we still hope that we have left to us a 'good son'.

The following day Aleck wrote to Mabel as soon as he received this letter and thus, his anxieties laid to rest, he set off two days later for Brantford and a well-earned vacation.

A week later he wrote to Mabel describing how he had been greeted like the prodigal son. Speaking of his father's changed attitude, he commented, 'If he has not killed the fatted calf for me, he has done everything else to make me happy and to show his affection for me.'[20] At Tutela Heights the warmth of an extended family soon engulfed him. There was Uncle David with his wife and four youngest children living nearby, as well as Carrie and her new husband. Eliza was in good form, radiant at her son's return, while Melville was brimming with news of his year's teaching at a ladies' college in Kingston. Aleck went off on a riding tour of southern Ontario and came home a week later, fully restored in mind and body. And to Mabel in late September he reported happily, 'My father and I have come together as we have not done for years . . . It is to me a new and delightful sensation.'

Eliza noted with relief that, compared with previous visits to Brantford, Aleck was no longer preoccupied with work. Of course, he occasionally jotted down various ideas as they presented themselves, but he did not let the problems of telephony obsess him as they had done before. The furthest he would go was to exhibit a couple of undulatory-current instruments at the local telegraph office, but he did not actually demonstrate them. The *Brantford Expositor* of 23 September reported enthusiastically that if a person sang or spoke into one instrument, not only the words would be heard at the other, but also the tones of the voice. The *Toronto Globe* four days later repeated this remarkable story. A lot of hard work would be needed before the telephone was an accomplished fact, but the Canadian newspapers accepted Aleck's claims without scepticism or reservation.

There was a serious purpose to this press publicity. Aleck's contract with Hubbard and Sanders only covered the United States rights, leaving Aleck free to negotiate the Canadian and British rights. To this end, Aleck approached George Brown, a neighbour in Tutela Heights and the proprietor of the *Toronto Globe*, in the hope that he would introduce him to Sir Hugh Allan of the powerful Montreal Telegraph Company. Brown, a native of Edinburgh who had founded the *Globe* in 1844, was arguably the most powerful man in Ontario. He had been prime minister (for a single day), twice refused a knighthood and, about this time, turned down the governorship of Ontario, preferring to wield power through his newspaper. His rabid anti-catholicism had made him very unpopular in Quebec, and he and Allan were politically poles apart. Consequently, Brown had no intention of putting his *bête noire* on to a good thing. Instead, he and his brother Gordon undertook to share the foreign rights themselves, provided that Aleck gave them guarantees protecting the non-American patent rights.[21]

On his return to Salem in October, Aleck sent George Brown a detailed description of his intermittent-current multiple telegraph (on which United States patents had already been granted or applied for), and also made a guarded reference to the undulatory-current concept which he now considered his most original and important. He emphasised that no hint of the latter had received any publicity in the American press and that he had, in fact, confided the matter to only two or three scientific friends.[22]

Soon after his return to the United States, Aleck began working on an American patent specification outlining his invention for the transmission of speech; but after devoting several weeks to this document he held back from filing his application, fearing that this might jeopardise a British application and mindful of his promise to Brown to avoid that. On the other hand, the Brown brothers failed to honour their end of the agreement and Aleck waited in vain for the promised contract and financial help. Having been paid in advance for the 1875–76 university session, Aleck was left with no alternative but to resume classes at the end of October, and consequently work on telegraphy was left in abeyance.

Aleck now concentrated on teaching, organising a teacher-training course in Visible Speech and drumming up sufficient private pupils to guarantee a regular income that would tide him over till the spring of 1876. He was still residing with the Sanders family at Salem and spending up to three hours a day working with little Georgie. Over the ensuing weeks he worked tirelessly on the teacher-training project, giving lectures, drafting advertisements for the press and sending out hundreds of circulars, negotiating with a Boston printer for the publication of Visible Speech manuals, and coping with his university classes. 'Telegraphy dormant! George Brown unheard from!' he reported laconically to his parents on 11 November, a few days before the teacher-training course was due to commence, adding jubilantly: 'Professional visitors are beginning to pour in . . . Every prospect of a *large* class.'

Telegraphy was not allowed to remain dormant for long. On 29 October Gardiner Hubbard wrote to Aleck aggrievedly, 'I have been sorry to see how little interest you seem to take in telegraph matters.' He suspected that Aleck's renewed enthusiasm for lecturing seemed to 'confirm the tendency of your mind to undertake every new thing that interests you & accomplish nothing of any value to any one,' and to emphasise his point he concluded, 'Your whole course since you returned has been a very great disappointment to me, & a sore trial.'[23]

Aleck managed to smooth Hubbard's ruffled feathers and started visiting the Cambridge house more regularly. Between visits, he also found time to write to Mabel two or three times a week. These letters, written on the spur of the moment, chart the ups and downs of this strange courtship. When Mabel (perhaps echoing her father) told him that his visits were probably hindering him in his work, Aleck was at pains to write that 'they are having just the *opposite* effect'.[24] A few days later he sent a near-hysterical letter pleading with her not to encourage him out of pity, but to let him know at once if she could not sincerely return his love. Inevitably the next letter had to pour balm on her wounded feelings at being suspected of thoughtless trifling.

Matters came to a head on 23 November. That evening Gardiner Hubbard, the blunt-spoken Yankee businessman, had a showdown with the younger man. Aleck was forced to choose between lecturing on Visible Speech and his commitments to telegraphy and Mabel (in that order). Furthermore, Hubbard offered as an inducement Aleck's living expenses if he took the latter option. In this last, he appears to have misjudged the young Scot. Aleck erupted with uncharacteristic fury. It was because he loved Mabel and prized Hubbard's respect that he would not accept any special favours. The existing agreement was perfectly satisfactory and he would abide by it. Nevertheless, he could not turn his back on Visible Speech, which had been his father's life's work and was now his also. He had become a teacher of the deaf because he was sorely needed, and that much had not changed at all. He had the power to free deaf and stammering children from what amounted to life imprisonment for no crime; he would not withhold it, at least not until he had qualified others to take his place. Interestingly, Aleck estimated that his income from teaching now amounted to about $5,000 a year, quite adequate for a man contemplating matrimony. He asserted stiffly that he was sorry that Hubbard did not like his profession, but he did not propose to change it. And if Mabel loved him, she would marry him anyway.

All this was said in the heat of the moment as Aleck made a grand exit from the Hubbard mansion; but later that night he sat down and wrote a letter to Hubbard in more reasonable language. Although he remained adamant regarding his profession, he apologised for any seeming disrespect and gratefully acknowledged Hubbard's 'sincere interest in my welfare independently of any pecuniary interest . . . in my inventions . . . Please bear with me a little longer.'

This blend of firmness and conciliation on Aleck's part was bolstered by Mabel's attitude. Angered and distressed at her father's clumsy attempt to make Aleck choose between her and his profession, she forced Gardiner to back down. Mrs Hubbard likewise forced the issue, telling Mabel that she should either give up Aleck altogether – or agree to be engaged to him at once. When Aleck called on the evening of 25 November, which was Thanksgiving Day as well as Mabel's eighteenth birthday, he was agreeably surprised to be told by the young lady that she loved him 'better than anyone but my mother', and that if that much satisfied him, she would be engaged to him on the spot.[25] Aleck seems to have reached the very nadir of despair around this time, and it was with some trepidation that he had called on her that evening. His immediate reaction to Mabel's declaration was characteristically canny: he reminded her of her youth and how little experience she had of other men. But Mabel told him that she knew that she would never find anyone else to love as well, or, for that matter, who would ever love her so intensely. Any lingering doubts on either side were banished by a kiss. Till the end of their days, Aleck and Mabel would always regard Thanksgiving as something very special to them.

Aleck was walking on air when he returned to the Sanders homestead. In bed that night he wrote two letters. First, to Mabel, he confessed, 'I am afraid to go to sleep lest I should find it all a dream, so I shall lie awake and think of you.' And to his parents he sent the joyful news: 'My heart is too full to allow me to write much to you tonight, so I scribble off only these few lines that you may known of my happiness.' And, for the first time, he signed his name 'Alec', dropping the final 'k' at Mabel's insistence. From then until the day he died he would be Alec Bell.

On 6 December Melville Bell wrote to his prospective daughter-in-law, expressing his 'great gratification' at the news and offering his congratulations, best wishes and a highly perceptive assessment of her matrimonial prospects. Even he acceded to the new spelling of his son's name:

> Alec is a good fellow and, I have no doubt, will make an excellent husband. He is hot-headed but warm-hearted – sentimental, dreamy, and self-absorbed, but sincere and unselfish. He is ambitious, to a fault, and is apt to let enthusiasm run away with judgement . . . With love you will have no difficulty in harmonising . . . I have told you all the faults I know in him, and this catalogue is wonderfully short.[26]

As a gesture of intent to his prospective father-in-law, Alec now lent Hubbard the specifications of the undulatory current to show to their patent lawyer Anthony Pollok, and he undertook to work on telegraphy four days a week from nine till two. Anxious not to jeopardise his British and Canadian rights, he refused Hubbard permission to apply for an American patent, until he had made a final appeal to George Brown over the Christmas holidays. As it happened, pressure of lecturing commitments, including free evening classes for adult deaf-mutes at Boston University, made savage inroads into the time apportioned for telegraphic work, and his fiancée now began to put her foot down, preventing him from resorting to the late-night laboratory sessions which had previously been his habit. A letter of 7 January 1876 to Mabel reveals his dilemma: 'I have been doing violence to my own instincts in the hope of working a reformation, but the result has been that I have been unable to do any serious thinking at all . . . and in the meantime telegraphy and everything else is at a stand-still.'

On Christmas Day, Alec arrived at Tutela Heights just as the family were sitting down to 'a regular merry old-fashioned Christmas dinner . . . with Turkey and Goose – and Plum-pudding all in a blaze – and Holly – regular English holly' as he reported to Mabel. After dinner he showed photographs of the Hubbard family, including one of Mabel's sister Roberta. Uncle David's son Charles was instantly smitten by the photograph. He stared at the portrait for several minutes before announcing as casually as he could that he had often wished to see Boston and that he thought he would ask his bank for a few days off to run down there and pay Alec a visit soon. In 1876 Charlie did, indeed, visit Boston and found that Roberta lived up to his expectations. They fell madly in love but their courtship suffered a severe setback when Charlie gave up his bank job in Canada. Without visible means of support (other than some vague secretarial employment from Alec) he was not a good prospect in the eyes of Gardiner Hubbard, who ordered the young man out of the house and forbade further communication with his daughter. In the end Mrs Hubbard effected a reconciliation; Charlie got a job in Boston, married Roberta and eventually became one of Washington's leading financiers.

Back in the winter of 1875–76, however, Charlie was of more immediate use to his cousin. Returning to his job in Toronto after the Christmas break, he telegraphed Alec that George Brown was in the city and wished to see him as soon as possible. Alec set off for Toronto immediately and after a long session with the Brown brothers agreed to let them have a half-interest in all his foreign rights, in exchange for the costs of taking out and defending these rights, plus a payment to Alec of fifty dollars a month until the patents were obtained, up to a maximum of six months. The relatively paltry sum was not for Alec's support but to pay for the rent of premises away from the Williams workshop where strangers (allegedly industrial spies in the pay of Elisha Gray) were believed to have been taking notes on his apparatus.[27]

Early in January 1876 Alec left Brantford and returned briefly to Salem. Now resolved to concentrate on telephony, he worked on the final draft of his American patent specifications and made copies of these and his earlier patents for George Brown to file on his behalf at the Patent Office in London. He was still spending several hours a day with Georgie Sanders as well as conducting classes at the university, so the vital paperwork on patents had to be done far into the night. All this turmoil took a toll on Alec's constitution. His frame of mind at this crucial time was vividly illustrated in a letter to Mabel:

> My afternoon at the University has been a very hard one, and I am so tired
> out and nervous that I feel it would be madness in me to goad my mind to

any serious work to-night . . . I have made various commencements – at different times during the past three months – upon the [undulatory current] specification that I feel to be so important – but it is no further advanced than it was in October![28]

Things could not go on like this. Alec needed a change of direction. Five days later, on 12 January, Mabel was indisposed. As her father was absent on business in Washington and her mother and Roberta had an evening engagement, Alec came over from Salem to Cambridge; while Mabel rested in her bedroom Alec conscientiously remained downstairs to keep an eye on the house. While waiting for Mabel's mother and sister to return he spent the time in Gardiner Hubbard's book-lined study, making a copy of the undulatory-current specification to send to Hubbard the following day. Around midnight Mabel rose from her bed and called down to Alec from the upper landing, urging him to stop work. Many years later she would recollect how 'he came running up all eagerness and begged that I leave him alone just that one night, for he was at last on the track of that hole in his telephone specification'.[29] She gave way, but got her own back soon afterwards by sending him a portrait which she had painted of him. When he unwrapped it he found a painting of a great white owl.

What Alec had suddenly remembered, while writing out the specification, was the principle of variable resistance which, by some oversight, he had omitted from the George Brown draft a few days earlier, even though it had formed a part of his previous Canadian theories. What jogged his memory will probably never be known, although it seems likely that he was reminded of this point by the spark arrester which he had devised at Brantford the previous September, and for which he would now write a patent specification. In the early hours, in Gardiner Hubbard's library, Alec drafted the vital clause:

Electrical undulations may also be caused by alternately increasing and diminishing the resistance of the circuit . . . For instance let mercury or some other liquid form part of a voltaic circuit. Then the more deeply the conducting wire is immersed in the liquid the less resistance does the liquid offer to the passage of the current. Hence the vibration of the conducting wire in a liquid included in the circuit occasions undulations in the current.[30]

The following day Alec sent the revised specification to Hubbard. Two days later he replied from Washington to say that Anthony Pollok, their patent attorney, was 'very much pleased' with it. He passed on a warning from Pollok that Alec should keep a tight lip on latest developments till the application had gone through. Meanwhile George Brown wired from Toronto asking Alec to meet him in New York on 25 January.

The intervening week was extremely hectic. On 16 January Alec began work on the spark-arrester specification and made arrangements for one of his student teachers to take over Georgie Sanders. The following day he moved into lodgings at Exeter Place in Boston, much more convenient for the university, and that night completed the spark-arrester specification. The two rooms were sparsely furnished, but very cheap, at only $16 a month. One room was swiftly converted into Alec's laboratory by the simple expedient of taking up the carpet and installing a plain deal kitchen table. 'I want a table upon which I can hammer and saw and carve to my heart's content, and a floor upon which I may spill acids without fear of damage,' he wrote to Mabel.[31]

On 19 January he made copies of his previous harmonic and autograph telegraph specifications for Brown. The following day he notarised a copy of the telephone specification and sent it to Hubbard and on the evening of 21 January he departed for New York. Four days later Alec and Hubbard met with George Brown who promised to submit the specifications to Sir William Thomson (later Lord Kelvin) when he got to Britain. As a token of good faith Brown then gave Alec fifty dollars as a down payment. In the event, it would be the only cash that Alex would receive from that source. Brown took ship for England the very next day. Five weeks later his brother Gordon belatedly informed Alec that the deal was off as the Browns did not reckon that Bell's invention was a commercial proposition in Britain.[32] It later transpired that, although George Brown had conferred with an electrical scientist in London about the harmonic telegraph, he had never thought the telephone worth mentioning. As Alec had delayed filing his application in the US Patent Office until he had a positive response from George Brown in England, one may imagine his chagrin on receipt of this news.

On top of that, he had a major setback when, on 16 February, Zenas F. Wilber, examiner at the Patent Office, formally notified Pollok and Bailey that Alec's application of 25 February 1875 for the harmonic telegraph was 'in interference with' Elisha Gray's application dated two days earlier, and Paul La Cour's dated 3 March that year. The matter could only be resolved by an enquiry into priority of conception, a process which was likely to be lengthy and very expensive. Hubbard must have wired the bad news from Washington; on receipt of this bombshell Alec had poured out his heart to Mabel who wrote to him at length that night, upbraiding him for his 'slowness and procrastination' which she felt lay at the heart of the problem. Then she continued:

I love you so much dear Alec I cannot bear that anyone should write to you and with too much justice, as my father has done. And I cannot bear that procrastination should rob you of the fruits of hours of hard study and of the great abilities God has given you. I know that ill health has the last week or two prevented you from working as hard as usual. But it seems to me when the thing to be done was so very important, when if it failed you lost the reward of past toil and suffering, you might *perhaps* have put even that aside for the time.[33]

Admitting that 'Procrastination is indeed my besetting sin', Alec replied the following day:

Help me, Mabel, to conquer it. I will not disguise from you dear what a blow this misfortune has been to me – for I had looked to this new patent to avoid all conflict with Gray – & to place the control of the new system of Telegraphy entirely in my own hands. I feel it more deeply than anything that has ever before happened to me – except one thing! And you know what that is . . . Just received a kind note from your father. If any telegram comes for me today please send it to the University tomorrow morning.[34]

Despite Alec's promise to the Browns not to file a telephone application in Washington till he had heard from England, Gardiner Hubbard had no such scruples. By the middle of February, when he had not heard from George Brown, Hubbard decided to go ahead without consulting Alec, and made a formal application regarding the undulatory-current and telephone patents on the morning of 14 February. A few hours later Elisha Gray's attorney William D. Baldwin entered a caveat for a speaking telephone on the principle of liquid variable-resistance. When apprised of this, Alec wrote to his parents, 'Such a coincidence has hardly happened before.' If ever there was an understatement, this was it.

Later Gray would testify that he had evolved the concept of the telephone from the winter of 1874–75 onwards, although he admitted that it was not till late in 1875 that the idea of a liquid variable-resistance transmitter had come to him. Interestingly, his thoughts on the matter were stimulated by seeing a device called the lovers' telegraph in a Milwaukee toyshop – two tin cans connected by a taut string. If one spoke into the can at one end, the sound was transmitted mechanically along the string and emitted through the open can at the other end. Gray's caveat envisaged the transmission of vocal sounds through an electric circuit using a water rheostat and an electromagnetic diaphragm receiver. This, of course, was pure theory, as Gray had not put his ideas to any practical test. What is remarkable is that Gray had never mentioned this telephone concept to a living soul until he had been in Washington several weeks and had frequently visited the Patent Office where talk of the Bell telephone specifications was rife. In fairness to Gray, it is probable that some vague notion of a telephone had been forming in his mind for some time, but was brought into sharp focus when he got wind of what Alec was about to patent. Moreover, Gray's caveat talked of using a series of diaphragms, each 'responding to a vibration of different rapidity and intensity' – oddly at variance with both the Bell specification and the lovers' telegraph which Gray claimed as his inspiration.

Even if one accepted Gray's own unsupported claim regarding the date of conception, Alec still had clear priority as the concept of the telephone had been clearly enunciated at Brantford in the summer of 1874. What was much more serious, however, was the timing of Gray's caveat. It was later shown that the caveat specification was not dictated, written out and copied until 14 February and that the Patent Office fee for the caveat was paid separately in order to meet the two o'clock deadline for that filing date, the caveat itself not actually being filed until some time later that afternoon. It was a close-run thing. Had the grant of the telephone patent been delayed on account of the Gray caveat, Alec and his partners would have been hard-pressed by prolonged legal hearings and might have been compelled to sell out their contested claim cheaply to Western Union which might then have deliberately suppressed the telephone in order to promote their telegraph interests.

On 19 February Wilber notified Pollok and Bailey that the Bell application had been suspended because of interference with a pending caveat. Five days later Pollok and Bailey wrote to Ellis Spear, acting commissioner of Patents, pointing out that the Bell application had been filed earlier on the same day as the interfering caveat and asking that the office records be checked to verify this fact. Wilber countered that the time of day was immaterial; but when the records were checked and Alec's application was shown to have been filed some hours before Gray's caveat, Spear overruled Wilber who consequently informed both Bell and Gray on 25 February that the interference had been dissolved.

This was by no means the end of the matter. Wilber now contended that Gray had filed a caveat on 27 January for the use of a continuous but varying current. Alec had planned to come to Washington on 29 February, but, at Hubbard's insistence, he arrived in the capital three days earlier and had an immediate meeting with Wilber, pointing out to the examiner that the principle on Gray's caveat was covered by a passage in his own application of February 1875. Wilber then permitted Alec to amend his application to clarify his nomenclature. Alec could now see light at the end of a very long tunnel. 'If I succeed in securing that Patent without interference from the others,' he wrote to his father, '*the whole thing is mine – and I am sure of fame, fortune, and success if I can only persevere in perfecting my apparatus.*'[35]

During his meeting with Wilber, Alec casually asked him what aspect of Gray's caveat had caused the interference in his application. Theoretically Wilber was bound by confidentiality not to reveal such details, but as the interference had been quashed he saw no harm in telling Alec that it was the matter of liquid variable-resistance. This seemed harmless enough at the time, but would later have grave repercussions and assume major proportions when Alec was embroiled in litigation with Western Union.

In his letter of 29 February 1876, quoted above, Alec told his father that he was assailed by self-doubt when Pollok and Bailey brushed aside his proposal to make an application in respect of his spark arrester, asserting that it had been anticipated by earlier patents. Furthermore, he was not only up against Gray and La Cour in the matter of the multiple telegraph but also one other whose name was withheld from him; 'But I have discovered it to be Mr Edison of New York, who has evidently been employed by the Western Union Telegraph Company to try to defeat Gray and myself.' William Orton, president of Western Union, had indeed commissioned Thomas Alva Edison to beat Bell and Gray to the 'speaking telegraph'. Edison, starting with the Reis device of 1861, had been exploring the possibilities of harmonic telegraphy and had even tried, without success, to devise a speaking telegraph. He actually got as far as filing a caveat on 14 January 1876 for a device using electromagnetism to make a diaphragm emit sound, but he later admitted that he was only thinking of the harmonic telegraph at that juncture. On 3 March Alec had a meeting with William Baldwin, Gray's patent attorney, in Pollok's office. Baldwin assured Alec that Gray had had nothing to do with the machinations, real or imagined, against him; and they concluded that Western Union lay behind the plot to set Bell and Gray against each other. Baldwin later reported to Samuel White, the dental millionaire who was backing Gray, that Bell seemed to like the idea of joining forces with Gray against Western Union. The young inventor struck Baldwin as 'intelligent, gentlemanly and well-disposed'.[36]

On that very day Alec celebrated his twenty-ninth birthday. The best present was the news that Gray had decided not to challenge Alec's claim, and four days later United States Patent 174,465 was formally issued. Mabel, having heard the good news from her father, wrote to Alec on 5 March marvelling that the justice of his claim had stood up to the 'colossal power' wielded by Western Union whose wily president she denounced as:

almost the most powerful man in this country, and willing to spare no expense, honest or dishonest, to conquer you. Just now too when Belknap's iniquity, coming after all those other stories and scandals, makes us feel as if there were no justice in such a sink of corruption as Washington.[37]

W.W. Belknap, Secretary of War, had only two days previously been exposed in a scandal that would rock the Grant presidency to its foundations. For six years his first and second wives (sisters who successively dominated the Washington social scene) had been taking kickbacks from a prominent contractor of Indian trading-posts. When this corruption was exposed Belknap had immediately tendered his resignation, which Grant accepted, but Congress was out for blood and the luckless Belknap was promptly impeached. On 5 March, in fact, the Belknaps were arrested when it was rumoured that they planned to take ship to Belgium which had no extradition treaty with the United States. In due course thirty-five senators voted for impeachment and twenty-five against; but as the motion failed to secure the necessary two-thirds majority Belknap walked free, to practise law in Washington and maintain his beautiful wife in Paris for the remaining twelve years of his life. The scandal was soon forgotten when other, even greater scandals involving the great and good erupted.

Mabel had commiserated with Alec when his spark arrester was jettisoned but urged him to keep a sense of perspective: 'So far as I can see from your letter it is Mr Gray more than you who is to be disheartened by the way the patent stands now.'[38] Certainly Alec's spirits were up one minute and down the next, as his personal letters to Mabel and his parents from Washington reveal. During these hectic days he was a house guest at Anthony Pollok's palatial mansion where he met the social élite of the nation's capital. The undoubted highlight of his time in Washington was the party which Pollok threw for Joseph Henry to renew his acquaintance-ship with the up-and-coming young inventor.

On 7 March, the day that one of the most valuable patents ever was granted, Alec returned in triumph to Boston. Hardly able to sleep that night, he was up early the following morning. Presently he was joined in his makeshift laboratory by Tom Watson and resumed his experiments with a reed receiver and a tuning-fork transmitter. In one experiment Alec took the electromagnet out of the circuit and replaced it with a small dish of water, one lead being placed over the rim and trailing in the water, while the other was connected to the handle of the tuning-fork. Alec vibrated the fork and partially immersed its prongs in the water. This produced a faint sound from the reed receiver, resulting from a current made undulatory not by induction but by the fluctuating resistance of the battery-powered circuit as the fork vibrated in the water and thus varied the area of its contact.

Although the hum was almost imperceptible, it was enough to rouse Alec's curiosity. He added some acid to the water to improve its conductivity, and the sound increased in volume. Next he enhanced the liquid contact of the stationary lead by affixing a brass strip to the end in the water, and the sound became very loud indeed. Substituting a handbell for the tuning-fork, and plunging it into the water after ringing, however, produced no sound at all. This led him to conclude that the vibrating lead's area of liquid contact should be small, and that of the stationary lead large. The less the vibrating lead was immersed, the greater would be the proportion of change with vibration, and therefore the more pronounced the effect. By the end of the day Alec had produced a rough sketch of a horizontal membrane diaphragm from the centre of which a needle dipped into a dish of water, the other lead lying at the bottom.

The following morning Tom set up a contraption along these lines and after lunch Alec sang into a hole at the top of a box with the diaphragm set in its bottom. The varying pitch came through on the reed receiver. Alec duly recorded that 'When Mr Watson talked into the box an indistinct mumbling was heard at [the receiver]. I could hear a confused muttering sound like speech but could not make out the sense'.[39]

On the morning of Friday, 10 March, Alec got his assistant to make a device with a brass pipe running into the water as the stationary lead, and a platinum needle projecting from the diaphragm. The box was replaced by a small chamber with a speaking-tube mouthpiece. That afternoon Alec and Tom tried out the new apparatus, adding sulphuric acid to the water in the dish. Tom stood in Alec's bedroom with the reed receiver pressed to his ear; at the far end of the corridor, behind closed doors in his laboratory, Alec spoke into the mouthpiece. A myth, first perpetrated by Watson in his autobiography published half a century later[40] and widespread to this day, asserts that Alec accidentally spilled some sulphuric acid on his trousers and involuntarily cried out, 'Mr Watson! Come here! I want you!' as he tried to mop up the corrosive liquid; and that Tom responded to the cry for help because he had heard it over the telephone. The truth, however, recorded by both men at the time, was rather prosaic. No acid was spilled and Alec spoke calmly and deliberately, as his detailed notes indicate:

> I then shouted into M[outhpiece] the following sentence: 'Mr Watson –
> Come here – I want to see you'. To my delight he came and declared that
> he had heard and understood what I said. I asked him to repeat the words,
> He answered 'You said – Mr Watson – come here – I want to see you.' We
> then changed places and I listened at S [the reed receiver] while Mr Watson
> read a few passages from a book into the mouthpiece M. It was certainly the
> case that articulate sounds proceeded from S. The effect was loud but

indistinct and muffled. If I had read beforehand the passage given by Mr Watson I should have recognized every word. As it was I could not make out the sense – but an occasional word here and there was quite distinct. I made out 'to' and 'out' and 'further'; and finally the sentence 'Mr Bell do you understand what I say? Do – you – un – der – stand – what – I – say' came quite clearly and intelligibly. No sound was audible when the armature S was removed.[41]

Incidentally, the first words spoken by telephone did not become immediately famous; six years would elapse before Alec's call to Tom Watson became a matter of public record, in the evidence given by Watson during litigation of August 1882.

7

Philadelphia
1876

My God, it talks!

Attributed to Dom Pedro II, Emperor of Brazil, 25 June 1876

Over the ensuing two months Alec worked tirelessly and incessantly to perfect his invention. First he strengthened the current by adding more batteries, but this merely created gas bubbles in the liquid, obscuring the vocal sound. In the end, he settled for two battery cells. A black deposit had to be scraped off the wire at frequent intervals, while splashes from the dilute acid perished the membrane. Gradually these problems were overcome: platinum was used for both transmitter leads while a simple wooden shield protected the membrane from splashes. At the same time Alec tinkered with the receiver, eventually devising an electromagnetic receiver with a steel reed attached to a membrane in a sealed chamber from which a hearing tube conveyed the sound to the ear.

On the Monday following the first successful transmission, Gardiner Hubbard and Dean Lewis Monroe called at Exeter Place to put Alec's claims to the test. Later, Alec would record that neither visitor could hear anything at first: 'Indeed both seemed at first rather sceptical, and I presume thought that the imagination had a good deal to do with the sounds.'[1] But when Monroe spoke into the transmitter, Alec and Tom Watson were able to hear his words clearly and wrote them down. The problem for Hubbard and Monroe lay in their inexperience in using the reed receiver; pressing it too tightly to their ears distorted and muffled the sounds. Even so, the sounds were not clear enough to be intelligible. Hubbard suggested that perhaps the transmitter needed work. Again, there was considerable trial and error before a greatly improved transmitter was produced, on 23 March, with a flared mouthpiece, like an inverted cone, over the diaphragm. At the same time, there were prolonged experiments with variable resistance, involving spiral leads, double points in series, different resistances and different liquids, but all this seemed to be leading nowhere. Baffled, Alec abandoned practical experiments while he reviewed his observations, analysed the theoretical variations and played with numerous permutations and combinations of voltage and resistance.

Alec's telephonic experiments were interrupted by other pressing matters. His father was scheduled to come from Brantford to Boston at the end of March to give a series of lectures, and Alec was preoccupied with organising them. Perhaps because the lectures were a huge success, Melville was in a mellow and expansive mood; father and son were now perfectly reconciled. 'I feel as if I had never known him till now,' wrote Alec to Mabel. 'It is a new pleasure to me to be able to talk freely and fully to him . . . I feel somehow as if it was your love that has brought us together.'[2] When Melville returned to Canada on 13 April, Alec confided to Mabel that his Exeter Place lodgings seemed empty without his father. It is probable that Melville had at long last realised that his gifted son had grown up. The old man was charmed by Mabel, the speech impediment that betrayed her deafness doubtless reminding him poignantly of his own courtship of Eliza, and he was impressed by Alec's amazing invention. For his part, Alec had a new self-assurance, still respectful but no longer overwhelmed by his brilliant father. Henceforward Alec and Melville treated each other as equals.

Although the variable-resistance transmitter powered by electricity would lie at the heart of the future telephone, Alec was not yet convinced that this was the ideal solution. Late in March he abandoned these principles and wasted considerable time and energy on experiments with a magneto transmitter which depended on the power generated by the sound waves themselves. Yet, on 23 March, he drew a diagram for a thin piece of acid-moistened sponge between two platinum plates, one fixed and the other vibrated by a membrane diaphragm with a point contact. Had he followed this line he might have ended with the pressure-sensitive solid conductor which eventually solved the problem, but such painstaking experiments would have taken considerable time and money, both commodities in very short supply at that crucial period. In desperation to find a satisfactory solution, Alec went off at a tangent; perhaps vibrating battery plates might do the trick, or failing that, platinum foil.

A major breakthrough came on 1 April when it occurred to Alec that the vibration of an imperfect solid conductor such as carbon in mercury might do the trick. The following day he obtained excellent results from plumbago, the graphite granules from a lead pencil, in a cup of mercury. This excited him so much that he could not sleep that night; at 2 a.m. he wrote to Mabel:

I try to stop thinking but it's of no use – I cannot get the reins of my mind! There is a picture before my eyes – a moving picture – a little lead-pencil vibrating in mercury! . . . I am only disheartened at the immensity of the horizons opened out to me . . . I feel like the first mariner in an unknown sea – uncertain which way to go.[3]

Alec persevered with the plumbago-mercury principle, off and on, for a further three weeks, but again he was sidetracked by Gardiner Hubbard who urged him to focus on the autograph telegraph. The immediate outcome was to verify that undulatory current would carry simultaneous musical notes which would have interfered with each other in an intermittent current. Melville likewise begged Alec to concentrate on the telegraph: 'Stick to the autographic till you bring it into practical use,' he wrote. 'Until then, I would suspend all other experiments.'[4] This seems to have been part of a concerted campaign orchestrated by Hubbard who also entreated Alec a few days later:

If you would take Mr Williams' man [Watson] as I proposed and work with him or let him work steady on *one thing* until you have perfected it you would soon make it a success. While you are flying from one thing to another you may accidentally accomplish something but you probably will never perfect anything.[5]

Twelve days later Hubbard's attitude hardened. 'If you could make one good invention in the telegraph you would secure an annual income as much as the Professorship and then you could settle that on your wife and teach Visible Speech and experiment in telegraphy with an easy and undisturbed conscience.' Even Mabel was recruited by her father to keep the young man in line, Hubbard persuading her to write to Alec on 6 May telling him that she would not marry him until he perfected the autograph telegraph. This letter almost broke Alec's heart. That night he wrote to her telling her, 'I want to marry you, darling, because I love you . . . and I wish to feel that you would marry me for the same reason.' Alec began to wish that he had never heard of telegraphy, if it was to come between him and his beloved.

As it happened, he was hard at work on the autograph telegraph during much of April and early May, continually experimenting with different writing fluids, the techniques of embossing and electrolysis, specifically in an attempt to deposit metal on marks made by pencil. These were blind alleys which consumed a great deal of time and did not produce any real progress towards the eventual goal. And on top of all that, there were his university and private classes to cope with, not to mention examination papers to be marked. He had just completed the marking when he learned that the matter of Gray's long-standing multiple-telegraph interference was about to be decided in Washington, entailing a considerable amount of time in writing out detailed statements covering each step in the evolution of his multiple telegraph system since he first thought of it in March 1875. Somehow, he also found the time to prepare the exhibit on Visible Speech which was to form part of the Centennial Exposition at Philadelphia celebrating the first hundred years of nationhood. It is hardly surprising that by the end of April Alec was prostrated once again by severe headaches and depression – 'worn out with work and anxiety' as he confessed in a letter to his father.[6]

Alec was at a crossroads. On the one hand he was within an inch of realising his goals with the autograph telegraph and the telephone. On the other, the pull of academe was strong. In February he had been tentatively approached as a possible director of the Perkins Institution for the Blind, and in April he was offered a professorship at the deaf-mute college in Washington. The latter prospect seemed very attractive, but Hubbard strenuously opposed it. 'If you were tied up to rules and hours,' he wrote, 'it would be very irksome and hard . . . You are not like other men and you must therefore make allowance for your peculiarities . . . If you could work as other men do you would accomplish much more . . . But you must overcome these habits by your own will, and not by rules imposed by a college.'

In this welter of conflicting interests it is astonishing that Alec still found time to take forward his telephone. Towards the end of March he finally abandoned his experiments with a liquid variable-resistance transmitter. It was Melville who observed that the receiver reed sounded loudest when it did not touch its electromagnetic pole, and this led Alex to try plucking it as a magneto transmitter, using a diaphragm receiver. Next he tried a magneto diaphragm device at both ends of the line and then a small, flat-coiled clock spring as the transmitter membrane armature. Using this instrument Alec spoke to his father who thrilled to hear 'Papa!' on the receiver.

Experiments with the telephone continued sporadically. On 2 May Alec demonstrated his magneto diaphragm telephones before Edward C. Pickering of the Massachusetts Institute of Technology and five professors from Harvard. In one room Alec recited Hamlet's famous soliloquy and in the other the scientists marvelled at the 'articulate sounds' emitted from the receiver. At the Hubbard residence on 5 May Alec rigged up a couple of improved instruments and clearly heard his prospective father-in-law declaim 'What hath God wrought', even noting that the diphthong came across perfectly. On 10 May the toughest test to date was a lecture before the American Academy of Arts and Sciences in the Boston Athenaeum. Ill at ease before such a distinguished gathering, Alec padded out his lecture with learned references, but what impressed his audience most of all was a practical demonstration. A few doors farther up Beacon Street, at Alec's room in the university, Mabel's cousin Willie sat at a telegraphic organ and, at a given signal, began playing psalms. There was a gasp from the assembled savants when the box on the table in the lecture hall began emitting the recognisable cadences of 'Old Hundred'. At the conclusion, the audience clapped wildly, something which the biologist Samuel Scudder (another of Mabel's cousins) had never experienced in all the twelve years he had belonged to the academy. The following day MIT asked Alec to repeat his lecture there at the end of the month.

On 22 May, at Exeter Place, using a double-pole magneto transmitter and a reed receiver, Alec was pleasantly surprised to hear that 'consonants and vowels were equally intelligible'. Until that time consonants had often been indistinct. Three days later he gave his talk at MIT and crowned this 'glorious success' by giving the first public demonstration of telephonic speech. A clock-spring membrane telephone in the hall communicated with another in a nearby house. The *Boston Transcript* of 31 May reported: 'Vowels are faithfully reproduced; consonants are unrecognizable. Occasionally, however, a sentence would come out with startling distinctness, consonants as well as vowels being audible.' Despite the mixed success of this demonstration, Alec wrote jubilantly to his mother: 'My name is sure now to be well known to all scientific men.'

On 10 May 1876, after five years of preparation, the Centennial Exposition opened in Fairmount Park at Philadelphia where the Declaration of Independence had been signed a hundred years earlier. The Exposition was by far the largest of its kind up to that time – three times the size of the Great Exhibition in London (1851) which was the prototype. More than 60,000 exhibitors from thirty-seven countries took part. Almost ten million visitors flocked that summer to see the Moorish horticultural hall, the quaint British pavilion (in the style of a Tudor mansion), the Swedish schoolhouse, the machinery hall and the vast US government pavilion covering two acres. The promenades and footpaths extended twenty-five miles; everything about the show was on a stupendous scale. Since the beginning of the year the entire country had been bombarded with Centennial lectures and sermons, concerts, dances, banquets and balls. The Centennial was in everyone's mind and on everyone's lips. Just as, a century later, the Bicentennial would help to divert attention from Watergate, so also the Centennial mitigated the worst of the Belknap, Babcock and Blaine scandals that rocked the Grant administration.

Gardiner Hubbard was a member of the three-man committee on the Massachusetts science and education exhibit, while Alec's old friend Percival Richards had been appointed agent for the committee. The education of the deaf formed a prominent part of the exhibit, and to this end Alec had been kept busy preparing the display on Visible Speech. Because he had missed the deadline for the scientific section of the Exposition, Alec squeezed his telephone and telegraph apparatus in as part of his educational display.

The opening ceremony was attended by Dom Pedro II. Then in his early fifties, the portly white-bearded Emperor of Brazil had a reputation for conscientious and enlightened rule. Ironically this would be his downfall, for his abolition of slavery in 1888 alienated the nobility and precipitated the revolution of November 1889 that forced him into exile. But in the 1870s he was at the height of his power, consistently sponsoring public improvements, fostering public education and assiduously patronising the arts and sciences. Following his appearance at the opening ceremony of the Centennial Exposition, by far the most important foreign personage to grace the event, Dom Pedro went on an extended tour of the United States. Early in June he came to Boston and, at Alec's invitation, visited the School for the Deaf on 14 June, conferred with Alec and Sarah Fuller and watched the children's classwork with the keenest interest.

Two days later Hubbard wired Alec, urging him to come to Philadelphia to be on hand when Sir William Thomson and other eminent world scientists judged the electrical entries. Hubbard was concerned that Elisha Gray, who had been in Philadelphia for the previous three months, might hog the limelight. This request could not have come at a worse time for Alec, up to his eyeballs in exam papers and schemes of work for the speech course at the university. Mabel pleaded, she implored, she bullied and cajoled him into going. Finally she drove him to the railway station. The following morning he wrote to his mother from New York: 'I had not the remotest intention of leaving Boston, but seeing how pale and anxious she was about it, I could not resist her and here I am. What I am going to do in Philadelphia . . . I cannot tell'. In New York he was met by Gardiner Hubbard who whisked him off to Philadelphia and booked him in at the same hotel as the three judges in the electrical section. That evening Alec met two of them (whether by accident or design is not known) and had the opportunity to discuss his work.

Professor James C. Watson of the University of Michigan later recorded that Alec

> stated to me in detail the character of his inventions . . . While sanguine as
> to practical results from his multiple telegraph, his great invention was the

speaking telephone, which he believed he had discovered, and in respect to which there was no rival claimant.[7]

At the very last moment, however, plans to reveal the telephone to the world were almost set at naught. Hubbard made a jocular remark that he would have to smuggle the telephone apparatus into the exhibition building, whereupon Alec felt obliged, on principle, to call it off and return to Boston immediately. Hubbard hastily backtracked, and produced the exhibition catalogue wherein Alec's name was entered against Visible Speech and Telegraphic and Telephonic Apparatus. Alec's over-reaction to Hubbard's little joke shows the fraught state of his mind at the time. Once he calmed down he actually began to enjoy himself. This episode was described in a letter to Mabel, in which he continued:

> I really wish you could be here to see the Exhibition. It is so prodigious and so wonderful that it absolutely staggers one . . . Just think of having the products of all nations condensed into a few acres of buildings . . . The Chinese are making a splendid show . . . How presumptuous of us to think ourselves so far superior to them. If I had only a little money to spare, I would buy some of the Chinese works of art for you.[8]

More importantly, Alec was rubbing shoulders with some of the greatest scientists of the period. He met Rudolph Koenig, inventor of the manometric capsule, demonstrating 'a splendid exhibit of tuning-forks and scientific apparatus'. Just how the conversation went we can only imagine, for Alec addressed Koenig in English and Koenig replied in French. Neither might understand the other's language, but their common interests in science transcended such difficulties.

On the very same day, Alec ran into Sir William Thomson as he was inspecting the Gray exhibit. Elisha Gray himself was hovering anxiously in the background as Alec proffered his card to Thomson. Sir William proved to be 'a splendid, genial, good-hearted and wise-headed looking man . . . What was my delight, when he addressed me, to hear a good broad *Scotch* accent tingeing his utterance!' Thomson was eager to inspect Alec's apparatus that day, but he was so preoccupied with the Western Union exhibit that he did not notice the time. Later he apologised to his fellow-countryman and said that he and the other judges would be coming on Sunday, 25 June, with Dom Pedro to examine Gray's instruments and asked Alec to have his ready for inspection at the same time.

Alec, slightly crestfallen, reluctantly agreed to this request. Elisha Gray had a decided advantage, having had ample time to prepare his instruments, whereas Alec's equipment was still arriving from Boston, and some of it had been damaged in transit. Nevertheless, Alec was confident that he would be able to cope. 'One thing I can stand my own upon, and that is *theory*,' he wrote to Mabel. 'I can *talk* and *explain* and Sir William will understand.' Hubbard had a word with Professor George F. Barker who was in charge of the Sunday scientific display, while Alec set to work on his damaged apparatus. He was now pinning his faith on the telephone, as he confessed to his parents. On Saturday evening Willie Hubbard arrived from Boston to lend moral and physical support. Gardiner Hubbard, worn out by his exertions in the searing heat, returned to Boston that same night.

Sunday, 25 June, was even hotter than the preceding days, and the midsummer sun beat down relentlessly on the deserted pavilions, closed to the public. As one man whose name would go down in history waited for his date with destiny, another was at that very moment riding at the head of the Seventh Cavalry to fatal confrontation with Sitting Bull and five thousand Sioux at the Little Big Horn. News of Custer's last stand reached Philadelphia telegraphically five days later, and cast a tremendous blight over the Exposition, but on Sunday itself nothing disturbed the utter stillness of the showground. That sunny morning several carriages rolled up to the Main Building, bearing Dom Pedro and the Imperial Brazilian entourage, Professor Barker and his coterie of scientists, officials of Western Union and the handful of exhibitors who were to demonstrate their inventions. There were about fifty people in all. The eminent scientists included the astronomers Henry Draper of New York and James Watson of Ann Arbor, the geodesist Julius Hilgard of the United States Coast Survey, the Canadian geologist Sterry Hunt, Rudolph Koenig, the brothers John and Joseph LeConte of Berkeley and Sir William Thomson.

This distinguished group, with the Emperor and Empress of Brazil in the forefront, congregated in front of the Western Union stand to listen to Elisha Gray lead off with a description of his exhibit. To Alec, perspiring profusely as the sun streamed through the glass walls and ceiling of the Main Building, it seemed as if his rival was droning on and on forever, though he noted smugly that, from time to time, Gray needed prompting from Barker who even had to help explain some of the more abstruse points of theory. So far as Alec could see, it boiled down to the fact that Gray's efforts at multiple transmission of Morse signals had failed. Of course, he had succeeded in transmitting musical tones, and the demonstration of this was as impressive as it was entertaining. As Gray's discourse concluded on this high note Alec frowned, then brightened up as a beaming Dom Pedro bore down on him and shook him warmly by the hand, thanking him effusively for the copies of Melville's book on Visible Speech.

In later years Alec himself embellished the account of what happened next, maintaining that only Dom Pedro's personal interest and intervention saved the day when the judges, overcome with the heat and having spent far too much time on the Gray exhibit, wished to call it a day. The Emperor had majestically commanded the judges to proceed to the far end of the vast building and mount the flight of steps to the upper floor where Alec's instruments were exhibited. But the letter which he wrote to Brantford on 27 June belies this. After describing his meeting with the Emperor, Alec added simply that 'Sir William and Dom Pedro then came to see my apparatus'. The truth is that Thomson, Watson and Koenig were by this time well aware of the importance of Alec's work and could hardly have waited any longer for a personal demonstration.

At the south end of the East Gallery Alec had laid out his exhibit on a table: harmonic multiple telegraphy was represented by two current-interruptors with their receivers fitted with the latest vibratory circuit breakers for operating Morse code. An electromagnetically vibrated diaphragm was fitted to a Koenig manometric capsule so that an undulatory current could be observed by means of a dancing flame and revolving mirror. Then there was the device which later became popularly known as the Centennial iron-box receiver containing a tubular electromagnet, the iron lid acting as a diaphragm. About a hundred metres away, on the far side of the Hook and Hastings organ exhibit, Alec had rigged up several different types of instrument: a variable-resistance transmitter and two electromagnetic transmitters, one with a single straight-cored electromagnet and the other having two side by side.

Firmly and confidently, Alec explained the principles of his harmonic telegraph, stressing how much simpler – and cheaper – it was than Gray's, and how the vibratory circuit breaker relieved the telegraphist of the tedium of trying to distinguish messages by their different pitch. Dom Pedro and Sir William successfully transmitted signals singly and concurrently. Two days later Alec described the occasion in graphic detail to his parents:

> I then explained the 'Undulatory theory' and offered to test the transmission of the human voice. I stated however that this was 'an invention in embryo'. I trusted they would recognize firstly that the pitch of the voice was audible and secondly that there was an effect of articulation.[9]

While Willie Hubbard remained in charge of the receivers, Alec went to the far end of the gallery and began singing into one of the membrane telephones. Thomson, seated at the table with the lid of the iron-box receiver pressed to his ear, was astonished to hear an unmistakeable melody coming from the instrument. He was even more startled when the song was followed by the words, 'Do you understand what I say?' Sir William cried out, 'Yes! Do you understand what I say? Where is Mr Bell? I must see Mr Bell!' Willie Hubbard went to fetch Alec, but Sir William sprinted after him and found the inventor still shouting into the mouthpiece of the membrane transmitter. 'I heard the words "what I say"', cried the eminent scientist excitedly. He asked Alec to sing again and recite a poem, and then scurried back to hear the results.

Now Dom Pedro pressed the receiver to his ear. 'I hear, I hear!' he exclaimed, and began repeating the words, 'To be, or not to be', which Alec was reciting. The oft-quoted ejaculation of the Emperor, 'My God, it talks!' appears in none of the contemporary eye-witness accounts and seems therefore to be quite apocryphal. Alec was still engrossed in Hamlet's soliloquy when he heard a clatter of footsteps and looked up to see the burly Emperor bearing down on him 'at a very un-emperor-like gait' followed by a gaggle of courtiers and scientists. At the receiving end others took it in turns to pick up the receiver and hear snatches of Shakespeare. Among the eager listeners was Elisha Gray who later testified:

> I listened intently for some moments, hearing a very faint, ghostly, ringing
> sort of a sound; but, finally, I thought I caught the words 'Aye, there's the
> rub'. I turned to the audience, repeating these words, and they cheered.[10]

For Gray there, indeed, was the rub. Later that day he called at Alec's hotel and the two inventors had a long and amicable conversation about the harmonic multiple telegraph. Significantly, the telephone was not at issue; Gray laid no claim to that. Writing to his parents two days later, Alec concluded that all matters of dispute between himself and Gray had now been satisfactorily resolved. 'We have decided that it may be advantageous to both of us to unite our multiple telegraph interests so as to control the Western Union Telegraph Company, if those associated with us can be brought to a mutual understanding.' The alternative, they conceded, would be protracted and costly lawsuits which would probably result in Western Union stepping in and buying up whatever part they wished. As it happened, the multiple telegraph interests were not combined; but this incident convinced Alec that Elisha Gray was 'an honorable man & an independent inventor – & that my suspicions were unfounded'.

Sir William wanted Alec to repeat his demonstration the following evening for the benefit of Lady Thomson; but Alec politely refused, saying that he had to get back to Boston that night, as he had an exam to set and invigilate the very next day. He arranged, however, for Willie Hubbard to repeat the performance for the Thomsons after the exhibition closed to the public on Monday night. To Willie fell the unexpected responsibility of transferring the telephonic equipment to the judges' pavilion at the behest of Professor Watson who now laid down an even more severe test. The transmitters were to be set up in a different building from that of the receiver. Fortunately Willie managed to send messages on both single- and double-pole transmitters without a hitch. Late that night he wired Alec: 'Sir William is entirely satisfied with the experiments. Never was more successful. A large number of sentences understood.'

Interestingly, no attempt was made to use the variable-resistance trans-mitter with a slender rod projecting from a membrane into a tiny cup of conductive liquid. At some point in the ensuing two weeks (before leaving Philadelphia on 10 July), Elisha Gray got his assistant to construct a model of the liquid variable-resistance transmitter which he had described in his caveat, and tested it with his own primitive 'sounding-box receiver'. The result was a total failure. It is possible that this experiment took place some time on Monday, 26 June, for Gray also attended the demonstration by Willie Hubbard that evening. Afterwards Gray discussed Alec's marvel with Barker and Watson and suggested that if the Bell telephone wires had been suspended tightly enough the results might have come from mechanical transmission. Professor Watson later recollected Gray claiming that there could be no other explanation, but Gray stoutly denied ever having said so. Despite any feelings or statements on the matter, Elisha Gray was clear in his own mind at that point in time that he had no grounds, legal or moral, for laying claim to Alec's invention, and it is highly significant that he carried out no further experiments in telephony during that year.

One thing was sadly lacking from the arrangements made by Gardiner Hubbard; he had neglected to inform the press. Only one report about the miracle of transmitted sound appeared up to September, and that was a rather lukewarm comment of 8 July in the *Boston Transcript* which had already provided some vague publicity on 31 May. By contrast, the *Scientific American* of 8 July merely reported that 'Dom Pedro has again visited the Exposition, and has made a minute survey of its contents. The marvelous work of the Walter press . . . is said to have astonished him more than all else'. A periodical might be forgiven for concentrating on the machinery that revolutionised the printing of newspapers, but the improved electrically-driven automatic press used by *The Times* in London had been around for some seven years. Other voluminous reports of the scientific and technical wonders of the Exposition, published around the same time, are equally silent on the matter of the telephone. It seems obvious that they were compiled in the early days of the Exposition, before Alec's instruments were so triumphantly demonstrated. Despite press silence, the news of the miracle of the age spread rapidly – appropriately, by word of mouth. Other scientists and interested laymen flocked to the East Gallery to see and hear the telephone, and within weeks professors from coast to coast were lecturing to their students about Bell's achievement.

Sending and receiving messages from one side of a building to another was one thing; putting the invention to practical use was another altogether. Flushed with success, Alec offered to transmit messages from Boston to Sir William in Philadelphia, if telephone instruments could be rigged up to the existing telegraph wires. This request was declined by the telegraph company, which was probably just as well for the technology had not yet been refined to the point at which such long-distance telephony was feasible. Alec appears to have succeeded in sending and receiving messages over telegraph lines between Boston and New Hampshire, a round distance of 120 miles, and this was sufficient to drive him on to even greater feats. He even envisaged sending telephone calls across the Atlantic, using the ocean telegraph cable, without a battery and relying solely on residual magnetism, but this was no more than a flight of fancy.

It is a mystery why it had never occurred to Alec to develop an all-metal transmitter diaphragm, despite the fact that he had previously toyed with the idea of using his iron-box receiver as a transmitter. Perhaps the poor performance of this instrument as a transmitter put him off the scent. By mid-July, though, he had considerably enhanced the performance of the membrane transmitter by increasing the size of the metal armature almost to the full area of the membrane.

The following day (12 July) Thomson, passing through Boston, called at Exeter Place and that evening he and Alec made another attempt to send a long-distance call over the telegraph wires. In the course of conversation, Sir William suggested that Elisha Gray in America, Paul La Cour in Denmark and Cromwell Varley in England were all working on the same lines as Alec on harmonic multiple telegraphy and exhorted him to join forces with Gray. Before they parted company Alec presented Thomson with a membrane transmitter and an iron-box receiver to take back to Britain. He returned to England shortly afterwards and described at great length the electrical marvels he had seen in Philadelphia when he delivered the opening address to the British Association for the Advancement of Science. Unfortunately he muddied the waters by referring to Elisha Gray's 'splendidly worked-out electric telephone' when he meant the multiple telegraph, whereas Alec's invention was described as 'the greatest by far of all the marvels of the electric telegraph'. Nevertheless, such a pronouncement from so eminent a scientist did much to enhance Alec's reputation. Meanwhile there was the relatively mundane matter of filing a report with the Exposition authorities responsible for awarding medals. Eventually Alec would, indeed, receive a gold medal from the Centennial Exposition in recognition of his achievement which, in the words of the presiding judge Sir William Thomson was 'of transcendental scientific interest', and this more than made up for any chagrin Alec may have felt at being urged to join forces with Gray over the harmonic telegraph.

Back in July, however, Alec once more showed his propensity for procrastination, this time irritating Gertrude Hubbard who would soon become his mother-in-law. To her husband she wrote on 14 July complaining of Alec:

> He has not yet sent in his report to the Bureau of Awards & I can't make him *do* it. He says that his brain won't work & he cannot make it. Then he has had applications from two Lecture Bureaus . . . for lectures on Acoustics & Electricity. He wants to lecture because he enjoys it, & as a matter of dollars & cents. Then he is crazy at the idea of Mabel's going away next winter & wants to be married. Then he would give up V.S. [Visible Speech] or the Telegraph; he says he cannot & I believe he ought not to try to carry them on together. Which shall it be? Which will pay immediately? Then he ought to go to Portland to see about starting a [public school for the deaf] . . . Then he wants to stop at Toronto & see George Brown, & he must be at Brantford on Tuesday – & more than all he wants to talk with you . . . Poor May will have a busy life if she attempts to keep him up to present duty . . . As to lecturing, I begged him as he valued his own & Mabel's happiness to stay at home & mind his proper business.[11]

Alec himself put this in perspective when he wrote to Mabel who was on holiday at Nantucket. He was then charging off at a tangent with a series of experiments in generating electricity that would result in the grant of a patent on 29 August, but it was a sheer waste of time and energy which Alec never subsequently exploited. 'Those experiments of the past few days have quite unsettled me,' he confessed to his fiancée, but he promised to get back to the principal job in hand. 'There is a sort of telephonic undercurrent going on all the while.'[12]

The university was in recess for the summer. With the madcap experiments in electricity concluded, Alec suddenly found himself at a loose end. Boston was unbearably hot, the temperature soaring into the nineties for a month on end. Alec, reared in the rigours of Scotland, could never tolerate the heat and humidity of the Boston summers. On 20 July he wrote to Mabel complaining that he was suffering from severe head-aches behind his left eye, and three days later he packed his bags and caught the train north. At Paris, Ontario, he alighted at one o'clock on a cool, starry morning and exuberantly tramped the ten miles to Tutela Heights.

Practical Developments
1876–77

There is a sumptuous variety about the New England weather that compels
the stranger's admiration – and regret. The weather is always doing
something there; always attending strictly to business; always getting up new
designs and trying them on the people to see how they will go . . .
Mark Twain, at a New England Society dinner, 22 December 1876

At his parents' home Alec found his uncle Edward Symonds (Eliza's
brother) and his three vivacious daughters, recently arrived from Australia.
The house was filled with laughter and jollity but Alec missed Mabel
sorely: 'Separation from you renders me as nervous and miserable as can be
imagined,' he wrote her three days later. This letter crossed with a letter
from Mabel, dated 26 July, in which she urged him to concentrate on one
thing at a time, and give top priority to the telephone. 'Try the lines
between Brantford and Paris, and do your utmost to induce someone to
take up your foreign patents and to allow you to go on working.' Alec
heeded this sound advice and asked Uncle Edward, on the eve of his
departure for Scotland, to seek out the Herdmans in Edinburgh and
enquire whether John or Ben Herdman might be able to promote the
telephone interest in the old country.

In the meantime Alec set to work to refine his equipment. Barely a week
after returning to Brantford, he hired a horse and buggy and drove the five
miles to the hamlet of Mount Pleasant where he installed an iron-box
receiver in the general store which also had the agency for the Dominion
Telegraph. That evening, most of Mount Pleasant's citizens congregated in
the store to witness Alec take a call from his Uncle David over the telegraph
wire from Brantford. Despite David Bell's superb articulation and rich,
resonant voice, only occasional words were intelligible. Several bystanders
took it in turns to press the receiver to their ears as others at the Brantford
end sang or recited poetry. The results were mixed, but at least it proved

that 'my undulatory current can be used upon telegraph lines', as Alec reported to Mabel the following day.

That evening was Edward Symonds' last at Tutela Heights, and the Bell homestead was gaily festooned with Chinese lanterns for a farewell champagne supper. The highlight of the evening was Alec's demonstration of his invention. On this occasion, he rigged three mouthpieces to the transmitter, so that he and two of the Symonds girls in one of the out-buildings could sing part-songs for the delectation of their hearers on the veranda. There was a serious undertone to this entertainment; it proved to Alec that:

> with the undulatory current a single transmitting instrument will suffice for *any number of simultaneous messages* – while with the intermittent current there must be a distinct instrument for each message sent . . . The more I think of it the more I see that the undulatory current is the thing.[1]

This comment betrays the confusion in Alec's mind between multiple telegraphy and telephony. Shortly afterwards he made a more impressive demonstration when he ran iron stove-pipe wire from Tutela Heights along the fence-posts at the roadside, to the nearest point on the Brantford-Mount Pleasant telegraph line and thence to the Brantford telegraph office four miles from the Bell homestead. At the telegraph office David Bell recited Shakespeare while one of his daughters and a local singer went through their repertoire of popular ballads. The successful transmission and reception was duly recorded by the *Brantford Expositor*, even if the reporter was more impressed by the list of dignitaries assembled for the occasion than the demonstration itself. The *Toronto Globe*, owned and edited by George Brown, relegated the event to the trivia column on page three, merely repeating the *Expositor* account. What would soon be hailed as the miracle of the age was dismissed as an entertainment which 'afforded much pleasure and information to those present'.

Undeterred by the inability of the press to appreciate his invention, Alec arranged an even more impressive demonstration on 10 August when he connected his iron-box receiver at Paris to the triple-mouthed transmitter at Brantford, a distance of eight miles. Jostled by a throng of excited onlookers crowding the Paris telegraph office, Alec listened intently to 'perfectly deafening noises . . . explosive sounds like the discharge of distant artillery . . . mixed up with a continuous crackling noise of an indescribable character'.[2] Through this jumbled sound, however, he could make out 'vocal sounds in a far-away sort of manner'. Luckily, he had had the foresight to make contingency plans and at a pre-arranged telegraphic signal high-resistance coils were substituted for low-resistance ones on both receiver and transmitter electromagnets. This produced an immediate improvement; the crackling interference was muted and voices came across clearly even if complete sentences were only wholly intelligible from time to time. Significantly, it was now possible to recognise the speaker's voice. Hitherto only disembodied, rather metallic voices had been heard. Alec discerned Uncle David, but then he heard the voice of his father who was not supposed to be at the Brantford office. An enquiry sent by telegraph elicited the response that Melville had just walked in off the street. Others came forward to speak and listen, and what had been planned as a one-hour demonstration stretched to three.

At the end of the month Alec moved back to Boston once more, finding to his dismay that the searing heat was unabated. Worse, there was a positive mountain of mail awaiting his attention. At the beginning of September the weather broke and Mabel, newly returned from Nantucket, proved an able and efficient secretary, opening letters and helping Alec to answer them. Perceiving that it was vital to press ahead with turning the telephone from an entertaining novelty into a commercial proposition, Hubbard and Sanders, at Alec's prompting, had arranged for Tom Watson to leave his job with Williams and work full time on the telephone project for three dollars a day, plus free board and lodging and a 10 per cent interest in all of the Bell patents. Conversely any patents taken out by Watson himself were to become automatically the property of the Bell Patent Association; as Tom eventually took out sixty patents he felt that he had made his fair contribution to the company. Tom now left his lodgings in Salem and moved in at Exeter Place, taking one of the attic rooms alongside Alec's. On 11 September work on the telephone was resumed in earnest. Mabel noted with relief that Alec seemed 'brighter and better than I have seen him for some time . . . His arrangements with Mr Watson are already a great relief and help to him'.[3]

Over the ensuing two weeks Alec and his assistant explored the possibilities of improved armatures for intermittent-current transmission, but this proved to be a dead-end and on 1 October Alec returned to the undulatory-current telephone. Going over his old notes he came across an entry for 11 July respecting the experiment with a large metal disc on the transmitter membrane. At that remove in time he could not remember why this line had not been pursued, so he now tried it again and found, as before, a vast improvement. Five days later, on Friday evening 6 October, Alec and Tom held the first two-way telephone conversation, using two membrane transmitters alternately as transmitters and receivers. One of these instruments had a large thin steel disc affixed to the membrane; clearly this was the way ahead. The following Sunday Alec wrote to Brantford to report this exciting breakthrough. The success of telephony was no longer an uncertainty: 'I *know* that my fortune is in my own hands. I *know* that complete and perfect success is close at hand.'

The following Monday a steel-diaphragm instrument was used at both ends and conversation was improved immeasurably. That evening Alec took one of these telephones to the Kilby Street premises of the Walworth Manufacturing Company, while Tom went with the other to the firm's factory in East Cambridge linked to the office two miles away by a private telegraph line. The instruments were connected and Watson tried to transmit but nothing happened. He had quite a job persuading the night-watchman to let him go over the factory to check the wiring. Eventually he found a telegraph relay which he bypassed and immediately transmission and reception were successful. Watson picked up the receiver and was deafened by Alec shouting testily at the other end and wondering what was causing the delay. Thereafter the dialogue settled down, each man writing down what the other said. The text was printed verbatim in parallel columns in the *Boston Advertiser*. The following day Alec wrote jubilantly to his parents of 'the proudest day of my life, as marking the successful completion of telephony'.

On Wednesday evening Alec reported the Boston-East Cambridge experiment to the American Academy of Arts and Sciences and allowed the members to try out the telephones for themselves. This momentous week was crowned on Friday, 13 October, by a lecture at Boston University; confounding the superstitious, Alec afterwards concluded that this was 'the best lecture I ever gave'. By contrast, he was at Framlingham the following day, lecturing on Visible Speech. The following Friday Alec dispensed with the transmitter membrane and tried thin steel sheeting as both armature and diaphragm, producing much greater clarity than ever before. Tom immediately constructed a couple of wooden-box transmitters, each with a six-inch-square steel sheet over the open end, close to an electromagnet pole, with a hole in the centre of the lid through which to speak and listen. Again, the experiment surpassed their wildest dreams; but then tragedy struck. Tom Watson went off to Philadelphia, still sweltering in an Indian summer, and there contracted typhoid fever which confined him to bed for two weeks. At this juncture Mabel was getting ready to leave Boston for a cross-country tour with her father who had been appointed chairman of a Federal commission of enquiry into the transportation of mail by railway. Making the most of the brief remaining time before her departure, Alec spent every available moment with Mabel, when he was not teaching at the university or drafting British patent specifications.

By mid-November Mabel was on her way west and Tom was back at work. The daily routine was rigorous, Tom waking Alec before seven and prodding him mercilessly until he rolled out of bed and dashed cold water in his face to come fully awake. During this period Alec secured the co-operation of the astronomer William A. Rogers who allowed him to use the telegraph network from the Boston Observatory (used during the day to transmit time signals to various businesses) at night for further practical experiments in which each of the telephone's components was tested and varied in turn in order to obtain the optimum combination. Alec spent his evenings at the Observatory while Tom remained at Exeter Place. A line ran from Exeter Place to the premises of Stearns & George whose electrical firm was one of the terminals of the Observatory network. An interesting development came when Alec gave Professor Rogers a steel-diaphragm telephone for his own use. Rogers would tap the disc and Alec would thus be alerted that the astronomer wished to speak to him. The refinement of a bell which would ring to summon the recipient of a call would come much later.

By 27 November Alec was making and receiving calls between Boston and Salem sixteen miles away, using the Eastern Railroad telegraph wire. The following day the *Boston Post* reported that 'Professor Bell doubts not that he will ultimately be able to chat pleasantly with friends in Europe while sitting comfortably in his Boston home'. That long-distance calls were, indeed, feasible, was demonstrated a week later when Tom Watson, at North Conway, New Hampshire, tried to converse with Alec in Boston 143 miles away, using the same railway telegraph line. Half a century later Watson recalled this experiment: 'We could hear each other, but the telegraph line was in such bad shape with its high resistance and rusty joints that the talking was unsatisfactory to both of us.'[4] That was a masterpiece of understatement. Alec's version of events, as related to Mabel three days later, was more graphic:

> A roaring rushing sound like wind mingled with the crashing of branches and all the noises of a storm utterly prevented us from hearing the faintest trace of Mr Watson's voice. It seemes as if a cyclone had been imported express by telegraph for the occasion.[5]

After a great deal of adjusting instruments, Alec's persistence was rewarded by hearing the faint, reedy tones of Watson singing 'The Last Rose of Summer' and a further thirty minutes' tinkering enabled the two men to conduct a fitful conversation. Clearly Alec had been unduly optimistic about the possibilities of long-distance calls. In fact, many years would elapse before trunk-calls became a practical proposition.

Meanwhile, the less spectacular experiments on the Boston-Cambridge line put the nascent Bell system to the test. Everything that could go wrong did so. There were interminable problems with leakage from an underwater cable, short circuiting of crossed wires, unexplained interference and weird background noises. Undeterred, Alec and Tom painstakingly and systematically checked the line and their instruments and dutifully logged the problems and their remedies. Alec accepted these trials philosophically as all good experience that would stand him in good stead in bringing the telephone to practical realisation. One of the discoveries in this period was that the hole in the box-lid was more of a hindrance than a help; better results were obtained by merely cupping a hand against the steel diaphragm or putting an ear to it, for transmission and reception respectively. Arguably the most important discovery, however, was that instead of sending a battery current through the electromagnet coil to magnetise an iron core, a permanently magnetised core would work just as well to provide the magnetic field needed for the diaphragm armature to generate an undulatory current in the coil. The wheel had come full circle, for this was anticipated by Watson's plucked reed that produced a mysterious twanging as far back as 2 June 1875.

This set Alec back on the track of using permanent magnets and eliminating batteries. The vast improvements in each constituent of the telephone in the interim seemed to make this more feasible. Tom, burrowing through the books on electricity in the public library, came across a reference to a quick-acting permanent magnet, consisting of a horseshoe magnet of laminated steel with soft-iron cores fastened to the ends to carry the coils. Tom fashioned a magnet of this type early in January 1877 and it was so efficacious that batteries could be eliminated altogether. It was only when variable-resistance telephones superseded magneto telephones in 1879 that batteries came back into their own.

Variable resistance continued to lurk in Alec's subconscious, although he seems to have conducted no further experiments with it at this time. Nevertheless, he was aware that variable-resistance transmission produced a much stronger signal, and with this in mind he and Tom worked shortly before Christmas 1876 on a miniature wet-cell battery 'about three times the size of a thimble'. Plans to experiment with this were postponed while Alec went off to Brantford for the seasonal festivities. Shortly before his departure from Boston he wrote to Mabel at length, reviewing the year's progress and looking forward into the future. He told her he was immensely bucked when a lecturer in Salem told him that telephony was a crowd-puller and that his audience applauded and cheered at the mention of Alec's name. He hinted that, before long, he wanted to make her his wife, once his financial security was settled.

> I want to get enough to take off the hardships of life and leave me free to
> follow out the ideas that interest me most. Of one thing I become more sure

every day – that my interest in the Deaf is to be a life-long thing with me. I see so much to be done – and so few to do it – so few *qualified* to do it. I shall never leave this work – and you must settle down to the conviction that whatever successes I may meet with in life – pecuniarily or otherwise – your husband will always be known as a 'teacher of deaf-mutes' – or interested in them.[6]

Warming to his theme, he outlined a plan for a network of day-schools for the deaf from coast to coast in all major towns and cities so that they could be taught and trained in their home environment. Alec would train the teachers and already he was working on setting up such day-schools in Chicago, Marquette (Michigan) and St Louis. But Alec's dreams were to be overtaken by the clamour of his latest brainchild.

Elisha Gray, writing to William Baldwin on 1 November 1876, had dismissed 'Bell's talking telegraph' as something of interest only in scientific circles, a beautiful toy which would never offer any practical advantage over the telegraph. But even by that date there were sections of the public clamouring for telephones of their own. Following press reports on the experiments of 9 October, Stearns & George were inundated with requests from the public who mistakenly believed that the electrical company were agents for telephone instruments. One firm placed an order for ten instruments to be delivered as soon as possible. Alec himself was overwhelmed with the deluge of letters from every part of the country from would-be purchasers. One of these was John Ponton, born at Edinburgh in 1842 and now resident in Pennsylvania where he edited the *Titusville Morning Herald*. Titusville had had the distinction, almost twenty years previously, of sinking the first oil well in America and more recently (1872) it had pioneered the natural gas industry. Now here was Ponton begging Alec for the right to introduce the telephone commercially into the Pennsylvania oil and gas fields. This was an exciting prospect, and to Ponton must be given credit for a practical suggestion that would have major repercussions on the development of the telephone. He suggested that, rather than have separate lines connecting each pair of subscribers, calls should be routed through a central telephone exchange. Alec wrote to Mabel ecstatically:

Ponton's plan is exactly what has always struck me as the most feasible method of bringing an immediate return. When people can order everything they want from the stores without leaving home and chat comfortably with each other by telegraph over some bit of gossip, every person will desire to put money in our pockets by having telephones.

Alec in due course passed on Ponton's proposals to Gardiner Hubbard to deal with. It will be recalled that his patent agreement with Hubbard and Sanders covered American rights only. The disappointment over George Brown was only a temporary setback and Alec was more determined than ever to secure overseas backers. Uncle Edward failed to make contact with the Herdman family, so Alec decided to approach the British actor-manager Dion Boucicault who was then playing in Boston.[7] He drafted an agreement on 10 November but, at the last moment, Boucicault had cold feet and declined to sign – a matter which he lived to regret bitterly. Filing patents in foreign countries was a necessary but expensive business, and Alec was now scrimping and saving the necessary cash for these overseas fees.

In the weeks immediately preceding Christmas 1876 Alec was working a twenty-hour day. Rising early at Watson's prompting, he would labour till late morning on the telephone project, returning to it after dinner in the evening and continue far into the night. From 11 a.m. till 6 p.m. he was at his day job, lecturing to students at the university, struggling to keep up with the latest developments and discoveries in the physiology of hearing, dealing with a vast correspondence that showed no signs of diminishing, and working on the scheme to establish day-schools for the deaf. He even found time to design a plaiting machine, a Christmas present for Gertrude Hubbard. Much of his daytime was taken up at this period with Shuji Isawa, who had been sent to Boston by the Imperial Japanese government specifically to study Visible Speech as a possible replacement for the *kata kana* syllabic alphabet as well as a medium for teaching deaf Japanese. Undoubtedly progress on the telephone was accelerated by having Tom Watson on the job full time.

On 23 December Alec packed his bags and travelled north. A cold which had been threatening for several days was at its worst by the time he reached Tutela Heights, and he was promptly bundled off to bed and cosseted by Eliza. Writing to Mabel on Christmas Eve, Alec commented ruefully, 'On Saturday I was a man, full six feet high with whiskers & moustache of the most unmistakeable kind, and within twenty-four hours I have dwindled down into a little boy once more!' By Boxing Day he had recovered and the following day set off for Boston again. By 28 December he was back to the demanding routine and on that day conversed from Cambridge with Watson in Boston, clearly and easily, over a distance of eight miles using the new quick-acting permanent magnets.

On New Year's Eve Alec was in Washington to give evidence before the hearing into the harmonic telegraph patent interference. The enquiry was held in Anthony Pollok's well-appointed office. For six hours (10 a.m. till 4 p.m.) without a break, in a clear, confident voice, Alec gave his testimony which was taken down by shorthand writers acting for him and Elisha Gray who, with his lawyer William Baldwin, was also present. Previously Western Union had pushed its claims based on the work done by Edison, but that had now been abandoned. Now, however, it appeared that the giant telegraph corporation had switched its allegiance to Gray. Alec was not worried at this development, fully confident that harmonic multiple telegraphy would be judged by posterity as merely the stepping-stone to the telephone. In fact, there were numerous practical problems which none of the contenders either envisaged or understood and which would delay the practical implementation of the harmonic telegraph for more than thirty years; not until the advent of the electrical resonant circuit, the electric wave filter, the vacuum tube modulator and the vacuum tube oscillator, could the ideas of the 1870s produce the frequency multiplex telegraph in the early years of the twentieth century. By January 1877 Alec was regarding the work on the harmonic telegraph as merely a stage in the evolution of the telephone. As such, it had already been surpassed by his latest invention.

This view was reinforced by the welcome news from Boston, a letter from Tom Watson enclosing diagrams of the latest, vastly improved, telephone instruments which he had made to Alec's specifications. This instrument, replacing batteries with compound permanent magnets, was the subject of a patent filed on Alec's behalf by Pollok and Bailey. They were not a moment too soon, for Percival Richards wrote to Alec shortly after Christmas to warn him that Professor Amos E. Dolbear of Tufts College had, independently, concluded that permanent magnets rather than electro-magnets were the answer, and that he was planning shortly to test his idea experimentally. Alec finished the detailed specification on 13 January; it was filed two days later and granted on 30 January (US Patent 186,787).

During his fortnight in Washington Alec, through Hubbard's influence, gained entrée to the War Department for whom he demonstrated the telephone, speaking from that office to the premises of an electrician some distance away. On 13 January he demonstrated the telephone at the Smithsonian Institution for the delectation of Joseph Henry and his daughters. The performance was repeated that evening before the Washington Philosophical Society; in his vote of thanks, Joseph Henry spoke warmly of 'the value and astonishing character of Mr Bell's discovery and invention'. Alec left Washington in triumph the day his second great telephone patent was filed, and had a rapturous reunion in New York with Mabel, travelling back to Boston in her company.

Not content to rest on his laurels, Alec was back to the old familiar routine early the following morning. On 21 January he wrote to Gardiner Hubbard (still in Washington) reporting further improvements:

by increasing the resistance of the coils, by converting the cover into a
sounding-box, and by supporting the magnet upon rubber, Watson and I
have increased the loudness of the sounds so much that they are audible all
over my experimental room . . . I believe we can make the vocal sounds of
almost any loudness we desire by increasing the resistance of the coils . . .
sufficiently.

The previous day the first telephone call in a foreign language was made
when Shuji Isawa brought two of his fellow-countrymen over from
Harvard. Kentaro Kaneko and Jutaro Komura conversed easily, proving that
the telephone could cope easily with Japanese. According to local tradition,
however, William Johnson (father of the poet Pauline Johnson) conversed
in Mohawk over the telephone at Brantford in the summer of 1876. As
Alec himself recorded the Japanese dialogue as the first use of a foreign
language on the telephone it seems more probably that Chief Johnson's
conversation occurred in the summer of 1877.

During the rest of January and the first two weeks of February 1877 Alec
and his assistant persevered with improvements in the telephone. By
increasing the thickness of the diaphragm the sound became clearer but
wasn't so loud. Increasing the diameter, however, increased the volume.
Taking this to its logical conclusion, Alec got Tom to fashion a diaphragm
from boiler plate, a quarter of an inch thick and two feet square. This would
have been utterly impractical in everyday use but it yielded no
improvement anyway and was promptly scrapped. Other avenues were
cautiously approached, then thoroughly explored. Eventually Alec
concluded that the magneto telephone was definitely the answer and he
gave up variable resistance.

Alec's involvement in these experiments tailed off when the spring term
opened and he was once again immersed in academic work. There are
frequent references (in his notes to Mabel) to the letters that continued to
flood in from every part of the country: more and more, Alec was being
importuned to give lectures to businessmen, civic groups, scientists and
educators, either on Visible Speech or telephony or both. On 31 January,
for example, Alec gave a most impressive demonstration of the power and
reliability of the telephone when he got Tom Watson to speak from
Malden, six miles north of Boston, to an audience of businessmen, railway
officials and electricians gathered on the premises of the Boston Rubber
Company. According to the *Boston Transcript*, they listened 'with rapt
attention to the voice of a fair cantatrice in Malden singing "The Last Rose
of Summer" with a distinctness equal to that attainable in the more distant
parts of a large concert room'.

Both Gardiner and Gertrude Hubbard were unhappy at Alec's preoccupation with public lecturing, which they felt was beneath his dignity, but Alec revelled in it. Besides, he sorely needed the ready cash which these lectures yielded. On 3 February he had written to ask his father for the loan of $200 in order to pay the foreign patent fees, but some unfortunate misunderstanding about the money resulted in a bitter correspondence in which Alec stiffly returned the cheque. 'Muddle, muddle, muddle!' wrote Melville with mounting exasperation. 'When will you learn wisdom and common sense?'[8]

What was so frustrating, above all, was that many of the letters that landed on Alec's desk were from businessmen and private individuals clamouring to buy telephones. Alec reduced this paperwork considerably by having postcards printed, on which he inserted details of the enquiries, and forwarded them to Hubbard at Washington to deal with; but Hubbard delayed taking positive action on these requests until Alec had perfected his telephone system. Moreover, Hubbard, astute businessman that he was, wished to put things on a proper commercial footing. Should telephones be sold outright or hired? The question of forming a public company was uppermost in his mind, but what proportion of funding should come from a share issue remained to be settled. Understandably, Hubbard wished to see these matters settled before a marketing strategy was launched; whereas Alec, oblivious to such mundane problems, was anxious to exploit his invention as quickly as possible. 'We could be making money *now* if we chose,' he complained to Mabel on 13 February.

Alec's sense of frustration was understandable. Only the previous evening he had given a demonstration at the Lyceum Hall in Salem before a packed audience who had paid good money to witness the miracle for themselves. Unfortunately, there was a technical hitch with the line lent by the Atlantic & Pacific Telegraph Company and twenty minutes after the lecture was supposed to begin Alec and Tom (back at Exeter Place, Boston) were still trying to establish communications. Mabel was in the audience that evening and was alarmed when the restive audience began stamping their feet; but eventually Alec strode out from the wings on to the stage and with superb showmanship slowly, deliberately, reverently almost, positioned a brown wooden box on the table. In an instant the stamping ceased and the room was silent. With impeccable timing and delivery, Alec outlined his researches to date and then began the demonstration simply with the sound of the intermittent current from Boston eighteen miles away – 'a noise very similar to a horn' is how the *Boston Globe* described it. This brought a hearty round of applause, but Alec held up his hand. Next he would demonstrate the transmission of actual music. Without the aid of an amplifier, the unmistakeable sounds of 'Auld Lang Syne' issued from the box and filled the hushed room, followed by 'Yankee Doodle'.

Warming to his subject, Alec tactfully made a fulsome tribute to his assistant, a Salem man, and this was Tom's cue to begin speaking. 'Ahoy! Ahoy!' Alec had borrowed this nautical expression – and would continue to open his telephone calls with it till the day he died. The public, on the other hand, would prefer 'Hello', a word that evolved after telephones came into general use but which was derived from the much older 'Holloa', 'Hollo', 'Halloo' or 'Holler' of the hunting field. The following day Alec wrote to Gardiner Hubbard, describing the occasion: 'As I placed my mouth to the instrument it seemed as if an electric thrill went through the audience, and that they recognized for the first time what was meant by the telephone.' On this occasion the first ever telephonic news report was included, when Tom Watson informed his hearers that the engineers on the Boston & Maine Railroad had just come out on strike. After the demonstration, Alec invited various members of the audience up on stage to speak to Watson and others at the Boston end. The Revd E.S. Atwood chalked up another first that evening by asking Tom whether it was raining in Boston. Tom replied in the negative, giving what must have been the first telephonic weather report. Next, Shuji Isawa spoke (presumably in English) and Watson immediately identified the speaker. That was probably not a difficult task, but when Watson named the speaker, the audience cheered appreciatively.

The meeting should have terminated at that point, but the audience refused to budge, even when the manager of the hall turned down the gas-light and Alec pretended to dismantle the telephone. About twenty men persisted in remaining, and thus witnessed Alec relaying verbatim to Watson the report by the *Globe* reporter. At the other end a stenographer took down the text from Tom's dictation and the following morning it appeared in the newspaper under the headline: 'SENT BY TELEPHONE. *The First Newspaper Despatch Sent by a Human Voice Over the Wires*'.

News of this lecture spread like wildfire and Alec was immensely gratified by the glowing accounts which appeared in many other newspapers far and wide. Not all of them were wholly accurate, of course, and some reporters let their imagination run away with them. The *Springfield Republican* thought that the telephone could even sway the outcome of the presidential election which had been extremely close and now depended on the outcome of contested returns from four states. Partisans on both sides were much excited and the country awaited the settlement of the dispute by 4 March. The newspaper predicted that if neither the Republican, Rutherford B. Hayes, nor the Democrat, Samuel J. Tilden, emerged a clear winner, then 'a half-dozen speakers by telephone might be enough for the new election'. As it happened, an electoral commission was created by Act of Congress and it voted by eight to seven in favour of Hayes who was formally declared the nineteenth president on 2 March. Alec gently pulled Mabel's leg over their political differences. She favoured Tilden whereas Alec would rather see Hayes in the White House. In the end, Hayes won by a whisker and would be the first American president to use the telephone.

More sober, less fanciful, were the accounts that appeared in *Leslie's Illustrated Weekly* on 31 March and the *Scientific American* of the same date. Even earlier, however, the story had been fully reported (3 March) in the London *Athenaeum* and *La Nature* of 21 April gave a Parisian audience a vivid report of *Le Télégraphe Parlant de M. A. Graham Bell*.

Although the audience had paid good money to attend the spectacular Lyceum lecture, Alec saw not a cent of it as he had agreed to give his services to the Essex Institute free of charge. In view of the success of this meeting, Alec suggested to the secretary of the Institute that he might give his demonstration again, on condition that he would gain the proceeds. The lecture was a sellout, 500 seats being sold at fifty cents each – ample reward for an evening's work as he gleefully reported to Mabel. Two or three evenings would free him from teaching during the spring term and then, by summer, the telephone itself would be making money for him. Invitations from two other organisations had come, and he proposed asking $200 for each.[9] The performance at Salem on 23 February surpassed the first lecture, Alec the consummate showman including a three-man backing group and a cornet player to enliven the entertainment. This provoked an even wider press response, including a perceptive article three days later in the *Providence Morning Star* of Rhode Island under the headline 'Salem Witchcraft' (an allusion to the infamous witchcraft trials of 1692). The report included an excellent pen-portrait of Alec:

> Mr Bell is a tall, well-formed gentleman in graceful evening suit, with jet-black hair, side-whiskers and moustache, light complexion, forehead high and slightly retreating, nose aggressive and black eyes that could look through a water commissioner . . . His scientifically beautiful utterance was of itself a pleasure worth going far for.

After paying for the hire of the hall and the costs of the musician and trio of singers, Alec netted $149, the first money he had ever earned directly from the telephone. His immediate reaction was to visit a Boston silversmith and commission a miniature replica of the telephone in silver, which set him back $85. Many years later Mabel would treasure it as 'perhaps the most historically interesting thing I have'.[10]

Alec's plunge into the lecture circuit was very timely, for it helped to counteract adverse publicity stemming from a report in the influential and widely read *Chicago Tribune* dated 16 February:

> The real inventor of the telephone – Mr Elisha Gray, of Chicago – concerns himself not at all about the spurious claims of Professor Bell . . . Mr Gray's claims . . . are officially approved in the Patent Office at Washington, and they have already brought in large returns in money as well as in reputation to the inventor. Talking by telegraph and other sport of that description Mr Gray has not paid much attention to as yet.

The bias of the *Tribune* towards a fellow Chicagoan is perhaps understandable, but the report was as inaccurate as it was irresponsible. In this context 'telephone' referred merely to Gray's intermittent-current transmission of tones, but of course the lay public were not to know that. On the other hand, the true telephone was put down as 'talking by telegraph', inferring that this was a frivolous side issue.

As luck would have it, only five days later Elisha Gray wrote to Alec seeking his permission to demonstrate the Bell telephone in a public lecture, to be held in the McCormick Hall on 27 February. Gray promised to give full credit to Alec, though he could not resist mentioning that 'I was unfortunate in being an hour or two behind you' in filing his caveat. But he concluded, 'There is no evidence that either knew that the other was working in this direction.' Alec wired an immediate rejoinder saying that he would give his permission provided that Gray repudiated the 'libel' in the *Tribune*, not only in his lecture, but in a letter to the newspaper itself. Gray replied the following day, saying that he had not seen the newspaper libel. He denied that he had ever spoken a word against Bell in the press and should not be held responsible for everything that appeared in the papers. Indeed, he went so far as to say that 'I have always defended you when I have heard disparaging remarks made about you . . . and am always willing to correct any wrong done you'. Back came Alec's immediate response, thanking Gray for his honourable conduct which he, for his part, had always reciprocated. But, he added, the careless use of the word 'telephone' had created misunderstanding and confusion. He was ignorant of the Gray caveat, was unaware that it pertained to a speaking telephone, and assumed that 'it had something to do with the vibration of a wire in water, and therefore conflicted with my patent'.

On 5 March Gray wrote at length, saying that he had now seen the *Tribune* article and conceded freely that it did Alec an injustice. He gave Alec full credit 'for the talking feature of the telephone' in his lecture. Then he added a paragraph which, when his chagrin over the telephone had deepened into lasting resentment, he would wish he had never penned:

Of course you have had no means of knowing what I had done in the matter of transmitting vocal sounds. When, however, you see the specification, you will see that the fundamental principles are contained therein. I do not, however, claim even the credit of inventing it, as I do not believe a mere description of an idea that has never been *reduced to practice* – in the *strict sense* of that phrase – should be dignified with the name invention.[11]

During April and May Alec delivered three public lectures in New York, three in Boston, and one each in Providence, Lowell, New Haven, Springfield and Lawrence. These were staged in much larger halls than the Salem lectures and were correspondingly more elaborate. In several of them, at least, two or three extra wooden-box receivers were installed above or behind the audience at strategic points in the auditorium, so that the transmitted sounds could be heard by everyone. The first, at Providence on 7 May, was unduly prolonged; due to problems with the snow-covered wires from Boston, Alec was obliged to treat his long-suffering audience to a marathon lasting more than an hour in which he traced the origins and development of the telephone from Reis and La Cour to Gray, with numerous digressions into the more arcane aspects of electromagnetism and sound. Eventually patience was rewarded, and the rest of the evening passed off without a hitch.[12]

Over the ensuing days Alec honed his public address technique, including a magic lantern to project diagrams and close-ups of telephone instruments on to a screen. After the practical demonstration he would conclude with a look into the future, at the infinite variety of uses to which the telephone would be put. Not for nothing did Gertrude Hubbard accuse Alec of emulating Barnum, when he enlisted the aid of the Boston Cadet Band and a quartet from Brown University, although an operatic duo was less successful because the Italian tenors refused to put their lips to the mouthpiece. It has to be admitted that the most successful turns were the tried and tested melodies on the telegraphic organ or a popular song rendered by Tom Watson. Tom's forte was the revivalist hymns of Moodey and Sankey which he belted out with more enthusiasm than tonal per-fection, but it had a powerfully emotional effect on his hearers. When the landlord at Exeter Place complained of the excessive noise and threatened to evict the singer, Tom devised the world's first telephone booth, contrived of blankets rigged over a barrel hoop.

At this remove in time it is difficult to appreciate just how sensational Alec's public lectures were. Time and time again the newspaper reports spoke of magic, miracles, witchcraft, the powers of darkness, of something weird and supernatural. The *Manchester Union* commented, 'Had the hall

been darkened, we really believe some would have left unceremoniously'
on hearing the first human sounds emanate from the mysterious box centre
stage. The same newspaper added, however, that this feeling soon wore off
and then the audience paid a somewhat more critical attention. Press
reports sometimes questioned the sound quality, and phrases like 'someone
a mile away being smothered' or talking with 'his mouth full and his head
in a barrel' tempered the generally adulatory tone of the stories. It was
generally conceded that the sounds became more coherent as one got more
experienced in using the telephone. By now Alec and Tom were adept at
understanding each other, even if the audience was often left in the dark.

Arguably the most important lecture of the series was that held at New
York on 17 May when William Orton of Western Union and Thomas
Eckert of the Atlantic & Pacific Telegraph Company, two of the sharpest
and most devious operators in the business,[13] were in a glittering audience
which included the principals of Columbia University and the Stevens
Institute as well as Cyrus W. Field, promoter of the Atlantic cable and a
British delegation led by William Preece, Chief Engineer of the Post
Office, who recorded that momentous day in his diary:

> During the day we sweltered in the Western Union building and during the
> evening we attended a lecture by Professor Bell on his telephone. We heard
> an organ distinctly that was played in New Brunswick 32 miles off, and
> conversed with a man there. Cyrus Field and I spoke and were answered
> clearly. It is a very wonderful performance and I am simply lost in
> amazement not so much at the performance itself as at the simplicity of the
> apparatus employed in producing the phenomenon.[14]

The following day Preece went to Menlo Park to visit Edison, 'an
ingenious electrician', and on 19 May he noted that 'Professor Bell came
and breakfasted with us and we had two hours interesting telephonic talk.
I hope to bring home with me a complete set to astonish the weak nerves
of the Britishers.'

In addition to the public lectures there were several private demonstrations. At Providence on 11 March Alec had put the telephone through its
paces before a very distinguished group of scientists who included Eli
Whitney Blake, professor of physics at Brown University and a great-
nephew of Eli Whitney, inventor of the cotton gin, and his friends John
Peirce and William F. Channing. Later these three would experiment with
telephones purely for the fun of it, promising Alec that any improvement
they came up with would be his for the asking, without financial obligation
or even acknowledgment. In the end they produced a number of minor
refinements which Alec, to his embarrassment, had already worked out for

himself. The most important contribution came from Peirce, a quiet, unassuming man, recently retired from the chair of physics at Brown University, who devised a greatly improved mouthpiece that later became standard for many years. Alec gave Peirce full credit for this, despite the latter's protestations that he wanted nothing but his own private satisfaction at having made a small contribution to a great advance.

In May 1877, however, Channing devised a telephone instrument small enough to be held in the hand. Alec had independently designed something similar around the same time using a narrow horseshoe magnet, whereas the Channing model used a straight bar magnet. This was adopted as the standard for commercial telephones during the period up to 1879 when variable-resistance instruments superseded the magneto type. Alec had previously used straight bar magnets in other telephones and, in fact, had already ordered just such a magnet for a second 'butter-stamp' telephone, so it is hardly surprising that he overlooked Channing's contribution. The other man, however, nursed a sense of grievance and appears to have complained loud and long to anyone who would listen. This was ignored at the time, but following Channing's death in 1901 an obituary in the *Alumni Register* of the University of Pennsylvania gave him sole credit for making the telephone 'commercially practicable'. Significantly, this claim was not repeated elsewhere.

Even before the telephone was a commercial success, recognition came to its inventor when he was elected to fill a vacancy (left by death) in the American Academy of Arts and Sciences. On receipt of this news Alec wrote home on 25 March, admitting that this 'has been for the last two years the summit of my ambition'. Just turned thirty, Alec was the youngest member of this august group, and Melville basked in reflected glory when he responded warmly two days later, 'You have fairly won the honour by rendering yourself one of the foremost men in the United States.' Mabel, who had already been responsible for Alec dropping the last letter of his name, now urged him to use his name in full for all public lectures and publications. 'Why do you let them speak of you as *A*. Graham?' she wrote on 6 April soon after the first lecture in Providence. 'I perfectly hate it when I think how handsome the full name is.' Alec replied two days later, saying that from then onwards he would style himself 'Alexander Graham Bell', and sign his name thus for the legion of autograph hunters.

Alec's hopes of making a sufficient sum from lecturing in order to give up university teaching were soon dashed. Frederic Gower, the youthful editor of the *Providence Press*, had organised the first highly successful lecture in Providence and this induced Alec to retain him as his business manager for the three Boston engagements. Gower was confident that the series would net at least $1,000 and perhaps as much as three times that sum; but in the event Alec barely cleared $150 after all expenses were met. Most of the losses were incurred by Gower lecturing simultaneously in another city, linked by telephone to the Bell lecture. Slowly it dawned on Alec that the inventor, rather than the invention, was what the crowds flocked to hear, but by the end of May even Alec's personal appearance no longer had the pulling power it once enjoyed. Superficially, the second New York lecture seemed a great success, but afterwards Alec discovered that Gardiner Hubbard had only filled the hall by giving away hundreds of tickets. Alec revelled in the public lecture, but the dwindling receipts at the box office were very disheartening. Disillusionment set in, swiftly followed by anxiety and psychosomatic ailments. Severe headaches were followed by a disturbing rash that covered his body. This attack of dermatitis was brought on by the disastrous lecture at Lawrence on 28 May when Alec and Gower stood before an expectant audience and could not coax a single sound from the wooden-box receiver. Watson, transmitting from Boston thirty miles to the south, later suspected that the telegraph operators along the route had found that they could pick up sounds by connecting their highest resistance relays and therefore listen in on the performance. The resultant silence, at Lawrence, was deafening and brought Alec's first essay in public lecturing to an ignominious end.

On 4 April the world's first regular telephone line commenced operation, connecting the machine shop of Charles Williams at 109 Court Street, Boston, with his home in Somerville. Alec wrote ecstatically to Mabel:

> I went into his office this afternoon and found him *talking to his wife by telephone*. He seemed as delighted as could be. The articulation was simply *perfect*, and they had no difficulty in understanding one another. The first Telephone line has now been erected *and the Telephone is in practical use!*

Inevitably this development was widely reported, and the clamour from businessmen and the general public for telephones increased sharply. As Williams manufactured the instruments on Alec's behalf he could scarcely be regarded as the telephone's first regular customer. That honour fell to a friend of Williams, Roswell C. Downer, a junior partner in the Boston merchant bank of Stone & Downer. About 1 May a couple of rented instruments were installed, linking the bank's office on State Street with Downer's residence in Somerville. Roswell and his younger brother Frank subsequently produced such a glowing, and unsolicited, testimonial that Gardiner Hubbard had part of it reprinted in a circular published later that month. The Downer brothers paid for the installation and the hire of the telephones some time in June 1877, so the first actual paying customer was

James Emery who paid twenty dollars in cash to Charles Williams on 30 May, as a year's advance rental for a telephone connection installed a week or two earlier, between his house and that of his brother Freeman in Charlestown. For eight days Williams kept the notes in his wallet until he could ask Hubbard how the money was to be accounted for. On 8 June the entry appeared in the Williams cash-book as 'To A.G. Bell & Co., telephone account from J. Emery, Jr., $20.00'.

Given Gardiner Hubbard's expertise and business acumen, it seems surprising that the formation of a proper company and a clear marketing strategy were so long delayed. Hubbard was strongly in favour of hiring out telephones, in order to retain a strict control over the system. Previous experience had taught him that such a policy, with rental charges, was preferable to outright sale. The latter course, which was just as vehemently advocated by Gertrude Hubbard (anxious to see a large influx of cash that would enable Alec and Mabel to get married), would have caused long-term problems, for there would have been nothing to prevent able mechanics and electricians from producing pirate telephones. In view of the simplicity of the instruments, this was a very real danger. A further complication was that Gardiner Hubbard, in the spring of 1877, was suffering from cash-flow problems aggravated by the pressing demands of the Internal Revenue Service. With a huge amount of back taxes to pay off and little or no income from his property as a result of the depression since 1873, he confessed to Anthony Pollok in July, by way of explaining tardiness in remitting legal fees, 'My money matters are entirely deranged by the adverse circumstances of the last few years'.

It may be that, as a result of these money worries, Hubbard made an approach to William Orton, in the spring of 1877 before the telephone was fully developed, and offered to sell all rights in the invention to Western Union for $100,000. The precise circumstances of the offer and its subsequent rejection are unknown, and it may be significant that there is no mention of the affair in Alec's voluminous personal correspondence. On the other hand, in his autobiography, Tom Watson alluded briefly to this incident, commenting on the disappointment he felt at the time when he realised that the chance of making a quick $10,000 from his telephone interest was slipping through his fingers.[15] Why someone as sharp-witted as Orton failed to grasp such a heaven-sent opportunity is the biggest mystery of all. The commonly accepted view is that he was so blinded by his hatred of Hubbard that he refused to relieve him of his financial embarrassment, even if it meant losing the greatest commercial bargain of all time. It is more probable that Western Union simply dismissed the telephone as 'a scientific toy' which could never compete with the telegraph. At the time when Hubbard was trying to negotiate with Orton,

Western Union was actually retaining Edison to produce his own refinements in the telephone. Edison, himself handicapped by deafness, was making good progress with a variable-resistance instrument, experimenting with various substances whose electrical resistance varied with pressure, and to this end his staff at Menlo Park, a hothouse of invention and discovery, tested no fewer than two thousand different materials. It was, in fact, Edison who discovered that carbon granules were the key to clear vocal sounds, and such were the improvements wrought by using a graphite disc that Edison could write with confidence to Peter A. Dowd of Western Union on 14 May, assuring him that he 'need have no alarm about Bell's monopoly'. Edison's confidence far outran practical realisation, for it was not until the following February that he was in a position to apply for a patent for his carbon transmitter. It seems likely that Hubbard got wind of Edison's experiments in the spring of 1877 and panicked into approaching Western Union when he saw the prospects of a vast fortune from the Bell telephone evaporating.

Hubbard was also sounding out other individuals whom he regarded as potential backers. One of these was Elisha Converse of the Boston Rubber Company with whom he had had business dealings in the past. Another was Henry Howard, Governor of Rhode Island, who is believed to have first heard of Alec Bell through his predecessor Henry Lippitt, whose daughter Jeannie, a deaf-mute, had benefited from Alec's teaching. Howard was not a well man, suffering from chronic heart disease, but he wrote to Alec on 16 February, saying, 'After seeing your deaf-mute school and your telephone, *I want to live*, if it is only to see what is coming out of it all!' He had more money than he knew what to do with, but he was fired by the notion of lending his name and his cash to some great endeavour. Howard was talking in millions of dollars, as Hubbard relayed to Alec; but a few days later Howard's enthusiasm waned somewhat: 'The commercial results of your inventions are as yet problematical.' He suggested that $10,000 immediate working capital would be ample at this juncture, and he hinted that he had other calls upon his valuable time, 'unless it is likely to prove an affair of magnitude'. Thereafter the plan to launch a company with Converse and Howard seems to have been dropped.

More promising was the plan of John Ponton to take a 9 per cent share of the business for an immediate cash injection of $10,000, but at the last minute this, too, was aborted when Ponton's Titusville bank failed. Nothing daunted, Ponton approached Hubbard in May with an alternative proposal, but this was rejected and in the end Ponton had to be content with the Titusville telephone agency. By this time Hubbard was on much firmer ground, with numerous offers coming in from other sources.

Meanwhile, the courtship of Alec and Mabel was moving forward. On

16 February Mabel wrote at length to her cousin Caroline McCurdy, marvelling that Alec ever came to her:

> Every day I see something new in him to love and admire. His wonderful talent and genius is but a small part of him. It is wonderful that he should be so clever, but far more so that he should not only be that but also so utterly without conceit of any kind, so very true, and as thoughtful for others as a woman, far more so than I.

Of course, such a paragon belonged more in the realms of fiction but it shows how smitten she was with Alec. Theirs had been a long engagement – over a year by this stage – and the delay in proceeding to a wedding was due in part to the hard-headedness of the Hubbards as well as the fluctuating confidence of the would-be groom. Early in May, when the prospects of a good living from the public lecture circuit seemed dazzling, Alec agreed to the Hubbards' suggestion of a June wedding. On 12 May Mabel wrote to her prospective mother-in-law. Alec had told his fiancée that 'like a true Briton his spirit all depends upon his having a good dinner' and she added that she was 'beginning to learn that my happiness in life will depend on how well I can feed him'. After the Lawrence public lecture fiasco, however, Alec postponed his nuptials again; Mabel was disconsolate one minute and trying the next to nag him out of his dithering and procrastination.

The frequent exchange of letters during this period minutely charts the ebb and flow of their relationship; all aspects of their future life together were carefully dissected and analysed. A potential problem was their different outlook on religious matters. While not being rigidly devout, Mabel had definite views on the subject, whereas Alec expressed profound doubts. In one exchange of correspondence Alec had frankly declared his agnosticism, stating that men should be judged by their conduct and not their religious beliefs. In response Mabel wrote a letter which reads more like a catechism, and the following day Alec did his best to answer her very searching questions. He hoped that there was a life after death but had no way of being certain, and he softened his confession by admitting that his religious beliefs (or lack of them) were 'a source of great grief to my poor mother who prays constantly for her misguided son'.[16] Later, when Mabel accused him of being blinded by science to the beauties of nature, he put her right: 'I catch glimpses of the harmonies of nature, of how one part fits into another like the wheel-work of a complicated machine'.[17]

Just when it seemed that the wedding would have to be put off indefinitely, fate lent a hand. Writing to Sarah Fuller, Alec described how William H. Reynolds, a Providence cotton broker, tempted me to negotiate with him for the sale of a part interest in my English patent on the telephone and he has kept me backwards and forwards between Boston and Providence for the last week or ten days arranging matters – but at last the matter has been settled, and I have sold him a portion of my patent for five thousand dollars cash. The result is that I shall leave Boston on the eleventh of July *with my wife!* We shall spend the summer and autumn abroad, returning in October. The wedding is to be very quiet and very few people are to be asked but I *must* have my dear friend Miss Fuller.[18]

A week later Alec splashed out on a costly piece of jewellery as a wedding present for his beloved, 'an exquisite cross of eleven round pearls, the prettiest he could find in Boston', Mabel reported radiantly to her cousin Caroline.[19] This extravagance reflected Alec's buoyant mood in light of the Reynolds deal. Coincidentally, enquiries about the renting of telephones were escalating, lines were being projected and plans for agencies in a number of towns and cities finalised; the time had come to put the rather informal association between Alec and his Boston backers on a more businesslike footing. On 9 July 1877 the Bell Telephone Company was created as a voluntary association, unincorporated and therefore without any declared capitalisation, through the medium of a declaration of trust in which Alec assigned all his telegraphic and telephonic patents, present and future, to Gardiner Hubbard as trustee with the responsibility for running the company's affairs. Five thousand shares and appropriate voting rights were apportioned between Hubbard, Sanders, Tom Watson and Alec Bell in the same ratio as their patent interests. Having disposed of some shares to Reynolds, Alec had 1,507 left, or about 30 per cent of the total. In addition to the pearl cross, he now made over 1,497 of his shares to his bride, keeping the remaining ten out of sentiment.

The wedding was, as Alec predicted, a quiet, family affair, the ceremony being performed at the Hubbard mansion on Brattle Street, Cambridge, in the very room where the young elocutionist had first set eyes on Mabel and sung into the piano for her father's amusement. It was a balmy July evening, filled with the scent of the Madonna lilies which the gardener had saved for the occasion.[20] Roberta and Caroline were bridesmaids, while the best man, appropriately, was Tom Watson, ably abetted by his assistant, Eddie Wilson. Watson recalled fifty years later his lack of *savoir faire*: 'We didn't know that at such occasions there was always a room for the men to dress in and as we were ashamed to wear our [white] gloves in the horse-car, we put them on behind a tree in front of the house before we went in.' [21]

Gardiner Hubbard's feelings as he handed Mabel over to her husband may be imagined: he was not losing a daughter so much as gaining a son –

and a valuable asset. A week before the wedding he wrote to Anthony Pollok:

> The telephones are doing very well. There are nearly 100 in operation in many different places, and they have not failed in a single instance . . . We shall soon begin to reap the rewards of Alec's invention.[22]

On 1 August the first shareholders' meeting was held in Boston. The five shareholders (who included Gardiner's brother Charles) voted themselves into office as the board of managers, Alec being elected Electrician (in charge of research and development), Tom Watson Superintendent (in charge of manufacturing) and Thomas Sanders Treasurer. In his capacity as Trustee, Hubbard delivered his first report to the board. There were now over 600 telephones in operation (the precise figure was, in fact, 778 according to Watson). Charles Williams had the Boston agency, while Frederic Gower had the rest of New England and John Ponton the industrial districts of Pennsylvania. Thanks to Hubbard's peregrinations on behalf of the Railway Mail Commission, agencies were about to come into operation all over the eastern states, from Ohio and Indiana to Florida, and plans were maturing to extend the system to Chicago and San Francisco. The future for the newly-weds seemed remarkably rosy.

9

Europe
1877–78

Man is the shuttle, to whose winding quest
And passage through these looms
God order'd motion, but ordain'd no rest.

Henry Vaughan, *Silex Scintillans. Man*

Ever since Napoleon's brother Jerome, the black sheep of the family, had eloped with Elizabeth Patterson of Baltimore in 1803 to Niagara Falls, this place of stupendous scenic beauty shared by Canada and the United States has been a mecca for honeymooners.[1] Alec and his bride journeyed thither the day after their wedding and from there travelled on to Brantford. There is no record of Alec carrying Mabel over the threshold of his family home, but his Symonds cousins broke oatcakes over the bride's head as she entered the house, apparently an ancient Scottish good-luck custom on which Melville insisted. Previously, Mabel had met Melville at Boston, but now she was introduced to Eliza whom she described, in a letter to her mother, as 'just as nice and kind as she can be, so bright and quick'.[2] The following day there was a huge party at the Bell homestead, some thirty neighbours being invited round to meet the new Mrs Bell and have a demonstration of the latest telephones. It was on this occasion that William Johnson spoke in Mohawk from Tutela Heights to some of his followers in Brantford.

While they were in Canada the industrial unrest in the eastern United States, which had been simmering for months, erupted in a wave of violent strikes and bloody riots in many towns and cities. This crisis had been a long time coming. The post-war boom had been followed by a slump triggered off by the failure of Jay Cooke, financier of the Northern Pacific Railway, in September 1873. As late as the summer of 1877, over 18 per cent of the railway mileage of the United States was in the hands of receivers, the iron industry was prostrate and mercantile failures assumed astronomical proportions. Gardiner Hubbard himself barely weathered this

166

crisis. The Boston & Maine Railroad strike which had been so dramatically announced by telephone in February that year, though itself short-lived, precipitated a wave of similar stoppages which paralysed the nation, and the return of Alec and Mabel to Cambridge at the end of July was marred by the disruption of the railways. News of the bloody street fights in the north-eastern cities reached the honeymooners as they passed through Montreal, on their journey home, where Alec took extraordinary precautions. As Mabel wrote to her mother-in-law on her safe return after an eventful journey, 'We were so doubtful about our chances of reaching Boston undisturbed that Alec bought a revolver with ammunition enough to kill a hundred men, he said. I think he was rather disappointed not to have a chance to show it off.' [3]

Pausing in Boston only long enough to attend the historic first meeting of the Bell Telephone Company shareholders, Alec and his bride took the train to New York. On 4 August, seven years and three days after he first set foot in the New World, Alec boarded the SS *Anchoria* bound for Plymouth. During the six-day crossing to England, Alec rose at 6 a.m., bathed and returned to his bunk till lunchtime. Afternoons were spent on deck, catching up on his reading, and when that was exhausted he turned his attention to the captain's navigation manuals. This led him to apply his hyperactive mind to inventing improved steering gear, though this line of research was never followed up. In the evenings there was a wide range of entertainment and Alec was the life and soul of the party, not only playing the piano for dancing and ship's concerts, but also demonstrating his wonderful invention. His luggage included telephone instruments and in no time they were wired up all round the ship.

The ship docked at Plymouth on 11 August. Shortly before they landed, Alec wrote to his mother: 'I cannot tell you what a longing I have to see again the places I remember so well, London, Bath, Edinburgh and Elgin. I don't know how it is, but Elgin bears the palm with me.' From Plymouth Alec and Mabel went straightway to Glasgow where Alec went 'perfectly wild' at being back in Scotland. He was euphoric, he was ecstatic, about all things Scottish, introducing Mabel to such culinary delights as the Scottish bap or breakfast roll. After a few days in the West of Scotland, where Alec demonstrated the telephone to a group of influential businessmen and Glasgow's civic dignitaries, they headed south again, first to Plymouth for the meeting of the British Association for the Advancement of Science on 20 August, and then to Bath which evoked very mixed memories, nostalgia being tinged by the bitter recollection of Edward's death which brought on a fearful migraine. Alec had recovered his equilibrium by the time they reached London. Here they went on a pilgrimage to Highgate Cemetery to commune with the spirits of his brothers and grandfather at their graveside. In this sombre, philosophic mood, Alec mourned the fact that most of his friends were dead and gone. This was an exaggeration, for there were still old friends aplenty to give the newly-weds a warm welcome to the metropolis.

They had a joyful reunion with Alexander Ellis, and later they spent some time with James Murray and his wife, not to mention their five children. Susanna Hull was still to the fore and eager to hear of Alec's experiences in teaching deaf children in America. And as news of their arrival in London spread, they were approached by Alec's old flame, Marie Eccleston, herself returned from Germany and recently married to a Mr McBurney, 'a little man with a brown beard and ghastly white face' as Mabel recorded. Marie herself was blooming, and seemed 'if anything younger and less stout than when he last saw her'.[4] Alec and Mabel travelled by train from London to Edinburgh in mid-September, visited the old home off Charlotte Square and toured all Alec's old haunts in and around the city.

A few days later they went north to Elgin and spent an idyllic week at Covesea where they rented a room in a fisherman's thatched cottage. Alec had some half-baked notion that it would be fun to rough it for a bit; he would catch fish and Mabel would cook it over an open fire. She, however, was not so sure:

> Neither one of us ever saw a fish cooked, much less ever did it ourselves. Alec appears to think it a very simple operation, but I have an idea that the fish has to be opened and cleaned, and a part of its inside taken out first.[5]

Inevitably, this chore was rapidly delegated to the fisherman's wife, leaving the young couple free to explore the cliff paths and the beach. Later they would both look back on that week at Covesea as one of the happiest they ever spent. The zest for the scenes of his boyhood gave Alec a prodigious appetite; writing to Eliza, Mabel noted with some apprehension that:

> Alec . . . is perfectly happy with his Edinburgh rolls, Scotch oatmeal porridge and red herring. Last night he swallowed a whole dish of finnan haddock which was intended for us both. In fact Alec is growing tremendously stout, and can hardly get his wedding trousers on now. I remember your warning long ago and scold just as hard as ever I can, but it is no use. Alec proposes buying a book, teaching fat men to grow thin![6]

On the last day they lingered on the beach. Alec was 'wild and full of fun, though rather ashamed that the inventor of the telephone should go wading', wrote Mabel to her mother, but she convinced him 'that he should not be the slave of his own position'.[7] By late August Mabel had missed a period, and at Covesea she was now certain that she was pregnant. Alec had originally planned that they should return to the United States in November, but this was put back on account of Mabel's condition, and then postponed indefinitely when the birth of the baby was imminent. Their daughter was born in London on 8 May and, after long deliberation spread over two weeks, named Elsie May, the first name being a Scottish contraction of Elizabeth after the paternal grandmother, and the second the name by which Mabel was familiarly known as well as the month of the child's birth. Commenting on the infant, Alec told his mother, 'Such a funny black little thing it is! Perfectly formed, with a full crop of dark hair, bluish eyes, and a complexion so swarthy that Mabel declares she has given birth to a *red Indian!*' And he added that he had lost no time in checking 'that all its organs of speech and sight and hearing are perfect'. Mabel told her mother that 'Alec is at once so fond of it and yet so afraid of the poor little thing, and he hardly knows how to hold it.' It was decided to delay the Atlantic crossing until Elsie had been weaned; in the end, in fact, the return to America would be put off until the end of October 1878, by which time she was almost six months old.

On coming to London early in September 1877 Alec and Mabel took rooms in Jermyn Street but when their original plan to return to Boston was put off Mabel insisted that they rent a house where she could have more privacy and Alec could pace up and down late at night without disturbing the other lodgers. By 27 November, therefore, they had moved into 'our own dear little home', as Mabel was pleased to call the seventeen-room, four-storey villa at 57 West Cromwell Road, South Kensington, which Alec leased, fully furnished, for £225 per annum, a colossal sum which he could not really afford, but he was shrewd enough to judge that it was important 'to make as good a show as possible' for business reasons. Mary Home, who had been Alec's grandfather's housekeeper for a quarter of a century, was hired as cook-housekeeper, and other staff, including a housemaid and, in due course, a nursemaid, were also taken on. This huge rambling house, set in more than an acre of grounds, would be their home for twelve months, apart from a few weeks in the high summer of 1878 when they retreated to a little country hotel in Middlesex where they were joined by Gertrude Hubbard and Mabel's sisters. While Alec was pre-occupied with telephone business, the women lazed away the long summer days 'lying on shawls spread out under the shade of some great tree in the meadow'.[8]

As soon as they were settled in their London mansion, Alec got down to serious business. In no time at all he was inundated with invitations to lecture, earning fees of £15 to £25 a time. With several engagements of this sort every week he more than covered his living expenses, but then there was a lull and he began to panic. For about a week there was rigid economy, Alec even being reduced to travelling third class on the trains; but then William Reynolds paid him the full amount for his share of the British patent rights. Alec promptly invested this windfall, the interest yielding sufficient money to give him a feeling of financial security. As time passed and his position became even more secure, Alec, while not becoming extravagant, would insist on the best he could afford. Mabel told him, when he was being finicky about hiring rooms in August 1878, 'Do you know, you have got the reputation among us [Hubbards] of being very particular, much more so than we. Why is that? You never have lived as well as we – a few years ago Papa was a very wealthy man, and we had our saddle and carriage horses and summer house in Newport, and yet we don't mind living cheaply, as you do.'[9] The Hubbards had their ups and downs and seemed to have adjusted to changing fortunes with equanimity.

The nocturnal habits which had made Alec a nuisance to fellow lodgers in Jermyn Street continued at West Cromwell Road. Worries about the telephone business, most of them quite unfounded, gave him many sleepless nights and a recurrence of those severe headaches which had plagued him in early life. Sleep would eventually come just before dawn, and then Alec would lie in bed till eleven o'clock or even later. Mabel, who was an early riser, eventually persuaded him to join her for breakfast at eight-thirty, but it was an on-going struggle:

> He often feels cross and headachy when I awake him and begs hard to stay in bed, but if I am firm, after breakfast the headache has quite disappeared, and he is bright and thankful he has been awakened . . . Yet it is hard work and tears are spent over it sometimes.[10]

An inability to get out of bed in the morning was not Mabel's only concern with her husband. Marriage obviously agreed with him – too well. In his bachelor days, especially in the previous three years when he was so preoccupied with his telegraphic and telephonic research, he had often been careless of eating regularly. Hyperactive in both mind and body, this six-footer had been as rangy as a beanpole. Now, however, a more sedentary lifestyle and regular meals began to have their effect. The gargantuan appetite that had been whetted by the caller air of Covesea had continued unabated after their return to London. At the time of his wedding Alec had weighed 165 pounds; by May 1878, ten months later, his weight had risen to 214 pounds. He then went on a rigid diet and succeeded in shedding a stone, but from then until the day he died he never got his weight below 14 stone, and at times would be as heavy as 18 stone. With increasing corpulence came hirsuteness. A heavy cold at the onset of winter dragged on intermittently till the following spring, and Mabel concluded that nature's muffler would be the best protection. At her insistence he let his side-whiskers grow. Full of beard and round of belly but tall and erect as ever, he emulated his Uncle David whom George Bernard Shaw once described as 'by far the most majestic and imposing-looking man that ever lived on this or any other planet'. Mabel eventually became resigned to Alec's obesity; he was impressive in public, and cuddly in private. By the end of 1877 she was confiding to her mother that Alec was

> just as lovely as ever he can be, and instead of finding more faults in him, as they say married people always find in each other, I only find more to love and admire. It seems to me I did not half know him when I married him.[11]

And Alec himself, writing to Gertrude Hubbard on 21 February 1878, agreed that 'we are enjoying life about as much as it is possible to do'. This idyllic domestic scene provided Alec with a much-needed refuge from the ups and downs of the telephone which, inevitably, continued to take up so much of his time.

Sir William Thomson had brought back from America in September 1876 a pair of 'gallows' telephones which he tried to demonstrate at the meeting of the British Association for the Advancement of Science at Glasgow that month; but the instruments had been damaged in transit and while he described the telephone as 'the greatest by far of the marvels of the electric telegraph' he was quite unable to get it working. Exactly a year later William Preece demonstrated the latest 'butter-stamp' telephones successfully at the BAAS conference held at Plymouth. Alec and Mabel had landed at that very seaport a few days earlier, and after their lightning trip to Glasgow, returned thither to take part in the meeting on 20 August. Gratified by the warmth of their reception, Mabel wrote home:

> Alec is really the chief person here, everyone seeks to do him honor, he has been introduced to all the great people, Lord this, Sir that, and all are anxious and eager to speak to him . . . When he went down to Table d'Hote that afternoon the whole large hall full of people turned around to stare at Alec.[12]

His demonstration and lecture were greeted rapturously and invitations to lecture flowed in. From then until the end of 1877 Alec would give a dozen major lectures, in some cases to audiences numbering over two thousand, as far afield as Aberdeen (25 September), Leeds (25 October),

Birmingham (29 October) and Glasgow again (7 November), as well as on several occasions in London, including two mammoth lectures before the Society of Arts and Manufactures on 1 and 20 December alone. In addition he arranged a number of stunts, including the use of the telephone to communicate between the coal-face and the pit-head at a Newcastle colliery, an incident that showed the incalculable merit of the telephone as a safety measure. In the same category was Alec's spectacular demonstration of communications between a ship and divers in the Thames. Alec himself donned a heavy rubber suit and copper helmet and conversed on the river bed with people on the surface, but had a bad attack of the bends when he was brought up too quickly.

On the last Saturday of 1877 Alec organised the world's first international telephone link. Through the good offices of Mr Bordeaux, superintendent of the Submarine Telegraph Company at Dover, he was able to hook up a telephone to the telegraph cable between St Margaret's Bay near Dover and the village of Sangatte on the French coast. The mayor of Dover and other civic dignitaries assembled in the little telegraph hut erected on the beach close by the borings of the Channel Tunnel, begun with such high hopes two years previously but since abandoned on account of the strenuous opposition of the War Office and the bitter rivalry of the South Eastern and Chatham & Dover railway companies. The successful communication by telephone was given additional poignancy because of the Tunnel fiasco, as *The Times* drily noted, contrasting 'a gross and material way of connecting the two countries . . . with the delicate communications we were about to establish'. The underwater line was twenty-two miles long and clearly intelligible speech was impossible against the constant hum of telegraph messages, but the parties at both ends contented themselves with singing 'Auld Lang Syne'. The rather plaintive melody of Burns's great song of parting appropriately brought this early experiment in international communications to an end; serious experiments with underwater telephone links were not resumed till 1891.

In 1864 Melville Bell had failed to interest Queen Victoria in Visible Speech, which he had offered to demonstrate to her at Balmoral; now, thirteen years later, Her Majesty herself expressed an interest in the telephone. On 11 December Alec was approached by Sir Thomas Biddulph, the Queen's private secretary, with a view to arranging a private showing at her retreat in the Isle of Wight, but plans were not finalised till 9 January. Much to her chagrin, Mabel (who had made a special trip to Paris to purchase a Worth gown worthy of the occasion) was not invited to Osborne, but five days later Alec took the train to Southampton and the ferry across the Solent and rigged up telephone wires connecting a hall in Cowes, Osborne Cottage (Biddulph's residence) and the Council Room at

Osborne House. That Monday evening, accompanied by Colonel William Reynolds, he was ushered into the Council Room where the elderly Queen in widow's weeds sat primly with her son and daughter, Arthur, Duke of Connaught, and Princess Beatrix. Later Alec wrote to Mabel describing the occasion. He found Her Majesty 'humpy, stumpy, dumpy' and was amazed to note that her ungloved hands were 'red, coarse, and fat as a washerwoman's and her face also fat and florid'. Despite her unprepossessing appearance, the Queen 'was genial and dignified and, all in all, quite pleasing'. Victoria herself merely noted in her diary under the date of 14 January that the telephone was 'most extraordinary'.

Alec began with a brief discourse on the origins and development of the telephone, before picking up the instrument and speaking to Sir Thomas Biddulph at Osborne Cottage. Then the Queen spoke to Sir Thomas and Lady Biddulph, before Kate Field, an American journalist hired by Reynolds to publicise the telephone, came on the line to sing 'Kathleen Mavourneen' and 'Comin' Thro' the Rye', followed by the epilogue from *As You Like It*. As Kate began singing the Queen happened to be looking away and Alec, used to the deafness of his mother and wife, instinctively reached out and tugged at Her Majesty's arm as he proffered the receiver. The Queen ignored this gross breach of etiquette and beamed sweetly at the young inventor.

Later calls linked Osborne House with Cowes, Southampton and finally London. At Cowes the line was supervised by Major Webber of the Royal Engineers who had lined up a quartet of singers composed of his daughter, Miss Strohmenger and Messrs Hamilton and Curwen who sang several part songs. At Southampton, William Preece stood by to converse with Alec and Reynolds. A bugle at Southampton sounded the retreat, and lastly an organ at London was played by a Mr Wilmot. The demonstration lasted from 9.30 p.m. till midnight.

Rather ambitiously, Preece had an orchestra and a choir lined up to bring the performance to a fitting climax with 'God Save the Queen', but the old problem of telegraph relays arose again and the line was not properly reconnected with Osborne until almost midnight, by which time the performers had long since packed up and gone home. In the end it was left to Preece to improvise by humming the tune as best he could. In the Council Room at Osborne, Queen Victoria, with the receiver pressed to her ear, was not amused. 'It is the National Anthem!' she cried, frowning, 'But it is very badly played!'[13]

Despite the non-appearance of the orchestra, the demonstration was pronounced a great success. Two days later, Biddulph wrote to Alec from Osborne:

My Dear Sir,

I hope you are aware how much gratified and surprised the Queen was at the exhibition of the Telephone here on Monday evening.

Her Majesty desires me to express her thanks to you and the ladies and gentlemen who were associated with you on that occasion.

The Queen would like, if there is no reason against it, to purchase the two instruments which are still here, with the wires &c, attached. Perhaps you will be so kind as to let me know to whom the sum due should be paid.[14]

Alec responded immediately, saying that he would be most happy were Her Majesty to accept a pair of telephones as a gift, and followed this promptly by despatching a handsome set fashioned in ivory trimmed with gold. The Queen's gracious acceptance was almost as good as the accolade of knighthood. It was widely reported and undoubtedly helped to boost interest in the telephone. Alec also installed a telephone in the gallery of the House of Commons so that parliamentary debates could be transmitted verbatim to a Fleet Street newspaper. Kate Field not only plugged the telephone in her regular columns in *The Times* and the *New York Herald* but wrote dozens of pieces for other papers and was instrumental in the placing of good telephone stories in all manner of periodicals. The Queen's request for the telephones nicely coincided with the great *Matinée Téléphonique* which Kate organised for the press, to 'get one general chorus of gratuitous advertising' on the eve of the opening of Parliament. A few weeks later Kate rushed out a little book entitled *The History of the Telephone* in which a fictitious 'Intercepted Letter' from an American lady tourist to a friend provided the connecting narrative for a wholesale reprint of Kate's articles and feature stories. She concluded with the speculation that some day light as well as sound would be transmitted and that, 'while two people, hundreds of miles apart, are talking together, they will actually *see* each other!' More than a century would elapse before videotelephone became a reality, but it was the sort of vision that Kate probably got from Alec himself. This booklet, which cost sixpence, was a best-seller and probably the earliest separate publication dealing with the subject.

Cashing in on the massive public interest in a phenomenon which, though widely discussed, was not yet commercially available, an enterprising toy manufacturer rushed out the Domestic Telephone, the contraption of two tin cans connected by a string which had earlier appeared in the United States under the name of the Lovers' Telegraph. Mabel was faintly irritated to find the London shops full of these gadgets:

Wherever you go, on newspaper stands, at news stores, stationers, photographers, toy shops, fancy goods shops, you see the eternal little black box
with red face, and the word 'Telephone' in large black letters. Advertisements say that 700,000 have been sold in a few weeks.[15]

Alec had put his faith entirely in his father-in-law, as trustee of the Bell
Telephone Company, to manage the rights of the telephone in Europe as
well as North America. Out of the monies which accrued from the rental
of instruments Alec and Mabel were to get an income of $3,000 a year,
while anything in excess of that sum was to be added to the principal until
it attained a ceiling of $200,000. Thereafter the whole of the income would
go to Alec and Mabel, while any children of the marriage would get the
principal (plus interest) in due course. Alec realised his own shortcomings
as a businessman and was quite happy to leave such matters in Hubbard's
hands. Nevertheless, this did not prevent him from doing whatever he
could to promote the telephone interest whenever and wherever he could.

William Reynolds arrived in England in September 1877 and took over
from Alec the responsibility for day-to-day enquiries about telephone
leasing. He negotiated with the Indiarubber and Gutta Percha Company
which already produced insulated telegraph wire to manufacture
telephones, but demand far exceeded supply, and soon unscrupulous
individuals were marketing do-it-yourself kits. Reynolds acted promptly
and vigorously to suppress these patent infringements and took the more
blatant offenders to court. Although the telephone pirates quickly caved in,
it is doubtful whether such legal action was itself legitimate. Sir William
Thomson, by fully describing the telephone at the BAAS meeting in
Glasgow in 1876 had, in fact, jeopardised Alec's right to a British patent. It
was by pure chance that the damage sustained in transit, and which had
made Sir William's instruments inoperable, led him mistakenly to publish a
diagram showing the iron-box receiver with its diaphragm attached to the
rim with a screw but bent away from it. This technicality enabled the
British courts to bend the law in the interests of justice and conclude that
the vital component, the metallic diaphragm, had not been legally
disclosed. To clinch the matter, Alec officially disclaimed certain non-
essential patent claims, but this provoked a spate of correspondence in *The
Times* during February and March 1878 in which he was accused of
stealing the telephone idea from Reis and Wheatstone, his disclaimers
being taken as admissions of guilt.

Even more damaging were the vociferous protests expressed in the
correspondence columns of the newspapers against the high cost of renting
a pair of telephone instruments. While Alec and his promoters were
charging £25 a year – almost a year's wages for the average working-man

at the time – pirates were *selling outright* passable imitations for twelve shillings a pair. Even when the pirate manufacturers added the cost of a Leclanché battery (which, at fifteen shillings, was actually more than they charged for the telephones themselves) the total outlay was only about a twentieth of the rental. This was bad publicity which even the ingenious and resourceful Kate Field could not readily combat, and it had a knock-on effect when a capitalisation of half-a-million pounds, planned by Reynolds in January 1878, was first delayed and then severely cut back in March when 55 per cent of the English patent was sold to a consortium for £10,000 cash and a similar sum in twelve months' time. Of this money Alec himself only got £500 for his expenses and services in Britain, though the family trust subsequently received a little more than £3,000.

On 25 March, two days after the inaugural meeting of the Electric Telephone Company of Great Britain, Alec circulated an open letter which admirably summed up his views on his invention:

> The Telephone may be briefly described as an electrical contrivance for reproducing in distant places the tones and articulations of a speaker's voice so that Conversation can be carried on by word of mouth between persons in different rooms, in different streets or in different Towns.
>
> The great advantage it possesses over every other form of electrical apparatus consists in the fact that it requires no skill to operate the instrument. All other telegraphic machines produce signals which require to be translated by experts and such instruments are therefore extremely limited in their application – but the Telephone actually speaks and for this reason it can be utilized for nearly every purpose for which speech is employed.[16]

Alec went on to compare its simplicity of operation with the complication of parts of telegraph machines and the expense of such instruments. Lines and wires could be laid along the network of gas and water pipes in large cities or by overhead suspension. Telephone links would be confined to cities to begin with, but he believed that:

> in the future wires will unite the head offices of Telephone Companies in different cities and a man in one part of the Country may communicate by word of mouth with another in a distant place . . . I am aware that such ideas may appear to you Eutopian [*sic*] and out of place, for we are met together for the purpose of discussing not the future of the Telephone but its present.

Initially he considered that telephones would be used by

banks, merchants, manufacturers, wholesale and retail dealers, Dock Companies, Gas Companies, Water Companies, Police, Fire Stations, Newspaper offices, Dispatch and public buildings and for use in Railway offices, in Mines and in Army, Navy and Post Office.

Alec urged the company to lease the lines and on no account to let control of them pass from its hands. Customers should be charged either a fixed annual rent or a toll based on the duration of calls. He strongly advocated the establishment of telephone exchanges in each town through which the calls of subscribers could be routed. And he recommended that, as a means of getting the system firmly established, certain large shops in each town should be granted a free trial period in order to encourage their competitors, as well as private individuals, to become subscribers.

Unfortunately, these admirable suggestions at first seem to have fallen on deaf ears and no move was made to implement them. For some time, therefore, telephones were rented out in pairs connected by steel wires, so that two individuals could converse locally. There were no switchboards to facilitate communication among a number of users, the calling devices were extremely crude and transmission uncertain at the best of times. A month later, however, Alec's old friend Adam Scott, whom he had introduced to Reynolds, obtained the position of secretary to the Telephone Company of Great Britain. He rapidly became the conduit of Alec's ideas and views to the company, thus relieving the inventor of such mundane matters; but Alec's seeming indifference to the company business undermined the confidence of the directors in him.

In one matter Alec showed that he could be just as positive and vigorous as ever when occasion demanded. In July a bill came before Parliament which sought to amend the Telegraph Act of 1869. That Act had effectively nationalised the telegraph companies and placed them firmly under the control of the Post Office, a situation that would continue until 1982 when British Telecom became a separate corporation. On 23 July 1878 Alec and Adam Scott lobbied MPs so successfully that the bill, which would have absorbed the nascent telephone business into the telegraph system, was defeated. It was not until 1912 that the British telephone service was nationalised, although the various companies were effectively under Post Office control from 1906 onwards.

Alec had not been resting on his laurels during his prolonged stay in England. He tackled the widespread problem of interference by induction by adopting a complete wire circuit instead of a single wire grounded at each end (as was the practice in the United States). In America, where telegraph wires were relatively few and far between, this was not a major headache, but in England, with its dense and largely urban population, the single wire system meant that the chattering of nearby telegraph wires often distorted or obscured the signals. To combat this, Alec came up with a process for twisting the outgoing and incoming wires around each other, the whole being encased in an insulating jacket. He patented this device in November 1877, but it later transpired that the same solution had been proposed as far back as the 1840s and as a result the Telephone Company of Great Britain refused to buy the patent. Other devices, including a call bell system and a galvanometer for measuring the intensity of a telephonic current, petered out for lack of support from the company's backers.

Mounting exasperation with his fellow directors came to a head in mid-July 1878 when Adam Scott brought to Alec's attention the fact that the company's general manager, McClure, was inefficient and dishonest. Not only was he dealing on the side but he was extremely lax in his attitude towards telephone and line rentals. Alec summarised his indictment of McClure in a confidential letter of 25 July to the directors, recommending that the manager be dismissed instantly and extolling the merits of Adam Scott as a replacement. The board of directors sacked McClure but ignored Alec's advice and appointed another man instead of Scott. This was the last straw. On 15 October Alec sent in his formal resignation as a director, on the grounds of 'gross mismanagement of the Company's business and the personal discourtesy with which I have been treated by the Board of Directors and by the Acting Manager'. Thereafter the British company drifted under the incompetent management of William Reynolds until the summer of 1879 when Gardiner Hubbard descended on it in his capacity as trustee of the Bell interest, shook up the entire administration and put new life into it. Proper networks and exchanges were opened all over the British Isles as a result. Oddly enough, separate exchanges were favoured for different professions, such as doctors and lawyers, but in 1881 they were amalgamated and absorbed into the newly created National Telephone Company. Hubbard returned to America with $50,000 in cash to swell the Bell trust, as well as shares in the reorganised company worth a further $100,000 by July 1880.

Elsewhere the Bell telephone system was enjoying mixed fortunes. *The Times* reported that the Persian ambassador had purchased a pair of telephones and shipped them to Tehran for the personal use of the Shah. The installation of telephones in the palaces of the crowned heads of Europe and Asia certainly generated international interest and helped to bring the invention before a wider public. On the other hand, the German patent was lost because Alec did not apply for it till August 1877, which was too late under German law. As a result the electrical firm of Siemens and Halske stepped in and manufactured telephones which they sold outright in vast quantities without a pfennig going to the Bell trust. As a consequence, Werner von Siemens has the credit for establishing the world's first *permanent* telephone lines, at Berlin in November 1877. Heinrich von Stephan, who doubled as the Imperial Postmaster General and General Manager of the Imperial Telegraphs, was quick to perceive the potential of the telephone and wrote enthusiastically on the subject to Chancellor Bismarck following experiments between Berlin and Friedrichsberg. As a result, long-distance lines were installed as part of the Reichspost and it was much later that private companies developed local feeder services.

However, the Austrian patent (which Alec and Hubbard thought they had lost because they had failed to make the necessary periodic payments) proved to be still viable when this market was developed in 1880, solely because the man to whom Alec had delegated powers of attorney had kept the patent alive out of his own pocket.

By late 1877 Thomas Alva Edison had developed his variable-resistance receiver to the point at which he attempted to break into the European market as a formidable rival to the Bell system. As usual, Edison's optimism outran his actual achievement, and a further two years would elapse before the variable-resistance system offered a viable alternative; but news that Edison was trying to gain a foothold in France goaded Alec into action. First he despatched telephones to a Frenchman who was angling for the telephone agency, and soon afterwards he crossed the Channel to demonstrate it in person, at the great Exposition Universelle in Paris. France was initially receptive to the idea; its popular press had been among the first to give prominence to the speaking telegraph at the time of the Dover-Sangatte experiment. Indeed, the Minister of War, having heard that Bismarck was using them, was clamouring for telephones of his own. But in December Cornelius Roosevelt (who had acquired an interest in the French rights from Hubbard) arrived in Paris to find the Bell patents in jeopardy due to late application, although Alec helped him to fight off the infringements and secure government backing.

Just when it seemed that the French interests had been protected, however, up bobbed Edison and Elisha Gray who had now joined forces under the aegis of Western Union and were publishing none too subtle insinuations in France impugning Alec's honour and integrity. This was an irritation that Alec had to live with; Preece himself had forecast that 'when once a thing is shown to be true, a host of detractors delight in proving that it is not new. The inventor is shown to be a plagiarist or a purloiner or something worse . . . Professor Bell will have to go through all this'.[17] Moreover, Frederic Gower, who had lost Alec considerable sums of money on the lecture circuit, had now moved to France and had succeeded in patenting a minor variation on the telephone which enabled him to operate a highly lucrative business offering the 'Gower system'. Once more, in his capacity as the trust's troubleshooter, Gardiner Hubbard came to the rescue and successfully negotiated a settlement with Gower, who promptly did the decent thing anyway by disappearing without trace during a cross-Channel balloon flight.[18] As a result of Hubbard's efforts, the Société Generale des Téléphones was formed in 1880, although it did not inaugurate a public service till the following year.

Sharp operators were only too ready to muscle in on the telephone business. Without Hubbard's vigilance the situation would undoubtedly have been much worse. As it happened, it was bedevilled by Alec's own actions in setting up agencies without always notifying his father-in-law.

There was a charming, homely approach to the global business which witnessed Melville getting three-quarters of the Canadian rights and Charles Williams the remainder, while Alec's Symonds cousins were awarded the Australian rights. Gertrude Hubbard was granted the Scandinavian rights, which she later sold to Mabel for $20,000 hard cash. Melly's widow Carrie, now the wife of George Ballachey, a Brantford farmer, was given the Italian rights. Other parts of the world were parcelled out among Uncle David and his family. The value of these rights varied considerably because in some cases the countries concerned either had no patent laws or the patent rights were time-expired; but it is clear that Alec intended that those nearest and dearest to him should share in the profits of his invention. Later on, many of these foreign rights were consolidated under the Oriental Bell Telephone Company and shares in this company apportioned to the family members in place of the original, rather vague, agreements.

In the autumn of 1878 Gardiner Hubbard, for all his business acumen, almost went bust. In desperation he turned to Alec to bale him out and the young inventor allowed his father-in-law to borrow from the trust funds. As a result, Hubbard successfully weathered the storm and eventually repaid the loan with interest. In the summer of 1880, however, what began as a minor disagreement over foreign rights escalated into open confrontation when Alec more or less accused Hubbard of mishandling a trust which had been set up for his own daughter and grandchildren. Hubbard was cut to the quick by this unreasonable outburst, but he showed commendable self-control and kept his dignity. Quietly he rebutted the accusation and reminded Alec that if it had not been for his timely intervention the British company would have gone to the wall. A suitably chastened Alec apologised and the potential rift between the men closest to Mabel was soon healed. Thereafter Alec steered well clear of involvement in the business. Within seven years the trust fund had reached its stated goal of $200,000, and when Hubbard died ten years later it was found that, under his able stewardship, it had more than doubled again.

William Preece's gloomy prediction about the host of detractors who would arise to counter Alec's claims came true just as the British telephone company was getting established. Western Union, under the direction of the devious William Orton, amassed a formidable array of counter-claimants and on 26 March 1878 filed a series of interferences against Alec's second telephone patent. All of them challenged Alec's priority, but two of them – Elisha Gray and Amos Dolbear – included a personal attack on Alec's integrity. These libels were repeated in an article which appeared in *The Times*, but Alec reacted philosophically when apprised of this. The following day he wrote to Mabel:

> Please don't be so distressed about that article in *The Times*. I am beginning to be quite troubled too, just because you are . . . Let the press quarrel over the inventor of the telephone if it pleases. Why should it matter to the world who invented the telephone so long as the world gets the benefits of it? Why should it matter to me what the world says upon the subject so long as I have obtained the object for which I laboured and have got you my sweet sweet darling wife? And why should it matter so very much to you and to my little Elsie so long as the pecuniary benefits of the invention are not taken from us – and so long as you are conscious of my uprightness and integrity?
>
> All questions of priority will soon be settled by the Patent Office . . . Truth and Justice will triumph in the end . . . Let others vindicate my claims if they choose but keep me out of the strife.[19]

Three weeks later his mood darkened. 'The more fame a man gets for an invention, the more does he become a target for the world to shoot at,' he wrote sourly to Mabel on 9 September. He was now disgusted with the whole sordid business. 'As for patents, if my ideas are worth patenting, let others do it. Let others endure the worry, the anxiety, and the expense.' At a time when Alec was increasingly disillusioned with the British company, the machinations of Orton and his associates were the last straw: he confessed that he was not really cut out for a business that had begun to make him 'irritable, peevish, and disgusted with life'. He added that he was 'sick of the telephone, and have done with it altogether, excepting as a play-thing to amuse my leisure moments'. Henceforward he would only dabble in the telephone 'from a love of science'. Alec was restless, frustrated and fretful. Soured by the calumnies of his detractors, he was almost suicidal at times. Ironically, part of the trouble was that he now had so much money at his command that he need never do a hand's turn for the rest of his life. He was aware that he was drifting, and implored his wife, 'Make me *work*, there's a good little girl – at anything, it doesn't matter what, only make me work, so that I may be accomplishing something.' Out of this personal crisis would evolve the passions that ruled his later life. First and foremost, of course, was the overwhelming desire to do everything he could to alleviate the wretchedness of the deaf; but lurking in the background was a strong hankering to involve himself in some other great field of scientific endeavour. Helping the deaf would take priority, but in the long run his lively mind would find other avenues to explore.

Increasingly, therefore, Alec took refuge in the field where his mastery was acknowledged. In November 1877 he had delivered a lecture on Visible Speech before the Philosophical Society of Glasgow, with his friend Sir William Thomson in the chair, and the following March gave a paper entitled 'The Natural Language of the Deaf and Dumb' at the Anthropological Society of London. At Glasgow in August 1877 Alec had renewed the acquaintance of Sir William who had courteously shown him round his laboratory. Thomson and Bell had an instinctive liking for each other; Sir William was doubtless aware of Alec's shortcomings in areas beyond acoustics (notably in mathematics) but respected his achievements in telephony. By contrast, Alec met James Clerk Maxwell at Cambridge on 4 June 1878. Though the introduction had been effected by Thomson, it appears that the two men did not take to each other. Maxwell, born at Edinburgh in 1831, left school in the very year that Alec was born, subsequently having a brilliant academic career at Edinburgh and Cambridge. In the year that Alec started at the High School, the youthful Maxwell was already professor of natural philosophy at Marischal College, Aberdeen, and later held the chair in physics and astronomy at King's College, London, retiring about the time that Alec began his studies at London University. He was called out of retirement in 1871 when he was appointed first professor of experimental physics at Cambridge, laying the groundwork for the great Cavendish Laboratory. Alec might have invented one of the wonders of the modern world, but Clerk Maxwell was an intellectual giant whose discoveries had ranged from colour photography to refraction of light. His greatest contribution lay in the field of electricity and magnetism; his magnum opus on the subject, published in 1873, was rightly described as one of the most splendid monuments ever raised by the genius of a single individual.

What precisely passed between the two men will probably never be known. Alec's letters and notebooks are remarkably silent on the matter, and the only clue comes from Maxwell's own subsequent comments on the telephone in which he was faintly dismissive of Alec Bell as a basic scientist. In fairness to both men, it should be noted that Maxwell, still in his forties, was in poor health and would, in fact, die a few months later.

Late in October, Alec gave a series of four lectures on speech at Oxford

University under the chairmanship of Professor Max Müller, the eminent philologist. Each lecture was packed out; such was Alec's skill as a communicator that both learned scientists and interested laymen could follow every detail clearly. Incidentally, this series conferred reflected glory on Boston University, whose president in his annual report said that it established a useful precedent for the exchange of professors between American and European universities.

While Edison was striving to surpass Alec's telephone, Alec was taking a long hard look at Edison's greatest achievement to date – the phonograph, which was launched late in 1877. Publicly Alec acknowledged it as 'a most ingenious instrument' but privately he was chagrined that Edison had beaten him to it. He had frequently remarked in his lectures that if some means could be found to follow the curves of a phonautographic tracing it might reproduce the sound that had made that tracing. At first he wished he had thought of indenting a substance, and from the indentations reproduced sound; later, like so many of the telephone claimants, he would be tempted to translate the wish into an accomplished fact. He even went so far as to consult Chauncey Smith, the Bell Telephone Company lawyer, and explore the possibility of interference in the phonograph patents from the telephone; but it was pointed out that Edison might equally well argue the opposite, and that this can of worms was better left unopened.

This did not deter Alec from examining the phonograph, assessing its shortcomings, and seeking ways of improving it. The early recordings were made on tinfoil sheets which rapidly deteriorated after a few playings. Alec's interest in the phonograph was aroused by its potential in the teaching of philology; he and Alexander Ellis examined the machine in April 1878 but soon found that it distorted vowel sounds. Alec was doubtless also spurred on by the fact that the Edison Speaking Phonograph Company had been established the previous January by none other than Gardiner Hubbard who saw nothing contradictory in collaborating with a man in one endeavour while opposing him in another. Edison himself was acutely aware of his brainchild's shortcomings; although it was marketed as a music box, he pinned his faith on it as a dictaphone and soon dropped it when electric light beckoned. The phonograph was in limbo and it would be left to others, including Alec Bell, to revive it and bring it to fruition.

One of Alec's wilder flights of fantasy was a spinning top which would cry out. The phonographic 'Swearing Top', he felt, would make an ideal Christmas novelty and he urged Tom Watson to put his mind to developing the idea. 'With the profits we can work at Flying Machines & all sorts of things next year in comfort,' he wrote on 12 August. Tom brought him down to earth, pointing out that the idea was impractical and not worth wasting his precious spare time. Nothing more was said on the matter.

Thirty years later Alec would indeed be working with flying machines. This had, in fact, been a lifelong obsession, ever since early boyhood when he had been transfixed by the effortless wheeling and soaring of gulls on Corstorphine Hill. Mabel's letters from Scotland in September 1877 vividly described this obsession. On 23 September, out walking near Aberdeen, he had watched the seagulls and his head 'since then has been full of flying machines'. At Covesea a few days later she wrote home:

> What a man my husband is! I am perfectly bewildered at the number and size of the ideas with which his head is crammed . . . Flying machines to which telephones and torpedoes are to be attached occupy the first place just now from observations of sea gulls . . . Every now and then he comes out with 'the flying machine has quite changed its shape in a quarter of an hour' or the 'segar-shape [sic] is dismissed to the limbo of useless things'.[20]

Observing the aerobatics of the rooks above Pluscarden Abbey, Alec made copious notes and detailed sketches, including an aeroplane of a startlingly modern appearance and a diagram for contra-rotating propellers powered by a lightweight 'oil or gas engine' (this, seven years before internal combustion!) and a 'parachute arrangement in case of accident to machinery'. A few days later he was working on the problem of vertical take-off and landing. The theories of aeronautics would run like a golden thread through his notebooks, off and on, for many years.

But it was ultimately in the field of vocal physiology that Alec was to feel most at home. It will be remembered that in the earliest telephone experiments Alec used identical instruments as both transmitters and receivers. Early in 1878 Professor David Hughes at London University had invented the microphone, having discovered that a loose contact in a circuit containing a battery and a telephone receiver might give rise to sounds in the telephone corresponding to the vibrations to which the contact was subject. Hughes constructed his microphone in the form of a horizontal carbon rod resting in grooves in two carbon blocks, the battery and telephone receiver being connected in series with these blocks. Immediately Alec was asked whether the microphone could be used to help the deaf. Back in Aberdeen that September he tested the microphone on a man who was very hard of hearing, rather than totally deaf. 'He held the telephone attached to the microphone to his ear,' reported Alec, 'and understood everything that was said, even when I went to the other end of the room, but when he took the telephone away he was helpless.' Herein lay the genesis of the electronic hearing aids of the present day, although it would be many years before science had advanced sufficiently to reduce the device to the required minuscule proportions.

The wheel came full circle during the Scottish trip of September 1878. Following Alec's lecture on Visible Speech at Glasgow the previous November he had been contacted by Thomas Borthwick, a Greenock businessman, who appealed for help in teaching his eight-year-old daughter and some other deaf-mute children in that town. Borthwick had unsuccessfully tried to persuade the Greenock School Board to set up an articulation school for them. Realising that such a project would only succeed if funded privately, Borthwick had been campaigning towards that end. Now he begged Alec to find him a teacher trained in Visible Speech or, better still, to come to Greenock himself and give the necessary instruction to some teachers. This was the sort of challenge that Alec could not resist. If Borthwick would guarantee a salary and organise the class, Alec would find a teacher. Greenock, he reasoned, would be ideal for the sort of pilot scheme he was already formulating for Chicago. The more he considered it, the more excited he became. It might, in fact, 'be likely to inaugurate a revolution in the method of teaching deaf-mutes in Europe', as he wrote to Borthwick. When the teacher from Massachusetts whom Alec had recruited for the task backed out at the last moment, Alec resolved to start the school himself, with the assistance of Mabel's former teacher, Mary True, who was then on holiday from a school in England and had agreed to help out.

At the beginning of September Alec went to Greenock and began teaching again. To Mabel he wrote on 5 September:

> I have been so happy in my little school, happier than at any time since the telephone took my mind away from this work . . . I have been waiting for months past for something to do. I have been absolutely rusting from inaction – hoping and hoping that my services might be wanted somewhere. Now I am needed, and needed here.

In fact, his 'little school' consisted of a disused storeroom at Greenock Academy containing the dust-laden effects of a long-deceased schoolmaster, but Alec rolled up his sleeves and set to work with his old panache. His pupils comprised only wee Jessie Borthwick and two other girls, but somehow they were symbolic of 'the *thirty thousand deaf-mutes of Great Britain*. I shall make this school a success if I have to remain till Christmas.' When the permanent teacher arrived three weeks later, Alec handed over with the greatest reluctance.

This had been one of the happiest times of his life, certainly in recent years, and was marred only by the fact that Mabel had been disinclined to join him. On 9 September he wrote to her reproachfully:

> It is a sorrow and great grief to me that you always exhibit so little interest in the work I have at heart, and that you have neither appreciated Visible Speech nor have encouraged me to work for its advancement.

This *cri de coeur* had the desired effect, for in later years Mabel devoted herself just as wholeheartedly to Visible Speech as Alec himself.

Alec left his heart in Greenock, and for many years continued to correspond with the teachers of the school he founded. Eventually it was taken over by the municipal school board but in its own way it achieved a great deal. The teacher appointed on Alec's recommendation in 1883 trained a number of others who took the oral method back to their own towns in Scotland and England. Indeed, its sterling work continues to this day.[21]

Greenock also gave Alec time to think, and get the hectic events of recent months into perspective. More than ever he was convinced that his true vocation lay not in invention so much as in carrying on a great humanitarian endeavour. 'Do you know, dear,' he wrote to Mabel, 'I think I can be of far more use as a teacher of the deaf than I can ever be as an electrician.' And to distance himself from the Bell Telephone Company in Boston he took ship for Quebec, where he disembarked, with Mabel, baby Elsie and Mary Home (retained as housekeeper and nannie) on 10 November. Alec had planned to take the train to Montreal and Toronto and thence to Brantford; but on the dockside that chilly morning was Tom Watson, a hunted look in his eye and an urgent plea on his lips.[22]

10

Patent Battles
1878–96

It is a maxim, that those to whom everybody allows the second place, have an undoubted title to the first.

Jonathan Swift, *A Tale of a Tub*, dedication

In December 1877 William Orton finally rejected all overtures from Gardiner Hubbard and took resolute steps to combat the Bell telephone system. Hitherto Orton had had a rather ambivalent attitude towards the telephone. Western Union had spent a vast fortune on developing the telegraph and establishing a nationwide network of lines and terminals and by 1875 was profiting richly from this investment. In an age when road, sea and rail communications were still slow and unreliable, the commercial expansion of the United States depended heavily on the telegraph. Within a year, however, Orton perceived the telephone as a serious threat: the fact that it did not require the long and arduous training in Morse code of the skilled telegraph operators, but could be worked quite simply by anybody, alarmed him. His immediate reaction had been to block Bell, hence the use of Elisha Gray as a means of interfering with the Bell patents. Later, Orton switched tactics, planning to develop the telephone and then sit on the idea while the telegraph was given a free hand. To this end he diverted Thomas Alva Edison from his work on the electric light bulb. This proved to be a more promising approach to the problem, and, in the long run, it would pose the most serious threat to the Bell system.

Orton's first step was to form the American Speaking Telephone Company which immediately set about acquiring the patents held by Edison, Gray and Amos Dolbear as well as anyone else who seemed remotely to be involved in telephony. The lines of battle were drawn in February 1878 when Edison patented the carbon-button transmitter and Hubbard set up the New England Telephone Company. In the same month, one of its subsidiaries, the New Haven District Telephone Company, established the world's first telephone exchange at 219 Chapel Street and within three weeks had fifty subscribers, listed in a single-sheet dated 21 February, the world's first telephone directory. The exchange was open from 6 a.m. till 2 a.m. but from 1 March onwards it was open all round the clock.

Perhaps the appearance of this directory, modest though it was, was the straw that broke the camel's back; for on that very day William Orton irrevocably severed all negotiations with the other side. Quite illegally, Western Union set up its own telephone networks and exchanges and undercut the Bell rental charges. During the spring and summer the war between the two companies escalated. Western Union lent heavily on the district telegraph companies, threatening non-cooperation on telegraphs if they linked up with the Bell telephones. There were allegations of Bell wires being cut and exchanges being sabotaged. The limitless resources of Western Union were pitted against the Bell network; only better quality instruments and the luck to be first in the field saved the Bell system from being overwhelmed by its titanic opposition.

There was a brief respite in April when Orton died suddenly; but the chain of events which he had set in motion continued to roll relentlessly towards a showdown in the law-courts. Western Union were now pinning their faith on Edison's variable-resistance carbon transmitter which produced much stronger (if harsher) sounds than the Bell magneto instrument. When it was discovered that Emile Berliner had filed a variable-pressure caveat on 14 April 1877, thirteen days before Edison's first carbon transmitter patent application, the Bell Company began wooing the German-born emigrant. In September 1878 Berliner was hired by the Bell Company in exchange for control of his caveat and inventions; armed with this, it filed an interference against Edison's transmitter which obstructed the issue so effectively that it was not until 1892 that Edison eventually acquired his patent. Moreover, the Berliner interference protected the Bell Company against its use of Francis Blake's carbon transmitter which was acquired in October 1878 and in operation three months later. In effect, Bell did to Edison exactly what Western Union would have done to Bell had Gray's caveat come before Alec's patent application. The two hours which had separated the application from the caveat on 14 February 1876 must have been the most crucial in the whole history of invention.

It had been a close-run thing, but the Bell patents were secure. They would be the chief defensive weapons in the ferocious legal contest that was about to unfold. One of the preliminary salvoes came in March 1878 when Western Union filed a batch of interferences. Within a few weeks Gardiner Hubbard was strongly recommending that the Bell patents be vigorously defended in the courts. Sanders counselled patience and caution, but after the Bell Company was formally launched and its backers pumped money into it, Sanders agreed that the time had come to fight off the competition. On 12 September, in the Circuit Court for the District of Massachusetts, the Bell Company petitioned for an injunction against Peter A. Dowd, an agent of the Gold and Stock Company which had leased Edison telephones as well as magneto receivers claimed to have been invented by Elisha Gray. Gold and Stock was, in fact, a subsidiary of Western Union which promptly picked up the gauntlet. This lawsuit would be only the first of more than six hundred which the Bell Company was obliged to contest over the ensuing eighteen years, but it was undeniably the most crucial.

The defence in the Dowd case rested mainly on Elisha Gray, but also, to a lesser extent, on Amos Dolbear who claimed to have devised, on 20 September 1876, a sheet-iron diaphragm and a straight-bar permanent magnet instead of an electromagnet. Both devices would have made a considerable improvement in the Bell telephone as it then was; and, of course, both elements were subsequently incorporated by Alec himself. Dolbear, however, claimed that his ideas had been passed on to Bell by a mutual friend, Percival D. Richards, who had contacted Gardiner Hubbard. Richards, on the other hand, would later admit that Hubbard told him that Alec had experimented with these features long before Dolbear had thought of them. Nothing daunted, Dolbear claimed that he was put off filing a patent when he was told that Alec Bell had already patented these devices. Although Hubbard denied having said anything of the sort to Richards, Dolbear continued to nurse a grievance and this dubious sequence of events was at the heart of his continual attacks on Alec's personal integrity. Alec later testified that when he heard of Dolbear's suggestions he had brushed them aside because they were nothing new. At any rate Dolbear did nothing to put his ideas into practice until February 1877 – but by that date Alec had already patented the metallic diaphragm and permanent-magnet telephone.

Dolbear weakened his case by writing to Alec (after his Salem lecture in February that year): 'I congratulate you, sir, upon your very great invention, and I hope . . . that you will be successful in obtaining the wealth and honor which is your due.' This was written before he discovered that Alec had only acquired his patent on 15 January. Later he would write to his friend, A. Winchell:

> As to Bell's permanent-magnet telephone, I *think* that a mutal acquaintance informed him as to what I was doing and before I could get in working order he, by the aid of a skilled electrician and working nights and Sundays, completed his and got it patented instanter, so I suppose that I shall lose both the honor and the profit of the invention.[1]

The truth of the matter is that Alec had thought of these improvements long before Dolbear came on the scene. At best, the information from Richards to Hubbard (and thence to Alec) of Dolbear's intentions could only have spurred Alec on to refine the practical invention and thus secure a patent. Indeed, Dolbear wrote to Alec in May 1877 in tones that do not suggest that he considered the latter to have stolen his ideas: 'How common it is, especially in telegraphy, for two or more persons to hit upon the same idea at the same time, without any knowledge of each other's work.' He went on to state that he had conceived the idea 'last fall', followed by some experiments 'early in Dec. last' – statements that contradicted his later testimony. In this letter Dolbear concluded that he was in the act of perfecting his invention 'when your invention of the same thing was made public' and although he had toyed with contesting the patent he could not afford to do so, 'therefore I beg you not to be uneasy in the slightest degree as to your claim'.

At this stage Dolbear wished to be on friendly terms with Alec and asked only that he would give him credit for independently arriving at the same conclusion, whenever Alec might lecture on the subject. On 8 July Alec did, in fact, write to Dolbear saying that he had been invited to give a paper on telephony before the British Association at Plymouth in September and wished 'to give credit where credit is due', adding that he would 'like exceedingly to have the opportunity of knowing what portion or portions of my invention you claim as your own in order to be able to allude to the matter in England'.

On receipt of this rather naïve letter, Dolbear went straightway to Hubbard's house and asserted his claim to both Alec and his prospective father-in-law. According to Dolbear, Alec conceded that Dolbear might have got a patent if he had applied for one ahead of himself (which proves nothing, as a profound statement); not surprisingly, Alec later denied having said anything of the sort. Dolbear, on the other hand, would deny that he had finally agreed to Alec's priority, although it is significant that, in a letter written later that day (at Alec's insistence) Dolbear was careful to omit priority of conception in spelling out his claims to recognition.

Three days later, Alec and Mabel were married. Once the young couple were safely on the high seas to Britain, Dolbear wrote to Hubbard demanding 'a share in the profits of this invention'. If his demand was not granted, he threatened to publish 'a small treatise on telephony' which would expose Bell and Hubbard. Furthermore, he hinted that he had 'good counsel and some parties around Boston' eager to contest the Bell patent of January 1877. Hubbard called his bluff, urging him to take the matter to court, but also pointing out that claiming undue credit in a book 'might be an injury to Mr Bell, for which no adequate atonement could be made'.

Dolbear did, indeed, publish his tract entitled *The Telephone*, now claiming dogmatically that 'the speaking telephone' was his invention and dismissing the Bell membrane telephone exhibited at Philadelphia as 'not a practicable instrument'. He was careful to avoid putting a specific date to his own supposed invention. Hubbard chose to ignore this treatise, which seems to have been something of a damp squib. The 'parties in Boston' were probably local officials of Western Union who encouraged Dolbear to contact Orton. As a result, Dolbear agreed to apply for patents on his telephonic inventions and assign them to Stock and Gold in exchange for a reimbursement of all expenses incurred, plus a third of any profits on these inventions and $25 a week as a research retainer. Two months later he applied for a patent, and having nailed his colours to the mast, he featured in the telephone patent interferences of March 1878 and subsequently in the Dowd lawsuit.

The matter of the interferences had reached a critical stage when the Bell family disembarked at Quebec on 10 November 1878. In the matter which was before the US Patent Office each party had only a brief time in which to make a deposition setting out claims and their chronology. If any party failed to meet the due deadline, he lost his case by default. If Alec did not file his statement in time, the case against Dowd would collapse. Although Tom Watson put the matter to Alec as forcefully as he could, the latter was reluctant to get dragged into the fight, still smarting from the trouble he had run into in England. Only when Tom, on behalf of the company, promised that Alec could leave his family at Brantford and travel on to Boston, all expenses paid, did he relent. With mounting anxiety (and in considerable pain from an abscess which had developed on the voyage) Alec returned to Boston on 14 November and immediately checked in at the Massachusetts General Hospital. From his bed he dictated his preliminary statement. He wrote at once to Mabel asking her for the keys to her escritoire in the Hubbard house: 'not that I have the remotest intention of publishing any of my love letters! I am only anxious to discover any statements that may help me to fix dates.' Though hampered as a result of not having access to his notebooks and other papers, Alec cudgelled his memory to marshal the facts in a logical sequence, inserting the precise dates as best he could. Though not as polished or perfect a document as he would have liked, his statement, dated 20 November 1878, was lodged in the nick of time.

With the light of battle in his eye, Alec worked feverishly on a second and infinitely more detailed document over Christmas and the New Year for the benefit of Chauncey Smith, the Bell Company attorney, and James J. Storrow, one of America's foremost patent lawyers, who was retained by the company to lead the prosecution.

The hearing opened on 25 January 1879 and lasted for ten months. The statements, depositions, witness testimony and legal arguments would fill two stout volumes. While Alec, with a research assistant supplied by the company, spent days on end in the Boston libraries painstakingly looking up every conceivable reference to earlier experimenters, Mabel came from Brantford in April and, with her cousin Mary Blatchford, pored over the vast quantity of correspondence and papers that had accumulated in her father's study, in the hope of gleaning some scrap which would help bolster her husband's case. This tedious exercise paid off handsomely when Elisha Gray's letter of 5 March 1877 came to light. This was most timely, for it enabled the Bell lawyers to confront Gray with his damning disclaimer of invention, during the hearing of his testimony. Gray had completely forgotten this letter and when asked to verify its authenticity he commented wryly to his lawyer, 'I'll swear to it, and you can swear at it!' The matter was clinched by a second letter written by Gray, this time to Professor James Watson and expressing disbelief on being told about the Bell telephone demonstrated at the Centennial Exposition. The inference was that, had Gray invented the telephone before Bell, he would not have expressed such incredulity.

Gray was the strongest weapon in Western Union's arsenal. By comparison, the claims of Amos Dolbear scarcely required serious examination. As for the other claimants whom Orton had signed up, they were permitted to present their testimony; even the assertions that Reis and others, now deceased, had anticipated the Bell discoveries were dutifully examined and duly dismissed. By contrast, the testimony given by Alec himself shone like a beacon of veracity. His examination and cross-examination was a legal marathon that lasted a full day. When one of the lawyers suggested a lunch-break at 2 p.m., Alec said flatly, 'I don't lunch,' and pressed on with his testimony. To be sure, Alec had the advantages of his elocutionary training and his formidable skills as a communicator; but he was also telling the truth, with nothing to hide. A few years later James Storrow would compliment him on the manly, forthright manner in which he put his case:

> You know how much I like to work with you because you are quick to catch an idea – but the real excellence of your deposition and its naturalness lies in the fact that in telling your own history you are telling the story of the man who invented, and who knew that he had invented, the electric speaking telephone.[2]

Alec's testimony of July 1879 ran to almost a hundred closely packed pages. He was David to Western Union's Goliath but the slingshot of truth toppled his mighty adversary. The Dowd defence was concluded in May while the lengthy rebuttal came to an end in September. Even before Alec was called upon to state his case, George Gifford, leading counsel for Western Union, realised that the Bell patents could not be overturned. In a bid to salvage something from the wreckage, he spent a week in negotiation with Chauncey Smith trying to work out some sort of compromise (much to the disgust of Alec and Mabel who were horrified at the wheeling and dealing going on around them). To his credit, Smith rebuffed Gifford's suggestion of an equal share for each side in the combined patents of both, but this cleared the way for direct negotiations between Western Union and the Bell Company. On 10 November 1879 the former conceded defeat. Western Union would relinquish its telephone activities and assign all its telephone patents to the Bell Company in return for a fifth of telephone rental receipts over the ensuing seventeen years (the period in which the original patents were valid). This was an excellent deal so far as the Bell Company was concerned; at one stroke they acquired the Edison transmitter and other important improvements, not to mention the Western Union networks, exchanges and customer base. Within days the value of the Bell stock almost doubled as a result.

Despite the decisive outcome of the Dowd case, the Bell Company was not left for long in uncontested enjoyment of its patents. The six hundred cases which it was obliged to contest over the ensuing two decades indicate the uphill struggle against pirates and infringers. In addition, the Patent Office hearings on telephone interferences dragged on till 1889 before being decided in Alec's favour. In the vast majority of the cases fought through the law-courts, Alec's deposition of 1879 was perfectly adequate to refute any argument the defence might put up; but in two cases Alec was challenged on specific grounds that required his personal appearance in the witness box.

The first of these was the Drawbaugh case in February and March 1883. It arose from the fact that Daniel Drawbaugh, 'Inventor, Designer and Solicitor of Patents', made extravagant claims in 1880 that he had, between 1866 and 1876, invented not only the Bell telephone but the Edison and Blake transmitters, the Peirce mouthpiece and many other notable improvements which, by 1880, had been incorporated into the telephone. Drawbaugh had, indeed, secured eight patents between 1851 and 1867 and by 1876 had sold rights in some of them for amounts up to $6,000. Yet he would later claim that he had failed to apply for patents on telephone inventions because he lacked the funds to pay the fees and provide working models.

In court Drawbaugh was asked to describe the mental and experimental processes which led him to the invention of the telephone and its subsequent improvements. In answer, he said blandly: 'I don't remember how

I came to it. I had been experimenting in that direction. I don't remember of getting at it by accident either. I don't remember of anyone telling me it. I don't suppose anyone told me.' Expert witnesses from the Bell Telephone Company swiftly demolished the Drawbaugh case; every one of his claims, it transpired, had been well established and was widely known prior to 1880. Furthermore, he was forced to admit that he had spent five days at the Centennial Exposition and consequently knew all about the Bell exhibit. When asked how it was that he had invented the telephone years earlier but had not mentioned this to a soul, Drawbaugh was at a loss to explain his silence.

What aggravated the matter was that Drawbaugh had sold his claims in 1880 to business backers in New York and Cincinnati who established the People's Telephone Company. Stock in this company was eagerly snapped up by many small investors, drawn psychologically to an organisation whose name implied that it was some kind of co-operative taking on Big Business. When that company began selling telephones in New York, it was promptly sued for infringement and the lawyers rubbed their hands gleefully. Bell's New York counsel, in fact, is believed to have earned over $50,000 in fees from the Drawbaugh case alone. Due to the peculiar nature of the case, Alec was obliged to give fresh testimony over a period of four weeks, most of this taken up with a very detailed cross-examination of his deposition in the Dowd case. It was his performance in this instance that drew forth the unstinted praise of James Storrow, previously quoted. Even so, the Drawbaugh case dragged on for eight years before judgement was given in Alec's favour. Though severely reprimanded by the court for his blatant falsehoods, an unrepentant Drawbaugh disappeared from the scene, with the $20,000 which he had netted from the People's Telephone Company more or less intact. He re-emerged briefly in 1903 when he claimed to have invented the wireless before Marconi.

Alec's last court appearance arose out of the curious litigation known as the Government case. It hinged on the misplaced ingenuity of Dr James W. Rogers of Tennessee who perceived that any legal challenge to the Bell patents, no matter how contrived, would protect infringers in fact even if the challenge was ultimately shown to be frivolous, so long as the legal process could be drawn out long enough for the patents to expire. Rogers employed his son, J. Harris Rogers, to draw up what purported to be plans for telephonic inventions. The younger Rogers was a competent electrician and no mean draughtsman, so the ploy succeeded for a time, thanks to Casey Young, a discredited ex-member of the Tennessee legislature who still had useful business contacts. Young set up a phoney business, the Pan-Electric Company; for an outlay of $4.50 for the use of the Tennessee state seal he created a capitalisation (on paper) of $5 million, and by cash inducements or promises persuaded several celebrities (including the Confederate general Joseph E. Johnston, who became president of the company) to lend their names to the letterhead. Senator Augustus Garland, former Governor of Arkansas, was the company's attorney, his chief remit being to persuade would-be investors to take up stock. The manner in which the company was floated and its stock sold was fraudulent, quite apart from the blatant infringement of the Bell patents. Cleverly, Rogers, Young and their cronies succeeded in pushing a bill through Congress enabling the Federal government to bring suit for the vacating of patents under certain circumstances. The bill passed the House of Representatives in 1884 but, despite Garland's efforts, failed in the Senate.

At that juncture, however, Grover Cleveland was elected Democratic President and suddenly Southern politicians were back in power. As his Attorney-General, Cleveland appointed Augustus Garland whose fellow directors in Pan-Electric asked him to sue, in the name of the United States, for the annulment of the Bell patents, on the grounds that Alec had obtained them fraudulently and was not the first inventor. Garland went off on a hunting trip, delegating the task of granting the request to the Solicitor-General (a Virginian). To keep everything legal and above board, President Cleveland submitted the question to the Secretary of the Interior (a Mississippian). Showing Southern solidarity, this minister took the line that whether the charges against Bell were serious or not, they implied fraud on the part of officials in the Patent Office, and for that reason the matter would have to be tested by means of a government lawsuit (at the taxpayers' expense) against the Bell Telephone Company.

The legal machinery got into gear in January 1887 and dragged on for nine years. Luckily, the attempt to prevent injunctions against infringers quickly collapsed. The Bell Company succeeded in obtaining injunctions against subsidiaries of Pan-Electric and the parent company decided not to contest the matter. Nevertheless, the government suit cost them nothing and, in fact, bought them valuable time by making their operations more plausible. Despite the exposure of Augustus Garland and his corrupt involvement with Pan-Electric in the *New York Tribune* and other newspapers, the Cleveland administration weathered the storm. A Congressional committee whitewashed the Attorney-General who retained his appointment. Eventually the case went all the way to the Supreme Court which upheld the Bell patents, even after they ran out. In the end the Government case ground to an ignominious halt, and when the government's chief counsel died in the summer of 1896 the case was tacitly buried with him. It was never formally settled.

The Government case rested on the assertion that Philipp Reis had invented the telephone and that this made Alec's claims false. Moreover, Alec had concealed the existence of the Reis telephone from Patent Office examiner Zenas F. Wilber. A much more serious charge alleged that Wilber had been bribed by Bell's lawyers to reveal the substance of Elisha Gray's caveat, so that it could be inserted into Bell's patent application, and to manipulate the papers on that fateful day so that Bell's patent application appeared to take precedence over Gray's caveat. Alec was accused of being an accessory after the fact. These grave allegations were splashed across the front pages of the newspapers and greeted Alec's return from a family vacation in Newfoundland and Cape Breton Island in October 1885. Instantly galvanised into action, he spent several days (and sleepless nights) composing a lengthy rebuttal in a ferocious letter to Augustus Garland, accompanied by a violent condemnation of the Attorney-General's own behaviour. Fortunately this draft was submitted to James Storrow who toned down the indictment of Garland, but more or less approved of the principal letter. Both documents, in their amended form, were then printed as a pamphlet and copies were circulated widely in the Justice Department and all the way up to the Oval Office itself. Alec's personal response had little effect on the conduct of the case but the pamphlet was a useful safety valve. He did not get to court until 1892, during which he spent the better part of eighty days, spread over the spring and summer, giving his most comprehensive testimony to date. In 1908 the Bell Telephone Company printed it in full 'because of its historical value and scientific interest'; Alec's testimony, examination and cross-examination filled no fewer than 445 pages.

So much for the prolonged litigation that came in the wake of the invention of the telephone; but the claims and counter-claims of rival inventors continued to reverberate for many years. Hardest done by was Amos Dolbear who felt that he had been 'outrageously swindled' on learning that Western Union, which had paid him $10,000 for his telephone rights in 1878, had been prepared to pay him ten times that sum. He, himself, admitted that he would have settled for $5,000, but that was beside the point. In 1879 he invented an electrostatic telephone, using a condenser instead of a closed circuit. This enabled him to form the Dolbear Telephone Company in 1881 but it was promptly sued by the Bell Company, whose rights were upheld by the Supreme Court in 1886. Continuing as professor of physics at Tufts College, he regaled generations of freshmen with the dramatic declaration that he had invented the telephone before Bell. After his death, a bronze plaque to this effect was affixed to the wall of Ballou Hall and is there to this day.

Elisha Gray nursed a grievance which erupted in 1885 with the extravagant claim that his counsel in the Dowd case had put up a sham defence, once the Western Union and Bell lawyers had begun working out a compromise. This was as illogical as it was ludicrous, for the counsel on both sides fought long and hard, and would not yield an inch. Inevitably William Baldwin, Gray's counsel, hotly denied the allegation, and the judgement of history is on Baldwin's side. The papers in the Dowd case indicate that the decision to compromise was made only *after* both Gray and Bell had delivered their testimony and the case was clearly going against Western Union. Gray's chagrin was intensified when Zenas Wilber naïvely admitted to him that he had let Alec Bell know the substance of the Gray caveat. Wilber, in fact, went further and swore an affidavit asserting that he had allowed Alec to examine the caveat in detail, which was certainly untrue. It is possible that Wilber was induced to perjure himself by agents of the Globe Telephone Company (which was also in contention with Bell in the 1880s), but the net result was to aggravate Gray's bitterness. Ironically, Gray was a much more prolific inventor than Alec Bell, and his seventy-odd patents (notably those of 1889–91 for the telautograph which transmitted facsimiles of handwriting) are believed to have netted him far more money than Alec and Mabel ever got from the telephone.[3] It should also be noted that while Alec enjoyed very mixed success in trying to interest the French in his invention at the Exposition Universelle of 1878, Gray was fêted by the French government during the same exhibition and awarded the Légion d'Honneur. His own fortune was gained through the Western Electric Company of Chicago and the supreme accolade came at the Columbian Exposition in 1893 when he was chairman of the International Congress of Electricians.

Gray, however, went to his grave nursing the bitterest resentment against the man whom he imagined had cheated him of his rights. On 21 January 1901 he drowned near Boston while conducting an experiment in the submarine use of electric bells. Shortly afterwards, a letter by him was posthumously published in *The Electrical World and Engineer*, stoutly maintaining that Wilber's disclosure of his caveat had shown Bell *how* to construct the telephone 'with which he obtained his first results'. Among his personal effects after his death was found a piece of paper on which he had written:

> The history of the telephone will never be fully written. It is partly hidden away in 20 or 30 thousand pages of testimony and partly lying on the hearts and consciences of a few whose lips are Sealed. – Some in death and others with a golden clasp whose grip is even tighter.

In the March issue of the magazine, G. Maynard stoutly defended Alec against the unjust allegations made by Gray. Alec's immediate response was to write to Maynard:

Ever since the commencement of litigation in telephone matters, I have been obliged to keep silence – my counsel always advising me that the *Courts* would look after my reputation and sustain my rights – which they have always done. This was pretty hard to do at first, and I can remember how I used to writhe – in silence – under the unscrupulous attacks which were made upon me. But as years went by I became callous and indifferent as to what people thought or said about me or the telephone . . . For some time past I have felt that the articles which have appeared in the public press demanded some reply, but I did not care to undertake it myself, and my old defenders have all passed away . . . I had almost reached the conclusion that the time had come for me to speak out in my own behalf, when the sudden death of Elisha Gray caused me to change my mind.

I had a very high respect for Elisha Gray, and have always had the feeling that he and I would have become warm friends had it not been for the intermeddling of lawyers, and the exigencies of law-suits . . . Whatever Mr Gray may have thought of me, I have always had the kindest feelings towards him; and it therefore seemed inopportune that I should say anything in conflict with his claims at a time when we are all mourning his loss.[4]

Having got that off his chest, however, Alec thought better of it and did not send the letter. Even to a staunch supporter such as Maynard, he felt that there were things that were better left unsaid.

11

After the Telephone
1878–86

Invention breeds invention.

Ralph Waldo Emerson, *Works and Days*

Alec's initial reluctance to return to Boston at Tom Watson's urgent request reflected his changing attitude towards his brainchild. How it must have irked him to be constantly dragged back into the courtroom to defend his reputation and integrity, long after he had ceased to take any active interest in the telephone. We have seen how his experiences in the latter part of 1878 had soured him in England; apart from the turmoil of preparing to do legal battle with the mighty Western Union in 1879, Alec found himself embroiled in the internal troubles of the Bell Telephone Company. Put simply, it was over-extended and under-capitalised. There was a severe cash-flow problem at the beginning of 1879 which within weeks had deepened into imminent bankruptcy. The situation was saved only by merging the parent company with its flourishing offshoot, the New England Telephone Company. Out of this was created a new National Bell Telephone Company with much greater capitalisation. Powerful financial backers now took over, and Gardiner Hubbard was elbowed out of his office of president and succeeded by William H. Forbes who actually impressed Alec immensely. Sanders resigned as treasurer though both he and Hubbard remained on the board of directors.

Significantly, Alec himself was not included in the new board, having stood down at his own request. He was quite content with the new capitalisation which left him and Mabel with 1,106 shares or just over a seventh of the total. This compared with a third of the original Bell Telephone Company stock, but the value of the new shares was infinitely greater. In December 1878 the value of Alec's and Mabel's stock was estimated at $50,000, but three months later it had risen to $65 a share, with a market value of $71,890. Mabel evidently thought that her shares

199

would never be worth more and had a premonition that the market was about to drop. On 9 March 1879, from her rented house in Washington, she wrote a near-hysterical note to Alec in Boston, urging him to sell immediately, 'please, *please, please, please, please, PLEASE PLEASE PLEASE.* Are you sufficiently impressed by the importance of the subject now? If you love me, *do* do something right away the moment you get this'. In the event, Alec sold only about three hundred shares – an action which ever afterwards he bitterly regretted, as the value of Bell stock continued to soar. Two months later, contrary to Mabel's fears, the value had risen to $110 a share, and in September it stood at $300. Alec evidently felt that his shares had now peaked, for he then sold a further two hundred, only to learn to his everlasting chagrin that the following day the price was being quoted at $337. Two days later, when the price passed through the $350 barrier, even Gardiner Hubbard had great difficulty in resisting the temptation to dispose of his holdings. In the end he was restrained solely from fear of bursting the bubble, and so he held on, to see the shares rise higher and higher. In October Alec sold fifty of Mabel's shares for $500 each and shortly afterwards another fifty at $525. Now they had over $150,000 in cash and still five hundred shares in the company. Alec felt that it would be prudent to hang on to his remaining stock, but early in November, when the price rose to $775 he sold a dozen. A week later, when the Bell Company announced its agreement with Western Union, Bell shares passed the magic $1,000 mark. When the company was re-organised in 1880 as the American Bell Telephone Company with 73,500 shares, exchanged at the rate of six to one for the old shares, Mabel found herself in possession of 2,975 new shares. The proceeds from previous share dealing was shrewdly reinvested in a broad range of bank and railroad stocks, yielding the Bells an annual income of $24,000. In 1881 Alec sold about a third of their remaining telephone shares, reinvesting the proceeds in United States bonds. Even so, such was the inexorable rise of telephone stock that the paper value in December 1881 was $75,000 greater than the stock held in December 1880. By 1883 Alec's investments were worth over $900,000, not to mention over $100,000 in the original trust fund, and the income from these investments was about $37,000. This figure remained more or less constant for many years thereafter. Contrary to popular belief. Alec was not a multi-millionaire; but he was financially independent and had the wealth to indulge every line of research to which his enquiring mind led him without the need to show profitability at the end of the day.

Alec's former assistant, Tom Watson, also did well out of the new arrangements and as the value of his stock rocketed he, too, found himself virtually a millionaire; but the heady days of experiment and the excitement of achieving a major breakthrough in communications were gone.

The new company could afford a full-blown research staff, just like Edison's establishment at Menlo Park, and Tom suddenly found that telephone research no longer had any appeal. In 1881 he resigned, took a year out to travel the world and broaden his outlook, and then, mentally reinvigorated, turned to farming before embarking on naval architecture and marine engineering which would absorb the remainder of his long and productive life.[1]

Alec himself was becoming rapidly disenchanted with telephony. On his return to Boston in November 1878 he had been fully occupied with preparing for the coming litigation. During this period he continued to draw his annual salary of $3,000, together with $1,000 each from Hubbard and Sanders. This arrangement continued until the company was reformed under William Forbes who began to put pressure on Alec regarding his abode, his terms of employment and, most importantly, the scale of remuneration. As to the first, Forbes wanted Alec to remain in Boston where he could control him, but he had bowed to the wishes of Mabel who had set her heart on moving to Washington. In 1879 Alec's father sold his Canadian rights to the National Bell Telephone Company for $100,000. This substantial sum freed Melville and Eliza from all financial worries; eventually they would leave Brantford and move south to be close to Alec and his family.

Despite the problems and worries of the Dowd case, Alec still found time to work on telephone improvements. During the latter part of 1879 and first half of 1880 he filed six patent applications dealing with simultaneous listening and speaking on one instrument, the twisted-wire circuit devised in England, a device for cutting a telephone in and out of the main circuit, a call bell and two variable-resistance transmitters. According to Mabel, Alec was spurred on to renewed efforts, stung by a casual remark by one of the new company men that 'the discovery of the telephone was an accident, and you can do nothing further'. As a result, Mabel urged her husband to 'bring out something no matter what, so it proves that that was not the end of you'.[2] Only the twisted-wire circuit, however, had any real practical application. Clearly, Alec's heart was no longer in the telephone. In July 1880 he and Forbes finally parted company, but there was still some residual interest in telephony. The following year Alec filed patents on an improved design of telephone cable and a receiver in which the current vibrated a diaphragm in passing through it, rather than electromagnetically. Neither of these patents offered sufficient advantage to be developed commercially. Ten years later, when Elisha Gray was making great headway with his telautograph, Alec's interest in the subject was briefly rekindled and he wrote to Mabel that 'my old autograph telegraph should be developed and perfected into a practical machine'.[3] But he does not appear to have followed this up, nor to have approached the company on the subject. In 1895–96 he turned his attention to the automatic switchboard. Seven years previously, a Kansas City undertaker named Almon B. Strowger had discovered that the operator on the local telephone exchange was the wife of a rival undertaker, and that she was diverting calls to her husband. To overcome this problem Strowger invented a system that would enable telephone users to dial numbers for themselves. The Strowger automatic exchange came into operation in 1889 and became the standard automatic system throughout the world until the 1960s when it was gradually replaced by electronic systems. Alec's idea was to do away entirely with the switchboard in the central exchange, and to this end he busied himself for the better part of two years, though he never progressed as far as filing a patent application. In June 1904 he was reported in the *Washington Evening Star* as predicting that some day 'there may be a system by which the subscriber can move certain buttons and call up whom he pleases . . . automatically'. Three-quarters of a century would elapse before digital key-pad telephones became commonplace.

During the preparation of his papers for the Dowd case Alec decided to write a detailed history of the telephone 'as a means of establishing my reputation upon an enduring foundation',[4] but, as Mabel commented in her diary on 6 March 1879, 'however hard and faithfully Alec may work on his book he cannot prevent ideas entering and overflowing his brain'. Soon he tired of this project and abandoned it, as malicious gossip spread surrounding the allegations of Elisha Gray. 'I am sick of the telephone and have done with it altogether,' he wrote to his wife in disgust.

That might be the case, but the telephone was not done with him. Never was a man more fortunate in his surname; it was onomatopoeic and had a ringing sound, it fitted well with the word 'telephone' itself and both as a name and as a logo it survives to this day in the telephone companies of America, while the slang expression 'give me a bell' is used in Britain as a synonym for a telephone call. But Alec was doubtless particularly proud of the fact that his name entered everyday language in the word decibel, denoting the standard unit of sound. This arose from Alec's invention, in 1879, of the audiometer, an instrument for measuring a person's hearing ability. Once again, Alec was being drawn inexorably back to his first love, the conquest of deafness.

Worry over the Dowd case left its mark on Alec; at thirty-two his once sable locks were now heavily flecked with grey and his full beard was already going white. At the same time, he was losing the battle with his waistline. But he carried himself well and over the ensuing decade he learned to accept his patriarchal appearance with resignation, if not good grace. Although, at that time, he had a marked aversion to having his picture published in the newspapers, it appeared so frequently that his appearance was almost as well known as that of the President of the United States. On one occasion this caused him some amusement. In April 1880 he and his wife and mother were travelling through North Carolina by train when the conductor approached him and asked him, 'Are you the inventor of the telephone, sir?'

'Yes,' said Alec.

'Do you happen to have a telephone about you? The engine has broken down and we are twelve miles from the nearest station.'[5]

Alec had to explain that, even if he had had a telephone instrument about his person, the conductor's idea was impracticable. It illustrates how, even at that stage, the public had an imperfect notion of his invention. Shortly after the telephone reached Montreal there was an outbreak of smallpox in that city. Soon the rumour was spreading that the dread disease was being carried down the telephone lines, and a violent mob intent on destroying the telephone exchange was only dispersed with difficulty by armed troops.

On 18 January 1881 Alec wrote to his father proudly announcing that his income in the previous twelve months had been about $24,000. 'We should be able to live on that,' he added smugly. The average manual worker earned about $100 a month, a twentieth of Alec's income. The average wage in Britain at that time was about half the American rate in real terms. In fact, although his investments subsequently yielded substantially more than that, Alec and Mabel were frequently hard up, and often had to dip into capital to make ends meet, or by borrowing against expected dividends. Gardiner Hubbard remonstrated with Alec in 1893 for not being 'as considerate in regard to your expenditures as you were ten or twelve years ago'. Mabel, in particular, was inclined to extravagance, and Alec was seldom willing or able to rein her in. In 1896 he wrote to his father-in-law approving of Hubbard's plan to reinvest the income from the trust fund, adding, 'it is the only way in which we can save anything'. In fact, over a period of forty years, from the early 1880s until his death in 1922, almost a million dollars were expended on Alec's research and experiments, despite the fact that this produced little appreciable income as a result. In the same period Alec spent almost half a million dollars on projects to help the deaf. In the 1880s the Bells joined Gardiner Hubbard in a quixotic venture at Moxee near Washington, a farming operation which was a steady drain on their cash, even if it did provide jobs for various Bell and Hubbard relatives. To be sure, there were occasional windfalls, such as the $200,000 which Mabel inherited from her mother in 1909 and the unexpected dividend of $22,500 from the International Bell

Telephone Company in 1901, but though the Bells lived well they did not live on the same lavish scale as the Rockefellers, Vanderbilts, Morgans and Carnegies (with whom they did not socialise anyway). When Alec stumbled across an article in *Cosmopolitan Magazine* in October 1889 which asserted that Mabel had a share in 'her husbands millions' and had the expectation of inheriting 'several millions more' from her father (whose estate, at his death in 1897, amounted to only about $500,000), he wrote to Mabel speculating cynically 'whether the wealth of the other ladies mentioned is as much exaggerated?'[6]

Another factor which has to be taken into consideration was Alec's open-handedness. Generous to a fault, he was often chided by Mabel for dissipating his cash in hand-outs to any plausible beggar or old friend down on his luck, despite the fact that Mabel had an almost superstitious feeling herself that 'no good can come of our wealth unless we try to do good to others besides ourselves with it'. In truth, Mabel would not have objected to Alec's impetuous generosity if they could really have afforded it. As the years passed, Alec was more and more content to let Mabel handle the purse-strings, and as a consequence the Bell papers contain numerous notes and memoranda in Alec's handwriting, passing requests for money to her with a pencilled annotation alongside. Gifts and unsecured loans might run to a hundred dollars here, two hundred dollars there; but over the years Alec's charity must have cost him dear. On one occasion he persuaded Mabel to part with $5,000 to an old friend of Melville's, to give him a fresh start in business after he had been ruined by a crooked partner. On another occasion he parted with a similar sum in a futile attempt to prevent his old friend and partner Thomas Sanders from bankruptcy. In later years he took an avuncular interest in his former pupil George Sanders, paying for his training and setting him up in his own printing works. Less personal, more public acts of charity included substantial donations to the YMCA, the Walter Reed Memorial Fund, the relief of Russian political exiles in Siberia in 1891 and of destitute Cubans after the Spanish-American War of 1898, and many, many more.

When Mabel and Elsie came south from Brantford in the spring of 1879 they rented a house in Washington while Alec looked around for a permanent residence in the capital. At this time William Forbes was urging him to return to Boston and in his letter of 9 March from Boston Alec wrote to Mabel that he was now resigned to leaving the 'quiet life in Washington' and settling in Cambridge. The Bells spent that summer in the Hubbard home on Brattle Street, a spacious, rambling mansion filled to overflowing with the extended family which included Mabel's cousins as well as her sisters. Elsie was now a toddler and beginning to speak. The following summer they returned to Brattle Street; Alec was singularly attached to the house in which he had first met his future wife and where he had demonstrated the singing piano which set him on the track of the telephone. Mabel was not as sentimental as her husband, and yearned to have a permanent home of her own. Both she and her parents urged Alec to settle in Washington. After a second winter there, Alec finally came round to the notion that Mabel was right after all, and in 1880 Gardiner Hubbard agreed that some money from the trust fund should be expended on a house in the capital. Even so, it would be a further two years before the Bells took the momentous step.

In the meantime, Alec was slowly re-establishing himself as an inventor. In 1880 he took on William Schuyler Johnson as his personal secretary, his primary role being to write up the very detailed accounts of each day's doings in the series of notebooks headed 'Home Notes'. This was a chore in which Mabel, and later Elsie, were also involved. Johnson, tall, spare, quiet-spoken and gentle, had come to Alec's attention through his younger brother who was a deaf-mute. He was very personable and the Bell family quickly took him to their hearts. He accompanied them on their European trip of 1881–82 but died the following year from cancer. Alec was grievously affected by his death: 'Is it not hard that a young man just beginning life with bright prospects and a hopeful future should die now?' he noted rhetorically.

Early in 1880 the French government made up for its earlier lack of enthusiasm for the telephone by awarding Alec the Volta Prize of 50,000 francs for his invention of the telephone. Alec promptly used his prize money (worth $10,000 or rather more than £2,000 at the then rates of exchange) to establish a workshop in Washington which he grandly christened the Volta Laboratory. A few months earlier he had hired a young man (actually three months younger than Tom Watson) named Charles Sumner Tainter who had served his apprenticeship with Charles Williams before switching to astronomical instrument-making. While Bell and Watson were slaving over the telephone, Tainter was travelling round the world, as instrument-maker to the expedition to observe the transit of Venus in the South Pacific (1874–75), and subsequently he had established his own workshop, providing instruments and apparatus for Harvard University. The primary object of research at the laboratory was the photophone which operated on the principle of sound transmitted in a beam of light using a light-sensitive selenium cell. At an early stage Alec was convinced that the photophone would far outshine the telephone, both literally and metaphorically; much of his energy and not a little of his fortune were to be squandered in pursuit of this chimera over the remaining years of his life. Although he did eventually succeed in transmitting sound through light, later renaming his invention the spectrophone and then the radiophone, it was never more than a curiosity, its range restricted to a few hundred yards. By 1897 transmission was extended to several miles, but was then totally eclipsed by the activities of Guglielmo Marconi. Ironically, the successful transmission of sound in the manner suggested by Alec Bell was eventually achieved by Professor A.O. Rankine during the First World War; Rankine revived the name of photophone to describe his invention, apparently unaware that Alec had coined the term thirty-five years previously.

One of Alec's close friends from the beginning of his Washington period was the Canadian-born astronomer Simon Newcomb who worked at the US Naval Observatory and the Nautical Almanac Office. In 1878 Newcomb was working on an improved version of the Foucault revolving mirror used to determine the speed of light when he learned that Midshipman Albert Michelson at the US Naval Academy in Annapolis had succeeded in just such a project. Michelson was transferred to Newcomb's department, and then in 1879 went to Europe to study physics under the great Helmholtz. From Berlin a year later he wrote to Newcomb telling him of his plans to determine 'the motion of the earth relative to the ether', the only snag being lack of funds to develop this exciting experimental project. Newcomb consulted his friend Alec Bell and he, developing an interest in the transmission of light and gravitational force, agreed to fund Michelson's experiments with $500 out of the Volta prize money. In April 1881 Michelson wrote Alec a detailed and painfully honest report, the nub of which was that the traditional view of the 'ether' surrounding the planet was false. Michelson had spent $200 so far, and he proposed to return the remainder. Alec immediately replied, 'I think the results you have obtained will prove to be of much importance,' and instructed the young man to keep the money. This was a tiny acorn, perhaps, but out of it would grow Michelson's impressive researches on the effects of the earth's motion on the velocity of light which would earn for him the Nobel Prize for physics in 1907. More importantly, his negative conclusions about the ether formed the starting point of Einstein's theory of relativity. Michelson was the first, but by no means the last, of the many promising young scientists whom Alec would fund and encourage.

Alec had invented the telephone while still in his twenties. It was his greatest achievement and he would never again equal it, far less surpass it, even though the rest of his long life would be devoted to scientific research and speculation. But he was, first and foremost, a great communicator. In later life he would serve as a publicist for ideas (notably aviation and eugenics) which would otherwise not have been taken seriously by the general public; and he would provide the financial and moral support for many a struggling young inventor. His voluminous notebooks over forty years reveal an astonishing range of ideas and potential inventions; nothing on such a scale had been conceived since the time of Leonardo da Vinci in the sixteenth century – with one notable exception. Alec's inventiveness was surpassed only by that of his rival, Thomas Alva Edison. The fundamental difference between them was that Edison not only had the ideas, but the discipline, tenacity, highly trained staff, equipment and vast technical resources to bring over a thousand of these ideas to practical, commercial fruition. Compared with Menlo Park, Alec's Volta Laboratory was a mere pygmy; where Edison was a hard-headed businessman as well as an inventive genius, Alec Bell was a dilettante. In half a century of active inventing, Edison would take out a staggering 1,033 patents. Alec, by contrast, would take out barely a handful after 1880, leaving it to others to develop his ideas to a practical conclusion. But just as Edison had leapfrogged Bell over the matter of the carbon-button transmitter, so too Alec would pick up an invention that Edison had discarded and make it into a commercial success.

In England in 1878 Alec had renewed the friendship of his cousin Chester – Chichester Bell, Uncle David's son. After an education in Dublin, Chester had studied chemistry and had subsequently taught the subject at the universities of Dublin and London. He had just the right academic background that Alec required, and was easily persuaded to cross the Atlantic in December 1880 and join his cousin at the Volta Laboratory.

Meanwhile, there were changes on the domestic front. On 15 February 1880 Mabel gave birth to a second daughter, three weeks premature but perfect in every way. Alec was preoccupied with his photophone at the time, but even he was forced to concede that no invention surpassed the wonder of 'this little, living mite'.[7] The baby was christened Marian, after Mabel's sister, but all her life she was known simply as Daisy.

Eighteen months later, while the Bells were spending the summer in Cambridge as usual, Mabel gave birth prematurely to a son who was promptly named Edward after Alec's late brother. Although strong and otherwise in good health, the baby had a breathing difficulty and expired after only a few hours. Alec never saw his son; at the time he was in Washington frantically trying to save the life of President Garfield.

Nominated by the Republican party after the thirty-sixth ballot, General James A. Garfield defeated Grover Cleveland to become the country's twentieth president and was inaugurated on 4 March 1881. On 2 July, while on his way to attend the commencement exercises at Williams College, the new president was shot in the back while walking through the Washington railway station by a disappointed place-seeker named Charles

Guiteau. The former Civil War general was forty-nine and in splendid physical shape and survived the assassination attempt; but what the madman Guiteau had begun, a long line of incompetent physicians and surgeons would eventually complete. Ignoring the precepts of Lister and Semmelweiss about scrupulous cleanliness, they prodded and probed into the gaping wound of the long-suffering president in vain attempts to locate the bullet. Only four days after the attempt on the president's life, Alec's friend Simon Newcomb publicly suggested that it should be possible to locate a metallic object, such as a bullet, through some kind of electrical or magnetic effect. Alec was in Cambridge when he read of Newcomb's suggestions in the press and promptly cabled him, offering his assistance.

Alec had, in fact, experimented in England with magnetic effects to locate buried or hidden metal, outlining the principles of what would later become the mine- or metal-detector. These experiments in turn had arisen from his researches into the earthing of telephone wires, and on his return to the United States he had suggested this to Gardiner Hubbard as a possible line for further exploration. Hubbard immediately saw the possibilities of such a device for detecting gold and silver, and encouraged Alec to pursue the matter. When he heard of Garfield's condition Alec began experimenting at Charles Williams's workshop in Boston, using the induction balance which Professor David Hughes had invented in London two years previously. At the same time, experiments along similar lines were conducted by Chester Bell and Charles Tainter at the Volta Laboratory, while Alec wired his old friends David Hughes in London and Henry Rowland in Baltimore for their suggestions. The matter became more urgent on 23 July when Garfield's condition suddenly worsened. Septicaemia from the infected wound was now spreading through his body and his temperature rose dangerously.

Progress with converting the induction balance into an effective metal detector was painfully slow. By 25 July Alec and his assistants had extended its range from two to three inches; Henry Rowland's suggestion of trying a condenser in the primary circuit gained them another half inch – not much, but sufficient for Alec to consider trying the device on Garfield himself. Early the following evening Alec and Tainter dodged past a crowd of journalists outside the White House and brought their apparatus to the president's bedside. Garfield was asleep, and this enabled Alec to work out the wiring of the bedroom for the experiment. Later he described the dramatic scene to Mabel. In the great bed, attended by a nurse who gently fanned him, lay the president:

> He looked so calm and grand he reminded me of a Greek hero chiselled in
> marble. He has a magnificent intellectual-looking head, as you know, with

massive forehead. As I remember him of old, his florid complexion rather detracted from his appearance, giving him the look of a man who indulged in good living and who was accustomed to work in the open air. There is none of that look about him now. His face is very pale – or rather it is of an ashen gray colour which makes one feel for a moment that you are not looking upon a living man. It made my heart bleed to look at him and think of all he must have suffered to bring him to this.[8]

Presently the president awoke and the nurse dressed his wound while Alec and Tainter finished their arrangements. At the crucial moment, however, the apparatus emitted only a spluttering sound. In vain, the doctors propped Garfield on his side and ran the instrument over his back, to no avail. Later Alec found that only one of the primary coils had been connected to the condenser. 'I feel woefully disappointed & disheartened,' Alec wrote to his wife that night, 'however, we go right at the problem again tomorrow.' Alec himself was laid low for a couple of days, but on 29 July he returned to the problem with renewed vigour. Using flat, overlapping coils, instead of conical coils, he succeeded in extending the range to five inches. Chester and Tainter worked feverishly to house the modified apparatus in a discreet wooden case and on the afternoon of 31 July the White House medical staff agreed to repeat the experiment the following morning. At nine o'clock that evening a reporter from the *Boston Herald* took Alec up on an invitation extended earlier that day and paid a visit to the little two-storey brick building partially concealed among trees and shrubs in the middle of a large lot fronting on Connecticut Avenue, barely half a mile from the White House.

The little mansion was brilliantly lit. Every room was in use, and all the windows were opened, so that the light streamed out as the air streamed in. A courteous colored serving man bowed his master's guest into the shadowed hall. Prof. Bell led me into the main room where stood his father and Sumner Tainter . . . In cabinets, on tables, chairs and floors were coils of wire, batteries, instruments and electrical apparatus of every sort. The light from the jets, burning brilliantly in the centre of the room, was reflected from a hundred metallic forms. It was reflected, too, from the smiling faces of the great electrician and his assistant, who saw success almost within their grasp . . . The room was full of metals, which disturbed the tone of the balance, and outside and inside, attracted by the light, 'annoying insects', as Prof. Bell called them, kept up a monotonous monotone.[9]

Alec's euphoria was severely dampened when the experiment the following morning was a resounding failure – literally, for instead of a precise sound which should have located the bullet he heard a feeble sound over the entire area. On 2 August, however, he discovered that the mattress of the president's bed was supported on steel springs. He immediately set up an experiment with a mattress and bedsprings to replicate the conditions in the president's sickroom but found that the springs had no material effect on the hearing distance. Baffled by the sound emanating from Garfield's body, Alec had to admit that he was beaten, and the mystery was never solved.[10] Although he never again had the opportunity to test his instruments on the dying president, Alec continued to experiment and eventually devised a telephonic needle probe that would have solved the problem; but Garfield was now wasting away and his physicians refused to submit him to further agony. On 6 September he was moved to his country home at Elberon, New Jersey, where he died thirteen days later.

During the first two weeks of August Alec commuted between his rented summer house at Pigeon Cove on the North Shore to the Williams workshop in Boston to continue his metal-detecting experiments. He was thus absent when Mabel suddenly went into labour and gave birth to Edward. Ironically, there was at that time no telephone by which he could have been summoned home. By the time he returned late that evening, little Edward was already dead. How the grieving parents reacted to this tragedy is not known, but we may guess that there was a certain amount of recrimination on Mabel's part and remorse on Alec's. The following year Mabel chanced upon President Chester Arthur at the casino in Newport and this triggered off a pang of regret. That night she wrote to Alec: 'but for Guiteau our own lives might have been different. You might not have gone to Washington, but have stayed with me and all might have been well.'[11]

Blaming Alec in this manner was unreasonable, if understandable. Mabel also blamed herself, as a letter to Alec a year later reveals. Commenting on the fact that she had punished Elsie for some misdemeanour by with-holding candy, she tried to explain to the little girl the principles of right and wrong and why it was sometimes necessary to accept punishment. 'I don't know what more I said, something it was about God's punishing me as I did her when I did wrong. How He had promised me a baby if I would be careful, but I had not been, and He took the little one from me.'[12] Alec himself had wired the sad news to his cousin Charlie, then in London, to insert a notice in *The Times* concerning the baby's birth and death.[13]

Something of Victorian attitudes to death is also revealed in the curious episode of little Edward's portrait. A young artist at Rockport was summoned the day following the baby's death to sketch the tiny corpse laid out in its coffin. The following November, when Alec took Mabel and his daughters to Europe as a distraction, he handed the sketch to the French artist Lobrichon and commissioned him to produce a small oil on canvas. Apparently Mabel was unaware of this painting at the time.

In the autumn of 1882 Alec and Mabel, after five years of marriage, finally had a permanent home, at 1500 Rhode Island Avenue in Washington, and to set the seal on this permanence Alec became an American citizen, taking the oath of allegiance on 10 November. It will be recalled that he took out preliminary naturalisation papers in 1874 to speed up his patent application, but he never took the final step until his nomination to the National Academy of Sciences seemed imminent. He was, in fact, elected to that august body a few months later.

An article in the *Washington Post* of 11 January 1887 described the Bell mansion as 'one of the largest and probably the most costly of the new houses in Washington, perfectly built and elegant in every appointment'. In fact this three-storey extravaganza in bright Pompeiian red brick was a riot of eclecticism, combining elements of the gothic, romanesque, italianate and baroque in a hopeless jumble of towers and turrets, flying buttresses and rococo gables. The original owner had unwisely given his architect a free hand and hang the expense, so that, even at the ridiculously low costs of 1879, this monumental folly had exceeded $100,000 which the owner could not afford. The net result was a forced sale to Gardiner Hubbard (as Bell trustee) for a sum reputed in the region of $99,000. Alec and Mabel then spent a further $28,000 redesigning the interior and furnishing it to their taste. Among its notable features were a billiard salon, a well-appointed library housing the books and papers of the late Joseph Henry which Alec had purchased from the great scientist's widow for $5,000, a music room with a concert-sized grand piano for Alec's use, a huge conservatory lined with majolica tiles and an oratory with expensive stained-glass windows. The house was fully wired for electric light and boasted the latest in steam central-heating which extended even to the capacious servants' quarters. This sprawling mansion, set in extensive grounds, occupied an entire block on Scott Circle, a stone's throw from the White House.

True to the adage 'new house, new baby', Mabel gave birth to a second son on 17 November 1883. Little Robert, however, was several weeks early and did not survive. 'Poor little one,' wrote Mabel in her journal three months later, when she could bear to contemplate this latest tragedy, 'it was so pretty and struggled so hard to live, opened his eyes once or twice to the world and then passed away.'[14] Several hours later Alec, oblivious to the tragedy, returned home from Hartford where he had been attending the convention of the National Academy of Sciences. Mabel had no more children, and she never got over the loss of her two sons, although she was only twenty-five when baby Robert died. It seems strange that her child-bearing should have come to such an early end. The fact that the births had all been premature suggests neo-natal problems, and although no subsequent miscarriages were recorded, some suggestion that Alec was concerned for Mabel's health is evident in a letter which he wrote her on 19 December 1887: 'I love you very much, my darling little wife, and wish indeed you could be blessed as you desire – *with safety to yourself*. I love you too much to risk your life.'

It will be remembered that Alec's cousin Charlie had fallen in love with Mabel's sister Roberta. Gardiner Hubbard strenuously opposed this affair and forbade the young man his house, but Gertrude Hubbard managed to bring her husband round and in due course Charlie and Berta were married. Charlie worked as Alec's secretary for some time before entering a banking career in Washington. His marriage to Berta was shortlived, for she died in 1885. Two years later, he married Grace, the youngest of the Hubbard sisters, and in due course produced a son named Robert. Mabel was thirty-six when she wrote to Alec that 'the touch of Robert's little hands on my face last night seemed to set some wheels going inside me that had been stilled a long while'.[15] This renewed a hankering to have a baby before it was too late. A few months later, having consulted a gynaecologist who told her that there was nothing to prevent her having a successful childbirth, Mabel again broached the subject: 'I can accept things philosophically when convinced there is no help for it, but I must be convinced first . . . This is my last stone unturned. Let me turn it, if in vain I will submit.'[16] There seems to have been some reluctance on Alec's part to tempt fate again, and no further children were born. Only when Elsie presented her with a grandson were Mabel's yearnings finally assuaged.

Along the way, however, Elsie gave them a great deal of heartache. As a very little girl she delighted her parents with her madcap antics and bubbling energy, but soon it dawned on them that Elsie was dangerously hyperactive. Her condition was eventually diagnosed as a severe case of chorea, an acute nervous disorder. She was entrusted to the eminent neurologist and novelist, Dr S. Weir Mitchell, inventor of the rest cure, and spent more than a year in his private sanatorium. A letter from Mabel to Alec about January 1891 sheds light on the alarming ailments to which the girls succumbed. 'Elsie,' she reported, 'is perfectly delighted at having diphtheria . . . and says "I have had everything Daisy has had, except typhoid fever and pneumonia".'

It was small consolation to Alec when the autopsy on President Garfield revealed that the bullet had been far too deeply embedded for even a five-inch radius of the induction balance to detect it. Ironically, it was not the bullet that killed the President, but sepsis in the wound and a ruptured aneurism in the splenic artery caused by inexpert handling of surgical probes. In October 1881 Alec successfully demonstrated the telephonic probe before a gathering of surgeons in New York City, and within five years this instrument was becoming standard equipment – though credit for it mysteriously passed to Dr John H. Girdner who had been one of the doctors present at the demonstration. Girdner at first acknowledged the great debt of medicine to Alec, to whom he wrote fulsomely on 15 December 1886, assuring him that his name would 'hereafter be coupled with Jenner, Wells and Harvey as suffering humanity's greatest benefactors'. In a paper which he published in the *Medical Record* on 12 February 1887, Girdner acknowledged his debt to Professor Bell; but in a subsequent paper eight months later, in the *New York Medical Journal*, Girdner omitted all references to Bell. Within three years he had set up in business, advertising 'Dr Girdner's Telephonic Bullet Probe', a claim that was repeated in his obituary in the *New York Herald Tribune* on 27 October 1933, where he was described as 'the inventor of the Girdner telephonic bullet probe, which was used universally for the removal of bullets before the development of the X-ray'.

Unlike the lengthy telephone litigation, Alec never seems to have bothered about Girdner's appropriation of his invention. There were plenty of others who knew the truth, and in 1886 he had the satisfaction of international acclaim, when the University of Heidelberg conferred on him an honorary doctorate of medicine for his contribution to surgery. In fact, Alec's telephonic bullet probes were universally employed as far afield as the Sino-Japanese War of 1894–95 and the Anglo-Boer War of 1899–1902, and even as late as the First World War his probes were often used to save lives at forward dressing stations where X-ray equipment was not available. Alec doubtless cast an indulgent eye over Girdner's activities, taking the philosophical view that anyone who helped to reduce the suffering of humanity could not be all bad.

Developing the bullet probe, even if it came too late to help James Garfield, helped Alec to expiate the feelings of guilt over the death of little Edward; but the child's respiratory problems goaded him into research on other lines which would ultimately benefit countless others. Turning aside from research into the photophone and the phonograph, he devised an airtight iron cylinder which fitted closely round the patient's torso. Air was forced in and out of the cylinder by means of a suction pump. By alternately increasing and decreasing the air pressure around the patient's chest the lungs were stimulated into action. A working model was constructed at King's College, London, and demonstrated at the Physiological Society early in 1882. In America, however, Alec envisaged the chief use of his device the resuscitation of people rescued from drowning, and for this reason it was not developed commercially at the time. Only a decade later, when it was fitted with a small engine to provide continuous and prolonged action, was its true value realised. Alec called this device a vacuum jacket, but it would later become more widely known as the iron lung. Who can tell how many victims of polio would owe their survival to this invention, especially in the global epidemic of the late 1940s?

The first audible reproduction of recorded sound was accomplished by Thomas Alva Edison in 1877, but twenty years previously Leon Scott had invented the phonautograph which provided a visual record of sounds by means of vibrations of a diaphragm. In the early 1870s the problem of translating sound into some visual medium had also exercised Alec Bell considerably as part of his research into impaired hearing. He was in London when Edison's phonograph became commercially available and, as previously noted, was quick to examine it as a potential aid to teaching the deaf, but found that the tinfoil records rapidly deteriorated after several playings. By 1881 Alec and his colleagues were taking a closer look at the phonograph and examining ways of improving it. Out of this developed what Alec termed the graphophone in which the sound recorded was produced by cutting instead of indenting the recording material, a process for which Tainter gets the credit. Edison himself had envisaged the use of wax cylinders but because he had failed to specify in his patent that the wax was to be *cut* rather than *indented*, the courts eventually upheld Tainter's explicit description, and this patent became the most lucrative single product of the Volta Laboratory. Furthermore, it was reasoned that a lateral cutting action (producing a zigzag effect) was preferable to the up-and-down action advocated by Edison, because lateral movement controlled the vibration of the needle. After considerable trial and effort, however, Alec and Tainter went back to the Edison system, though Tainter ultimately concluded that their attempts at lateral cutting had failed because the zig-zag grooves were much too large and their pickup too heavy for the energy of the sound waves. It would be left to Emile Berliner (in 1887) to develop lateral cutting and make it a commercial success.

The problem of rapid deterioration in play was overcome by applying a process of electro-deposition. Interestingly, Alec anticipated the much later development of the tape-recorder by suggesting some system of magnetic action to eliminate direct contact with the record surface. On 25 September 1881, shortly before he departed with his family for Europe, Alec tested a device in which a fine jet of compressed air was directed into the lateral-cut grooves of a wax record and the sounds picked up quite clearly: 'There are more things in heaven and earth, Horatio, than are dreamed of in our philosophy. T-r-r- I am a Graphophone and my mother was a Phonograph.' A graphophone, together with a phonogram (as Alec dubbed his form of record), a detailed description of the invention and a transcript of the recorded message, were placed in a sealed box and despatched to the Smithsonian Institution on 20 October. While the Bell family were abroad, Tainter and Chester Bell pursued their experiments with sound reproduction. Tainter subsequently described this hectic period:

> We made many experiments with etching records and also with electro-plating or building up of the record; with various arrangements for bringing in some auxiliary power to work the cutting style; with various methods of reproducing the sounds without contact with the record (magnets, air-jets, and radiant energy were used for this purpose). Different shaped cutting styles and those not adapted for cutting were tried. Much time was devoted to electrotyping, moulding and making copies of records. Records were made by means of photography, and by sensitive jets of liquids. We experimented with stearine, stearine and wax, stearine and paraffin, wax and oil. We tried many forms of reproducers making records of music by direct transfer of the vibration of the sound board. We made records by jets of semi-fluid substances (including maple syrup) deposited on the recording surface, also records on narrow strips of paper coated with wax-like composition; records on wax-coated paper, disks and tubes, with many forms of machines for using wax-coated disks and cylinders, with many forms of recorders and reproducers for wax-coated cylinders and with various forms of speaking and hearing tubes.[17]

In the end the breakthrough came in February 1882 when Tainter devised a much lighter, and more flexible, pickup or floating stylus which moved in response to the undulations of the grooves. This was combined with much finer grooves which increased the recording capacity of the cylinder and also produced much better sound quality. Although both magnetic and jet pickups were patented, the direct-contact floating stylus was eventually deemed to be the most practical solution. After his return from the European trip in May 1882 Alec added his own input to the experiments with the graphophone, but this was a period in which he was frequently distracted with other matters such as the telephonic bullet probe and the vacuum jacket. Furthermore, he was frequently absent from Washington, so that much of the day-to-day work fell on Chester and Tainter. In the end, although Alec was associated with the others in the patents for non-contact reproducing devices, the crucial patent covering the engraving or incising principle was issued in the names of Chichester A. Bell and Charles S. Tainter alone. Even this was not wholly satisfactory to Tainter who felt, with a measure of justification, that the Bell name had only been added to the patent to ensure the commercial success of the venture. This, however, had no effect on the share of the profits which the three associates received from the commercial application of the invention. In fact, responsibility for coupling the Bell and Tainter names in the patent application rested with Anthony Pollok. Alec himself was absent on his summer vacation in Newfoundland and Nova Scotia when the application was filed, so he was in no way responsible for his cousin's name appearing on the patent. He was invariably punctilious about such matters, and, as Tainter would have been the first to admit, Alec always gave Tainter exclusive credit for the invention.

In 1885, when the patent application was pending, Alec and his associates put out feelers to the Edison Speaking Phonograph Company about a possible merger of interests. The Phonograph Company, which Edison had bought back from Gardiner Hubbard, was in suspended animation. Nevertheless, it was vital for the Volta Laboratory to join forces with Edison's company if further progress were to be made with the phonograph or graphophone. Edison demanded three-quarters of the joint interest and when this negotiation predictably broke down he determined to out-invent Bell and his associates whom he dismissed as a bunch of pirates – though Edison himself had no scruples about pirating Tainter's floating stylus when he returned to the matter of making improvements in the phonograph.

The Volta Laboratory dissolved its original agreement in January 1886, being replaced by the Volta Graphophone Company, incorporated in the state of Virginia as a holding company for the patents. In the new company Chester was joined by his younger brother Charles. Subsequently a consortium of Washington court reporters, who had found the slim, wax-coated cardboard cylinders of the Volta Company extremely useful, organised the American Graphophone Company which acquired the Volta patents by exchanging part of its shares for those of the Volta Company. These shares were divided between the Volta associates, each of whom received a quarter, with a second quarter going to Alec as the original backer. Alec sold one of his quarter shares soon afterwards for $100,000 which he handed over to Melville to administer as a trust fund for researches relating to the deaf, but he retained the other share. The income from Tainter's shares provided that young man with financial security for the rest of his very long life and towards the end, when he was in his eighties, he received a number of honours and awards that recognised his achievements of the early 1880s. Chester Bell went back to Britain in 1886 and he, too, enjoyed a comfortable and worry-free life off the income from his share, marrying in 1889 and raising a family of six on the proceeds, dabbling and tinkering with experiments that never led anywhere, right up until his death at Oxford in 1924.

Early in 1883 Alec returned to the problem of the electrical transmission of signals. He rigged up a boat on the Potomac with trailing terminals at the bow and stern and sent a strong intermittent current between them. Another boat, similarly equipped, about a mile distant succeeded in picking up these signals with a telephone receiver. Although this fell far short of wireless telegraphy or radio telephony, it is idle to speculate where this line of research might have led, had Alec pursued it further. Two years later he pondered on the feasibility of using adjustable metal strips to cast the shadow of a particular sound wave form, and then reproduce the sound by means of the photophone. 'If the above invention can be perfected, it will be a greater achievement than the telephone, photophone, or spectrophone,' he wrote in his notebook.[18] What Alec was groping at so crudely would eventually be realised eighty years later, as the electronic sound synthesiser. As in so many of his other visions, he was several generations ahead of his time. Brimful of ideas, but charging off in different directions, flitting from one project to another and only too easily distracted, Alec at thirty-eight was at the mid-point of his life; but already all his best work was behind him.

12

Washington and Beinn Bhreagh
1887–1900

Nothing great was ever achieved without enthusiasm.
Ralph Waldo Emerson, *Circle*

In the early hours of 10 January 1887 fire broke out at the Bell mansion. Through a cracked chimney-flue the dying embers from a grate on one of the upper floors had got at the roof joists. It was still pitch dark on a cold winter's night when a passing patrolman saw tongues of flame licking the top of the mansard roof. Alec was away from home at the time, but Mabel was alerted to the danger when her little dog leaped on to her bed. By the time she was fully awake the District of Columbia fire department had swung into action and the conflagration was contained on the top floor. Inevitably, much of the furnishings and contents of the house suffered irreparable damage from the fire hoses. Miraculously, Alec's library with its priceless contents survived, but his study was a mess; what papers and manuscripts had not been pulped by the water were by morning cased in ice several inches thick.

At daybreak the Bells' housekeeper, with commendable presence of mind, recruited a posse of young men from a nearby boarding-house to clear up the mess. One of the helpers, an eighteen-year-old black youth from Virginia, struck the housekeeper as being of above average intelligence and he was given the responsibility of salvaging the papers in Professor Bell's study. In this casual if dramatic manner Charles F. Thompson slipped into a lifetime's service in the Bell household. Later that day Alec himself came home to survey the appalling scene, and almost forty years later Thompson would vividly recall his first impressions of his future employer as 'a tall, heavily built man with black hair and beard streaked with gray . . . With a genial smile, he shook my hand as if he had known me for years . . . That handshake electrified my whole being'.[1] In turn, Alec was impressed by the alert young man who could decipher his notes, and emphasised the importance of preserving every shred of paper that had figures and diagrams on it. Thompson carried out this formidable task so diligently that he was immediately hired as Alec's personal servant and general factotum.

Alec and Mabel lost no time in redecorating and renovating their mansion as tastefully as ever. By March 1889 a reporter for an Illinois newspaper was describing a visit to the house a few weeks earlier and, in particular, to Alec's sanctum under the mansard roof where he worked every day from one o'clock until four the following morning. A narrow door led into the study from the book-lined library:

> In the study, books are everywhere. An easy lounge [chaise longue] lies in front of the fire, and a globe stands in one corner. At a common flat walnut desk, sitting on an office chair cushioned with green leather, Mr Bell works. The desk is covered with books and papers . . . A porcelain hand with letters pasted upon it lies at one side, and this, I am told, is an invention for teaching deaf children to converse with each other by touching certain spots on the hand, which represent letters . . . Mr Bell has the dark complexion of a Spaniard. His face is full and regular, and his forehead very high and whiter than the rest of his face. His hair is thick, and its colour is that of oiled ebony. His face is covered with a full, black beard, which curls and twists, and his eyes are a soft, velvety black. He dresses usually in business clothing, and he is democratic in his manners.[2]

The description of Alec's hair and beard is oddly at variance with the evidence in photographs from 1880 onwards; perhaps the reporter felt it more diplomatic to overlook the premature greyness in a man who was approaching his forty-second birthday. By the time this report was in print, however, Alec had already sold the house on Scott Circle to Levi P. Morton, recently installed as Vice-President of the United States. The fire had robbed the Bells of their enjoyment of this house and both were soon anxious to get away from it. The Morton family held on to the house for fifty years and when not in personal occupation they let it to a succession of eminent personages, including the Russian ambassador Count Arturo Cassini, the politician Elihu Root, the inventor and engineer John Hays Hammond, and Ogden Mills, Assistant Secretary of the Treasury. Morton paid Alec $95,000 for the house, representing a considerable loss on the original outlay. When the Mortons sold it in 1940 they received exactly the same sum which, allowing for inflation over the intervening half century, was an even greater net loss.

The two following winters were spent in a rented house on Nineteenth

Street, but in the summer of 1891 Alec and Mabel began the construction of a new house at 1331 Connecticut Avenue, just below Dupont Circle and across the way from Hubbard Gardiner's imposing mansion.[3] On the adjoining section, Alec's cousin Charles J. Bell was erecting his own residence in a manner befitting the rising Washington banker that he was. Alec's new home was a three-storey mansion of red brick and grey stone, much simpler, better proportioned and more elegant than the Scott Circle extravaganza. It was as well appointed as ever and over the ensuing thirty years Alec and Mabel furnished it in a manner that reflected not only their eclectic tastes but their indefatigable globe-trotting. Alec had an annex added specially to accommodate the eminent men who congregated at his house every Wednesday evening during the winter months. Eventually Bell's Wednesday gatherings would become one of the cultural phenomena of Washington. Fewer than two dozen men came together at any one time, but they represented the intellectual élite of the nation's capital – politicians, senior government officials, scientists, artists, writers and musicians. Over them, Alec presided in a gracious, genial manner. He often played the piano for their entertainment, usually solo, but sometimes accompanied by eminent virtuosi of the violin or cello. Washington's cultural development in the closing years of the nineteenth century was meteoric. By 1900 it boasted ten scientific societies with a total membership in excess of four thousand. Pre-eminent was the Cosmos Club which catered to men of science and letters alike. Alec became a member in 1880, but his role in this august society appears to have been purely passive.

Melville and Eliza Bell disposed of their house at Tutela Heights in April 1881 and moved south to be near their son and daughter-in-law in Washington, settling about a mile from Alec in a house on Thirty-fifth Street in Georgetown. Melville was then sixty-two, but Washington was to be his home for a quarter of a century. The three Symonds sisters, Eliza's spinster nieces, lived with them, and not long afterwards Melville's brother David and his wife purchased the adjoining property. Their daughter Aileen (who had once rejected an offer of marriage from George Bernard Shaw no less) kept house for her parents. One of the abiding memories of Georgetown was the sight of the two elderly brothers, looking for all the world like biblical patriarchs, with their black clothing and long, snow-white beards, strolling along the street to and from Saturday markets with shopping-baskets on their arms. At the back of Melville's house was a dilapidated stable which Alec did up and converted into a laboratory. Thereafter, whenever he was in Washington, he would come over every afternoon, visit his parents, and spend several hours pottering about in his little workshop.

★

For all that Washington was the capital of one of the world's most prosperous and rapidly developing countries, it had many drawbacks. It was founded in 1800 in a swamp, much of which was well-nigh impassable. In 1839 it was described as 'a large, straggling village reared in a drained swamp'. By the 1870s, when Alec Bell first visited it, Washington had grown enormously as a result of the recent War between the States, but it was exceedingly backward in all municipal improvements. The public buildings and grounds were sadly neglected, the streets were ankle-deep in mud or swathed in choking dust depending on the season, the undeveloped areas were undrained swamp and the sewerage was worse than useless. Only after the administration of the city was reformed in 1874 was any material progress in the infrastructure effected. In winter, Washington had a bracing climate, but in summer the heat and humidity combined to make it a very unhealthy place. In the early 1880s Alec and Mabel would return to Massachusetts and spend their summers on the North Shore; later they would take extended vacations in Newport, Rhode Island or among the mountains in western Maryland.

In the summer of 1885 Melville suggested a sentimental pilgrimage to Newfoundland where he had lived in 1838–42. Gardiner Hubbard liked the idea, for it gave him the opportunity to take a side trip to Glace Bay in Nova Scotia where he had a longstanding financial interest in the Caledonia coal-mines. So the combined Bell and Hubbard clan spent that summer in Newfoundland and Nova Scotia, and in Cape Breton Island, the most northerly part of the latter province, they truly found a home from home. Here lived a race which had not only preserved their Scottish accents but even spoke Gaelic. The climate and scenery were so reminiscent of the Scottish Highlands that Alec was immediately enchanted. Armed with Charles Dudley Warner's guidebook to Baddeck, the Bells strolled up the street to the Telegraph House Hotel. Almost half a century later Maude MacKenzie would recall sitting on the hotel veranda and seeing the tall, imposing figure ('the handsomest man I had ever seen . . . with his wonderful head of black hair liberally sprinkled with white') accompanied by his wife ('a slender, graceful woman, with the gentlest manners, her sweet sympathetic face framed in the most beautiful soft brown hair').

If Baddeck fell in love with them, the Bells fell in love with Baddeck. Mabel committed lyrical descriptions of the place to her journal:

> This morning we drove to the New Glen, and saw forest-covered hills, undulating valleys with trim, well-kept fields and neat little houses, pretty streams . . . Baddeck is certainly possessed of a gentle restful beauty, and I think we would be content to stay here many

weeks just enjoying the lights and shades on all the hills and isles and lakes.[4]

Baddeck had everything that Alec craved: fresh sea air, limitless expanses of sea and the rugged grandeur so reminiscent of Scotland. Moreover, it was sufficiently remote from the importunings of the endless patent litigation and the demands of Washington society. Here Alec could idle and daydream without interruption. The tranquillity of Baddeck was underscored by the unpleasant allegations of the Pan-Electric conspirators that assailed Alec on his return to Washington that autumn. Small wonder that he often yearned for the soft, cool atmosphere and the peacefulness of Baddeck, and often he would while away the tedious winter months in the city dreaming and planning. The following summer Alec and Mabel returned to Baddeck. Already their half-formed dream was beginning to take shape, in the capable hands of Arthur W. McCurdy, a local businessman through whom they purchased fifty acres at Redhead. For the time being, the Bells leased and subsequently bought a cottage on the Baddeck side of the bay, but over the ensuing seven years they bought up all the land on the Redhead promontory. In 1889 Alec chose a Gaelic name for his peninsular retreat – *Beinn Bhreagh* – meaning 'beautiful mountain'. Pronounced 'ben vreeah', this was easier to get one's tongue round than *Cnoc Mhaiseach* (beautiful hill), which was the alternative suggested by a local scholar.

As a first step, Alec erected 'The Lodge', a house near the point which would be their summer quarters while the main residence was completed. Alec personally selected the site on the promontory, with cliffs on three sides and a steep, heavily wooded hillside on the fourth. According to family tradition, Alec selected the view from each bedroom window by surveying the scene from a perilously rickety two-storey scaffolding mounted on a hay-wagon. Despite her poor sense of balance, a concommitant of her deafness, Mabel insisted on accompanying her husband on this hazardous operation. A firm of architects in Boston was hired in 1892 and the construction carried out by a local building contractor for $22,000. When it was completed in November 1893, the *Halifax Chronicle* ran a feature with the headline 'The Bell Palace at Baddeck' with the subheading 'Said To Be The Finest Mansion in Eastern Canada'.

Although the newspaper described the general architecture as 'after the French chateau', this failed to do justice to the vast, sprawling two-storey structure, with its conical turrets and Scots-baronial crow-stepped gables, assorted balconies, loggias, porches and promenades, the whole ensemble topped out with cedar shingles on the roof. It was exuberant rather than elegant, but above all eminently practical for it was designed to accommodate the extended Bell-Hubbard family with all its ramifications. In its heyday, in the early years of the twentieth century, it housed four generations numbering upwards of two dozen adults and children, and not counting numerous servants. It boasted thirty bedrooms and a dozen public rooms, including the drawing-room which was reminiscent of a baronial banqueting hall. And of course it had a huge book-lined study for Alec, with an enormous lounging sofa by a bay window where he could reprise the daydreams of his youth at Tutela Heights and survey the magnificent panorama of Great and Little Bras d'Or Lakes and the myriad wooded islands of St Patrick's Channel.

Gradually, over the years, Alec and Mabel explored the surrounding countryside, going for long tramps through the wooded hills or undertaking strenuous trips by rowing-boat. When their Washington friend George Kennan, a leading explorer and naturalist, discovered a cluster of lakes in the mountains thirty miles north of Baddeck in 1893, he purchased government land there and built himself a log cabin. The following summer the Bells visited the place and soon afterwards erected their own cabin half a mile away. Later they joined with their friend, the astronomer and physicist Samuel P. Langley, in buying up all the land around the lakes to prevent the depredations of the lumbermen. For more than twelve years, the Bells, Kennan and Langley spent every September in this wild, remote spot, boating and fishing and exploring the primeval forests.

Alec also acquired a large houseboat which he christened the *Mabel of Beinn Bhreagh*. At first he used it to explore the Bras d'Or Lakes, but later he had it permanently moored in a little inlet near Beinn Bhreagh and connected to the shore by a footbridge. This became Alec's hermitage and over the years, as he added to its amenities, it became virtually another cottage on the estate where he would vanish all weekend. In addition, as the estate expanded by judicious purchases of the surrounding land, the range of buildings reflected the astonishing diversity of Alec's interests. There were workshops and a laboratory, housing for the scientific staff, wharves and boathouses, extensive stabling, a dairy, a warehouse, a windmill and cottages for a gardener and a shepherd. Mabel planted an orchard and this became a consuming interest for Gardiner Hubbard in his declining years. Beinn Bhreagh, by the early years of the twentieth century, was a thriving community, boasting a wide range of farming, livestock and gardening interests; but it was the Nova Scotian equivalent of a dude ranch whose running expenses invariably outran its income. When Gardiner Hubbard raised the matter of a deficit in excess of $10,000 in 1895, Mabel responded defiantly, with little hint of apology:

I am not at all troubled about our financial condition. It is much better than it was this time last year, and our income is large enough for any reasonable family . . . It is only that we always spend before we get our money . . . I can't see why we shouldn't have a good time with our money while we are young enough to enjoy it.[5]

That philosophy was also pursued relentlessly in other directions. While not at Washington or Beinn Bhreagh, the Bells indulged their wanderlust by travelling the world. Between 1880 and the beginning of the twentieth century they toured Britain and Europe six times, overwintering there in 1881–82 and again ten years later. In addition, they paid an extensive trip to Mexico in 1895 and three years later went to Japan and the Far East. Up to the end of the nineteenth century Alec and Mabel travelled together, but in 1901 Mabel undertook a trip to Europe without him. Long before then, however, increasingly time was spent apart as their interests diverged. They remained a loving and devoted couple, and the periods apart were assuaged by long and detailed letters which give the biographer an *embarras de richesse*, charting Alec's hopes and ambitions, heartaches and yearnings, and revealing a great deal, both in their attitudes towards each other and towards external factors and other people.

Their differing temperament and outlook, for example, coloured their perception of the places and peoples encountered on their travels. Mabel never lost her sense of wonderment at the colourful, exotic and bizarre scenes which she saw, smelt and touched, and her letters and journals are replete with graphic descriptions of magnificent sunsets, stupendous scenery and quaint folk customs, made all the more poignant when one remembers that the chronicler took all this in in complete silence. Alec, on the other hand, was more drawn to the outward signs of human endeavour and achievement, especially anything of a scientific or technical nature. Above all, the methods of educating and caring for the deaf were of consuming interest. Although innately modest and self-effacing, Alec relished the fame and recognition which the telephone had brought him, and he also took an almost childish delight in meeting celebrities of all sorts. But in spite of his genial, bluff appearance to the world at large, Alec remained essentially a loner, only truly at home within the family circle or in the company of a handful of trusted friends of long standing.

As he entered middle age in the closing years of the nineteenth century, the negative side of his fame became more apparent to him. To the world at large he seemed as willing as ever to grant interviews to journalists, especially if this gave him the opportunity to promote one or other of his pet causes, but privately he grumbled at having to make speeches or dress up for some public occasion. In 1898 he was informed that the Emperor of

Japan would grant him an audience the following morning at ten o'clock, and that he was to be dressed in full evening dress, white gloves and silk top hat for the occasion. When Charles Thompson gave him this news, Alec pulled a face and said, 'Charles, are you kidding? Do you really mean I am to put on that horrid outfit at ten in the morning? Good Lord!' Thompson succeeded in rousing Alec at what, for him, was an ungodly hour of the morning, got him into his 'horrid outfit' and packed him off to the Imperial Palace. On returning to his hotel later, Alec went off to bed without a word to anyone, and slept till two in the afternoon, when he awoke and asked when the American consul was coming to take him to the Emperor. As he became fully awake, however, hazy details of the morning came back to him, but when he recalled the Emperor's haughty mien, he commented, 'Well, I am glad I was not awake.'[6]

In Washington, despite the Cosmos Club and the Wednesday soirées, Alec became increasingly solitary and aloof. Even his own wife and daughters felt somehow remote and cut off from him at times. This may be partly explained by the 'absent-minded professor' syndrome – a total preoccupation with whichever idea or invention was of paramount importance at any given moment – but it also reinforced traits of character which had been present since Alec was a boy. His son-in-law David Fairchild would sum this up shortly after Alec's death in 1922 when he wrote of him, 'Mr Bell led a peculiarly isolated life; I have never known anyone who spent so much of his time alone.' This shrewd observation was borne out of the habits which became more accentuated as Alec got older: in Washington a working day that ran from noon till four o'clock in the morning, then the severely proscribed social scene at Beinn Bhreagh and the almost hermitic weekends aboard the houseboat where he deliberately sought the total silence which had engulfed his wife since early childhood, relieved only by the sough of the winds and the plaintive cries of the seabirds. Alec was a night owl, sluggish and somnolent before lunchtime, increasingly active and animated as the afternoon progressed and only fully alert in the wee small hours, when he was given to long nocturnal rambles at Beinn Bhreagh or solitary tramps through the silent streets of Washington. His habit of playing the piano far into the night – to the disturbance of other members of the household – also became more deeply ingrained with the passage of time.

Quite early in their marriage Mabel had tried to force Alec to conform to normal hours of rising and breakfasting, but as time passed she realised the hopelessness of the case. Nevertheless, from time to time, especially if he disturbed the children by his midnight piano solos, she would nag him about his strange nocturnal habits: 'Please, please, if you love me, work in the daytime and not at night, Alec. I am frightened and don't see what we are coming to,' she pleaded in an undated note. Now and again he did his level best to fall in with her entreaties. In December 1891, for example, he twice climbed up and down the mountain at Beinn Bhreagh in a desperate bid to find sleep by midnight, but three hours later he was still as wide awake as ever and writing despairingly to Mabel: 'To take night from me is to rob me of *life*. No more useless reform for me as yet.' Before turning in at four o'clock, Alec would prowl around the sleeping house. On nights when there was a full moon he would draw curtains or place screens to shield his family from its baleful light. It goes without saying that he always took care to blot out the moonlight from his own bedroom, lest by some unlucky chance it should fall across him as he lay sleeping. This fear apparently went back to that incident in early childhood when he lay ill in bed with scarlet fever and was terrified by his mother's cloak.

As early as the mid-1880s, Mabel was remonstrating with Alec when his natural aloofness extended to his own daughters. In an undated letter about 1885, she wrote to him, hearking back to the death of her sons and once more trying to rationalise this tragedy as some sort of penalty for Alec's indifference and her deafness:

> Your children need you; their characters are unfolding and they are a puzzle to me. All our lives we may regret that you were too absorbed in irregular night work – tending where? – to give them the care I cannot. I believe in God. Perhaps the reason our boy was taken from us so early was that we have not done our duty by the children we have . . . Why was our wealth given us if not to give *you* time to make up to *your* children what they lose by their mother's loss.

Even if Mabel had not constantly reminded him, Alec was aware of this tendency, and viewed it introspectively from time to time. Early in May 1890 he attended the funeral of George Sanders's aged grandmother who, it will be remembered, had been a mother figure to Alec at a crucial point in his life. Depressed by the funeral, he wrote to Mabel:

> I feel more and more as I grow older the tendency to retire into myself and be alone with my thoughts. I can see that same tendency in my father and uncle in an exaggerated degree – and suppose there is something in the blood. My children have it too, but in lesser degree – because they are younger I suppose. You alone are free from it – and you my dear constitute the chief link between myself and the world outside.[7]

On the face of it, is seems ironic that Alec saw his deaf wife as his chief conduit to the outside world; indeed, many of the people who knew Alec through the Washington social and intellectual circles in which he moved so effortlessly would have been surprised at this self-assessment. He could, and did, make a great effort when required, and Mabel constantly laboured to push him out into society, often against his innate tendencies. From Paris she wrote to him in London:

> Accept all the invitations to dinner you get and meet all the great men you can – I want to hear all about them. I always feel as if you were my second self and all the gorgeous people you meet I meet too, and enjoy far more than if I really met them. Never mind a little dyspepsia. We'll go home to Cape Breton and live on bread and milk the rest of the summer.[8]

Sometimes she tried flattery, and found it quite efficacious in forcing him to come out of his shell:

> I am always so awfully proud of you when we go to parties. There's not another man in Washington unless it's Justice Gray who is as distinguished-looking as you. I don't mean handsome, doubtless there are plenty prettier than you, my husband – I'm nothing if not impartial! – but none that look so evidently somebody. I always expect the listlessly polite face of the hostess to change and light up when you come, and the look of interest to deepen when your name is announced.[9]

Even when they were together, Mabel often resorted to the written word when she wanted to convey her thoughts and feelings to her husband. In 1889, for example, she wrote:

> I wonder, do you ever think of me in the midst of that work of yours of which I am so proud and yet so jealous, for I know it has stolen from me part of my husband's heart . . . I live in hope that you will not quite forget me, and that we may pass many another summer like the last when we had thoughts and interests in common.[10]

And four and a half years later she reproached him:

> I realize as I see Mamma and Papa, Grace and Charlie together how little you give me of your time and thoughts, how little willing you are to enter into little things, which yet make up the sum of our lives.[11]

In the spring of 1895, Alec and Mabel went off on an extended trip through Mexico. On this occasion the girls were left behind, and as a result this jaunt was like a second honeymoon. Their love was rekindled, and for a time Alec gave his wife his undivided attention. Shortly after their return to Washington, Mabel and the girls departed for Europe while Alec headed back to Beinn Bhreagh. There he discovered a letter which Mabel had left for him. In it she wrote:

> I want to tell you how very happy I am that we have had these last six weeks to ourselves for ourselves. I had wanted you so much and I felt that the only way I could hope to have you really was to go away with you . . . You were very, very good to me all the time.[12]

Alec was deeply moved by this note, and opened his heart to her in reply:

> You have made me very, very happy, my darling, during all our wedded life, and I too enjoyed these few weeks alone with you in Mexico, although I fear you did not think so. I meant to give you pleasure, but pleased myself instead. I meant to devote myself to you, but the scientific men and old mines, etc., were all for me. I fear that selfishness is a trait of my character. I can see it very clearly in others, but I do not recognize it in myself until too late. It was selfish in me to let you all go to the other side of the world without me, for the sake of my experiments and the Convention.[13]

Alec's growing egocentricity was also evident in his dining habits. By the 1890s, preoccupied with the many interests that took up his time, he absented himself from the family circle until dinnertime, when he would make a brief appearance and then vanish once more into his own solitary world. First there was the incident of the fussy English china tableware to which Mabel was so partial, but to which her husband took an instant dislike, mainly on account of its somewhat bizarre decoration of various insects. Eventually he succeeded in having it replaced by a relatively plain French set with a gold rim and a simple monogram. 'At long last I can enjoy my dinner without imagining a caterpillar or a moth in every spoonful of soup!' he confided to Charles Thompson. In the mid-1890s, as his full beard reached the proportions of an old Testament patriarch, he overcame the problem of depositing his soup all over it by adopting various glass drinking-tubes. Tubes with a fine gauge were preferred for sucking tea and coffee out of a cup, while a coarse gauge was used for getting soup from the plate into his mouth fairly neatly. The same ploy was efficacious in dealing with stews and troublesome gravies. Mabel probably thought this custom rather repulsive, though she chose to attack it on the grounds of hygiene, arguing that it was impossible to clean these tubes satisfactorily. Alec ignored this, and in the end Mabel gave way. For his part, Alec could never understand how this latest, brilliant invention of his failed to find any enthusiasm among the rest of his family.

On one score at least Mabel could be thankful; her husband was very abstemious. Occasionally, if attending some social function, he would tentatively sip a glass of wine or perhaps toy with a light beer, but alcohol made him dyspeptic and inclined him to fuzziness. Whisky he abhorred, while brandy – by the teaspoonful – was sparingly confined to medicinal purposes when he had one of his severe headaches or was fatigued after a long hike through the forests.

Alec was a voracious reader, and at both his Washington house and Beinn Bhreagh he boasted libraries containing thousands of volumes. In February 1879 he had purchased a set of the *Encyclopaedia Britannica*, ninth edition, and vowed to read it from cover to cover. Whether he achieved this self-imposed task is nowhere recorded, but it was in line with his gargantuan appetite for miscellaneous information of all kinds and an almost childlike wonderment about all manner of natural phenomena.

After several years of lying fallow, his inventiveness resurfaced in 1889. Four years earlier he had moaned to Mabel that Washington was no place in which to carry out experiments and he looked back nostalgically to his time in Boston when the Williams workshop was such a powerhouse of invention, but he ended by consoling himself: 'Don't urge me to work any more for money. The subjects I long to work at are nearly all unremunerative in their nature . . . Our income is good enough.'[14]

Mabel continued to encourage him and in December 1889 he re-activated his laboratory in the little brick outbuilding behind his father's house in Georgetown, taking on a new assistant named William H.D. Ellis, initially to help with statistical work but subsequently to work on physical experiments. About the same time he was joined by Arthur McCurdy, son of the Baddeck businessman who had helped him purchase the Redhead land. Young McCurdy's first task was to take down Alec's random thoughts in two parallel sets of notebooks headed 'Lab Notes' and 'Home Notes', divided solely by the place where they were dictated. Eventually this series would run to 210 volumes, covering the last thirty years of Alec's life.

In spite of his disclaimer to Mabel, Alec had in mind a project which would generate a great deal of cash if it were successful. This was a practical process for making copies of phonograph records. By the spring of 1890 he had perfected a method of moulding the indented cylinders from the original masters using a waxy substance which he termed ozokerite. The idea was sound in theory, but there was a snag: the copies did not always come away cleanly from the mould. Instead of concentrating on this technical hitch, however, Alec went off at a tangent on something completely different, a scheme for using agate cement to take a printing impression from photographs. 'Here at last is a subject at which we can work together,' he wrote jubilantly to Mabel in June 1890. 'My previous inventions have been to you all sealed things, relating to the world of sound, but this will bring us together in a common interest.' This project likewise ran into technical difficulties and was similarly abandoned.

In the ensuing decade Alec made little attempt to invent things which had a commercial viability. Typical of the flights of fancy in this period were his experiments of 1891 with thought transference. He devised coils of wire which he placed around his head and that of his long-suffering assistant Ellis, linked by wires charged with an electric current, in the vain hope of transmitting thoughts from one brain to the other. He briefly revived his photophone, now renamed the spectrophone, and dreamed of seeing by electricity. Five years later, when Wilhelm Roentgen unveiled his X-rays, Alec flirted with this concept but could find no practical method of taking the matter further. In 1895–96 he toyed with the notion of boats with revolving hulls to reduce water resistance at high speeds, and in the same period dabbled in a gadget for distilling fresh water from fog or moist sea air, with the laudable aim of producing a device that could be fitted to lifeboats. None of these pipedreams produced anything tangible, certainly nothing that was worth the expense of Patent Office fees.

A recurring theme of the notebooks of the 1890s, however, was Alec's random thoughts on a subject which would eventually round off his career as an inventor in fine style – the development of a heavier-than-air flying machine. During the same period, moreover, Alec was heavily committed to his life's work for the deaf; from this and his experiments with sheep-breeding at Baddeck developed an interest in heredity and eugenics. Because of their importance these subjects are discussed in separate chapters. But in addition there is the invaluable contribution which Alec made to the advancement of science in general which must be put on record.

In some respects, Alec was a scientist *manqué*. As far back as the spring of 1879 he had his sights set on the position of physicist at the Smithsonian Institution, in succession to Joseph Henry who had died on 13 May 1878. To that end he prepared a paper entitled 'Vowel Theories Considered in Relation to the Phonograph and Phonautograph' for the National Academy of Arts and Sciences. Sending a copy of this paper to Spencer Baird (who had succeeded Henry as Secretary of the Smithsonian), Alec commented that he hoped 'to show the scientific men here that I have a special familiarity with the subjects that were Prof. Henry's chief objects of study'. Although the paper was well received, and subsequently published in the *American Journal of Otology*, it transpired that the Smithsonian lacked the funds to appoint a new physicist. Only an application to Congress for a special appropriation would answer the case, and although Gardiner Hubbard offered to lobby on his behalf, Alec declined as a matter of principle. Over the ensuing five years he contributed a number of papers recording his work on the photophone, spectrophone, induction balance, telephonic probe and vacuum jacket.[15] Subsequently there were a few papers on aspects of heredity (discussed in Chapter 14), but effectively Alec's serious contributions to the literature of science ended in the mid-1880s. In later years he was content to keep his scientific musings to himself, though he did come quite close (in 1889) to producing a paper on energy conservation that would assuredly have been almost a century ahead of its time.

On the other hand, he was immensely proud of his election to the National Academy of Sciences in 1883 and attended its meetings and conventions regularly and diligently. In the ensuing years he contributed five papers to its transactions, all but one ('on Apparent Electricity Produced in an Apparatus by the Pressure of the Atmosphere') on aspects of heredity. He also served on six *ad hoc* committees but in 1897 he turned down the suggestion that he should take on the treasurership of the Academy.

The financial support which Alec gave to young Albert Michelson was by no means his only practical contribution to the advancement of science. In 1880 John Michels began *Science*, a weekly periodical aimed primarily at the scientific community. Although conducted on a shoestring it lost money from the outset, but for eighteen months the deficit was made good by Edison. In April 1881 Alec sent Michels a copy of his National Academy paper on the reproduction of sounds by radiant energy and Michels promptly published it, ahead of the *American Journal of Science*. On 18 July that year Michels wrote to Alec suggesting that he should form a small stock company to take over publication of the magazine. Unfortunately, the offer came just as Alec was totally preoccupied with his attempts to save the life of James Garfield, and apparently he never got around to replying. When Edison withdrew his financial support at the end of 1881, Alec was in Europe. Somehow Michels managed to keep the struggling paper going and renewed his appeal to Alec the following summer. On 9 June he wrote to Alec again, enclosing a copy of his latest prospectus which announced boldly: 'SCIENCE is essentially the medium of communication among the Scientists of America . . . SCIENCE enters into competition with no other scientific journal; it was established to fill a void that has been long felt.' The first claim was merely wishful thinking, but the second was true enough, as the *American Journal of Science* had become increasingly élitist, and predominantly given over to lengthy papers on aspects of geology, to the detriment of the sciences in general. At the other end of the spectrum, to be sure, there were several popular science magazines, but there was nothing that catered specifically to the scientific community. Alec had seen the British equivalent, *Nature*, and admired it greatly; and, besides, the notion of going one better than his great rival Edison rather appealed to Alec's combative nature. As a result, he and Gardiner Hubbard responded favourably to Michels' latest offer.

Originally they planned to retain Michels as editor, but the consensus among scientists in Washington was that the magazine could only succeed were he replaced by a writer with impeccable scientific credentials. In the end Michels sold the name and goodwill of the magazine to Hubbard for $5,000, and Samuel H. Scudder was appointed editor, with an annual salary of $4,000, guaranteed for three years. Scudder was distantly related to Hubbard but he was also eminently qualified, being 'the greatest scholar and most charming writer among the American entomologists' as the *Dictionary of American Biography* described him. Moses King of Boston agreed to serve as publisher. Alec put up most of the $25,000 for this venture, but Hubbard looked after the business side. The Science Company was incorporated late in 1882. Originally Hubbard suggested that Alec should be the company president, but the latter felt that, with so much telephone patent litigation still pending, it would be wiser if he kept in the background, otherwise *Science* might be regarded as a propaganda weapon in the battle. In the end Alec pursuaded Daniel Gilman to fill this role. This proved to be a prudent move; even so, there was considerable suspicion at first regarding Alec's ulterior motives, but this evaporated as the magazine was shown to be impartial. In the end, Alec's numerous contacts and friendships in the scientific world ensured that the magazine got a ready supply of well-written, authoritative, up-to-the-minute articles.

Publication had come to a halt in June 1882 but was resumed on 9 February 1883. From the outset Scudder stated clear aims: 'To increase the knowledge of our people, to show our transatlantic friends our real activity, to gain among intelligent people a knowledge of the true aims and purposes of science, and to elevate the standard of science among scientific men themselves.' This far exceeded the rather modest target proclaimed by Michels, and from the beginning the new-look *Science* was a vast improvement. Most importantly, thanks to Alec's input, Scudder was able to pay his contributors whereas Michels had relied on purely voluntary contributions. Although the circulation of the new magazine rose steadily, it fell far short of the figure required to cover the annual running costs, while the revenue from advertising plummeted because the limited circulation failed to generate the kind of response that advertisers were expecting. After a few months, Moses King resigned as publisher and at the end of the first year the deficit amounted to $19,000, which would have left the original capital of $25,000 woefully depleted. Alec and his father-in-law injected a further $10,000 into the business, and braced themselves to continue pumping in cash on an even greater scale, until the circulation and advertising improved. In the second year running costs rose to $30,000 whereas income did not exceed $5,000. This pattern continued for a decade, and would prove a considerable drain on Alec's resources. Discouraged by his feelings of inadequacy, Scudder resigned in 1885, although Alec pleaded with him to soldier on. He was replaced by N.D.C. Hodges, a professional journalist who made up for his lack of scientific eminence by his dogged determination to make the paper a success. Late in 1891 Alec and Hubbard transferred ownership of the magazine to their indefatigable editor, but continued to bale him out financially. This situation continued till 1894 when the American Association for the Advancement of Science undertook to subsidise the magazine. By that date support for *Science* had cost Hubbard $20,000 and Alec three times that sum.

In the same year Hodges transferred ownership to James McKeen Cattell, a psychologist with decidedly entrepreneurial flair. After twelve months the AAAS reneged on its arrangement, but the enterprising Cattell persuaded the Macmillan Company to shoulder the burden of running costs in exchange for unlimited advertising space. This arrangement continued well enough until 1900, when the AAAS belatedly recognised *Science* as its official organ. Since then, it has never looked back and it has now become the world's pre-eminent scientific periodical. In 1899 Cattell wrote to Alec to express 'the great indebtedness of American men of science for your great gift to science in America'. That $60,000 could never have been so well spent.

At an informal meeting at the Cosmos Club in Janaury 1888 Gardiner Hubbard launched another venture which was to have a major impact not only on his own life, but on that of his son-in-law and his eldest granddaughter. He founded the National Geographic Society at Washington 'for the increase and diffusion of geographical knowledge', and assumed office as its first president. During the nine years of Hubbard's presidency (terminated only by his death) the society remained small in numbers and pedestrian in outlook. Its members were largely confined to the Washington area and its journal, the *National Geographic Magazine*, was ponderous and pretentious, solid text relieved by few maps and even fewer line drawings. It seemed destined to struggle for survival, just as *Science* had done. Early in 1897 Hubbard invited Professor Edwin Augustus Grosvenor of Amherst College to lecture to the society about his experiences in Turkey, where he had been professor of European history at Robert

College in Constantinople from 1867 till 1890. In 1891 he had returned to the United States to take up a similar appointment at Amherst where, in due course, his identical twin sons Edwin and Gilbert would receive their higher education. Professor Grosvenor distilled two decades of his life in the Ottoman capital into a two-volume book, *Constantinople*, the manuscript of which was typed by fifteen-year-old Gilbert. This scholarly, well-written book was made all the more remarkable by its lavish illustrations, 230 photographs taken by the professor being included.

During his brief sojourn in Washington in connection with his lecture to the National Geographic Society, Professor Grosvenor stayed with Alec and Mabel, and regaled them with stories of his remarkable sons who were one of the best tennis doubles ever to play for Amherst. Soon afterwards, the Grosvenor boys graduated with the highest honours. Edwin would have a brilliant career as a lawyer, and Gilbert was expected to follow his father into teaching. By the spring of 1897 Elsie Bell had blossomed into a handsome young lady with the sultry beauty and raven locks which led her to be often taken for a Spaniard. Grosvenor's sons visited the Bell home around that time and were both smitten by her, but Elsie, it seems, already had a suitor, a young Washington architect called George Totten. Already established in his career and definitely going places, Totten had the edge over his younger rivals. Alec and Mabel considered George a very suitable catch; the only snag was that Elsie seemed indifferent to him. Mindful of the fact that Mabel had not been quick to respond to Alec's first advances, Elsie's parents were not unduly concerned. In the summer, however, the Grosvenor boys graduated, and Elsie and her sister Daisy accepted the invitation, extended by Mrs Grosvenor, to attend the graduation ceremony. The brothers were the outstanding students of their year, both athletically and scholastically, and their graduation attracted considerable coverage in the national press.

When George Totten turned up at Beinn Bhreagh that July, Mabel promptly wrote to Amherst and invited Edwin and Gilbert to join the house party. It would prove to be a contest for the hand of Elsie Bell. The progress of the courtship of her elder daughter was faithfully charted by Mabel in her letters to Alec and her mother from early August till the end of September. 'The Grosvenor boys . . . are certainly fine fellows, clever and manly with no nonsense about them,' she wrote approvingly at the end of their visit. George had shown himself to be 'really a nice fellow, kind and gentle and up to anything . . . Alec likes him.' And she added later that he had 'won all hearts except the only one he cares about'. Thereafter, George Totten seems to have dropped out of the picture. By the end of the year even Gilbert Grosvenor felt that he was getting nowhere with the rather self-possessed Elsie. He was by that time getting started in his career as a teacher, at the Englewood Academy for Boys in New Jersey where he taught French, German, Latin, algebra, chemistry, public speaking and debating, and the demands of such a busy curriculum left him little time to brood over his love life.

In December 1897 Gardiner Hubbard died at the age of seventy-five. Considering the very poor opinion he had had of Alec as a businessman, it is ironic that in the last years his life Hubbard had come to rely more and more on his son-in-law and found that he possessed remarkable organisational skills as well as a shrewd business sense. Latterly, Alec had been closer to Hubbard than ever, intimately associated in the promotion of *Science* as well as in the struggling Geographic Society. On Hubbard's death, therefore, Alec was unanimously elected president in his stead.

At that time, however, Alec was preoccupied with experimental work on aircraft and he was unable to give the fledgling society the care and attention it deserved. As a result, membership dropped sharply, from fifteen hundred to fewer than a thousand, the life membership reserve was depleted and a deficit rose alarmingly. By the beginning of 1899 the society was in a parlous state. It was then that Alec galvanised himself into action. Quickly targeting the problem, he decided that the magazine needed to be transformed into a paper that would catch the eye of the general public. He realised that a periodical put together by eminent but amateur editors could never get anywhere and he felt that it was vital to recruit some young man who would brighten it up. So strongly did he feel about this that he was prepared to pay the salary from his own pocket if he could get the right person.

It is not known whether, or to what extent, Elsie prodded her father in the right direction, but at any rate, on 19 February 1899, Alec wrote to his friend Dr Edwin Grosvenor at Amherst:

> As President of the National Geographic Society I am on the lookout for some young man of ability to act as Assistant Secretary of The Society, and manage, under the direction of our Editorial Committee, our monthly publication, 'The National Geographic Magazine'.
>
> In this connection your two sons recur to my mind. I do not know whether the position contemplated would be in the nature of an advance on the positions they now occupy, or whether it would be consistent with their aims in life – and therefore write confidentially to you before approaching either of them upon the subject. If, as I understand, they contemplate ultimately going into law – the opportunities for study here are unrivalled, and the duties of the position would not be of so exacting a character as to prevent them from pursuing any studies they desire.
>
> The present Editor of The Magazine, an expert geographer, serves

without remuneration, but he finds himself so overburdened with work as statistician to the Agricultural Department that he desires to resign the Editorship. He would remain, however, on the Editorial Committee and give his active assistance to his successor. We are now contemplating the advisability of placing The Magazine in the hands of one only salaried officer, the Assistant Secretary, making him the Managing Editor to get out The Magazine with the assistance of the Editorial Committee.

I am afraid, however, that our present Assistant Secretary would not be competent to conduct The Magazine. He is a married man, and we pay him a salary of $1,200 a year. I have thought that perhaps for the same salary we could secure an unmarried man of superior ability by applying to the Presidents of our universities.

Some bright college graduate just beginning life would probably find in this position a stepping-stone to something better, and be able, while here, to pursue some post-graduate course of study while earning his livelihood.

Under the proposed plan the members of the Editorial Committee would provide the original material for The Magazine, the Managing Editor simply applying to them for material as needed. The chief duties of the Managing Editor would be the *arrangement* of the material and the reading of proofs – but he must also have sufficient literary ability to be able to write himself in an emergency, and sufficient judgement in quoting from our exchanges. Of course, in all this he would have the assistance of the experts upon the Editorial Staff who would always be glad to be consulted. Either of your sons would, I am sure, have sufficient ability for the position, but of course I do not know what their present prospects are, or whether such an opening would prove attractive to them.

We shall make no change for some months yet, and in the meantime no harm can come from consulting you upon the subject . . . [16]

With this he enclosed a specimen copy of the magazine. Alec's notion that this would be a part-time job with plenty of time for studying law on the side seems quaint and old-fashioned when one realises that it takes a staff of almost two thousand hard-working people to carry on the society's work at the present day. Even more amusing, in the light of subsequent events, was his notion that the position might be 'a stepping-stone to something better'. By this time Gilbert's courtship of Elsie was making some progress. Whether Alec was aware of this and chose to ignore it, or was oblivious to the way things were going, is not known. Perhaps he was determined to appear even-handed in the matter of appointing the editor. He followed up the letter to Professor Grosvenor by writing identical letters to the boys:

My dear Friends:

  Will you kindly look over the enclosed communication to your father and let me know whether either of you would consider the proposition to become Assistant Secretary of the National Geographic Society, and Managing Editor of The Magazine, if such a proposition should be made to you.

Edwin, now nearing the end of his post-graduate law course, yielded to his brother, who was combining his teaching at Englewood with the finals for his Master's degree at Amherst. The appointment with the National Geographic must have seemed a dawdle compared with the exacting duties of a teacher, so Gilbert accepted with alacrity. On 1 April, All Fools' Day, 1899 he reported for duty in Washington, and wondered whether the joke was on him, when Professor Bell personally showed him round his cramped working quarters, half of a tiny rented room on the fifth floor of a building (long since demolished) on Fifteenth Street, opposite the US Treasury. Despite Alec's blandishments, the young man was not to have the title of managing editor; instead he was designated assistant editor and assistant secretary, but in spite of the title the responsibility was all his. Many years later Gilbert recorded his dismay when he beheld the scene:

> The little space of which I, age 23, the only employee, was to assume charge, was littered with old magazines, newspapers, and a few books of records, which constituted the only visible property of The Society. The treasury was empty, and had incurred a debt of nearly $2,000 by expenditure of life-membership fees to keep alive.
>
> The Society was not so poor as it seemed, however, for its management, inspired by Alexander Graham Bell, had a revolutionary idea: 'Why not popularize the science of geography and take it into the homes of the people? Why not transform the Society's magazine from one of cold geographic fact, expressed in hieroglyphic terms which the layman could not understand, into a vehicle for carrying the living, breathing, human-interest truth about this great world of ours to the people? Would not that be the greatest agency of all for the diffusion of geographic knowledge?'[17]

At the end of a month's probation, Gilbert's appointment was confirmed for one year, at a salary of $100 a month (paid personally by Alec for five years). Within eighteen months, Gilbert was managing editor in name as well as fact, a position he would hold until 1954. In 1920 he would become president, and in 1954 chairman of the board, retaining this office until his ninetieth birthday, in 1966, presiding over an organisation which grew from a local society into a truly universal institution. Many years after he became editor, Gilbert would reflect that what probably secured the job for him was the fact that his father's book had been so well illustrated. That may well have played some part in Alec's choice, but it is clear that he himself had very positive views on how the magazine should develop. As early as 14 July 1899 Alec had written to Gilbert, urging that the magazine should have 'a multitude of good illustrations and maps'; and a few months later he sent a memo: '*Motion* interests . . . Run *more dynamical pictures* – pictures of life and action – pictures that tell a story "to be continued in our text"!!'

In fact, Alec had formed the opinion that a picture was worth a thousand words, long before he had come across Professor Grosvenor's *Constantinople*. In 1894 Samuel McClure, casting around for some way of keeping his own struggling magazine from going under, came up with the brilliant idea of a series of articles on Napoleon who, as the centenary of his First Consulship approached, was enjoying unprecedented public interest in America. It so happened that Gardiner Hubbard had, since 1880, been accumulating a prodigious collection of paintings, engravings and ephemera associated with Napoleon and his spectacular career. McClure got to hear of this and secured Hubbard's co-operation in the series on the life and times of Napoleon written by Ida Tarbell. The series was a runaway success and thereafter *McClure's Magazine* never looked back. In succeeding years, therefore, McClure was firmly wedded to the idea of using as many pictures as possible. As the nineteenth century drew to a close he was widely regarded as the most successful of the magazine publishers, and consequently a recognised authority on what sold magazines. Inevitably, he had the ear of Alec Bell, and this was to lead to a head-on confrontation between him and the youthful editor.

Meanwhile Gilbert was making good progress in other directions. Within weeks of taking up the editorship of the magazine, he was invited to join the Bell family on a picnic to Great Falls and Cabin John, a noted beauty spot. Mabel recorded in her diary that 'Gilbert really needed the outing. He said he was played out. I think Elsie is seriously considering him.' A few days later Mabel wrote to Alec, 'The more I see the boy, the more I am impressed with the idea that he will be a successful man. I like the way he talks . . . He is wholly absorbed in making a success of the paper.' But she was perplexed that Gilbert could be 'so perfectly self-possessed when his lady-love is near him . . . I am sure you weren't.'72[18] As for the girl herself, Mabel noted apprehensively in the spring of 1900 that 'she thinks she will probably decide to marry Gilbert, but she is so perfectly matter-of-fact about it that I am sure she is not a particle in love with him.'[19] But Mabel's fears were groundless. On 30 August 1900 Gilbert formally proposed marriage and was accepted. 'I've got her at last and she won't get away,' he wrote triumphantly to his father. They were married in the city of Elsie's birth, at King's Weigh House Church, London, on 23 October 1900. It was to be a happy marriage, ended only by her death sixty-three years later.

While the young couple were honeymooning in Europe, Alec seized the opportunity to make some sweeping changes in the magazine. To be fair, it appears to have been the members of the ten-man executive committee who persuaded Alec that the advice of McClure – 'the Midas of the ten-cent magazine' – should be heeded. McClure recommended that the name of the magazine be changed – geography had no appeal for the public. Never mention the society in it, and give up trying to build circulation by membership of the society. The road to success lay in the street-corner news-stands. Finally, publish the magazine in New York; no popular magazine ever came out of Washington. Heeding this wrong-headed advice, Alec had the magazine transferred to New York, where the January and February 1901 issues were published.

As soon as he stepped off the ship from Europe in December 1900, however, Gilbert, with his bride in tow, went straight to the publishing office and asserted his authority in no uncertain terms. Back in Washington he confronted the executive board with the unpalatable truth that production costs had soared since the move to New York, while circulation had shown no commensurate increase. Gilbert's plea was answered and the board applauded him for his resolute stand. With the issue of March 1901 the magazine was safely back in Washington, where it has been ever since.

Gilbert was vindicated when the circulation began to rise steadily. Within a year membership of the society had doubled, and the board signalled its approval by voting their young editor $800 per annum on top of the $1,200 which continued to come out of Alec's own pocket. He switched from a solid page format to double columns and made adroit use of photographs. It should be stated that, shortly before Grosvenor took over the editorship, Alec was already injecting new life and more vivid pictures into its solid pages. In particular, a photograph of a bare-breasted Filipino girl harvesting rice was published at Alec's insistence; prudery yielded to geographic truth, but doubtless it did sales no harm either.

Within a year of taking office as president, Alec advocated a move into more salubrious premises. He recommended 'a building – a library, worthy of the Society, and headquarters a little more respectable than . . . the two little lumber rooms in the Corcoran Building.' In 1900 the society purchased a lot at the corner of Sixteenth and M Streets and in the spring of 1902 the foundation stone of the Hubbard Memorial Hall was laid with full masonic honours, five-month-old Melville Bell Grosvenor holding the trowel.

13

The Deaf Shall Speak

To instruct the deaf no art could ever reach,
No care improve them, and no wisdom touch.
Lucretius

Today Alexander Graham Bell is best remembered as an inventor, with the telephone as his lasting achievement. His contribution to science, largely financial, is far less well known, but it was crucial at the time and deserves to be more widely appreciated. While he revelled in the epithets of inventor and scientist often applied to his name in the popular press, Alec himself regarded as his main contribution to humanity his work with the deaf. It was his deep-seated concern and compassion for a section of the handicapped community which seldom got understanding or sympathy from the general public which ruled his life and governed his actions at all times. Even the telephone, which the deaf could never use, owed its genesis to his unique understanding of the physiology of hearing. Apart from the telephone, an abiding interest in the deaf would lead Alec into other strange byways, such as his pioneering studies of heredity and eugenics, and to some extent his work on the graphophone and the photophone was inspired indirectly by his ongoing commitment to the deaf. But all this was peripheral to the work that was at the very core of his being, and which would continue to absorb a considerable amount of his time and money till the day he died. Alec's role as a humanitarian, so completely overshadowed by his one really great invention, has not received the general recognition it deserves. During his own lifetime, moreover, his methods were not always understood, and, indeed, they would earn him a great deal of calumny and opprobrium, every bit as damaging as the attacks on his integrity and reputation during the prolonged telephone patent litigation.

It was popularly believed that a person who was deaf was, *ipso facto*, also dumb. The term deaf-mute was commonly used for all persons who had never acquired the habit of speech because of severely impaired hearing as well as those who were congenitally deaf, or had become deaf through illness in very early life. Even worse, there was a tendency to equate deaf-mutes with idiots and lunatics. This was the situation prevailing in the mid-nineteenth century, when Alec was a boy. Even where a relatively enlightened and liberal attitude existed, very little was done for the deaf. Systematic attempts to teach the deaf to communicate by means of signs only developed in the eighteenth century. About 1760 the Abbé de l'Epée opened a school in Paris and almost simultaneously Thomas Braidwood established a school at Edinburgh. The first public school for the deaf was opened in Bermondsey, London, in 1792 and thereafter similar schools were opened in many cities in Europe and America. In all of these establishments the inmates were taught to communicate by means of signs: either the natural signs which develop almost instinctively as part of body language, or the conventional signs invented by the Abbé de l'Epée and others. These systems enabled the deaf to converse, often with an amazing degree of dexterity and speed, with those who had been trained in the same method, mostly other deaf-mutes. Imprisoned by their deafness within their own tiny silent world, these people were condemned to communicate with others in the same condition.

That a deaf person was dumb only because he or she had never been taught to use the vocal chords was a notion developed during the nineteenth century, although it has a surprising antiquity. The Venerable Bede, no less, recorded in his *Ecclesiastical History* how John, Bishop of Hagulstadt (Hexham), in the year 687 taught a deaf man to pronounce words and sentences; but this was regarded as a miracle. A few isolated cases of similar miracles were recorded through the centuries, but it was not until the end of the eighteenth century that Samuel Heinicke established a school where the deaf were taught to speak, and to understand the speech of others merely by closely watching the motion of the vocal organs. By great patience, perseverance and kindness, Heinicke enjoyed a modicum of success with a handful of pupils, even though their speech was laborious and contorted, usually too loud and frequently harsh to the ear of the untutored. By the middle of the nineteenth century Heinicke's articulation system was widely used in the deaf schools of Germany and Austria, but it was little applied or understood in Britain or America, as it was believed that the English language was not as adaptable as German for this purpose. German teachers considered that articulation was necessary for the acquisition of thought, and were confident that it could be taught to the great majority of the deaf and dumb. In England, on the other hand, most teachers held the opposite opinion. The oral method gradually crept in during the course of the nineteenth century, but was confined to the 'semideaf' – those whose hearing was not totally impaired and those who had lost their hearing through illness in puberty or adulthood.

In the case of the women closest to Alec, his mother had lost her hearing when she was thirteen. Consequently her speech was normal, but because she never took the trouble to learn the art of lip-reading she could only receive communication through signs. In the case of Mabel, rendered deaf by an illness in early childhood, there was some residual speech; and on this Alec gradually built, to the extent that, in maturity, Mabel's speech was reasonably distinct and discernible even to perfect strangers. She was also skilled at lip-reading, so much so that those who had never met her before were quite unaware of her affliction. This also explains why Mabel preferred the company of hearing people and had a marked aversion to being with other deaf people, an attitude which sometimes pained Alec who considered it a form of selfishness.

In 1857 the Columbia Institution for the Deaf and Dumb was founded in Washington, with Edward Miner Gallaudet as its director. Gallaudet was then aged twenty, but in the realms of deaf instruction he was something of an infant prodigy. His father, Thomas H. Gallaudet, had founded the first permanent school for the deaf, at Hartford, Connecticut. Though Edward was only fourteen when Thomas died, he carried on where his father had left off. Energetic, highly intelligent and possessed of great charm and self-confidence, Edward so impressed the Congressional committee that when the choice of a director for the first national school was being mooted he was unanimously selected. He would remain as head of this prestigious institution for fifty-three years, witnessing its name change in 1864 to the National College for Deaf-Mutes and then, in the 1890s, to Gallaudet College in memory of his father. Apart from following in the footsteps of a famous father, Alec and Edward Gallaudet had much in common. Both had a deaf mother, and both had initially been sceptical about lip-reading. In 1867 Gallaudet toured Europe, examining the methods used to teach deaf-mutes. On his return to Washington he reported:

> Nothing in my foreign investigations has led me to question the character of the foundation on which the system of instruction pursued in our American institutions is based. It is plainly evident, from what is seen in the articulating schools of Europe and from the candid opinions of the best instructors, that oral language cannot, in the fullest sense of the term, be mastered by a majority of deaf-mutes.[1]

Within a few years, however, he had modified his views after seeing the progress made at the Clarke School in Northampton where the oral method was used exclusively. It will be remembered that one of the prime instigators of this school was Gardiner Hubbard whose eight-year-old daughter Mabel was one of the first pupils. Gallaudet subsequently recommended that speech and lip-reading should be taught in all schools for deaf-mutes if at all possible, bearing in mind the aptitude of the individual pupil as well as the abilities of the teacher. At one stage he even went so far as to recommend the articulation system as a substitute for the sign methods, anticipating the fears (later expressed by Alec Bell) that it would be all too easy to fall back on sign language as an inferior substitute for speech.

So far so good; but in the 1870s the spectacular success of young Professor Bell caused the pendulum to swing away from the traditional methods. The oral method was introduced into a few of the existing institutions and several schools were established in which the 'German system' was used exclusively. Armed with Melville Bell's Visible Speech, the oralists advanced their cause with all the zeal of medieval religious fanatics. Gallaudet now revised his position; wishing to be fair-minded and even-handed, he counselled the continuance of sign language as a teaching aid, and even suggested that if children wished to communicate with each other in the playground, there was no harm in reverting to signs. Out of this he evolved what he termed the Combined Method, in which signs (the Natural Method) could be combined with speech (the Artificial Method).

In this, Gallaudet appeared to be taking a pragmatic, commonsensical view of the problem and, as the outstanding figure in the education of the deaf, his views commanded considerable respect. He was ten years older than Alec and the younger man admired his singleminded devotion to helping the deaf. Soon after he first came to the United States, Alec had toyed with the idea of joining the staff of the National College. After he settled in Washington, he often ran across Gallaudet, especially at the Cosmos Club of which Gallaudet was a founder member. Gallaudet was on intimate terms with the Hubbards, and from January 1880 onwards, he dined with Alec and Mabel from time to time. They also met at the homes of mutual friends and were on good terms. Later that year Gallaudet was instrumental in conferring on Alec the first of his many honorary degrees.

Where the two men first drifted apart and then became deadly antagonists, however, was in their respective attitudes towards the teaching of the deaf. Gallaudet was a firm believer in segregating the deaf from other children because he believed they would feel happier and more at ease with their own kind. To Alec this was almost an admission of defeat, like Gallaudet's unfortunately labelled compromise between signs and speech, which Alec contemptuously dubbed the Sign Method because, in practice, that was the feature on which it seemed to rely. Instead, he firmly believed that, even when it was necessary to instruct deaf children separately from their peers, it was essential that they should mingle freely in the playground and after school hours, in order to develop their skills of articulation. It was for this reason also that Alec was so keen to establish day-schools for the deaf, so that they could practise their speaking skills with parents and siblings in a normal family environment, instead of being packed off to special boarding-schools where they had little contact with normal speakers.

The rift between Bell and Gallaudet began imperceptibly, but was made public one evening in 1881 when, according to Gallaudet's diary, they had a good-humoured verbal sparring match at the home of a mutual friend. At first they agreed to differ, each respecting the other's rights to his own opinions. On 2 December 1884 Alec wrote to Gallaudet to set the record straight:

> Not only do we find all shades of opinion represented in the ranks of the profession, but we also find a very general feeling of respect and friendship existing among those who entertain the most opposite views. Yet we are still engaged in discussing and rediscussing the questions that were discussed & rediscussed by other teachers before we were born. The experience of the past indicates that these discussions & controversies may continue . . . to the end of time *without settlement* unless some new element can be introduced into the problem.

And he concluded that they should collaborate to gather the facts from which the theories would emerge as a matter of course. This spirit of tolerance and objectivity continued for a further eighteen months. At the four-yearly American Convention of Instructors of the Deaf in the summer of 1886, attended by advocates from all factions and shades of opinion, it was unanimously resolved that:

> earnest and persistent endeavors should be made in every school for the deaf to teach every pupil to speak and read from the lips, and that such effort should only be abandoned when it is plainly evident that the measure of success attainable is so small as not to justify the necessary amount of labor.

In spite of this laudable resolution, however, the numbers of pupils taught the oral method declined during the following year. Alarmed at this retrograde trend, Alec wrote passionately to Gallaudet:

> I wish you could realize, as I do, how important even imperfect articulation is to a deaf person. I have daily – hourly – experience of its value in my own home, and my heart bleeds for the speaking young men at the College who

are placed under deaf teachers with deaf companions . . . It is the boast of
the advocates of the Combined Method that [it] *includes all methods*; and yet
the National College . . . excludes from its curriculum the subjects of
speech & speech-reading – while the majority of its graduates are semi-
mutes! Take away . . . this undoubted reproach . . . Excuse my warmth of
utterance. I can only write as I feel.[2]

Having got that off his chest, Alec probably felt much better, but it only
polarised opinion. Gallaudet and Bell kept their own counsels, in public at
least, but their respective supporters felt no constraints. The Gallaudet
faction viciously attacked Alec in the press, denouncing his opinions as
'ranting' or 'the vaporings of an idle brain'. This campaign of vilification
continued for several years. Alec professed to be unmoved by these attacks.
In 1891 he wrote to Mabel: 'I suppose I have grown callous and thick-
skinned . . . I cannot realize that I am the person attacked, but look upon
myself somehow as a third person.'[3] And he shrugged off this continual
sniping as 'evidence of victory . . . You don't throw mud until your
ammunition has given out'. But although he professed cool detachment,
the jibes wounded him deeply, and when someone rushed to his defence
in the public press, or wrote him a sympathetic letter, he was greatly
moved.

The showdown came in 1889 when Alec travelled to Britain to give
evidence before the Royal Commission on the Condition and Education
of the Deaf and Blind. Gallaudet himself had gone to London two years
earlier to give his testimony in favour of the Combined Method, and Alec
was originally allocated a single day in order to rebut Gallaudet's statement.
Alec, with all his debating skills as finely honed as ever, created such a
dramatic impression before the hearing that he was invited to return the
following day in order to answer some of the supplementary questions
which had arisen as a result. In the end, his testimony spread over four days,
during which he coped successfully with over six hundred questions,
carefully elucidating abstruse technical points. Ever the superb
communicator, he had his audience in the palm of his hand. Even when
some of the questions were biased or unsympathetic, he fielded them
confidently and with unfailing good humour. It was a remarkable *tour de
force* and his printed evidence is regarded to this day as the most
comprehensive statement of his philosophy, aims and ideals regarding the
education of the deaf. Afterwards, and at his own expense, Alec had the
transcript of the hearing printed for dissemination in libraries and
institutions. In so doing, he wrote to Gallaudet for permission to
incorporate his testimony in the interests of balance and fairness, adding,
'Honest controversy never hurts truth, and that is what we are after – both

of us – I am sure'. Gallaudet responded nobly; giving his permission he wrote back, 'We *are* seeking to arrive at the *truth* & to use a little current slang I think we shall both get there ultimately.'

Up to this point, despite the antics of their partisans, Gallaudet and Bell had behaved towards each other in a gentlemanly manner. But in January 1891 Gallaudet applied to Congress for an appropriation of $5,000 in order to set up a teacher-training school at the College. Alec is supposed to have viewed this proposal tolerantly when it was first mooted a few months previously, but by the time Gallaudet's bill was before the House, Alec had come out in fierce opposition. In his evidence before the Royal Commission three years earlier he had expressed himself firmly against a special training school for teachers of the deaf on the grounds that it would 'tend to the perpetuation of some one method'. What he meant was that such a school would tend to favour Gallaudet's Combined Method or worse. If the trainee teachers were, as he suspected, deaf themselves, they would inevitably teach their future pupils by the sign methods, and so the clock would be turned back. Articulation would have no room in such a scheme. Gallaudet tried to defuse Alec's opposition by assuring him privately that no deaf students would be admitted to the training school, but Alec thought that such a promise was worthless.

Inevitably the ensuing controversy turned nasty. When Alec testified before the Congressional committee that the Gallaudet bill would lead to the deaf teaching the deaf, Gallaudet took this to mean that Bell was accusing him of lying, or at least of making false promises. This goaded him into joining in the public bitterness. Before an audience of deaf students in Minnesota, he declared emphatically:

> Bell was not satisfied with the muddle he had already made by meddling in affairs that did not concern him, and wrote letters to all the schools and institutions in the country, that were so worded as to misguide those not informed, and also contained several untruths, that were untruths to his knowledge.[4]

In his reminiscences recorded in 1923, Charles Thompson recalled how one of Alec's friends had suggested that he invite certain congressmen to dinner in order to win them over. Alec reacted to this violently. 'If the facts presented to these gentlemen do not convince them of the merits of this case, they can go to blazes!' he cried, thumping his fist on the table. Lobbying congressmen over a good meal, then as now, was accepted practice, but Alec shrank from anything that did not come up to his own uncompromisingly high standard of ethics. Gallaudet's attacks on his probity hurt him deeply; subsequently Gallaudet backed down, and privately admitted that he had gone too far, but he never recanted publicly. In the end the matter was settled by a compromise, and Alec supported Gallaudet's bid for an increased funding, specifically for the appointment of articulation teachers at the College. Gallaudet then established his Normal Department anyway, committing it to the Combined Method; but as a result of the rumpus raised by Alec he took care to bring in articulation instructors and to refrain from admitting deaf students to that department.

It was not in Alec's nature to harbour grudges or resentment and, bowing to pressure from mutual friends, he quickly patched up the squabble with his acerbic opponent. In response, Gallaudet invited Alec to attend the 1893 commencement exercises. On the face of it, everything seemed peace and goodwill again, but privately Gallaudet confided to his diary, 'The hatchet is buried, but I know where it is.'

Alec's firmly held views about integrating deaf and non-deaf children outside the realms of special instruction were reinforced by the experience of the little school which he had established in Greenock. In June 1881, T. Jones wrote from Greenock saying that 'the plan of holding classes in the regular school building where the pupils would associate with hearing children [outside classes] . . . is accomplishing all you had hoped for it.' In May 1882, during the European trip that followed little Edward's death, Alec had paid a visit to Greenock and inspected progress at the deaf school, reporting that evening to a large audience that 'A little day-school like this one is to my mind the ideal.' His comment that it was much cheaper than supporting pupils at a boarding-school drew appreciative applause.[5]

Alec returned to America brimming with enthusiasm for the similar school which he hoped to establish in Washington. It opened on 1 October 1883 and after a few days in temporary accommodation it moved into a small brick building on Scott Circle which he had leased. The little house was old, but it had the merit of extensive lawns where the children could play. The running costs were cannily covered by sub-letting the ground floor of the building to a kindergarten; this served a double purpose, for it allowed Alec's pupils to mingle with hearing children at playtime. The upper floor was occupied by the deaf school. There was an open-plan classroom, almost a century ahead of its time; instead of the grim regimentation of desks and benches common at that time, a low table was the focal point, round which the children gathered in a relaxed, informal manner. Pictures and ornaments, games, toys and books were scattered around, and there was a large bay window overlooking the lawn and the street; everything was designed to stimulate the senses of sight and touch on which the pupils relied for their contact with the world.

To begin with Alec had six pupils, the day-to-day instruction being in the capable hands of Gertrude Hitz, daughter of the Swiss consul general,

John D. Hitz. Alec and Gertrude devised 'whiteboards' – panels with a ground-glass surface on which brightly coloured pictures and letters could be affixed, alongside writing in a charcoal pencil. Later Gertrude devised 'a museum full of common things', each tagged with its name in Visible Speech and standard English. Before the month was up, Dr Bell's Experimental School had been inspected by a reporter from the *Washington Star* who wrote a very sympathetic and favourable article. Within six months Gertrude could report to a convention of articulation teachers that speech was gradually taking over from word cards in conversation, lessons and games. Alec also established a class for parents, friends and other interested parties so that the school routine could be augmented outside school hours. This also served to disseminate information on Alec's teaching methods and articulation theories.

Just when the little school was achieving tangible results, however, Gertrude left to get married, and her successor, a Miss Littlefield, lasted only a few months. These were serious blows; Alec had hoped to secure a permanent teacher who would grow with experience, but instead he was forced to shoulder more and more of the daily burden himself. As he said himself, he 'sacrificed every occupation that could interfere with . . . devoting all my time and all my thoughts to my school'. The *coup de grâce* was administered by the Pan-Electric conspirators; preparing for the coming litigation in the Government case now left Alec little time for his school. In desperation he recruited a couple of mothers and a young teacher with no training or experience in working with the deaf. Inevitably this measure proved inadequate, and with the greatest reluctance he was forced to close the school at the end of November 1885.

Alec was devastated by this failure, telling Mabel that he felt as if his whole life had been shipwrecked. Pathetically, he asked her to accompany him to Boston on the Government case 'to keep him from an accident' – the nearest he ever came to admitting to suicidal tendencies – and for a while he clung to her, feeling 'as if I am all he has left', as Mabel noted in her diary. She now began to feel guilty about the school's failure, as she had nagged him about its high cost relative to the paltry return from pupils' fees and the kindergarten rent, and had later drawn his attention to the ineptitude of his stop-gap teachers. Afterwards she blamed herself for the school's closure. Not long after Alec's death, Mabel confessed to the writer Fred DeLand that she was 'always sorry' about it. All the evidence suggests that the decision was Alec's and his alone and, given all the circumstances, unavoidable. Two years later he assuaged his sense of failure by renaming his Volta Laboratory the Volta Bureau. The change of name signalled a shift of emphasis from science and invention to 'the increase and diffusion of knowledge relating to the deaf'. The work of the Bureau belongs more properly to the next chapter, as it tackled the problem of deafness from the standpoint of possible hereditary links and used statistical and genealogical methods for this purpose.

Gallaudet's jibe that Alec was meddling in affairs that did not concern him stung him but did not surprise him. Gallaudet, for so long *the* pillar of the establishment where deaf matters were concerned, did not consider his younger adversary as a *bona fide* teacher of the deaf, and eventually, in 1895, he would succeed in excluding Alec from membership of the American Convention of Instructors of the Deaf. Long before then, however, Alec could see which way the wind was blowing, and resolved to form a break-away movement. Late in 1883 he had come to the conclusion that there should be a national society for the promotion of articulation, with the aim of establishing day-schools for the deaf, a long-cherished ambition. By January 1884, however, he modified his aims, concentrating on the spread of the articulation method and abandoning his plans for day-schools because most teachers were firmly opposed to them at the time. For the moment, he was content to proceed carefully, but as an interim measure he planned to organise an articulation section at the next Convention in 1886. At that Convention he was pleasantly surprised by a well-nigh unanimous resolution in favour of speech training, and so he decided to put the proposed articulation section on hold for the time being, in order not to spoil the new mood of amity that prevailed. In the intervening four years good relations between Gallaudet and Bell and their respective factions deteriorated. When the Convention met in August 1890 the articulation section emerged, fully-fledged, but on the very next day (when this was met with an unfavourable reaction) Alec announced that he was setting up an entirely new organisation, the American Association for the Promotion of the Teaching of Speech to the Deaf. Gallaudet, during the period when the gloves were off, once reduced a deaf audience to helpless laughter by writing this jaw-breaking title on a long blackboard, accompanied by flourishes and pirouettes. The AAPTSD was incorporated under the laws of New York State in September 1890, funded by an endowment of $25,000 provided by Alec.

The association which Alec founded amid the rancour of the traditionalists would occupy a very large part of his time and energies throughout the rest of his life. Ever afterwards he would remain true to the principle of promoting the teaching of speech, but he was entirely pragmatic as to how this goal should be achieved. Far from adopting any narrow, doctrinaire stance, he advocated the use of *all* methods – oral, manual or some combination of the two. Thus teachers of the sign methods were welcomed so long as they expressed an interest in teaching speech. Over the years, the association broadened its aims to embrace everyone and anyone interested in the subject, whether they were teachers or not. During his personal involvement over a period of thirty-two years, Alec was punctilious about giving all shades of opinion and all methods of teaching a fair hearing, although he himself never wavered in his conviction that oralism was the best. And he demonstrated his flexibility and adaptability when he abandoned his long-cherished ambition for day-schools, on the grounds that such a campaign would dissipate the association's resources or divide its members. It reached a stage where Alec steadfastly blocked an official association commitment to day-schools, and as a result of this *volte face* some of his most ardent partisans resigned in disgust. Alec, however, had a much broader picture in view, hoping that by a policy of moderation he would some day effect a rapprochement with Gallaudet and his allies.

As president, Alec launched the association in fine style, with a ten-day convention at Lake George, upstate New York, in July 1891. Sweetness and light, hope and harmony were the keynotes of the lively meetings at which Gardiner Hubbard was one of the outstanding personalities. A hundred and fifty teachers, social workers and administrators from over twenty schools and institutions took part in the proceedings. On the third day Alec wrote enthusiastically to Mabel: 'It is a glorious success . . . I feel that a great work has been inaugurated here.' She herself attended on the last two or three days. The convention at Lake George the following July attracted an even larger attendance. In July 1893, the convention was held in Chicago to coincide with the Columbian Exposition and, with all the distractions of that prestigious world fair, it was decided to confine meetings to social affairs. In 1894, and at five other summer meetings held at intervals between 1896 and 1912, instruction in the oral method and other aspects of speech were resumed. One of the highlights of the 1894 meeting, in fact, was a paper contributed by Mabel herself entitled 'The Subtle Art of Speech-Reading', described by Fred DeLand as 'brilliant and absorbing . . . so far ahead of the time that it may still be read today as a modern and authentic exposition of speech-reading'.[6] When the association was compelled, through a shortage of funds, to abandon annual conventions, a forum for the exchange of information and opinion was provided in the shape of the *Association Review*, later renamed the *Volta Review*, after Alec presented his Volta Bureau to the association in 1909. The 1912 convention was the last to provide formal courses of instruction in Alec's lifetime.

When the association's journal was renamed, Alec appointed a new editor, Frederick K. Noyes, whose first responsibility was to increase it from five to twelve issues a year. To achieve this, he took on as assistant his lanky red-headed Yale classmate, Sinclair Lewis, but after six months on fifteen dollars a week Lewis left to become a reporter in New York, before going on to better things as a novelist and winner of the Nobel Prize for literature. Noyes himself moved on in 1912, having only managed to raise the magazine's circulation to a thousand a month. Casting around for a successor, Alec hit upon Fred DeLand, an amateur writer who had caught his eye with an article entitled 'Pioneer Telephone Exchanges' in 1905. DeLand, then in his fifties, was treasurer of several telephone companies and an ardent student of early telephone history. At that time Alec had written to him to compliment him on the 'accuracy and range of know-ledge displayed . . . concerning my work'. Thus encouraged, DeLand went on to write a book *Dumb No Longer*, describing Alec's work for the deaf. On 31 January 1912 Alec wrote to Harriet Rogers, full of wonderment at this man, whom he had never met, but who 'seems to know more about me and what I have done than I know myself'. When Alec learned that DeLand was recovering from a nervous breakdown and was out of work, he approached him and offered him the editorial post on a temporary, stopgap basis. DeLand came to Washington and after a spell as interim editor became librarian of the Volta Bureau. In 1914 he became permanent editor, serving in that role till 1920, and as superintendent of the Bureau till 1921. Once he found his feet, he achieved the seemingly impossible task of making the magazine appeal to the general reader as well as the professional.

In the earlier years, at any rate, the Bell–Hubbard clan was well to the fore at the association's annual conventions, Alec's parents also taking part. Inevitably Alec, with his worldwide celebrity and majestic appearance, dominated the proceedings, although he tried to play this down. Indeed, when the war with the Gallaudet faction was at its height, Alec deliberately took a back seat, and in July 1893 he handed over the presidency to Philip Gillet. This was a diplomatic manoeuvre, as Gillet was a confirmed advocate of the Combined Method. This conciliatory gesture was not lost on Gallaudet who heartily approved of the appointment, although inevitably some of Gallaudet's supporters denounced Gillet as a traitor. During Gillet's presidency, the AAPTSD and Gallaudet's Convention put out feelers towards each other, with a view to amalgamation, but the negotiations broke down in 1895, neither side willing to concede to the other. When Gillet resigned the presidency in 1899 on grounds of ill health, Alec took over for a second term. By 1904, when he demitted office, membership of the association had more than doubled. He continued his ardent support of the association right up to the day he died, and over the intervening period he campaigned continually on its behalf, and contributed at least a further $25,000 to its funds. Proof of its efficacy lies in the fact that in 1890, when the association was formed, fewer than

40 per cent of all deaf pupils were being taught speech. By the time of Alec's death, thirty-two years later, the proportion had risen to over 80 per cent, and in the ensuing period it would rise to almost 90 per cent, only those pupils who failed to make headway in speech falling back on the sign method. Moreover, Alec lived long enough to see the word 'dumb' removed by federal law from the titles of all schools and institutions for the deaf. Today the American Association is by far the largest organisation in the world dedicated to the training of the deaf to speak and lip-read.

When the proposal to merge the two bodies broke down in 1895 there was a resurgence of bitterness and recrimination. Gallaudet then wrote to a supporter, 'It seems a great undertaking to do up Professor Bell, but I think it must be done.' At the convention's meeting in Flint, Michigan, in July, Gallaudet gave a lengthy paper raking over the ancient squabbles, particularly Bell's opposition to his Normal Department, the merger failure and some petty bickering that had arisen at Chicago two years earlier over the nomenclature of methods and the control of an exhibit at the Exposition. In summing up, Gallaudet denounced his adversary as 'an unprofessional, narrow-minded, despotic propagandist and intriguer for pure oralism'. Gallaudet considered that he had been relatively mild in his reproof (Alec not being present to defend himself), but his partisans took the hint and declared 'war to the knife'. Alec dismissed this ranting, concluding charitably that his opponent was suffering 'monomania against myself'. Alec eventually prevailed in his bid to get a hearing at the convention and, without yielding to the temptation to lash out at his enemy's persecution complex, he simply refuted Gallaudet's interpretation of his motives and policies and deplored the spirit of strife which had developed among workers in the common cause. 'He spoke as if inspired,' wrote Sarah Fuller. 'Not a word of retaliation, not a thought of anything but entire truth . . . He lifted the entire audience into a broader, better, clearer atmosphere.' Alec's statesmanship eventually defused the situation, even though Gallaudet was re-elected president of the convention and retained that office until his death twenty-two years later.

While Alec was prepared to adopt a conciliatory approach to Gallaudet, Mabel was outraged at his treatment of her husband, and wrote to him, formally severing their social ties. Gallaudet responded with a dignified, contrite note, accepting her decision with regret, affirming his regard for her and her husband, and denying that his Flint speech had been intended as a personal attack. Characteristically, it was Alec who made the first move to heal the breach. In August 1900 he invited Gallaudet to join him in support for better treatment of the deaf in the decennial census, and the following day Gallaudet attended a Literary Society meeting at the Bells' home. 'I hope the hatchet is finally buried now,' wrote Gallaudet in his diary.

A month later both men attended a world congress on deafness, staged as part of the Exposition Universelle in Paris. Something of their old friendly rivalry emerged at a meeting when Gallaudet urged the adoption of his Combined Method in Europe. Alec admitted to Mabel that he had 'a high old time' exposing the flaws and defects in this proposal. This time, however, Gallaudet was unruffled. At a luncheon for delegates Alec made a speech in English and asked Gallaudet to render it for him in French. 'He seems to be an orator in French as well as in English,' wrote Alec approvingly. 'I must do him the justice to say that his translation was admirable and bettered the original.' The peace was well and truly sealed on 4 July 1903, when Gallaudet wrote to Alec concerning the exhibits for the education and welfare of the deaf at the forthcoming St Louis World's Fair: 'If any partisan feeling has existed anywhere, I trust it may pass away.'

Over the years, therefore, Alec learned to moderate his views and retreat from an extreme stance. This was also evident in his attitude towards schools. Having abandoned his original dream of a nationwide network of day-schools, he fell back on the notion of day-schools as complementing, not replacing, boarding-schools. In fact, he was on very good terms with most of the boarding establishments, especially those that were well disposed towards speech training. He was assiduous at visiting oral classes, readily giving advice when requested and helping with administration, recruitment and staffing. In 1898 he was elected to the Clarke School Board of Corporators, in succession to his late father-in-law. Three years later, he even prevented the closure of the Wisconsin state boarding-school when this was advocated by one of his own partisans in the day-school cause. Alec came to the view, however, that there were many positive aspects to day-schools which the boarding system could not match. In particular, the child attending a day-school would be compelled to exercise his or her speech skills, no matter how defective, in getting along with hearing children and family members in the domestic environment. Playing with brothers and sisters was the most powerful incentive to persevere with lip-reading and speech. To Alec, the ideal solution would be small day classes, with a high teacher-pupil ratio, which would be more cost-effective than boarding-schools.

What was working well at Greenock would eventually be exported to America where it came to be known as the Wisconsin system, because that state was the first to embrace it. Prime mover was Robert C. Spencer, a Milwaukee businessman whom Alec later extolled as the man who had done more to promote the teaching of speech to the deaf than anyone else in the country. In 1884 the National Education Association held its annual convention at Madison, Wisconsin, and Alec was favourably impressed by Spencer who had, some five years previously, led the campaign to organise a state society for speech training. In February 1885 Alec returned to Madison and spent two weeks testifying before state committees, drafting reports and writing an impassioned plea to the state legislature. Even Gardiner Hubbard had to concede that, when it came to persuading politicians to his way of thinking, Alec had a golden tongue indeed. As a result, Spencer's bill was passed and, under his supervision, became the model for other states to emulate. Generous state subsidies enabled day-schools to open in Milwaukee and other Wisconsin cities. Alec toured the state in 1895 and again the following year, with a gruelling schedule that included giving numerous public lectures and demonstrations, as well as visiting all the deaf schools and inspecting their teaching methods closely. Spencer proved to be a veritable impresario, much to the disquiet of Alec who grumbled to Mabel about his 'distribution, before my face, to all these audiences of pamphlets containing my picture and commendatory notices of myself that make me feel like a Dime Museum freak'.[7] By 1900 Wisconsin had fifteen day-schools for the deaf and Alec had concluded that 'the Wisconsin system is the most important movement of the century for the benefit of the deaf'.

Over the last three decades of his life Alec campaigned indefatigably on behalf of the education and welfare of the deaf in the broadest sense. To this end, he visited every state of the union and every province in Canada, as well as many countries in Europe and latterly other parts of the world, minutely examining teaching methods and practice. Above all, he enjoyed visiting schools and seeing the children at work and play. To the youngsters, this huge, bluff figure with the long snowy beard must have seemed like Santa Claus in plain clothes. On one such occasion Alec wrote from Providence, Rhode Island, to Mabel, telling her how he played up to this fanciful notion:

> I accepted the situation and described in graphic terms my driving over the tops of the houses. Pandemonium reigned for a time, and the children were much puzzled to know how so big a body could come down so small a chimney. I taught them the word 'squeeze' so that they will never forget it!!! I'm afraid that half of the school will write to me before Christmas and I shall have to visit the school in appropriate costume![8]

He gave freely of his time, advising and encouraging, writing letters and articles, making speeches and giving public lectures. As a propagandist and communicator he was without equal; no cause was ever so ardently championed or so well served. Despite the private reservations of some in the Gallaudet camp, Alec was scrupulous in avoiding bias. His support was glady granted to any campaign regardless of his personal preferences, and latterly he was just as ready to do battle for a deaf school using the Combined Method as he was for a speech-training school. Furthermore, he refused to obtrude his own views unless invited to do so by legislative committees and other responsible bodies.

Early in his career Alec had recognised the value of gaining the co-operation of the parents of deaf children, and he fully appreciated the help which he had received from the Sanders and Hubbard families which extended far beyond the bounds of their children's deafness. When that indomitable old campaigner, Sarah Fuller, approached him in 1894 to help organise a permanent body for the parents of the deaf, he came at once to Boston. The following year the Boston Parents' Education Association for Deaf Children was chartered 'to bring together parents and teachers having a common interest in the pupils'. The Boston Association formed the model for similar bodies in other cities across the United States. It was uphill work, especially in the early years, and the organisers had to fight against the apathy, ignorance and even hostility of parents, especially from the working classes. Nevertheless, within four years, fifteen associations had been formed and were already proving invaluable in the struggle through the state legislatures to secure better conditions and understanding for the deaf.

One project which was particularly dear to Alec's heart was the day-school movement in Chicago. He lent his weight to the campaign of the local parents' association which culminated in 1899 when state aid was granted for day-schools and the unpopular superintendent of the state institution was replaced by an abler and more sympathetic man. When the city erected a splendid school to accommodate deaf and hearing children in separate classrooms but bringing them together at playtime, according to the scheme advocated by Alec four decades earlier, the institution was named the Alexander Graham Bell School. By that time many awards and honours had come his way, but Alec prized this one above all the others.

In 1037 John of Beverley was canonised largely because, as Bishop of Hexham 350 years earlier, he had made a deaf man speak. This miracle was as nothing compared with the feat of Annie Sullivan in immeasurably improving the lot of people who had the double misfortune of being both deaf and blind. Although he was on the periphery of this work, Alec played a not inconsiderable role in it. His earliest encounter with the blind-deaf came in February 1876 when he attended the memorial service for Samuel Gridley Howe, late head of the Perkins Institution for the Blind in Boston, and was introduced to little Laura Bridgman, the school's most celebrated pupil. At the age of two, Laura had been stricken by illness which robbed her of her senses – smell, taste, sight and sound. Consigned to the institution as a human vegetable, she had at least the consolation of a remarkable teacher in Samuel Gridley Howe who managed to strike a responsive chord in the girl's heart. At the memorial service for her dead teacher, little Laura cried aloud, and her anguished cries struck deep in Alec's heart. It was an experience he never forgot.

Eleven years later, he was approached by Captain Arthur Keller, a former Confederate officer turned newspaper proprietor in Tuscumbia, Alabama. Like Laura, Keller's daughter Helen had been struck down by severe illness at nineteen months which left her without her sight or hearing. Shortly before her seventh birthday her father brought her to Washington to meet Dr Bell. Alec was immediately struck by the lively child, obviously excited by the novelty of the journey and stretching out her hands to feel and touch the objects around her. He could not help contrasting the eagerness in her sightless face with the sadness of her father. Years later Helen herself would recall that first meeting. She had sat on the great man's knee and felt his watch strike. Above all she had experienced a great feeling of his tenderness and sympathy and she loved him for it: 'But I did not dream that that interview would be the door through which I should pass from darkness into light.'[9]

At Alec's suggestion, Captain Keller got in touch with Michael Anagnos, the director of the Perkins Institution. Anagnos was already aware of this case, having been approached by a friend of the Keller family who was then a student at the Lawrence Scientific School in Cambridge. It seems that Helen's mother had read of the Perkins Institution and the strange case of Laura Bridgman in Charles Dickens's *American Notes*. Anagnos himself alerted one of his most promising graduates to the possibility that she might be able to help. Annie M. Sullivan was then aged twenty, scarred by four years' incarceration in the poorhouse of Tewkesbury, Massachusetts, and partially sighted as a result of trachoma in early childhood. Whatever her physical handicaps (she would eventually become totally blind), Annie was an exceptionally gifted young lady, above average in intelligence and possessed of the rare qualities that made her a born teacher. She was just the person to take the little blind-deaf girl in hand. On 3 March 1887 – Alec's fortieth birthday – Annie arrived at Tuscumbia. Helen would later celebrate that date as her 'soul's birthday'.

From the outset Alec took a keen interest in Helen's development. Not content with giving advice to her parents, he kept in close touch with both Helen and Annie, who were to be numbered among his dearest friends. Credit for working the miracle, of course, lies with the remarkable Annie Sullivan, but there were times when she despaired of making any progress, and it was then that Alec was always ready with a kind word and unobtrusive help in many forms.

When Annie settled in at the Keller home in Tuscumbia, she was confronted with an unruly, fractious child, given to irrational and frightening tantrums, the rage of frustration and futility. On 20 March 1887, however, Annie wrote to Alec: 'A miracle has happened, the wild little creature of two weeks ago has been transformed into a gentle child.' On 5 April came the historic breakthrough to Helen's understanding that things had names, and by July the little girl was beginning to write the letters of the alphabet. In 1888 Alec was deeply touched to receive a letter which Helen herself had written. 'Dear Mr Bell,' it said simply in large, childish lettering, 'I do love you.' Later he furnished a photograph of her and one of her letters to a New York newspaper and overnight Helen became a national celebrity. Alec was quick to perceive that locked inside that sightless head was a sharp intelligence. 'Through her,' he wrote in 1891, '[the public] may perhaps be led to take an interest in the more general subject of the Education of the Deaf.'

Not surprisingly, the press hailed Helen's progress as a miracle; Mark Twain, no less, lauded Annie as 'the miracle worker'. More soberly, Alec regarded Annie's achievement as a brilliantly successful experiment. 'It is . . . a question of instruction we have to consider, and not a case of supernatural acquirement.' On 7 May 1890 he had a long interview with Helen herself in order to quantify this acquirement and quizzed Annie for explanations, especially of Helen's quite extraordinary command of colloquial English. He discovered that the key lay in Annie's constant spelling of natural, idiomatic English into Helen's hand without pausing to explain unfamiliar words and constructions, and in encouraging Helen to read books in Braille or raised type, relying on the same method to explain any new words and phrases as they occurred. This, in fact, closely followed the way in which all children effortlessly pick up language as they develop.

At the association's meeting in July 1891, Alec gave each delegate a handsomely bound *Helen Keller Souvenir*, a compilation of essays by Annie Sullivan, Sarah Fuller (who had recently given Helen her first speech lesson) and others, which he had edited. At Alec's expense Annie and Helen attended the 1893 meeting in Chicago. Helen experienced the Columbian Exposition through the hands of Annie and Dr Bell, a highlight being a visit to the stand where Alec had replicated his Centennial Exposition display of the telephone in 1876. At the association meeting teachers of the deaf had ample opportunity to observe the lively teenager at close quarters. The following year Annie Sullivan submitted a paper giving a vivid, yet objectively factual, account of her work and the relationship which had developed between her and her famous pupil. In 1896 Helen herself addressed the association: 'If you knew all the joy I feel in being able to speak to you today, I think you would have some idea of the value of speech to the deaf . . . One can never consent to creep when one feels an impulse to soar.'

Annie Sullivan, who achieved so much with her gifted pupil, put matters in their true perspective when she wrote:

> It was an immense advantage for one of my temper, impatience and antagonisms to know Dr Bell intimately over a long period of time. Gifted with a voice that itself suggested genius, he spoke the English language with a purity and charm which have never been surpassed by anyone I have heard speak. I listened to every word fascinated . . . I never felt at ease with anyone until I met him. I was extremely conscious of my crudeness . . . Dr Bell had a happy way of making people feel pleased with themselves. He had a remarkable faculty of bringing out the best that was in them. After a conversation with him I felt released, important, communicative. All the pent-up resentment within me went out . . . I learned more from him than from anyone else. He imparted knowledge with a beautiful courtesy that made one proud to sit at his feet and learn. He answered every question in the cold, clear light of reason . . . with no trace of animus against individuals, nations, or classes. If he wished to criticize, and he often did, he began by pointing out something good I had done in another direction.[10]

And Helen herself never forgot the great debt she owed Alec. On 5 July 1918, she wrote to him:

> Even before my teacher came, you held out a warm hand to me in the dark . . . You followed step by step my teacher's efforts . . . When others doubted, it was you who heartened us . . . You have always shown a father's joy in my successes and a father's tenderness when things have not gone right.

It is small wonder that Elsie and Daisy sometimes felt twinges of jealousy at their father's feelings for Helen. On more than one occasion in the ensuing years things had not gone right for Helen, but Alec was always there to give her that helping hand. In 1891 Helen wrote a short story entitled 'The Frost King' as a birthday tribute to Michael Anagnos. He subsequently had it published, and was immensely embarrassed when it was exposed as a piece of plagiarism. In fact, it closely resembled in story line and language a fairy tale published in the early 1870s. Annie had never come across it, nor was it to be found in any of Helen's books, but eventually it transpired that the story had been read to Helen at the home of a friend while Annie was away, some three years previously. Incredibly, the board of governors of the Perkins Institution ('a collection of decayed human turnips' is how Mark Twain savagely described them) interrogated the bewildered and frightened child at great length, denying her the moral support of her teacher who was sent out of the room. Eventually this portentous body came to the conclusion that Helen had unwittingly called up the story from her remarkable memory rather than from her imagination as she had supposed. This inquisition had a traumatic effect on the eleven-year-old; for many months she could not bear to handle a book, let alone read one, and it shattered her growing self-confidence for years, despite the fact that Margaret Canby, the author of the fairy tale, recorded that Helen's story was no plagiarism but 'a wonderful feat of memory and an improvement on the source'. To Annie she added, 'Please give her my warm love, and tell her not to feel troubled over it any more.' Mark Twain was more trenchant: 'To think of those solemn donkeys breaking a little child's heart with their ignorant damned rubbish about plagiarism! I couldn't sleep for blaspheming about it last night.' Characteristically, Alec regarded this distressing incident with scientific objectivity. Having helped Annie to track down the Canby original, he observed, 'We all do what Helen did; our most original compositions are composed exclusively of expressions derived from others.' He added that Anagnos had 'failed to grasp the importance of the Frost King incident . . . A full investigation will throw light on the manner in which Helen has acquired her marvellous knowledge of language – and do much good.'[11] Fortunately, Helen got over the experience and between 1902 and 1938 would write six books which reflected her indomitable spirit. The first of these was her autobiography entitled *The Story of My Life* which she dedicated to Alexander Graham Bell, 'Who has taught the deaf to speak and enabled the listening ear to hear speech from the Atlantic to the Rockies.'

Helen later got tuition at the Horace Mann School in Boston, under Sarah Fuller, and at the Wright-Humason Oral School in New York, not only learning to read, write and talk but also becoming exceptionally proficient in the normal school curriculum. Eventually she would acquire a mastery of several European languages, as well as a broad, cultural education. Up to 1894 her education had been at special schools, but she confided to Alec that she had a 'strong desire' to go to an ordinary school with non-handicapped classmates. Alec considered this carefully before giving his backing. He told Captain Keller that Helen would need some kind of interpreter, but he undertook to rally Helen's friends and admirers to underwrite the outlay of such an experiment. In due course Helen was enrolled at the Cambridge School, and Annie came along too, in her role as interpreter and companion. Helen was an extremely diligent student, determined to outshine her classmates, so much so that the headmaster, Arthur Gilman, felt that she was overdoing her studies to the detriment of her health. Gilman regarded Annie as a Svengali-type figure and tried to separate Helen from her beloved companion. When he turned to Alec to aid and abet him in this wrong-headed decision, Alec prevaricated. When Annie, on the other hand, approached him, he acted immediately, sending his friend John Hitz to look into the problem. Subsequently Alec wrote to Gilman saying that nothing could justify parting Helen from Annie, except evidence that Annie was in some way unfit for her charge. As to that, his conversation with Helen had revealed her to be 'a living testimonial to the character of Miss Sullivan'. Helen's mother came from Tuscumbia to Boston to check the matter for herself. Finding her daughter in excellent health and determined to stay with Annie, she agreed with Hitz and Alec that Gilman was wrong. No attempt was ever made to part them after that. In 1900, when Helen was about to enter Radcliffe College, a well-meaning friend tried to dissuade her, saying that she could put her talents to better use by running a school for deaf-blind children. Once again, Alec intervened in no uncertain terms and this idea was nipped in the bud. Helen went to Radcliffe and in 1904 graduated summa cum laude.

In the summer of 1901, at the end of her first session at college, Helen came to Beinn Bhreagh. One of her most treasured memories in later years was the night she spent on the houseboat with Elsie and Daisy, and their midnight swim on the moonlit lake. In the meadow overlooking the lake, Alec introduced her to his latest passion, kite-flying, and told her of his great dream of giving mankind wings. One breezy afternoon she helped him fly his kites:

> On one of them I noticed that the strings were of wire, and having had some experience in bead work, I said I thought they would break. Dr Bell said 'No!' with great confidence, and the kite was sent up. It began to pull and tug, and lo, the wires broke, and off went the great red dragon, and poor Dr Bell stood looking forlornly after it. After that he asked me if the strings were all right and changed them at once when I answered in the negative. Altogether we had great fun.[12]

Over the years Alec showed Helen many little acts of generosity and kindness. Typical was the $194 which he slipped her in 1905 so that she could surprise Annie with a wedding gift when she married the writer John Macy. When Captain Keller died in 1896 Alec sent Helen $400. These were modest sums compared with the money contributed by Helen's friends and admirers who were more affluent than Alec was and not so involved in other good causes. But what he gave her was invaluable. Her biographer and friend, Van Wyck Brooks, put it succinctly when he wrote: 'More than anyone else, during those early years, it was Alexander Graham Bell who gave Helen her first conception of the progress of mankind'.[13]

In a letter of 5 July 1918 Helen asked Alec if he would consider playing himself in a film that was about to be made of her life. He was then seventy-one, in poor health, even more reluctant than ever to leave Beinn Bhreagh in summertime, and quite averse to appearing in a moving picture; but he was touched by her letter and replied two weeks later saying that 'It brings back recollections of the little girl I met in Washington so long ago.' But, he added, 'You will have to find someone with dark hair to impersonate the Alexander Graham Bell of your childhood.' Against his inclinations, however, he agreed to appear with her in one of the later scenes, if shooting could be delayed till the hot summer weather was past. He was immensely relieved when he was not summoned in the end, which was perhaps just as well as the film was a fiasco, both as drama and historical record.[14]

14

Heredity and Eugenics

When Nature has work to be done, she creates a genius to do it.
Ralph Waldo Emerson, *Method of Nature*

The third of the Alexander Bells to make a name for himself in the realm of speech, Alec was always conscious of the abilities which had come to him from his distinguished father and grandfather. How much he knew about his ancestry is debatable, as speculation on more distant forebears is nowhere to be found in his voluminous notes or correspondence. He would surely have been aware of Bailie Bell and his interests in the printed word. He might have been startled to discover that there was a distinct possibility that he and Thomas Alva Edison may have been distantly related, for the seventeenth- and eighteenth-century parish registers of St Andrews are liberally sprinkled with Adiesons, Edisones, Eddysons, Eadisons, Edesons and Edisons, several of whom intermarried with Bells.[1]

The publication of *The Descent of Man* by Charles Darwin in 1871 caused a furore on both sides of the Atlantic. Alec was an immediate convert, an issue on which he crossed swords with his parents who held firmly to what they read in the Bible. This kindled Alec's interest in heredity, though it was not until his return from Britain late in 1878 that he turned seriously to this subject when the Massachusetts State Board of Health recruited him to help gather statistics on inherited defects, so that the laws of inheritance might be better understood. Armed with a bundle of questionnaires and stamped addressed envelopes, Alec painstakingly wrote off to the superintendents of asylums and institutions across the country, seeking data on the deaf, and he regularly appealed for information in the *American Annals of the Deaf*. The response, however, appears to have been sporadic and meagre, and consequently the annual reports of the state board in the three successive years were silent on Professor Bell's findings. Alec was not in any way discouraged, and quietly over the ensuing years continued to collect data on the deaf, especially in regard to their marriages and the resultant offspring. In particular he collated material supplied from the Hartford and Illinois institutions about their former pupils. In the midst of this, the United States government's decennial census of 1880 was much more detailed than before, and got together a panel of experts to evaluate the various reports arising from its findings. From the report on 'Defective, Dependent and Delinquent Classes' Alec extracted sufficient additional data to produce a paper for the National Academy of Sciences in November 1883, entitled 'Memoir upon the Formation of a Deaf Variety of the Human Race'.

In England, Francis Galton had been inspired by his cousin's thought-provoking *Origin of Species* (1859) to study anthropology and apply his Gradgrindian obsession with statistics to this subject. Galton's prodigious labours in heredity and the application of statistics to human attributes led to a remarkable series of publications including *English Men of Science* (1874) in which he carefully analysed the backgrounds and pedigrees of leading scientists, *Inquiries into Human Faculty* (1883) and *Record of Family Faculties* (1884) which laid the foundations for the science of eugenics, a term which Galton coined in 1883. In later years he was to become heavily involved in the study of fingerprints and anthropometry, but returned again and again to eugenics and heredity in such seminal works as *Noteworthy Families* (1906), and finally collected his essays on the subject three years later. The thrust of Galton's philosophy was that the productivity (that is the birth-rate) of the 'fit' should be promoted and encouraged. By the same token, the productivity of the 'unfit' should be restricted, by prohibition of marriage and, if that did not work, then by compulsory sterilisation. The downside of Galton's theories, taken to their grimly logical conclusion, would see half of the states in the Union enacting compulsory sterilisation programmes for the mentally defective, not to mention the deadly ruthlessness of the 'solution' to the problem in Nazi Germany. Along the way, eugenics would statistically proclaim the superiority of the white races and the inferiority of the black, and use the intelligence quotient to 'prove' the superiority of the upper and middle classes and the inferiority of the working classes. For these reasons eugenics has been largely discredited nowadays, but around the turn of the century it was taken very seriously and, indeed, earned Galton the knighthood conferred on him by Queen Victoria in 1900.

Galton's American counterpart was Richard Dugdale who published in 1875 the most influential work on heredity, a detailed study of the Jukes family which had produced a staggering array of mental defectives, alcoholics, degenerates, no-hopers and outright criminals over several generations. It was Dugdale's frightening conclusions, more than Galton's more objective analyses, that influenced the hereditarian thinking in the United States over the ensuing sixty years and provoked the desperate response of sterilisation that reverberates even to the present day. Few of the 'unfit' characteristics itemised by Dugdale could be measured objectively or classed as congenital; rather it could be argued that the depraved environment of the Jukes family was largely to blame. Nevertheless, thinking men (including Alec Bell) saw enough in Dugdale's revelations to realise that there might be some correlation between heredity and certain mental and physical defects.

Dugdale would be no more than the springboard to Alec's studies of congenital deafness. While this handicap was usually worse than the deafness arising from illness (because the victims in many cases had learned to speak before the onset of the illness), Alec quickly recognised that there were different degrees of congenital deafness. Because it was less obvious than other inherited defects, deafness did not attract the same stigma as other handicaps and was therefore less likely to be glossed over in family tradition. Moreover, because the need for special schooling had been recognised since the beginning of the nineteenth century, if not earlier, records were available that would help him to pinpoint actual cases of congenital deafness. This, then, was the burden of Alec's paper to the National Academy. While at pains to point out that he needed more data to complete his research, he came to the conclusion that deaf parents had a much higher proportion of deaf children than did the population as a whole. Of 2,262 congenital deaf-mutes in his study, 54.5 per cent had deaf relatives. Marriage records indicated that, unlike those with other defects, the deaf strongly tended to marry other deaf people. From this, Alec argued that deafness could be inherited and that it tended to propagate itself, hence the rather startling title of his paper. Alec shrank back from advocating prohibition of marriage for the congenitally deaf, merely recommending that they should be warned of the risks beforehand. When he encountered George Sanders at his grandmother's funeral in 1890 he was taken aback to discover that George had fallen in love with a deaf girl in whose family congenital deafness went back at least four generations. He tried to warn Lucy Swett that if she married George, she was shortening the odds in favour of having deaf children. Lucy argued that George would probably marry a deaf girl anyway, and she would rather be that one. To Mabel Alec confided rhetorically, 'Will lovers ever consider the good of those that will come after them?' George and Lucy married the following year and after Thomas Sanders lost his fortune Alec continued to take an avuncular interest in the young couple.

Alec, typically, urged that the most humane solution to the problem of the congenitally deaf would be to broaden the scope of their lives, through speech-training and day-schools where they could mingle with their hearing peers. Out of friendships in the wider world would come mixed marriages. His paper also included the sentence: 'If we could apply selection to the human race we could produce modifications or variations of men', which shows that he arrived independently at the same conclusion as Galton in his *Inquiries into Human Faculty* published about the same time.

At this juncture Alec did not attempt to work out precise laws of inheritance for deafness. Abbot Johann Gregor Mendel had carried out experiments in the gardens of his monastery and established the dominant and recessive characteristics of the culinary pea. In 1866 he published his theories which would lay the foundations for the science of genetics, but they excited little or no attention from the scientific world at the time. Mendel, in fact, died in obscurity in the very year that Alec's first work on heredity was published. International recognition of Mendel's pioneering work did not come until 1913, when his papers were translated into English; but a decade earlier Mendelian genetics were independently rediscovered, and revolutionised thinking. Back in the 1880s, however, Alec had nothing precise to go on, beyond a vague notion that congenital deafness had an alarming tendency to recur generation after generation in the same family. Even worse was his discovery that hearing persons in a family prone to deafness could transmit the defect to their children. All he could emphasise at that stage was the vital necessity of encouraging the deaf to marry into hearing families where the odds of recurring deafness would be diminished. This sounds uncannily like the Mendelian theory of dominant and recessive characteristics, though Alec could not have known anything of the abbot's research at the time.

Unfortunately, the title of Alec's paper boomeranged on him; by appearing to overdramatise the problem he was not taken as seriously as he should have been. Furthermore, it antagonised many of the deaf, the very people he sought to help. The situation was aggravated when irresponsible journalists took the title out of context and claimed that Professor Bell was demanding that the deaf should not be allowed to marry. Even worse, this damaging allegation was perpetuated in such influential periodicals as the *Deaf-Mutes Journal* and *American Annals of the Deaf*, and it was not until 1887 that Alec got the opportunity to set the record straight, when he gave a lecture before the Literary Society of the National College for Deaf-Mutes. Even so, the canard persisted for many years thereafter.

When Alec gave his 1887 lecture he had the assistance of Edward A. Fay, professor of languages at the College and editor of *American Annals of the Deaf*. Not only did he translate Alec's speech into sign language for the benefit of the audience, but he published it in order to correct the earlier misunderstanding. The following year a periodical dealing with charities began gathering data on marriages of the deaf and in 1889 passed this material over to Fay. In this rather casual manner he embarked on what was to be the greatest work of his life. He compiled a detailed questionnaire which elicited a very good response. Alec repaid the favour by handing over all his own data and provided much-needed cash to fund the research and pay the wages of assistants, although Fay himself undertook the task on a purely voluntary, unpaid basis. Over the ensuing six years an enormous amount of data was amassed and analysed. In the end Alec also paid for the publication in 1895 of Fay's findings in *An Enquiry Concerning the Results of Marriages of the Deaf in America*. This detailed work was based on records of 4,471 marriages in which one or both partners were deaf, and it reinforced Alec's findings of 1883.

While there was little evidence of congenital deafness in the offspring of hearing parents, almost 30 per cent of the children of congenital deaf-mutes were themselves deaf. The proportion was even higher in cases where one or both parents had deaf relatives. Conversely, even when both parent were congenitally deaf, their children ran much less risk (4 per cent) of deafness if neither had deaf relatives. Consanguinity of parents was a potent factor, considerably increasing the probability of deafness in children, even without deaf relatives. Fay also concluded that the deaf were just as likely to marry other deaf people, regardless of the type of schooling they had had. Sympathy and shared problems tended to bring them together, no matter whether they had attended day-schools or boarding-schools or had received speech-training. As the question of marriage was only one of the factors governing Alec's advocacy of day-schools and speech-training, Fay's findings did not alter his views on those subjects.

It is no exaggeration to say that Alec's paper of 1883, together with Fay's expansion of 1895, represents the 'soundest and most useful study of human heredity produced in nineteenth-century America. By that token it may also be reasonably counted Bell's most notable contribution to basic science, as distinct from invention.'[2]

Alec was not content to leave it at that. Soon after the publication of his 1883 paper he began to follow it up with a detailed study of deafness as it recurred in several generations of certain families. The parishes of New England had registers going back to the early seventeenth century in some cases, and this material proved to be a goldmine for his research. For example, he was able to follow the Lovejoy family from 1644 onwards and analyse the pattern of deafness found in its members almost two hundred and fifty years later. On Martha's Vineyard he found Squibnocket, an isolated community in which a quarter of the population was deaf, and on the same island he chanced upon an amateur genealogist with thousands of files, one for each old Vineyard family, which enabled Alec to trace the communal deafness back to a common seventeenth-century ancestor. As this work assumed greater importance, Alec hired Annie E. Pratt, a trained genealogist with the same zeal for the chase. On 22 May 1887 he wrote to Mabel with the news that a ninety-six-year-old Lovejoy had been located and that 'Mrs Pratt is to start off at once to the boundaries of Maine and New Brunswick to interview the old lady while there is yet time'. In Halifax, Nova Scotia, Alec tracked down yet another branch of the Lovejoy family. Annie Pratt subsequently carried out research for Alec's monumental history of speech-training in America, which he published serially in the *Association Review* between 1900 and 1904.

As Alec's trawl through the voluminous family records of New England progressed, he hired John D. Hitz, the father of Gertrude who had taught in Alec's deaf school. Recently retired as Swiss consul general, this gentle patriarchal figure would act as librarian and researcher until his death twenty-two years later. 'No one is better fitted to help me and encourage me in this work than yourself,' wrote Alec on 15 October 1888. 'There is labor enough in this work to afford you employment for a long time to come.' Through his association with Alec, Hitz came to know Helen Keller and Annie Sullivan and corresponded with them both far more fully than Alec ever did. Installed in a room on the upper floor of the Volta Laboratory, he sorted, classified and filed an enormous amount of vital statistics, parish records, census cards, genealogies, local and family histories, deaf school reports, books, manuals, reports, treatises and long runs of the relevant periodicals on deafness and genealogy. In 1887 it was Hitz who suggested that this part of the Bell enterprise be named the Volta Bureau; Alec readily agreed, and bestowed on Hitz the title of superintendent. The trust fund was renamed the Volta Bureau Fund and earmarked for the Bureau's support, apart from the $25,000 apportioned to the AAPTSD in 1890.

Melville and Eliza Bell had until now taken little interest in what went on in the converted stable at the back of their house, but family history was a subject that intrigued them both and thereafter they took a very active role in the Bureau, helping Hitz to gather, sort and file the papers that flooded in from all quarters. Inevitably the mass of paper soon overflowed into Melville's house and Alec was faced with the urgency of erecting a new building adequate to the purpose. Melville (who possessed more of the qualities of showmanship than his son) argued in favour of something really impressive that would be worthy of the Bureau's name and aim, and when Alec demurred Melville put $15,000 of his own money into the enterprise. In the spring of 1893, on a site across the street from their house, the elder Bells looked on with satisfaction while twelve-year-old Helen Keller turned the first sod. By the end of the year a splendid building in the neoclassical tradition was erected, with a façade of yellow brick and sandstone and a flight of stone steps leading up to a portal framed by massive columns. Over the ensuing fifteen years the Volta Bureau grew in stature and reputation. By the time Hitz died in 1908 it ranked as one of the world's leading centres of information on all aspects of deafness, a position reinforced following its merger with the AAPTSD at the end of that year.

A major find, and one that had impelled Alec to hire John Hitz, was the original census forms of the federal government, all the way back to 1790 when the decennial census of the United States commenced. In 1886 Alec discovered this vast quantity of paper, occupying more than a thousand volumes but scattered and disarrayed, strewn over the floor of a dusty cellar in the basement of the Patent Office. Alec persuaded the Secretary of the Interior to have these priceless documents properly arranged and stored. Over the ensuing three years he pored over the musty volumes and extracted a considerable amount of genealogical data from them. It seems that no one had ever considered such a use for them; indeed, they had several times come perilously close to being scrapped. In 1889 Alec brought the existence of this archive to the attention of the Massachusetts Historical Society which, in turn, spread the word to other societies. Alec campaigned vigorously against various motions before Congress to junk all census records as soon as they had been tabulated. He argued cogently that the published tables used only a proportion of the raw data collected, and he predicted that scientific and other learned bodies would, in future generations, deplore such vandalism. When a motion to destroy the census records came before the House of Representatives in May 1895 Alec lodged a formal protest saying that:

> The schedules for 1900 will be as interesting to the students of history in 2000 as those of 1800 are to students at the present day . . . When new questions are raised, and an answer to them is sought, it will be necessary to go over the former records again, in order to secure the proper basis for comparison.[3]

Alec's argument won the day and the records were saved for posterity. For over a century, therefore, they have been the basis for genealogical research in the United States; but without the persistent interest of Alec Bell they might have disappeared long ago.

Alec's involvement with the census records led to him being consulted in the framing of the section of the questionnaire dealing with mental and physical defects in general, and deafness in particular. The census of 1880 had been couched in terms which either produced imprecise answers or provoked the antagonism and hostility of the person being questioned. In December 1888, at the request of a Senate committee, Alec submitted forty-two specific suggestions for making the 1890 census of the deaf more accurate and useful. In particular, he railed unsuccessfully against the proposal to put 'the Insane, Feeble-Minded, Deaf and Dumb, and Blind' together willy-nilly in a single report, although this was mitigated when Edward Fay was appointed as special agent in charge of that category, the first time it had been entrusted to a recognised expert on the deaf. Alec assisted Fay in working out the precise details of the relevant section of the census forms. After the 1890 census he salvaged the supplementary records which were about to be consigned as waste paper, and had them safely lodged in the Volta Bureau Library.

Throughout the 1890s Alec systematically worked on the annual reports of the deaf schools, supplemented by occasional questionnaires. As the 1900 census approached, he was offered the task which had been assigned to Fay a decade earlier, and he gladly accepted. This time he succeeded in getting Congress to entitle the report 'The Blind and the Deaf'. Preparing for the 1900 census was one thing; processing all the relevant data arising from it would take up a considerable amount of Alec's time over the ensuing six years, so much so that he grew to loathe it. 'The question of Census versus Laboratory is ever before me. I hate this census with a personal hatred,' he wrote to Mabel on 13 November 1904, and she in turn wrote to Gilbert Grosvenor a month previously, 'I feel it is taking from Father time and strength he cannot spare.' Alec turned down the invitation to work on the 1910 census, and as a result the task was assigned to someone who had no expertise in deafness. Alec's conscience was pricked when the relevant report appeared in 1915: 'a perfect fizzle, not at all comparable to any former census' is how he described it to Fred DeLand.[4]

Alec's inventiveness was put to good use in the run-up to the 1890 census, when he devised a machine that would sort punch-coded census cards, 'based upon the principle of turning the cards around an axis by the motion of a rod in a slot punched out of the card at different angles', as he described it in a letter to Mabel on 16 December 1889. This was nothing new, for Charles Babbage, the father of computers, had designed an 'analytical engine' using punched cards as far back as 1854. Babbage's machine, however, was never completed but it appears to have inspired Herman Hollerith whose electrically operated tabulating machine was invented in 1890. Alec never patented his device, and when Hollerith's machine was adopted by the Census Bureau to process the data collected in 1890 he accepted it philosophically: 'it seems to be an ingenious and practical method', he noted in December 1890. 'I do not propose to push my own method.' Ten years later Alec examined a Hollerith machine in the

Census Bureau and worked out a method of counting electrically 'without the necessity of sorting the cards', which was based on his earlier research into an automatic telephone switchboard. Alec dubbed his system 'combinatorial branching' and, in fact, it anticipated the binary system at the heart of modern computer science. Had he persevered with this idea one wonders whether he might well have revolutionised the world far more than he did with the telephone; but tantalisingly his notes at this point concluded with the words 'Have no more time to make fresh notes' and the following day, 27 December 1900, he went off at a tangent with his project to distil fresh water from sea fog.

Somewhere in Darwin's writings Alec had stumbled across a report that blue-eyed cats were prone to deafness. In 1884 he sent a note to *Science* recording the fact that he had so far come across three blue-eyed cats and, yes, they were indeed quite deaf. Alec kept a male and a female cat for several years in the hope of breeding from them but no kittens ever materialised. After he acquired Beinn Bhreagh, however, Alec's interest in animal heredity was rekindled by Thomas Sanders who bred horses and sheep on his Vermont farm and seems to have encouraged Alec to try his hand at stockbreeding. In 1889 Alec procured a number of Merino sheep from Vermont and was intrigued, in the following lambing season, to find that half the births in his little flock were twins. At that time twin-births in sheep were unusual. When Alec examined the twin-bearing ewes and discovered that a high proportion of them had more than two nipples, he was certain that he had stumbled across an important genetic phenomenon. Years later he would wish that he had stuck to the blue-eyed cats.

The abnormally endowed ewes had only a vestigial third nipple, but this was sufficient to encourage Alec in his attempts to develop a strain of ewe in which the third nipple would produce milk and in which twin-births would become the norm rather than the rare exception. With visions of vastly increasing lamb and wool productivity, Alec set to work with his customary zeal. In an undated Sunday letter of the early 1890s Mabel commented to her mother: 'He has thrown himself into these breeding experiments with all his characteristic interest and absorption and thoroughness of detail.' Every sheep was numbered, given a coded ear punch and weighed regularly, every detail of its life and pedigree being meticulously tabulated. On top of Beinn Bhreagh there sprang up a veritable village of sheep pens of his own scientific design, which Alec whimsically dubbed 'Sheepville'. Here were the octagonal sheep barn, the precisely measured sheep runs, the freeze-free watering troughs of his own invention and the instruments which he produced for testing wool strength and extracting the lanolin. The sheep became Alec's ruling passion for several years – a passion not shared by his wife and daughters whom he often nagged into accompanying him on his daily inspection of Sheepville. During this prolonged period Alec's life revolved around his precious flock, ensuring that he would be at Beinn Bhreagh for the lambing season. On one occasion he even broke off a European tour to rush back to Beinn Bhreagh for this crucial event, before recrossing the Atlantic and continuing with his tour. Although he employed shepherds, Alec felt that he could not trust them to give the flock the loving attention he lavished on it. And he was right; for on one occasion most of the flock perished in a blizzard when the shepherd neglected to get them into their pens overnight, and on another many of the sheep were savaged by wild dogs.

Alec's dogged perseverance paid off, to the extent that he eventually developed a strain of ewes with at least four milk-producing nipples; but by 1904 he was forced to admit to the National Academy of Sciences that 'the multi-nippled sheep have not proved to be more fertile than normally nippled sheep; and the proportion of twins born has been quite small'. Far from giving up, though, he was determined to concentrate on the twin-bearing characteristic and research along these lines would continue a further decade. In 1915 he gave the best of the flock to a young farmer (who disposed of them five years later), and sold the rest by auction. Next day Alec discovered that Mabel had, surprisingly, acquired them, through a proxy bidder, and proposed to continue the experiments, with or without his help. In the sheep barn that morning, as he contemplated Mrs Bell's new flock, he was overheard to say furiously, 'I thought I was THROUGH with those damn sheep!'[5] True or apocryphal, Alec on reflection seems to have been rather pleased that the all-consuming hobby of the past quarter-century was still around, and in fact he continued with undiminished zest his search for the holy grail of a multi-nippled flock that would be a 'true twin-bearing stock'. That, at least, was his firm belief to his dying day. After his death, Alec's copious notes and records were sent to the Harvard geneticist William E. Castle and he concluded that the extra nipples had indeed become strongly hereditary in the flock, though it was unclear whether this had any bearing on increased milk yield or a propensity to bear twins. The University of New Hampshire's agricultural experimental station took a ram and thirteen ewes from the flock and carried on Alec's breeding experiments until 1941, after which the US Department of Agriculture continued them till 1944 before disposing of the flock. In its final report, the Department reluctantly concluded that 'the multi-nipple character has no practical value in sheep production'.

Alec's work with sheep may not have been as fruitful as he had hoped, but it brought him membership of the American Breeders' Association, established in 1903 by university biologists and geneticists. This, in turn, led him into the eugenics movement which was gathering momentum at that time. Twenty years earlier, his paper suggesting that the human race might be modified by conscious selection put him in the very forefront of eugenics. Now he was drawn into the eugenics movement which was launched in England in 1901 by the octogenarian Galton who, in his old age, had concocted a philosophy that was a hodge-podge of racism, élitism, Darwinism, Mendelism and social reform. Six years later the American Breeders' Association, taking due cognisance of the spread of this philosophy, established a Committee on Eugenics 'to investigate and report on heredity in the human race and to emphasize the value of superior blood and the menace to society of inferior blood'. Some sixth sense must have warned Alec, for he turned down the chairmanship of this august body; instead this post went to David Starr Jordan, chancellor of Stanford University and an eminent biologist, but he served on the committee alongside such distinguished scientists as Luther Burbank and Charles Henderson. Alec, along with Jordan and Henderson, was re-appointed in 1909, and served as chairman of the sub-committee on hereditary deafness.

In the autumn of 1903 Gilbert Grosvenor contacted David Fairchild, a botanist with the Department of Agriculture, who had recently returned from a trip to the Persian Gulf on behalf of the Office of Seed and Plant Introduction. Fairchild's distinguished reputation had gone before him, and Grosvenor thought he might make an ideal lecturer for the forthcoming season of the National Geographic Society. He was surprised, on meeting him, to find that Fairchild was not the elderly greybeard he had imagined, but a boyish figure in his early thirties. Alec attended Fairchild's lecture and afterwards invited him to one of his Wednesday evening dinners. Fairchild was bowled over by the older man's 'vigor and kindliness' and many years later he would recall feeling 'immediately at ease, as one does with any really great and simple character'.[6] Late in November 1904 Elsie Grosvenor invited Fairchild to dinner, where he sat next to her sister Daisy, recently returned from studying art under the great Norwegian-American sculptor, Gutzon Borglum. Daisy and David saw a great deal of each other that winter; and in the following spring Daisy would drive him round the countryside in her electric car at a sedate twelve miles an hour. Late in April that year they got married and lived with Alec and Mabel until their house was completed in 1906, on a forty-acre woodland site in Maryland. Their first-born, on 17 August 1906, was aptly christened Alexander Graham Bell Fairchild. Grown to manhood, he too would be an eminent figure, like his father and his grandfather and his Bell forefathers, thus underscoring Alec's beliefs in heredity, although Sandy, as he was generally known, would make his mark in entomology.

In 1913 David Fairchild was elected president of the American Breeders' Association, and Alec collaborated with him in drafting the articles of incorporation of the society which was shortly afterwards renamed the American Genetic Association. In subsequent years Alec was an enthusiastic supporter of its *Journal of Heredity*, to which he contributed a number of papers on sheep-breeding and eugenics. The word, coined by Galton from the Greek meaning 'well-born', has since acquired a pejorative ring as mentioned earlier, due to its links to the murderous Nazi programme of the 1930s which aimed at wiping out the retarded and anti-social and ended up with the extermination of six million Jews. It has to be admitted that Alec, along with everyone else interested in eugenics at the turn of the century, believed that different ethnic groups had different levels of intelligence and ability. But while he subscribed to the general view of the superiority of the Anglo-Saxon peoples – tall, blond and blue-eyed – he himself was the living embodiment of a much older Celtic race: tall, long-headed, fair-skinned yet black-haired.

Within the first decade of the twentieth century, racism had permeated the eugenics movement on both sides of the Atlantic. In America it often manifested itself in calls for severe restriction on immigration, at a time when Ellis Island was operating at full capacity processing 'the huddled masses yearning to breathe free'. Alec's published work on eugenics made only vague and casual references to restriction on immigration on ethnic grounds, and then only in so far as he felt that it was desirable to make careful, objective studies before any groups were presumed to be undesirable on grounds of heredity. At a time when many self-styled eugenists were clamouring for the exclusion of Italians, Slavs and Jews and the restriction of black Americans, Alec showed himself totally free of racial bias. Among the close friends whom he admired and respected the most may be numbered Guglielmo Marconi, the hydrofoil designer Enrico Forlanini and the educational reformer Maria Montessori, which gives the lie to any suggestion of a bias against Italians. As for anti-semitism, Alec could number among his closest friends and associates the German Jew Emile Berliner and the Polish Jew Albert Michelson. As for negrophobia, the most vicious aspect of American racism, no one could ever accuse Alec of that. On his third day in the United States he had commented sarcastically on the white American prejudice against intermarriage, and throughout his life had been an outspoken champion of black social and political equality. Charles Thompson had ample evidence of his employer's colour-blindness, recalling the time in 1904 when a Halifax hotel refused him admittance because of his race; he had never seen Alec in such a towering fury as a result. Travel broadened his mind even further. Alec's interest in eugenics was solely for the benefit of the human race as a whole. By 1915, however, he was becoming decidedly uneasy about 'our eugenic cranks', and he strongly condemned any proposal to interfere with the marriage of 'undesirables', which he considered impractical anyway. Eugenics, for him, remained simply a science which might some day lead to the development of a healthier and more intelligent human race.

Latterly his researches in this field concentrated mainly on the question of longevity and whether this was an inherited trait. To this end, in 1914, he established the Genealogical Office of the Volta Bureau for 'the collection and preservation of genealogical records pertaining to long life'. Here the obituary columns of the newspapers were carefully studied and data extrapolated. Alec himself made a detailed study of the Hyde family of Connecticut from the seventeenth century onwards and published his findings in a pamphlet in 1918. Longevity, he concluded, was not heritable in itself, but probably related to some heritable qualities of vigour or resistance to disease.

His own family provided ample evidence of this, from his nonagenarian great-grandfather Andrew Colvill onwards. Grandfather Alexander Bell had lived to seventy-five and Melville reached the ripe old age of eighty-six. Alec's mother Eliza lived to eighty-seven, but, almost ten years older than Melville, she predeceased him, dying on 5 January 1897 in her Georgetown home. Three years earlier, she and Melville had celebrated their golden wedding in fine style, and in 1896 Gertrude and Gardiner Hubbard reached their jubilee also. Twelve months after Eliza's death, Melville, then seventy-nine, married a fifty-four-year-old widow, Harriet Shibley, whom he had arranged to meet after seeing her photograph in the home of an Ontario friend. It was a happy match and Melville, despite his years, had all the vigour of a man half his age right to the end of his life, with all his faculties intact. Gardiner Hubbard also died at the age of seventy-five, and Mabel's mother might have lived very much longer than her eighty-two years had she not been fatally injured in the spring of 1909 when her chauffeur-driven vehicle collided with a streetcar.

In March 1897, two months after his mother's death, Alec reached a milestone of his own. At fifty, he was possessed of the same full mane of white hair and long, bushy white beard as his father. A photograph taken shortly after the birth of Elsie's son, Melville Bell Grosvenor, on 27 November 1901, shows the young mother and infant with Alec and his father alongside. The two men could have been brothers, although twenty-eight years separated them.

15

Conquest of the Air

They shall mount up with wings as eagles
Isaiah, xxxviii, 31

Since early boyhood, when he had watched the gulls wheeling and soaring over Corstorphine Hill, Alec Bell had been fascinated by flight. The gulls at Covesea and the aerobatic rooks at Pluscarden twenty years later had rekindled this fascination and for a time Alec's head was filled with flying machines. From time to time thereafter he would return to the subject and record his thoughts and sketches in his notebooks, but it was not until 1891 that he took up aviation really seriously. Over the ensuing quarter of a century it would be a recurring theme and ultimately his crowning obsession.

His interest was rekindled by Samuel Pierpoint Langley, himself one of the most remarkable scientists of nineteenth-century America. Born in 1834 of good Pilgrim stock, he went straight from Boston High School at the age of sixteen to Chicago where he practised as an architect and civil engineer. At the age of thirty he accompanied his brother to Europe where he travelled for a year and broadened his education. In 1865 he was appointed assistant at Harvard observatory and a year later became professor of mathematics at the US Naval Academy where he reorganised the observatory. At thirty-three, he was appointed director of the Allegheny observatory in Pennsylvania where he spent twenty fruitful years, building up an international reputation as an astronomer. In 1887 he left Allegheny to take up his appointment as secretary of the Smithsonian Institution in Washington. Here he would spent the remaining nineteen years of his life, continuing his astronomic researches as well as administering what was even then one of the world's most prestigious centres of learning.

Sun-spots and solar energy are what Langley is chiefly remembered for today, but he also played a fundamental part in the history of aeronautics.

He was, in fact, the first man to offer a clear explanation, backed by experiment, of the manner in which birds are able to soar without appreciable motion of their wings: birds, he reasoned, used the ordinary fluctuations of air currents to keep themselves aloft. It was as simple as that. From these observations in the Allegheny Mountains, Langley progressed to qualitative experiments with the lift and drag of a plane surface moving through the air at a measured speed. In Washington he built a long-armed, whirling table fitted with a recording dynamometer and in April 1891 gave a lecture at the National Academy of Sciences where he demonstrated this strange device. Alec was out of town at the time, but on 21 April Mabel wrote to him:

> I wish you were here if only to attend the National Academy meetings and to hear the discussion on Professor Langley's flying machines. Of course the papers treat him more respectfully than they would anyone else, still they cannot resist a sly joke now and again.

At Beinn Bhreagh by late May Alec had devised an aerial propeller and was testing its lifting capabilities. In mid-June, despite his aversion to the heat and humidity, he was back in Washington, impelled by his desire to meet Langley and discuss his flying machines. His pilgrimage was richly rewarded. 'Langley's flying machines flew for me today,' he reported excitedly to Mabel on 15 June. 'I shall have to make experiments upon my own account in Cape Breton. Can't keep out of it. It will be all UP with us someday!'

Alec's earliest practical experiments were with horizontally rotating propellers, anticipating the helicopters of a much later period, and included one spectacularly unsuccessful trial of a model with powerful steam jets mounted at the tips of the rotor blades. From 1892 till the end of 1897 he carried on more sustained and extensive experiments at Beinn Bhreagh, usually from May till late November or early December. Of course, many other ideas and activities crowded his busy schedule in that period but, unlike his experiments with fog distillation and even the automatic switchboard, flight riveted his attention for weeks on end. Even during that memorable second honeymoon in Mexico in the spring of 1895, Alec's head had been filled with aeronautics. During a train journey through the sierras he jotted down: 'Soaring buzzard's wings turned up at tip . . . surface air almost calm . . . moved in spiral . . . horizontal velocity not less than 30 feet per second.'

Perusing Alec's notebooks today, one cannot help smiling at some of his more jejeune ideas which ranged from springs to rockets as a means of propulsion, though here and there we find notions which would one day become practical. Although most of his early experiments were with helicopters, he also worked on the problems of a streamlined monoplane of startlingly modern appearance. Rockets misfired or blew up the model, while free-flying rotors did spectacular back-flips before plummeting earthwards. Alec was not deterred by these failures. 'The more I experiment,' he wrote in 1893, 'the more convinced I become that flying machines are practical.'

By the 1890s aeronautics had a long history. Balloons had been flown successfully since 1783 but until Parsifal and Zeppelin developed dirigibles at the end of the nineteenth century they had little practical application because they could not be accurately navigated. Heavier-than-air machines had exercised the minds of Leonardo da Vinci and Francis Bacon but after G.A. Borelli concluded that the strength of a man's muscles was insufficient to lift a machine into the air and keep it there, interest in the subject waned. It revived early in the nineteenth century, with the development of steam engines. Sir George Cayley, the father of British aeronautics, built a strange contraption in 1809 combining elements of the aeroplane and helicopter, before turning to balloons with manually operated propellers some years later. W.S. Henson's aerial steam carriage of 1842 was a monoplane with an enormous wingspan, but its 25 h.p. steam engine was not powerful enough to lift the machine off the ground. Steam engines were just too heavy in proportion to their power. Experimenters then turned to models, and six years later J. Stringfellow's aeroplane, a monoplane fitted with twin propellers, was the first to take to the air. Thomas Moy's aerial steamer of 1874, fitted with a tiny 3 h.p. engine, was the first powered aircraft to lift off, although it only managed a few inches before it sank to earth again. The most promising models of the period were those constructed by Alphonse Pénaud and propelled by a screw driven by the torsion of an indiarubber cord. To give this cord suitable length it was fitted to a rigid rod, emulating the fuselage of later aircraft, and to give this device stability he added what he called an automatic rudder but which was, in effect, a small horizontal wing serving as the tail unit. Pénaud's 1871 monoplane, in fact, bore a remarkable resemblance to the aircraft developed almost half a century later, and it is a mystery why the aviation pioneers did not persevere with this pattern. Instead, every inventor did his own thing, relying on flights of fantasy as much as the flights of birds. Not surprisingly, the men who tinkered with these devices, more weird than wonderful, were invariably dismissed by their contemporaries as madmen, cranks and dreamers.

Alec's preoccupation with helicopters stemmed from the experiments of Cayley whose arrangement of two windmills of gull feathers revolving about a vertical axis had actually flown some distance in 1796. These tiny models worked well enough and for a time Alec seriously considered marketing them commercially as toys, with the aim of funding serious research on full-sized helicopters. He was continually baffled by the problem of increasing the size until the machine was capable of carrying a man, but the ratio of weight to lift eluded him. During the 1890s he and Langley collaborated closely, the latter even travelling to Beinn Bhreagh in the summer months to compare notes. In May 1895 Langley, the mathematician, poured cold water on one of Alec's ideas and this temporarily crushed him. He must have communicated this to Mabel, then travelling in Europe with her daughters. From Paris on 28 May she wrote to him, 'If Mr Langley has changed your ideas, why then I can't see why you should not come over.' Alec, however, stayed put, and a month later Mabel was writing encouragingly, 'I do so want your name associated with successful experiments in flying-machines.'

Exactly a hundred years after Cayley's gull-feathered helicopter came the first real breakthrough when, on 9 May 1896, Langley succeeded in flying a steam-driven model from Quantico, Virginia, a distance of 4,200 feet across the River Potomac. This was a remarkable achievement at the time, although the sixteen-foot model was pilotless and had no means of controlling either take-off or landing. Alec, from a rowing-boat in midstream, witnessed the biplane catapulted into the air, and heard the roar of its little steam engine as it hurtled overhead. Three days later he wrote a jubilant letter to the editor of *Science*, likening the flight to that of 'an enormous bird, soaring in a great spiral to a height of a hundred feet, travelling half a mile, and then when the steam gave out, settling unhurt on the water as slowly and gracefully as . . . any bird'. A second trial was equally successful. Alec was now more convinced than ever that the day of manned flight by heavier-than-air machines was just around the corner. That day he penned a brief congratulatory note to Langley which, coming from the man who had invented the telephone, was praise indeed: 'I shall count this day as one of the most memorable of my life.'

For both men it was a case of back to the drawing board, but with renewed vigour and excitement. Lacking Langley's mathematical expertise, however, Alec found the routine of endless experiments and precise measurements very taxing. By October he had come to the conclusion 'that a great deal has yet to be learned concerning the best way to combine aero-planes or aero-curves – so as to gain the full benefit of the surfaces'. Significantly, it was during the same period that he turned increasingly to the problems of the automatic switchboard, almost as a form of light relief.

Charles Thompson has left a vignette that illumines the friendship and collaboration between the ebullient Scotsman and the shy, reserved bachelor scientist. Speaking of a summer at Beinn Bhreagh, when the two men cruised on Alec's houseboat, he described how:

> I have seen them sitting on deck under the awning for hours and hours, neither of them uttering a sound, but both of them eagerly watching the seagulls soaring about the boat. I remember one day Professor Langley said suddenly, in a raised voice, 'Isn't it maddening!' 'What's maddening?' said Mr Bell. 'The gulls!' said Professor Langley. 'I was thinking they were very beautiful,' Mr Bell replied. They both eyed each other for a moment and then laughed heartily. Professor Langley always appeared buoyed up in spirit when leaving after these summer visits.[1]

Alec warmly supported Langley in many other ways; not the least was by acting as his propagandist. Left to his own devices, Langley would have shrunk from publicity of any sort, but where Alec was often diffident about his own achievements he had no such qualms about singing the praises of his friend. The very first volume of *McClure's Magazine* (1893) contained a lengthy interview which Alec gave a reporter on the subject of flight:

> I have not the shadow of a doubt that the problem of aerial navigation will be solved within ten years. That means an entire revolution in the world's methods of transportation and of making war. I am able to speak with more authority on this subject from the fact of being actively associated with Professor Langley . . . in his researches and experiments.[2]

McClure's reporter found Alec's enthusiasm quite infectious. 'Professor Bell has the happy faculty of expressing great ideas in simple words,' he wrote, concluding perceptively, 'His black eyes flash, and they seem all the blacker contrasted with his white hair; the words tumble out quickly, and those who have the good fortune to listen are carried away by the magneticism of this great inventor.' Following Langley's experimental flights in May 1896, Alec told a reporter from a New York paper:

> The problem of the flying machine has been solved. Those who read this article are reading the fulfilment of a world-old dream . . . Fifteen years ago a man who had the temerity to deliver a serious lecture on the prospects of navigating the air would have ruined his professional reputation by the indiscretion. Now the much-derided 'cranks' are having their innings.[3]

Strangely enough, Alec's old friend Sir William Thomson, now Lord Kelvin, appeared less than enthusiastic about these flying experiments, when he met the Bells at Halifax during a tour of North America in 1897.

Mabel recorded that he was 'greyer than when I last saw him twenty years ago, but otherwise the same kindly, loveable, simple man'. Kelvin, talking to Alec, 'expressed regret that he was going into aeronautics. Alec took issue, and Lord Kelvin . . . drew him aside and plunged right into scientific talk right there in the midst of the crowd'. Mabel herself wrote to the great man the following day, defending her husband's involvement. After returning to Britain, Kelvin replied:

> I was quite sure that your husband would not go on in respect to flying machines otherwise than by careful and trustworthy experiment. Even if the result is to demonstrate to himself that a practical useful solution of the problem is not found . . . When I spoke to him on the subject at Halifax I wished to dissuade him from giving his valuable time and resources to attempts which I believed, and still believe, could only lead to disappointment, if carried on with any expectation of leading to a useful flying machine.[4]

On the face of it Lord Kelvin's negative attitude to aeronautical experiment seems out of character with the modest, self-effacing and kindly person that he was; but it was his very kindliness that impelled him to adopt this stance. He was undoubtedly motivated by the fact that, the year before his visit to Canada, he had been a horrified witness to the death of a young colleague at Glasgow University. Percy Pilcher, a lecturer in naval architecture, had been experimenting with man-carrying gliders, often hurling himself off the steep bank above the river from which Lord Kelvin took his title. Both Pilcher and the German Otto Lilienthal had been experimenting along similar lines, and both met their death in 1896 when their machines crashed out of control.

The day after Kelvin wrote to Mabel, the Spanish-American War had broken out, and by the time the letter reached its destination the American press was agog with the exploits of Admiral Sampson's North Atlantic squadron as it scoured the seas for the Spanish Armada, under Cervera, which had left Cape Verde and was intent on a showdown with the gringos in the Caribbean. When the Spanish battle fleet succeeded in eluding the American blockade and reached Santiago de Cuba on 19 May, the American public were roused to a frenzy. It was during this crucial early phase of the campaign that Alec gave serious thoughts to the use of aircraft for reconnaissance and bombardment when he wrote, 'I am not ambitious to be known as the inventor of a weapon of destruction, but I must say that the problem – simply as a problem – fascinates me, and I find my thoughts taking more and more a practical form.'[5]

Nothing that Lord Kelvin had said or written to him would deflect Alec from an ambition that now seemed within his grasp. As in so many of his earlier inventions and scientific speculations, however, he was now side-tracked. On the other side of the globe a young Australian named Laurence Hargrave was apparently achieving great results with combinations of box-kites. Out of this would evolve the double banks of aerofoils which provided the basis of the biplane. By June 1898, therefore, Alec was convinced that the solution to the problem of manned flight lay in the development of giant kites: 'The importance of kite-flying as a step to a practical flying machine grows upon me,' he wrote to Mabel. In the year that Langley achieved his first powered flights at Quantico, sixty-four-year-old Octave Chanute devised a quintuple kite. Later he would reduce the banks of wings to a triplane and then a biplane. The kite construction seemed to give a far greater degree of stability than monoplanes or rotating blades. Man-carrying box-kites had also attracted serious military attention in England where they would, for a time, eclipse balloons as a medium for aerial reconnaissance; but these devices were tethered to the ground and did not afford the free flight which Langley, Bell, Lilienthal, Chanute and others sought. By May 1899 Alec was reporting progress:

> The Laboratory Annex was so filled by the big kite that there was no room for experiment. Just fancy, a kite 14 feet 7 inches long by 10½ feet wide and 5 feet 2 inches high! A monster – a jumbo – a 'full-fledged white elephant' . . . I am no longer young, and the experiments on which I have been engaged for years should be completed sufficiently for publication, so that younger men can take up the thread of research . . . Don't take me any more away from my work until it is finished – or I am![6]

But a few days later he was confessing to his wife that he did not know how to proceed. By now it had dawned on him that the air drag in kites was such a fundamental problem that he was veering back to his original idea of helicopters. Perhaps wings should be eliminated and lift obtained simply by angling the propellers upwards. Alec was floundering; he would continue to dither between the helicopter and the kite for some time. Reflecting on his countless notes going back over many years, he began to doubt whether the problem of flight would ever be solved. Yet, as he had so confidently predicted in 1896, the solution was, indeed, just around the corner. His achievement, at this early stage in aeronautics, was to have buoyed up his friend Langley when he was assailed (as he frequently was) by self-doubt. And Langley, in turn, would inspire others. In 1898 two bicycle mechanics in Dayton, Ohio, named Wilbur and Orville Wright pored over all the available literature on kites and flying models. In due course they wrote to the Smithsonian Institution for advice, and Langley promptly responded by sending them copies of all his writings on the subject.

The jumbo-sized kite that Alec described to Mabel was a box-kite of the Hargrave pattern. Fortunately for Alec – and Baddeck – no hurricane of sufficient strength ever blew over that windswept area to lift this monster off the ground. Alec was still pondering the mystery why it was possible to get a small kite or a model aeroplane airborne, but when it came to a machine large enough to carry a man it remained stubbornly earthbound. Simon Newcomb provided an answer in the September 1901 issue of *McClure's Magazine*. In this he expostulated that if the scale of a working model were enlarged, the wing surface would increase only as a *square* of the linear dimension, whereas the volume, and hence the weight, would increase as the *cube*. This was untrue, as Alec quickly surmised, for it presupposed that every element of the aircraft would be increased proportionately in each dimension. Newcomb also erroneously assumed that there would be no change in design as the weight and speed of the aircraft were increased. Nevertheless, Alec had to concede that his old friend Simon had a valid point, even if he was less than happy with Newcomb's concluding jibe: 'No builder of air castles for the amusement and benefit of humanity could have failed to include a flying-machine among the productions of his imagination.'

Alec's solution to the problem was to build a number of relatively small box-kites connected by a rigid framework. Where the box-cells were joined, edge to edge, they shared the same piece of the framework where two had been required previously. Thus a multicelled kite actually weighed less in proportion to the area of its surfaces than did a separate cell. From this he progressed to considering the shape of the individual cell. In his notes for August 1899 he reflected, 'There is a good deal in equilateral forms. Quite independently of this – a triangle is *braced*.' Two years later he had developed this concept to the stage at which he was constructing kites that resembled a triangular prism rather than a box. The triangular open ends required no bracing, whereas the Hargrave boxes had to have diagonal braces and struts to prevent distortion; this added to their weight and wind resistance. Hitherto triangular kites had been dismissed as far less efficient than box-kites, but now their greatly reduced drag more than made up for their less effective conformation. In March 1902 Alec wrote a memo to himself: 'Avoid rectangular elements – let everything be built up of equilateral triangles.' A few days later he made tetrahedral cells out of folded paper and fitted them together to see what forms emerged, but thought no more about this casual experiment until 25 August when, at Beinn Bhreagh, he was suddenly conscious of a great discovery.

Earlier that day he had fashioned a 'triangular stick', trimmed into what he termed 'a perfect equilateral cone, each of the four faces constituting equilateral triangles'. Then he described it more accurately as:

> A figure composed of 4 equilateral triangles having 4 triangular faces
> bounded by 6 equal sides. Wish I could describe this solid form properly as
> I believe it will prove of importance not only in kite architecture – but in
> forming all sorts of skeleton frameworks for all sorts of constructing – a new
> method of architecture. May prove a substitute for arches – & bridge work
> generally.

He included a rough diagram, but added in frustration, 'Can't draw it'.
Then he indulged a flight of fancy:

> Whole structure so solid & so perfectly braced by its construction that it
> may be treated as a solid body. Only needs support at the three extremities
> of its base. Structures of this sort may be used in place of arches for bridges
> – ceilings of large buildings &c. It lends itself to metallic structure. All the
> parts can be made of metal – & made cheaply . . . It needs no solid core.
> Can we not try it by casting it in lead? Flat parts could be stamped out of
> sheet metal if desired.

And at the foot of the page he doodled a steam train chugging over a
bridge of this tetrahedral construction. Coming down to earth momen-
tarily, he concentrated on tetrahedral kites which combined simplicity,
strength and lightness with aerodynamic stability. By November Mabel was
becoming apprehensive: 'Alec continually more wrought up over his kite
experiments than I like.' That day he completed a large H-shaped kite
composed of tetrahedral cells and the following day he successfully tried it
out in a windswept meadow. A few weeks later he wrote a paper on the
subject and submitted it in April 1903 to the National Academy of
Sciences. By the autumn of that year he was confident that if he did not get
a motorised aircraft off the ground within the twelvemonth, someone else
would. He predicted as much in an interview which appeared in the *Boston
Herald* on 29 September, as well as features by Gilbert Grosvenor in the
New York Herald on 1 November, the November issue of *Popular Science
Monthly* and the *New York Tribune* of 26 November.

Alec's prediction was based not only on his own work, but on the
progress being made by Samuel Langley, who had been given a grant of
$50,000 from the War Department in 1898 to develop a man-carrying
aeroplane. Putting in $20,000 of his own cash, Langley hired a young
engineer named Charles M. Manly whose specific task was to design an
internal combustion engine light enough to power the aircraft. Manly
designed a five-cylinder, water-cooled, radial engine weighing 125 pounds
and developing 52 h.p. Before testing the full-scale engine in a man-
carrying aircraft, however, Manly succeeded in scaling it down to a quarter

of the size, and used it successfully to fly a model aircraft in August 1903. Langley, unduly sensitive to criticism and ridicule, alienated the press by trying to bar them from his trial flights. Consequently, when Manly eventually took to the air in the full-sized aircraft on 7 October 1903 – and promptly plunged into the water at the end of the launching platform – the farce was hooted with derision from the assembled pressmen, who promptly dubbed the aircraft 'Langley's Buzzard'. When the second attempt, on 8 December, ended even more spectacularly with the wings collapsing and the machine itself totally wrecked by the clumsy efforts of the recovery crew, the assembled journalists and photographers fell about in helpless laughter. The resultant newspaper ridicule broke Langley and hastened his death in March 1906. At his funeral, Alec delivered the eulogy, declaiming, 'His flying machine never had an opportunity of being fairly tried, but the man and his works will permanently endure.' Langley lived long enough, however, to see his dream come true and to be acknowledged on his death-bed as 'a pioneer of this important complex science'. Only nine days after the collapse of the Buzzard, the Wright brothers made their first powered, man-carrying flight at Kill Devil Hill near Kitty Hawk, North Carolina.

Wilbur and Orville Wright had succeeded with a modified form of a Chanute biplane glider, to which they had added an elevator or horizontal rudder for steering the machine in the vertical plane, and flexing the trailing edge of the main planes to vary the lift on either or both at will in order to maintain balance in the air. The first flight lasted only a few seconds, but by 1905 they had made forty-five flights – in the longest of which they remained in the air for half an hour and travelled a distance of twenty-five miles.

Meanwhile Alec was still hard at work. Far from giving up now that the Wright brothers had attained the long-cherished goal, Alec redoubled his efforts. Although they had beaten him to the draw, Alec was utterly without the chagrin and resentment which had embittered Elisha Gray over the telephone. Magnanimously he told a newspaper reporter, 'The impossible has come to pass in aerial navigation and I am proud of the fact that America leads the world in that matter. To the Wright brothers, of Ohio, belongs the credit.'[7] When the brothers came to Washington later that year they were pleasantly surprised by the genuine warmth of Alec's welcome.

The Wrights had merely proved that manned flight was possible; there remained a great deal of work to be done before flying could be regarded as reliable and safe. First of all Alec had to determine the optimum size of a tetrahedral cell, and after a great deal of trial and error with various sizes he settled on a ten-inch cell as the standard unit. A major advantage of a multicelled kite was that the centre of pressure on each small cell moved only a fraction of the cell's length as the angle of flight changed, and this gave Alec's flying machines a much greater degree of stability. The drawback about these massed cells was their enormous drag. Nevertheless, Alec concentrated on safety and stability, reasoning that more powerful engines would eventually be developed that would compensate for the loss of lifting power. By the end of 1904 he had devised a structure with a single multicelled wingspan and a short horizontal tail. When it took to the air it resembled a great soaring bird, so Alec named it the *Oionos*, the Greek bird of omen.

Through 1904 and 1905 Alec persevered with his multicelled system, buoyed up by the thought that the Wrights had not made any material improvement in their machine which was essentially a powered glider. By November 1905 he was ready to test-fly his latest creation, waiting only for a wind strong enough to get it airborne. When a gale struck Baddeck, however, it made the bay impassable and the local men could not get round to Beinn Bhreagh to assist with the launch. This freak of nature almost crushed Alec at a crucial moment when he had built his hopes on success. 'He looked gray when he came home,' noted Mabel, 'wrote a short note dismissing the staff and closing the laboratory, turned his face to the wall and never spoke again that day or night.' The storm eventually abated and Alec succeeded in gathering sufficient men for a successful test with a smaller model. The following month he assembled a giant model, made up of no fewer than thirteen hundred cells, and christened it the *Frost King*. Just after Christmas he photographed Neil McDermid, a burly local man, dangling precariously from the tethered machine at a height of about thirty feet in a mere ten-knot breeze. Later Alec reported to the National Academy of Sciences that he could build 'structures composed exclusively of tetrahedral winged cells that will support a man and an engine in a breeze of moderate velocity'.[8] At the same time, he was investigating and examining different types of small, light petrol-driven engines to determine which would be most suitable for his aircraft. His assistant, Hector McNeil, had now worked out a method of mass-producing tetrahedral cells and, according to Alec, was planning to start up a manufacturing business in this line. In an article for the *National Geographic Magazine* in 1903 Alec explained the tetrahedral principle:

> It is applicable to any kind of structure whatever in which it is desirable to combine the qualities of strength and lightness. Just as we can build houses of all kinds out of bricks, so we can build structures of all sorts out of tetrahedral frames, and the structures can be so formed as to possess the same qualities of strength and lightness which are characteristic of the

individual cells. I have already built a [sheep] house, a framework for a giant wind-break, three or four boats, as well as several forms of kites, out of these elements.

Ironically, it was Mabel who nagged Alec into applying for a patent, and she herself negotiated with Philip Mauro, the patent attorney, to set the business in motion. 'Alec would never have done anything more than talk about it, I am pretty sure,' she wrote later.[9] The Patent Office, taken aback by the deceptive simplicity of the principle, delayed taking a decision, but eventually, on 20 September 1904, granted Patent No. 770,626 for 'Aerial Vehicle or Other Structure'. This and a kite patent granted earlier that year were the first that Alec had received since the graphophone patent in May 1886, and the first in his name alone since a minor telephone improvement was patented in 1881. In the long run it was not its aircraft application that made the tetrahedral principle so important, but its general application as a space frame in building construction. Nevertheless, making the idea commercially viable proved to be difficult and time-consuming. In October 1904 Alec wrote to his cousin Charlie, proposing that he should establish a patent-holding corporation like the one he had organised for the Volta Associates' graphophone patents, but Charlie demurred. Early in 1906 Mabel consulted an engineer but he did not consider the Bell system an improvement over that then in use for heavy construction projects, though he thought that it might be feasible for light constructions such as footbridges, water towers and the reinforcement of concrete arches; and he liked the concept of mass production of standardised structural members. The matter remained in abeyance until May 1906. Significantly, it was Mabel, rather than Alec, who recruited the right man for the job of working out the fine details and dealing with supplementary patents as they arose.

The young engineer whom she hired was Frederick W. Baldwin, born in 1882 (which would have placed him between Edward and Robert, had they lived). Nicknamed 'Casey' after the popular ballad 'Casey at the Bat' as a tribute to his baseball skills, Baldwin was an athletic all-rounder, a graduate of the University of Toronto, a skilled yachtsman and crazy about aeronautics. He was introduced to the Bells by Douglas McCurdy, Arthur's younger son, who was a special favourite with Mabel. Shortly after he graduated, Casey joined Douglas and the two of them set off for Beinn Bhreagh. Casey had meant to stay about two weeks; he was still there when he died forty-two years later.

Alec could not have been better suited. Casey was Tom Watson and Sumner Tainter all over again, but infinitely better qualified that either, with a good degree in electrical and mechanical engineering. Alec and

Mabel took to him instantly; modest, self-effacing, cheerful, lively and intelligent, Casey was the son they never had. He had the skills and disciplines that Alec had never found the time to acquire, yet he was ever-responsive to the older man's flights of imagination, and flexible enough to adjust to them, or tactful enough to steer Alec in the right direction. To prepare himself better for what would be his life's work, Casey spent some time at Cornell University in 1906. When he returned to Beinn Bhreagh in the autumn he set to work on the construction of the tetrahedral tower, a gigantic tripodal structure on the summit of Beinn Bhreagh. The tower, intended to show the world what could be achieved by the use of tetra-hedral space frames, was formally inaugurated on 31 August 1907, and dozens of guests gasped at the view from the observation platform, over the Bras d'Or Lakes six hundred feet below. In due course Gilbert Grosvenor published a well-illustrated account of it in the *National Geographic Magazine* while Casey himself wrote it up for *Scientific American* in October that year. Despite favourable publicity, however, this tetrahedral structure failed to excite commercial interest. The patent expired long before the idea was taken seriously. When the tetrahedral space frame principle was widely adopted thirty years later, it appeared to have been independently reinvented, and Alec Bell never received the credit, nor the royalties, that should have been his.

In September 1907 Alec embarked on an ambitious project which was to have important results. In addition to Baldwin and McCurdy, Alec recruited Lieutenant Thomas Selfridge, a young artillery officer who had developed an interest in aviation and who had visited Alec in Washington that spring. Later Alec persuaded his friend Theodore Roosevelt, President of the United States, to second Selfridge to Beinn Bhreagh as an official observer for the War Department. A graduate of West Point in 1903, Selfridge had the same rigorous scientific training as Baldwin and McCurdy, and the three of them brought a much more professional approach to Alec's aviation programme. These three young engineers were presently joined by a fourth. Glenn H. Curtiss, like the Wrights, graduated from bicycles to aeronautics but along the way had also become national motorcycle champion (1903) and the fastest man on wheels, at 136 m.p.h. (1907). He formed his own company to manufacture small, lightweight engines for bicycles and then found that they were also being fitted into dirigible balloons. In 1906 Alec, casting about for a suitable engine for his aircraft, ordered one from Curtiss. Although it did not meet the purpose, Alec must have been sufficiently impressed, for he ordered a more powerful one and offered Curtiss $25 a day and his expenses if he would come to Beinn Bhreagh and deliver it in person. In July 1907 Curtiss made the trip and was so fired by Alec's enthusiasm that he became an immediate convert to aviation. After putting his business affairs in order, he returned to Beinn Bhreagh as the group's engine expert. At twenty-nine, Curtiss was rather older and infinitely more mature than the others, but without their education or breeding. Consequently, this rather shy, dour young man never quite entered into the boyish camaraderie. Orphaned at a very early age, his nearest relative was his only sister; she was deaf, and this seems to have given him a special place in Mabel's affections.

Mabel, in fact, was the driving force in what became the Aerial Experiment Association, and it was she who put up the $25,000 capital for the project which was to commence on 1 October 1907 and run for twelve months. Alec was the unsalaried chairman, Baldwin and McCurdy received $1,000 per annum, and Selfridge as a serving officer was unpaid. A measure of the importance given to Curtiss was the fact that his salary was on the scale of $5,000 per annum while he was at Beinn Bhreagh, and half that rate while he was absent on his own company business.

The AEA humoured Alec by concentrating at first on the *Cygnet*, a tetrahedral kite of 3,400 red silk cells. On 6 December 1907 Selfridge burrowed into this honeycomb and was towed out into the Little Bras d'Or Lake. When the steamboat attained top speed in the teeth of a twenty-knot wind, the lashings were cut and the kite rose majestically on its towrope, reaching a height of 168 feet where it hovered for seven minutes till the wind dropped. Then it sank 'gently as a butterfly' and settled on the water, but Selfridge (who could not see what was happening) failed to disconnect the tow in time and the kite was dragged to pieces. At the meeting following this fiasco, Alec gracefully acceded to the views of his young colleagues: for the time being they would experiment with Chanute-style gliders. Privately, however, Alec resolved to build a bigger and better *Cygnet* and test it the following summer with an engine.

Work on the project continued at Beinn Bhreagh till January 1908 when the team moved to the Curtiss workshops at Hammondsport, New York, in search of better weather. By early March manned glider trials had progressed so successfully that it was decided that each of the four young men should design and build an aeroplane. First to make the attempt at powered flight was Selfridge's little biplane *Red Wing* (so-called on account of the red silk covering its wings, left over from the previous year's tetrahedral kite experiments). Selfridge was in Washington at the time on army business and, anxious to test the aircraft on frozen Lake Keuka before the ice thawed, it was Casey Baldwin who had the job of taking it aloft. Unlike Langley and the Wrights, who had an aversion to letting the press or public witness their experimental flights, the showman in Alec ensured that there was a good turnout for the trial. Octave Chanute himself was present on 12 March and later credited Baldwin with 'the first public exhibition of the flight of a heavier-than-air machine in America'. Casey, in fact, flew only about a hundred yards, at an altitude of ten feet, before a tail strut buckled and he was forced to land. Five days later he tried again, but a gust of wind tipped the flimsy craft over and it crashed. Both the machine and its engine were irretrievably damaged but Casey escaped without a scratch.

This mishap, however, produced a positive result. To give the aircraft lateral stability, Alec suggested that the tips of the upper wings should be hinged and moved in opposite directions to each other by means of wires attached to the pilot's shoulders. By this concept Alec had arrived independently at the aileron (later it was discovered that the French had already anticipated this), proof that his inventiveness was by no means diminished with the passage of the years. The ailerons were incorporated in the second aircraft, designed by Casey Baldwin and named the *White Wing* because the red silk was exhausted and white cotton had to be substituted. In place of the ice-skids, this machine was fitted with a light tricycle undercarriage. Several flights were made between 18 and 23 May, each of the young associates taking it in turn to pilot it. Alec, at sixty-one, was too old to emulate them, but he watched with mounting satisfaction as the flights became longer and higher, attaining a record of a thousand feet. Like its predecessor, this machine was totally wrecked as a result of a crash, but miraculously no one was hurt.

The flights of both aircraft got considerable press coverage and were well documented in photographs, but it was the début of the third plane which got the greatest publicity. This was the *June Bug* built by Glenn Curtiss who profited from the trials and errors of his colleagues to make a number of improvements in design and construction, notably the use of varnish to seal the fabric. In the last week of June, Curtiss made several flights, one of which exceeded the one-kilometre distance stipulated for the *Scientific American* trophy, the first to be offered for heavier-than-air flight. Alec was absent at Beinn Bhreagh when the AEA staged a friendly contest on 4 July for the trophy, but Daisy and David Fairchild were among the thousand spectators who saw Curtiss and his 'strange, white, flying apparition' take the prize. On receipt of the good news, Alec immediately cabled his patent attorneys to check out the *June Bug* for patentable features. They concluded that the ailerons, shoulder controls, tricycle undercarriage and combination of steerable ground wheel and rudder should all be patented. A few weeks later Orville Wright complained that the ailerons infringed the Wrights' wing-warping patent of 1906, in which it was clearly described as 'any combination whereby the angular relations of the lateral marginal portions of the aeroplanes [the wings] may be varied in opposite directions'. In spite of this sweeping claim, and the prior French use of ailerons, the latter were included in Patent No. 1,011,106 for a 'Flying Machine', granted on 5 December 1911 to all five AEA members as joint inventors.

After the *June Bug* success, Alec persuaded Casey to return to Beinn Bhreagh and help him build his tetrahedral 'aerodrome' (the term coined by Langley for his machines), while the others remained at Hammondsport to help McCurdy with his aircraft. Douglas constructed a machine with a more powerful engine, improved ailerons and rubberised balloon fabric which gave the plane its name of the *Silver Dart*. In September, Selfridge was ordered back to Washington for the army trials of the Wright aircraft at Fort Meyer, Virginia. On 12 September Orville established a new endurance record by keeping his machine in the air for an hour and a quarter. Five days later Thomas volunteered to be Orville's passenger on a prescribed two-man flight. The aircraft crashed, severely injuring the pilot and wrecking the plane, but Thomas Selfridge died of his injuries a few hours later, earning a dubious place in the history of aviation as the first aeroplane fatality. Mabel took his death very hard and wrote immediately to her husband:

> I can't realize it, it doesn't seem possible. I miss the thought of him so . . . Give my love to them all, and let's hold tight together, all the tighter for the one that's gone. Casey called me the 'little mother of us all' and so I want to be.

As the original AEA agreement was due to expire at the end of that month, Mabel offered to put up another $10,000 and extend the project a further six months. The others assented readily and so Douglas completed his machine, tested it briefly at Hammondsport in December and then shipped it to Baddeck. On the afternoon of 23 February 1909 McCurdy's *Silver Dart* rose from the ice of Baddeck Bay and, witnessed by a large crowd, flew about half a mile at a speed of forty miles an hour. This was the first heavier-than-air flight in Canada, and the first by a British subject anywhere in the British Empire. (The first flight by a British subject had been made by Baldwin in the United States the previous year.) The following day Douglas flew round the bay, a distance of more than four miles and the best flight by an AEA machine so far. During the ensuing fortnight he made several cross-country flights up to twenty miles in duration. The last flight was made on 29 March, the finale being a circle of three and a half miles at an altitude of fifty feet. Two days later the AEA agreement expired. Late that evening Alec, Baldwin and McCurdy met in the great hall at Beinn Bhreagh for the formal wind-up of the Association. Before a roaring fire, as Alec recorded:

Casey moved the final adjournment, Douglas seconded it, and I formally put it to a vote. We hardly received the response 'aye' when the first stroke of midnight began. I do not know how the others felt, but to me it was really a dramatic moment.[10]

Charles Bell was appointed trustee of the AEA's patents and other assets. The total investment had consisted of Mabel's $35,000, plus $3,000 spent by Alec on printing a bulletin of the Association's activities. In settlement of the latter debt, Alec took the *Silver Dart* but promptly handed it over to McCurdy and Baldwin. To Curtiss he gave the *June Bug*. Curtiss formed his own aircraft company and would go on to make a fortune, despite the setback of prolonged litigation with the Wright brothers. Alec gave testimony about the work at Hammondsport but, with bitter memories of the long drawn-out telephone litigation, refused to appear as an expert witness at the hearings in 1914 on the grounds that he was not well enough qualified. The following year the AEA patents were adjudged free of interference and in 1917 were sold to the Curtiss Company for $5,899.49 in cash and $50,000 of Curtiss stock. Shortly afterwards, the federal government purchased both the Wright and Curtiss patents, the latter being sold for two million dollars.

In the aftermath of the AEA, Alec persuaded Baldwin and McCurdy to remain at Beinn Bhreagh. They formed the Canadian Aerodrome Company and in the summer of 1909, along with the *Silver Dart*, built *Baddeck No. 1* and *Baddeck No. 2* in the hope of securing a contract from the Canadian army. The military authorities, however, insisted on testing the machines on a rugged cavalry field. On 2 August, after three successful flights, the *Silver Dart* hit a knoll while landing and was completely wrecked. Miraculously Baldwin and McCurdy crawled out of the wreckage unscathed, but it was a severe blow to the trials. When *Baddeck No. 1* had trouble a few days later with a new frontal elevator and sustained some damage, the military's enthusiasm evaporated and no contract materialised.

Meanwhile, Alec continued work on tetrahedral kites, especially after Selfridge's tragic death. He was more convinced than ever that the tetrahedral principle was vital to the stability and safety of aircraft. To this end he and Casey designed and built *Cygnet II* but McCurdy's attempts to get airborne in February and March 1909 failed. From July 1909 till February 1910 Alec laboured on a new *Oionos*, a triplane with large triangular prism cells between the layered wings, but even with a more powerful engine, this machine obstinately refused to leave the ground. Experiments with more conventional biplanes continued during the autumn and winter, but in the spring of 1910 Casey and his wife Kathleen went off on a round-the-world trip with Alec and Mabel, while Douglas went barnstorming with Curtiss, and the Canadian Aerodrome Company quietly faded from the scene.

Over the winter of 1911–12 Alec gave aviation one last shot. When Douglas returned from his year with Curtiss, Alec set him to work on a much more advanced tetrahedral aircraft, *Cygnet III*, a huge honeycomb mounted on a Curtiss tricycle, with a Curtiss elevator and tail unit. On 9 March 1912, just after Alec's sixty-fifth birthday, Douglas revved up and sent the ungainly machine hurtling over the slush. As it gathered speed, he 'felt some squirming' and immediately throttled back. Subsequently it was found that there was a break in the tracks in the wet snow, showing that the machine had been airborne for about twelve inches. On the strength of this McCurdy sent Alec a telegram: 'Congratulations on technical flight of tetrahedral aerodrome *Cygnet III* this morning'; but this, arguably the shortest flight in the history of aviation, was not enough to encourage Alec to go on. *Cygnet III* was well named, for this was Alec's swan-song, so far as aviation was concerned. A few days later, Douglas made one last attempt at flight from the ice of Baddeck Bay but in the end the 'aerodrome' simply collapsed with the strain.

16

Active to the End

There is a silence where hath been no sound,
There is a silence where no sound may be,
In the cold grave –

Thomas Hood, *Sonnet. Silence*

With his consuming interests in the deaf, sheep-breeding and aeronautics, Alec led a very busy life. He wrote and he lectured and he entertained like-minded cronies. In 1898, through the good offices of Samuel Langley, he was appointed a regent of the Smithsonian Institution but he soon found that this had little more than social status. Six years later, however, he was in a position to make a valuable contribution. Having discovered that the remains of the Institution's founder, James Smithson, were in a Genoese graveyard threatened by encroachment from a quarry, he campaigned for their repatriation, and subsequently he and Mabel travelled to Italy to superintend the disinterment and transport the body back to the United States in a fitting manner.

In old age Alec began writing articles that popularised science, especially among children. For a time he wrote under the pen-name of H.A. Largelamb (an anagram of his name) but after several such articles had appeared in the *National Geographic Magazine* the truth leaked out and thereafter he stuck to his own name. He was a painstaking correspondent, unfailingly courteous in replying to the myriad would-be inventors who approached him for advice about their pet projects. In between times he and Mabel travelled extensively but as time passed she often went without him. She was in Britain again over the winter of 1900–1, for the marriage of Elsie and Gilbert Grosvenor, and a few months later witnessed the funeral procession of Queen Victoria. They both travelled to Britain and Europe in 1906, 1907 and 1909, and in 1910 they embarked on a grand round-the-world trip which took them to India, the Far East, Australia and

New Zealand as well as the far west of Canada. Business commitments, and later the outbreak of the First World War, put paid to globe-trotting for ten years, but there would be a last sentimental trip to Scotland in 1920, when Alec and Mabel revisited the haunts of their honeymoon.

The Aerial Experiment Association was a turning point for Alec, now in his sixties. Whereas he had worked on equal terms with Chester Bell and Sumner Tainter in the Volta Association, he was now working with young men less than half his age. If Mabel was the little mother, then he was the coach, to borrow a football term which Baldwin and McCurdy would have understood. His shock of white hair and large snowy beard heightened the impression of a man of advanced years. This was a matter which Alec was forced to accept, though at times he found it hard. When he was forty-eight, a newspaper reporter had once described him as well preserved for a man of seventy, and in later years he and Melville were often taken for brothers. But hair and beard were mere superficialities; those who knew Alec better recognised in him the vigour and stamina of a much younger man. Mabel had long since given him up as a hopeless case, especially where his hearty appetite and addiction to tobacco were concerned. Occasionally she nagged him about the size of his monthly cigar bill, and urged him to take more exercise, but all that running about on the meadows of Beinn Bhreagh hauling on kite-strings must have had a beneficial effect. Photographs of him in the 1900s show a tall figure – not unlike George Bernard Shaw, in fact. Mary Blatchford, Mabel's cousin, writing in 1911, described him:

> He is a magnificent figure of a man, and his dress – always the same – becomes him wonderfully. He wears long grey, coarse knit stockings with knickerbockers – or knee-breeches – of grey tweed with a loose jacket plaited and belted. For dinner he simply changes the grey jacket for a white waistcoat and black velvet jacket, and behold him resplendent! The other evening he danced for us, and whether it was a Scotch jig or a Highland fling, or an original-made-up-on-the-spot caper I do not know, but it was a *great show.*[1]

With the death of his father in 1905, Alec assumed the mantle of family patriarch. Elsie and Gilbert Gosvenor would eventually have two sons and five daughters, while Daisy and David Fairchild would have a son and two daughters. Mabel was particularly attached to the boys: 'All the plans, the hopes, and the ambitions that have lain buried in the graves of my own little sons sprang to life with the coming of each of my three grandsons,' she wrote poignantly to Gilbert on 19 September 1915, for this formed part of the letter of condolence on the death of five-year-old Alexander Graham

Bell Grosvenor. Mabel must have felt that the tragic history of the early 1880s was repeating itself. Fortunately both Melville Bell Grosvenor and Alexander Graham Bell Fairchild were to live long and distinguished lives. Alec too derived immense pleasure from his grandchildren, who called him 'Grampie' or 'Gampie'. Melville, the eldest, was probably Alec's favourite, and he has left the most vivid and affectionate memories of his grandfather, whether kite-flying or canoeing at Beinn Bhreagh or enjoying more sedate pleasures in Grampie's Georgetown laboratory. Both Gilbert Grosvenor and David Fairchild were absorbed with the pursuit of their respective careers, and it was inevitable that their children, turned loose at Beinn Bhreagh, saw more of their grandparents in their early, formative years. These were happy times for Alec and Mabel, and the clan remained close-knit. The many photographs from the first two decades of the new century showing this extended family at Beinn Bhreagh invariably have Alec and Mabel in the centre of the group with the youngest grandchildren on their laps, surrounded by Elsie and Daisy and their husbands and elder children.

About the time that the Great War broke out, fourteen-year-old Melville was sent to Beinn Bhreagh to live with his grandparents, just as Alec had gone to London to live with his grandfather. The time spent at Baddeck over the ensuing months nicely rounded off Melville's education. During his stay, he helped the old man with his statistical tables, thereby improving his arithmetic. Gilbert had stipulated that the boy's reading and writing should not be neglected, and in due course Alec reported:

> Melville has been a great comfort to me here and quite a companion . . .
> although it must have been very lonely for him without any young people
> of his age to play with . . . Melville has developed his GREAT AMBITION
> IN LIFE, which is to be an editor like his father . . . I have encouraged him
> in this and he has now produced three issues of the great new popular
> magazine known as 'Wild Acres Weekly'.[2]

After graduating from the United States Naval Academy shortly after the war, Melville would join his father and devote his life to the great institution which his grandfather and great-grandfather had started and which his own son, Gilbert Melville Grosvenor, would continue in his turn – five generations in the service of the National Geographic Society.

Alec, who never lost his childlike wonderment at everything around him, was firmly opposed to regimentation and rote in education. In the little deaf school in Washington, for example, he and Gertrude Hitz had encouraged the pupils to respond to the external stimuli of pictures, objects and their surroundings. He adopted the same approach with Melville and, to a lesser extent, his other grandchildren. He was therefore intrigued to learn, from Daisy, of the spectacular success which Dr Maria Montessori was having along similar lines in Italy. Samuel McClure, who (despite the *National Geographic* episode a decade earlier) was an intimate friend and now a regular attender at Alec's Wednesday soirées, was also an ardent devotee of the Montessori Method which he publicised in his magazine. The notion of educating children by making them think for themselves and developing their powers of observation and reasoning appealed immensely to Alec and he tried an experiment, with five-year-old Sandy Fairchild and his three-year-old sister Barbara as guinea pigs. Early in 1912 they were joined by half a dozen neighbours' children in what Alec was pleased to call the 'Children's Laboratory', a class conducted by Roberta Fletcher who had been trained in the method.

The following summer Miss Fletcher travelled with the Bells to Beinn Bhreagh and established, on the upper floor of the warehouse, the first Montessori school in Canada, enrolling five Grosvenors, two Fairchilds and five local children. Alec was fascinated by the children's dramatic progress and took part in regular discussion groups with parents and Miss Fletcher. Later Mabel sponsored her and Anne E. George (Dr Montessori's leading American disciple) in opening the first fully-fledged Montessori school at the Bell's Washington home during the school year of 1912–13. In the following spring Mabel was elected president of the Montessori Educational Association; subsequently she purchased a house on Kalorama Road and leased it to the Association for a much larger Montessori school that autumn. McClure brought Maria Montessori herself to America in December 1914 and arranged a lecture tour whose climax was the grand Washington reception which the Bells organised on her behalf. In the spring of 1915 the Montessori Educational Association launched its magazine and elected Alec as president. A reaction set in by 1916, however, and the Montessori Method came under increasing fire from traditional educationists. There was also an ugly racist and sectarian undercurrent which attacked the movement because it was Italian (and therefore Catholic). Unfortunately, as the World War intensified, contact with Italy was weakened and, without the personal support of Dr Montessori herself, the Association foundered. By 1919 it had ceased operations and it would be many years later before the Montessori Method regained a foothold in the United States. Nevertheless, the weight lent by Alec and Mabel ensured that the debate on the nature and content of children's education was opened up.

At Beinn Bhreagh, Arthur McCurdy, who had been Alec's private secretary and closest confidant for fifteen years, left in 1905 to start up a photographic equipment business. For nine years Alec made do with a succession of temporary secretaries, but in 1914 he hired a local girl, Catherine MacKenzie, newly graduated from a convent school. She stayed with him until his death eight years later, and in 1928 would publish an affectionate biography of her illustrious employer. Many of the anecdotes pertaining to Alec's last years were derived from this source. Catherine's duties included reading the *New York Times* to him every day, taking down dictation of letters and notebook entries and keeping his office in the manner he required. What struck her particularly about his working methods was his insistence on the precise dating of all records, both written and photographic, a lesson which he had learned from the prolonged battles over the telephone patents.

After the *Cygnet* experiments, Casey Baldwin stayed on with Alec as manager of both the Beinn Bhreagh estate and the laboratory, with a salary of $2,500 per annum and a free house. It might be argued that Casey could have done better for himself, but he was perfectly content to remain in this backwater of Cape Breton where he could indulge his passion for sailing and the outdoor life. It was his interest in boating which gave Alec's inventiveness another direction. One day in October 1906 he asked Casey: 'Why should we not have heavier-than-water machines as well as lighter-than-water? I consider the invention of the hydroplane as the most significant of recent years.'[3] A few weeks later he drew a vessel of the type now known as a hydrofoil.

Alec's term 'heavier-than-water' referred to the fact that such a vessel, in motion, is sustained not by its displacement but by the lift of its hydrofoils, the blades acting in water as aircraft wings do in air. The concept was not new by any means; it had been successfully demonstrated on an English canal as long ago as 1861, and Alec probably read of it in the March 1906 issue of *Scientific American*, in an article by William E. Meacham who had been working on the principle for some time. Alec and Casey did not begin experiments with hydrofoils till the summer of 1908, and then only as a potential medium for aeroplane take-off in water, based on the work previously done by the Italian inventor Enrico Forlanini. Later, however, they examined the possibility of developing hydrofoil boats. Tests of such vessels continued intermittently through the summer and autumn of 1909. Although the world tour of 1910–11 interrupted experimentation, Alec and Casey took the opportunity to confer with Forlanini while visiting Italy. Mabel described to Elsie how:

> Both Father and Casey had rides in the boat over Lake Maggiore at express
> train speed. They described the sensation as most wonderful and delightful.
> Casey said it was as smooth as flying through the air. The boat . . . at about

45 miles an hour glides above the water . . . being supported on slender
hydro-planes which leave hardly any ripple.[4]

On their return to Beinn Bhreagh late in the summer of 1911, Casey
designed and built a hydrofoil boat which he and Alec called a
'hydrodrome' and designated HD-1. With its aerial propeller and stubby
biplane wings, it resembled a stunted seaplane, zipping across the lake as if
about to lift into the air at any moment. Over the ensuing winter it was
stripped down, redesigned and rebuilt, then tested from July to October
1912; before it fell apart (probably from metal fatigue) it attained speeds up
to fifty miles an hour. Rebuilt as the HD-2 and unfortunately christened
Jonah, it failed to match the previous speeds before a structural failure
crippled it in December. While these trials were proceeding, Alec suddenly
had an idea for hydrofoil sailing boats. Casey was quick to point out that
even the fastest sailboats could not achieve the speeds required to lift the
hull out of the water by hydrofoils. Nevertheless, Alec continued to play
with the notion of vessels given aerodynamic lift by means of horizontal
vanes or sails, and went on to fantasise about large passenger ships
skimming smokeless across the Atlantic on the wings of the breeze.
Accordingly, the summer of 1913 was occupied with trials of models
designed along these lines.

In the spring of that year, Casey designed and built the HD-3, a more
powerful and structurally more robust version of its predecessor. At first all
went well. That summer Prince Albert of Monaco anchored his yacht
Hirondelle in Baddeck Bay, and Alec laid on a demonstration for him. Casey
roared across the bay with the throttle full open; striking a slight wave, HD-
3 soared into space and somersaulted before plunging into the sea.
Fortunately the speed was not so great that damage was sustained on
impact. Further trials in the autumn were disappointing and Casey
diplomatically suggested to Alec that the time required to prepare the boat
for experiments in 1914 would be far better spent on testing the hydrofoil
sailboat. In the event, that turned out to be little more than a pipedream,
but before Alec could return to the problem of powered hydrofoils, the war
had intervened, and everyone had more important matters on their minds.

In December 1899, when the Spanish-American War was at an end and
America was launched as a major power in the Pacific as well as the
Caribbean, Alec had given a newspaper interview in which he admitted to
being 'pessimistic regarding the future of the British Empire and the
English people'. By the beginning of the twentieth century he regarded
himself as first and foremost an American, although he probably spent most
of his time in that most Scottish of Canadian provinces, Nova Scotia. He

was punctilious in avoiding any political involvement in Canada, much to the disappointment of Charles Tupper who tried to enlist his support during his election campaign of 1896. Alec maintained an apolitical stance in the United States as well, on good terms with presidents and politicians regardless of their party affiliation. He heartily endorsed the progressive Republicanism of Theodore Roosevelt whose immediate successor, William Howard Taft, president in 1909–13, was a cousin of the Grosvenors. When Roosevelt turned against his old friend and successor, and ran against him for the presidency in 1912, Alec's loyalties were divided. At a dinner in Philadelphia in February 1912, however, Alec was electrified by the speech made by Woodrow Wilson, the Democratic candidate who, profiting from the Roosevelt-Taft split, romped into the White House. Later Alec recorded that Wilson's speech 'was the finest I have ever listened to' and on the strength of it he became a convert. Even Gilbert Grosvenor followed him, deserting family ties and registering as a Democrat in the autumn of 1914 because, in the current world crisis, he felt that the President needed all the support he could get.

Something of the radical outlook of his grandfather and Uncle David inevitably rubbed off on Alec. Since the 1870s, for example, he had been an outspoken advocate of equal rights and opportunities for women and, in this regard, had frequent arguments with Mabel who had a surprisingly old-fashioned attitude. Even when he eventually convinced her of the justice of giving women the vote, she argued that this should be restricted to ladies of education and property. 'The ignorant have as much right to be represented as the educated,' he countered. 'I believe in universal suffrage, without qualification of education, sex, color, or property.'[5] Nine years later, Mabel had come round to his way of thinking, and she and her daughters participated in the national convention that presented a monster petition to Congress in April 1910. On Alec's sixty-sixth birthday he and Mabel cheered lustily as the Women's Suffrage Parade marched along Pennsylvania Avenue to the White House. Elsie and the Grosvenor children followed the parade in their car, but Daisy was actually on one of the floats in the procession. In March 1914 Alec chaired a public meeting on the issue, introducing himself as 'the first suffragist in our family'.

The question of divided loyalties arose in August 1914 when Britain and much of Europe were plunged into war. A few months later, in the wake of the sinking of the *Lusitania* by a German submarine, Alec wrote, 'I am not one of those hyphenated Americans who claim allegiance to two countries.'[6] Nevertheless, his adherence to Wilson's call for strict American neutrality must have sorely tested him at times. At least half of each year was still spent in Canada, where Alec was exposed to the flag-waving patriotism and the frenetic campaigns to aid the war effort. The war's immediate effect on Alec was to inhibit a return to research on hydrofoils, on the grounds that he, as a neutral, should not engage in work that might have some military benefit to one of the belligerents. In the summer of 1915, however, the Bells organised a garden fête to raise money for the Red Cross. Two and a half years later, on 6 December 1917, Alec was startled when the ground shook. It was not an earthquake but the reverberations from the greatest disaster to hit Canada. A Norwegian steamer, leaving Halifax harbour with a relief cargo for Belgium, collided with an incoming French ship laden with 3,000 tonnes of high explosives. A tenth of the city was devastated by the blast, hundreds of people were killed and many thousands more were rendered homeless. Alec and Mabel packed spare bedding and clothing for the survivors while Casey led a contingent from Baddeck to build temporary shelters for the homeless.

By that date Alec's dilemma as a neutral was over. After the United States entered the war he took up experiments in underwater sound detection with his old vigour. Sadly, he soon discovered that his expertise in telephony was more than a mite rusty, and he had not kept abreast of developments in the past quarter of a century. Likewise, his ideas for a projectile that would put out a small rudder towards the end of its trajectory, so that it would leap in a series of diminishing upward swoops like a stone skimming the surface of a pond was dismissed by his friend Charles Walcott of the Smithsonian before it even got as far as the War Department. Independently, of course, Barnes Wallis would use the principle of bouncing bombs to destroy the Ruhr dams. As a theoretician, however, Alec was on safer ground. Twenty years earlier he had imagined fleets of aircraft bombing Cervera's Spanish fleet; now he addressed a convention of the Navy League, prophesying that the day of the big battleships was rapidly coming to an end. Soon, naval battles would be fought and won in the air. It was a notion that destroyed General Billy Mitchell, the pioneer of US military aviation, court-martialled in 1925 for criticising the War and Navy departments, but was learned all too well by the Japanese in their attack on Pearl Harbor.

In February 1917, following the German announcement of unrestricted submarine warfare which made American involvement in the conflict inevitable, Alec returned to research on his hydrodromes. On 8 April, two days after the American declaration of war, he left Washington for Beinn Bhreagh, spurred on by the Navy Department's plea for fast patrol vessels as submarine-chasers. Alec offered to build two hydrofoil boats for this purpose, but the Navy turned him down. 'It fell like a bomb into the camp and shattered all our plans,' he noted despairingly, but Mabel offered to put up the money anyway, and Alec got the Navy to promise to lend a couple of 400 h.p. Liberty engines. Work on the HD-4 began late in the summer of 1917 but was sadly hampered by naval intransigence. The promised Liberty engines failed to materialise, and when the far less suitable Renault 250 h.p. engines were earmarked instead, they did not reach Beinn Bhreagh until July 1918. Somebody suggested that HD stood for 'Hope Deferred'. The first trials got under way in October 1918 and although the Renault engines could only produce a top speed of fifty-four miles an hour, the design of the vessel looked very promising. Eventually, in July 1919, the Navy released two 350 h.p. engines and these were duly fitted to the HD-4. On 9 September 1919 the latest hydrodrome set a world marine speed record of 70.86 miles per hour, a record that stood for ten years. In 1920 Alec finally succeeded in getting observers from both the US Navy and the British Admiralty to Baddeck to watch the HD-4 in action. Although both delegations reported very favourably, neither the British nor the Americans placed any orders, and the great Naval Disarmament Conference of 1921 applied the death knell. That autumn the HD-4 was dismantled and its great grey hull left to rot for decades on the shore at Beinn Bhreagh.

Bell–Baldwin Hydrodromes Limited, the company which Alec had formed to acquire the patents of Forlanini and Peter Cooper Hewitt, as well as operating a working agreement with William Meacham, applied for its own patents, and on 28 March 1922, shortly after Alec's seventy-fifth birthday, a joint patent was granted to him and Casey on certain original features of their design. At the same time, they were granted a patent on a method of preventing the fouling of hydrofoil sets, one for features of a hydrodrome which never got beyond the design stage, and another for a device to change the angles of hydrofoil blades. These were Alec Bell's last patents, taken out forty-seven years after his first had been granted.

In February 1887, on the eve of his fortieth birthday, Alec had firmly rejected an invitation from Mrs M. Lincoln who wished to produce a biography of him: 'So far as I am concerned, I prefer a post mortem examination to vivisection without anaesthetics.' Almost thirty years later he responded to a request from the publishers Little, Brown and Company that he write his autobiography with the statement that 'I am as yet too much interested in the future and the development of new ideas to give the time to a book of this character.'[7] He shrank from the idea, for it seemed to signal the end of his useful life. At forty he feared it; at seventy he continued to resist it. The same attitude impelled him to reject an invitation from the film producer Carl Laemmle in 1915 to allow newsreel footage of himself to be used in a documentary about 'the ten most prominent men in the country'. Similarly, he turned down his old friend Fritz von Sumichrast who wished to include a pen-portrait of him in a book entitled *Living Leaders of the World*. Alec demurred on the grounds that 'publicity of this sort would be distasteful to me'. This did not prevent him from looking back, at least once, on his long and eventful life. On 4 April 1904, when he was urging his son-in-law Gilbert to make a career out of writing, he wrote:

> Circumstances arise that bend our lives hither or thither against our will. But our lives are bent, not broken – there is always continuity of growth. In looking back over my own life I realize how different has been the result from anything that I aimed at, and yet I can recognize continuity in the whole; one occupation has fitted me for the next, and that again for the next.

So far as can be ascertained, this was the only occasion on which he took stock of his past life, until early in 1922 when his wily son-in-law managed to get an article from him for the *National Geographic Magazine*. This developed out of an address given before a young audience, to whom Alec confided some reminiscences of his own youth. Gilbert Grosvenor was present on that occasion and got a stenographer to take his words down verbatim. Then, aware that Alec was short of ready cash to send a donation to the Clarke School for the Deaf when this was requested, Gilbert suggested that the National Geographic Society could send a cheque in his name, provided he would consent to the publication of his lecture. Shrewdly, Gilbert had touched on Alec's Achilles' heel, and so the address, revised by Gilbert, appeared in the March 1922 number under the title of 'Prehistoric Telephone Days'.

For one who was so reticent about authorising a biography in his lifetime, Alec was a biographer's dream, for part of his legacy was a vast amount of diaries, notebooks, letter copy-books and other papers, invariably dated precisely. He developed the habit of retaining every scrap and filing it methodically, right down to the least significant piece of ephemera, such as circulars, invitations, greetings cards and even his grandchildren's artless scribbles. It was as if he were keenly aware of his historic importance and wished posterity to have the fullest picture of his life and times in documentary form. His last secretary confirmed this when she wrote, 'All the years I was with him, I felt Mr Bell's constant mindfulness of posterity and his biographer, in everything he wrote, and in a good deal he did. The sense of an audience is very evident to me in all his Home Notebooks.'[8] This was taken to its ultimate in the *Beinn Bhreagh Recorder* which Alec started in July 1909 as a family newsletter but which eventually developed into a research bulletin, house organ and news magazine. As the years passed, the *Recorder* grew in size and scope, eventually incorporating a considerable amount of Bell family history and reprints of Alec's earlier writings. Originally produced in seven typewritten copies, it was later duplicated in an edition of twenty for family and friends. Copies were also deposited at the Volta Bureau and the Smithsonian Institution. By the time of Alec's death, the *Recorder* had grown to twenty-five bound volumes, each of four or five hundred pages. In March 1922 Gilbert Grosvenor persuaded Alec to deposit his vast personal archive at the National Geographic Society, setting aside a Bell Room in Hubbard Hall for this purpose. Seventy years later, this invaluable record of one of the most interesting figures of the nineteenth and twentieth centuries was transferred to the Library of Congress, where it is now more easily accessible.

In his later years there came echoes from the past. In 1905 Alec was present at Portsmouth, New Hampshire, at the signing of the treaty which brought the Russo-Japanese War to an end, and there he renewed the acquaintance of Komura and Kaneko, the Japanese students at Harvard whom he had met in the 1870s through Shuji Isawa, the Boston student who had been the first to speak a language other than English over the telephone.

Two years earlier, he got in touch with the Fore River Ship and Engine Company in Braintree, Massachusetts, in the hope of getting them to take on as a shipbuilding apprentice a deaf boy in whom he was taking an interest. When he saw the name of Thomas A. Watson on the company's letter-head he wrote, 'Are you my old friend Thomas A. Watson of Salem, Mass?' Back came a friendly response, saying that he had been following the kite-flying experiments with interest, would gladly interview the boy, and would like to show Bell round the Fore River yard. That autumn, however, Tom Watson was ejected in a boardroom coup before he could give his old friend the guided tour. Watson lost a fortune in this episode, and had the chagrin of seeing Fore River going on, during the First World War, to secure destroyer contracts worth millions of dollars. He lived comfortably on the income of a trust fund which he had wisely established at the time of the telephone windfall, and devoted the rest of his life to literature, the arts and travel. Alec kept in touch with him from 1903 onwards and on 25 January 1915 joined with him in the historic link-up when the transcontinental telephone line was completed. Alec in New York and Tom in San Francisco waited for the signal, then Alec spoke first: 'Mr Watson, are you there?' Woodrow Wilson joined in, from the White House, and congratulated Alec on 'this notable consummation of your long labors'. Then a replica of the Centennial telephone of 1876 was connected to the line at New York and Alec repeated those memorable words 'Mr Watson, come here. I want you.' Back came the riposte that it would take at least a week to get there.

The following year Boston celebrated the fortieth anniversary of that first telephone conversation. Alec unveiled a plaque at Exeter Place commemorating 'The First Complete and Intelligible Sentence by Telephone, March 10, 1876' and another at 109 Court Street, site of the Williams workshop, proclaiming that 'Here the Telephone Was Born, June 2, 1875'. At a celebratory luncheon at Boston University and a City Club dinner afterwards, Alec regaled his audiences with anecdotes of those far-off times. Not to be outdone, Brantford (which now rejoices in the epithet of the Telephone City) erected an impressive memorial to him, which the Governor-General unveiled on 24 October 1917. Later the same day he also dedicated the Bell homestead at Tutela Heights and Mabel and Alec posed happily for photographs on the edge of the bluff where his 'dreaming place' had been. 'Under yon roof of mine the telephone was born,' Melville had claimed, and to this day the house is preserved partly as a memorial to the Bell family and partly as a museum of early telephone technology.

In 1910, during the world tour, Alec met his old flame Marie Eccleston in Melbourne. Her husband, a banker who had lost all his money in a bank crash, had recently died and the widow McBurney was eking out a precarious living by giving piano and singing lessons. 'She doesn't look as if there were much money in her profession,' wrote Mabel, 'but she is a bright, plucky, energetic woman.'[9]

The man who had never completed a university degree course received a dozen honorary doctorates, and for this reason was often referred to as Dr Bell, although he himself never used the title. In 1906 he returned to Edinburgh to receive a doctorate from his alma mater and spent two weeks in the city, looking up the Herdmans and other old friends, and taking Mabel round his old haunts. He was disappointed to find that Trinity, which once had been open countryside, was now heavily built over. Even Milton Cottage had been altered and enlarged beyond all recognition.

Time was also catching up with Alec himself. Apart from severe headaches and recurring pain in his left ankle, he was remarkably fit, given his disregard of advice from wife and doctors alike to watch his diet and cut back on his heavy smoking. Ben Herdman and John Hitz both died in 1908, and later the same year Charles Williams succumbed to pneumonia. Thomas Sanders died of a heart attack in 1911. 'I begin to feel very old,' wrote Alec in a letter of condolence to George Sanders. 'You are about the last remaining link connecting me with those happy Salem days.'[10]

In March 1915 John Jamieson, a contemporary at Edinburgh High School, wrote to Alec from London saying that, out of 135 pupils in their class, he could trace only twenty-five still alive. In the same year, Alec had the first intimation of his own mortality when diabetes was diagnosed. Before Banting's discovery of insulin, this wasting disease was incurable and fatal. Fortunately, in Alec's case, it was identified at a very early stage and he was given a dire warning from his doctor to change his diet drastically. Both Mabel and Charles Thompson did their level best to ensure that he adhered to this strict régime, but from time to time Alec would go on a binge, either raiding the refrigerator in the dead of night, or slipping into pastry-shops in Washington to gorge himself on apple-pie and cream. Fred DeLand noted that Alec had got much thinner, when he saw him in 1916, though Alec assured him that he had never felt better in his life. Writing to Mabel from Beinn Bhreagh in April 1917, he confided: 'John McDermid makes me walk every day.' In the same year he became president of the Clarke School's board of governors and regularly spent a day or two there whenever he journeyed to or from Nova Scotia. As late as mid-1922 he delivered a couple of lectures on Visible Speech there.

In October 1920 Alec made his last trip to Britain. On this sentimental journey he was accompanied not only by Mabel but also their fifteen-year-old granddaughter Mabel Grosvenor and Alec's secretary Catherine MacKenzie. In London they visited Chichester Bell and Adam Scott before motoring to Bath and other places associated with Alec's younger days. Then they took the train to Edinburgh where Alec haunted the City Library, poring over old newspapers and directories for snippets of family history. When he told Chester that their grandfather's brother had been a brewer, his cousin reproved him for dredging up 'facts that are not so creditable to the family', but Alec riposted that the lowlier the start, the prouder was the rise. He took his granddaughter to see his birthplace in South Charlotte Street and later drove her out to Corstorphine Hill but he realised that he was now too old to scramble up it one last time. This depressed him, as did the realisation that so many of his old friends were dead and gone. In a rather sombre frame of mind he took the train north for a farewell visit to Elgin. The Bells stayed at the Station Hotel and hired a car to visit Pluscarden Abbey. He was horrified to find that its grassy floor had been concreted over and that an ugly wooden cage had been erected around the tower. Later they drove out to Lossiemouth and on to Covesea where he and Mabel had spent their idyllic honeymoon, but the fishermen's cottages were deserted and in ruins, and he could not identify which of them had been their holiday home. Many years later they would be restored and are now occupied again, but the scene that blustery day in November 1920 only added to Alec's depression. As they were catching the train back to Aberdeen, however, he perked up when a reporter from the local newspaper breathlessly caught up with him and was granted a brief interview in the carriage. On the railway platform a man was using the public telephone, oblivious to the fact that its inventor was seated only a few feet away. Something of Alec's old spirit returned, and he answered the young man's questions with humour, even giving him his views on Prohibition which had recently begun in the United States.[11]

Alec and his family headed back to London, cash running low and his spirits even lower. They were all set to go to Southampton to board the ship back to America when word reached him that Edinburgh Corporation had decided belatedly to make him an honorary burgess. Immediately, his spirts soared, the sailing was cancelled, and the Bell party headed north again. He was in splendid form when he addressed the pupils of his old school, and revelled in 'the medieval pomp and pageantry' of the City Chambers where Mabel and her granddaughter proudly watched him receive his burgess ticket in its ornamental silver casket. Alec's voice was as strong and mellifluous as ever as he made his acceptance speech: 'I have received many honours in the course of my life, but none that has so touched my heart as this gift of the freedom of my native city.' And it must have gladdened his heart to read in *The Scotsman* the following morning that not even Sir Walter Scott had brought more honour to Edinburgh.[12] Back in London a few days later, his euphoria had vanished. To a reporter he confessed: 'I visited Edinburgh, but I was a stranger in my own land . . . My advice to those who have remained away from home and contemplate returning for a farewell visit is – don't.'[13]

Back on the other side of the Atlantic Alec soon recovered his equilibrium. At his beloved Beinn Bhreagh he immersed himself in experiments and research. As a result of the diabetes he lost a great deal of weight and now felt the cold rather than relished it. Over the winter of 1921-22, therefore, he and Mabel toured the Caribbean. In the Canal Zone the acting governor put his car and yacht at their disposal. In the Bahamas Alec even went down into Ernest Williamson's Photosphere, descending through a narrow tube to the steel chamber on the seabed to observe marine life. In Jamaica he drove round the island most of a day in a fruitless search for the grave of a seafaring relative who had died there at the beginning of the nineteenth century, and everywhere he went he called on officials, toured schools and studied government publications. But in Venezuela he was overcome with the heat and fatigue and had to cancel a visit to the Caracas School for the Deaf. On the way home they stopped off in Florida, with the Fairchilds at Coconut Grove. From here, Mabel wrote to Elsie on 14 February 1922, 'I guess our travelling days are pretty well over now, and I am glad we had this trip to remember.'

Before embarking on the Caribbean tour, Alec had given an interview to Mary B. Mullett who wrote an article about him entitled 'How to Keep

Young Mentally'. She quoted him as saying, 'There cannot be mental atrophy in any person who continues to observe, to remember what he observes, and to seek answers for his unceasing hows and whys about things.'[14] He told her that he was currently engaged on improving the photophone, and discussed his ideas for air conditioning, the conservation of waste heat from stoves and roof-top solar energy panels, dramatic evidence of the fact that his mind was as inventive as ever. His last serious endeavour was, like the photophone, a device that he had first considered many years previously. From 1920 till midsummer 1922 he worked on the problem of distilling drinking water from fog and sea water; his last notebooks are replete with sketches, diagrams and data on a variety of devices. Ultimately Alec decided that the most practical of them would be a shallow tray about a metre square with a sloping glass lid on which moisture condensed from sun-warmed sea water beneath it, and down which the distilled drops trickled into a container. On 23 February 1922, shortly before his seventy-fifth birthday and despite the fact that he was debilitated by diabetes and fatigued after his Caribbean trip, he wrote to Gilbert Grosvenor from Coconut Grove saying 'I am just starting on water distillation experiments at low temperatures, and as I think of trying to patent the apparatus, am avoiding publication at the present time.' He was still staying with the Fairchilds when he celebrated his birthday. It was the last great gathering of the clan and Alec rose nobly to the occasion. Among the many greetings he received there was a card from his old friend Emile Berliner who, like Alec, was independently wealthy from the invention of his early life (the gramophone) and who had more recently been dabbling in aeronautics.

Refreshed and rejuvenated by his stay in Florida, Alec returned to Washington in the spring. He acquired the latest wonder of the age, a wireless set, and installed it in his study. Characteristically, he examined it carefully and wondered whether it might be possible to invent some device which would enable people to listen to the radio without the need for headphones. Physically he was haggard and in poor shape but his enquiring mind was as sharp as ever. Forty-five years earlier Alec had once admitted to Mabel that he feared that his greatest achievement, coming so early in life, might condemn him to a long anticlimax. A nagging fear that this had, in fact, been the case lay at the heart of his chronic reluctance to sanction biographies. He need not have worried. He could have sat back and leisurely enjoyed the wealth which the telephone brought him. Instead, he busied himself with science, invention, eugenics and the deaf, and continued to strive to the very end. It was entirely in character that his last project was motivated by humanitarian principles, to save the survivors of shipwreck from the agonising death brought about by thirst or drinking sea water.

In June the Bells went back to Beinn Bhreagh for the summer, and soon Alec was immersed in his research on sheep-breeding. On 11 July, what would be the last issue of the *Beinn Bhreagh Recorder* was produced, and concluded with an article about the lambs born that year to 'Mrs Bell's Multi-Nippled Twin-Bearing Stock'. He had some fresh ideas on tetrahedral construction which, combined with previous work on hydro-dromes, would lead him and Casey Baldwin to light, fast, strong hydrofoils which could be used as naval towing targets. Late in July he observed Casey's trials with a model of the hydrofoil target and, meticulous as ever, recorded the details in his notebook.[15] Up to 29 July Alec pottered about with the sheep and then sat up half the night as usual, reading and writing.

The following day there was great excitement when David and Daisy Fairchild arrived, a few days earlier than expected. They were horrified to find Alec too weak to get up from his chaise longue unaided. At lunchtime his appetite had gone; Mabel commented on 'his last hard service to me' when he tried to eat because she wanted him to, but he just could not take more than a mouthful. A doctor was hastily summoned from Baddeck and he concluded that the diabetes had affected Alec's liver and pancreas. By evening, Alec rallied and was more like his old self, sitting on the sofa reading a novel and chatting. David Fairchild asked him if he thought that his debility might be electrical in character and if life might not have an electrical basis. Alec shrugged and said softly, *'Je ne sais pas, Monsieur. Je ne sais pas.'*

The following day Alec stayed in bed, semi-conscious, occasionally murmuring confusedly, as he usually did when Charles Thompson tried to waken him. On the afternoon of 1 August, however, he felt much better, but when he tried to dictate notes to Catherine MacKenzie he found the effort beyond him. 'Don't hurry,' said someone. 'I have to,' he replied with a wry smile and continued:

> I want to say that . . . Mrs Bell and I have both had a very happy life together, and we couldn't have had better daughters than Elsie and Daisy or better sons-in-law than Bert and David, and we couldn't have had finer grandchildren.

He wrestled with the problem of making financial provision for his daughters in the context of Mabel having legal title to the great bulk of his property, but was assured that this would be sorted out. Finally, as his strength ebbed away, he gasped, 'We want to stand by Casey as he has stood by us . . . want to look upon Casey and his wife Kathleen as sort of children.'

Alec sank back into semi-consciousness. Mabel sat at his bed-side holding his hand, and now and again he squeezed hers, opened his eyes and smiled at her. At midnight David took over the vigil while Mabel rested on a sofa nearby. About two o'clock in the morning David felt his father-in-law's pulse fade and called Mabel to her husband's side. Alec's breathing grew slower and more laboured. When she spoke his name, he opened his eyes for the last time and smiled wanly. 'Don't leave me,' she implored. He could not speak. Instead his fingers made the sign for 'No'. Even after his pulse could no longer be detected, Mabel could feel his fingers moving in a last feeble attempt to communicate. Silence enveloped him at last.

The day of Alec's funeral, 4 August, was misty and overcast. The previous day workmen had blasted a hole out of the solid rock below the tetrahedral tower on the summit of Beinn Bhreagh. In the house, Alec's body was laid out in his favourite grey corduroy jacket and tweed knicker-bockers in a coffin of local pine lined with aircraft fabric. From near and far family and friends came to Beinn Bhreagh and congregated informally. At Mabel's insistence, no one wore black; the women were in white dresses and the men in their summer suits. John McDermid loaded the coffin on his buckboard and drove up the hill. A large crowd gathered on the summit and sang the hymn 'Bringing in the Sheaves'. A local girl sang a verse of Stevenson's 'Requiem' and the Presbyterian minister recited Longfellow's 'Psalm of Life'. Everyone intoned the Lord's Prayer and then the coffin was lowered. At that precise moment, 6.25 p.m., all telephone communication throughout the United States ceased for one minute as a mark of respect. Then Sandy Fairchild and little Bobby Baldwin raised the Stars and Stripes and the Union Jack on temporary flagpoles and everyone trooped back down the hill.

Mabel subsequently had the tower demolished lest it fall into disrepair. She meant to erect a more permanent memorial to her husband's tetrahedral principle on the spot, but she herself died only five months later, on 3 January 1923. She had never got over his death. She was interred alongside Alec, above whose grave a simple tablet gave his name and dates, with the appellation of 'Inventor' and (as he had requested) 'Died a Citizen of the United States'.

Both Elsie and Daisy lived into their eighties. David died in 1954 at eighty-five, while Gilbert survived till 1966, past his ninetieth birthday. From their eight married grandchildren have sprung numerous progeny. Beinn Bhreagh remains family property, but in 1956 the Canadian government erected, on a fourteen-acre site overlooking the Bras d'Or Lakes, the Alexander Graham Bell Museum at a cost of $375,000. The architect, O.H. Leicester, paid his own tribute to Alec by using tetrahdral space frames in its construction. Appropriately, the museum was dedicated to Casey Baldwin, Douglas McCurdy, Glenn Curtiss and Thomas Selfridge.

In the same year the AAPTSD was renamed the Alexander Graham Bell

Association for the Deaf. It has gone from strength to strength and is now the world's largest organisation for the welfare and education of deaf people, with a wide range of activities ranging from international symposia to publications on all aspects of deafness.

Alec would probably have turned in his grave at the spectacle of *The Modern Miracle* made by Twentieth Century Fox in 1939, with Don Ameche as Alec, Loretta Young as Mabel, Henry Fonda as Tom Watson and Charles Coburn as Gardiner Hubbard. In more recent years, at least two television series have done more ample justice to the inventor of the telephone, and highlighted the many other aspects of his remarkable career.

None of Alec's descendants bears his surname, but the Bell System of America, with over a million employees, would eventually become one of the world's largest enterprises, and in the Russian Arctic is an island called Graeme Bell [*sic*], thus named in 1932. His name has been enrolled in the Hall of Fame of New York University, and alongside Curtiss and Selfridge in the Aviation Hall of Fame in Dayton, Ohio. But he needs none of these memorials; his name will endure so long as hearing people use the telephone and the deaf converse in speech. The man who brought sounds out of silence will never be forgotten.

Notes

1. Edinburgh, 1847–62

1. The parish registers of St Andrew's and St Leonard's record seven generations of the family, back to Alexander Bell and Beatrix Fyfe whose son John was born in 1657.
2. Parish registers of Dairsie, Leuchars and Balmerino
3. Parish registers of St Andrew's and St Leonard's, which show that he was baptised David only. He himself added Charles at some subsequent date.
4. Parish registers of Dundee and Monifieth, Angus; testimony of Revd Dr Alexander MacLachlan in the lawsuit between Alexander Bell and William Murray.
5. Bell v. Bell, Court of Session Records, Extracted Processes, no. 58, February 1833, S.R.O.; Revised Case of *poor* Alexander Bell, 6 July 1832, S.R.O.; Revised Condescendence, 30 July 1832; Re-Revised Condescendence, 4 April 1833. Report of Trial in the Action of Damages for Crim. Con., Alexander Bell v. William Murray, 16 December 1833.
6. An impressive tombstone in Balmerino parish cemetery near Gauldry, erected by AGB in 1909, touchingly mentions his grandmother Elizabeth, 'wife of Alexander Bell', although she was actually interred in St James's burying ground at Cupar, Fife.
7. Eliza Grace Symonds was born at Alverstoke, Hampshire, on 15 October 1809. In the 1861 Edinburgh Census, however, she gave her age as 42, the same as her husband, although she was actually 51. Her mother was born Mary White at Portsea on 3 November 1786 and married Samuel Symonds at Gosport Holy Trinity Church on 28 November 1808. After Eliza Grace came Charles (1811), James White (1814) and Edward Stace (1816), all born at Gosport.
8. Edinburgh Census, 1841; Edinburgh Directory, 1842–43.
9. Edinburgh Directory, 1844–45, p486: advertisement headed STAMMERING AND OTHER VOCAL DEFECTS.
10. The frequent moves of the Bell family around the south side of Charlotte Square in the 1840s confused the issue when, in 1936, the question of erecting a memorial to AGB was being mooted. See correspondence on the subject in *The Scotsman*, 23 July 1936. A temporary wooden plaque, erected in May 1937, was replaced by the engraved stone slab on 24 November 1937.
11. Reminiscences of AGB in *Beinn Bhreagh Recorder*, VII, pp180–4, hereafter referred to as *BBR*.
12. Robert V. Bruce, *Alexander Graham Bell and the Conquest of Solitude* (London, 1973), p21, hereafter referred to as Bruce, illustrates 15 South Charlotte Street, on the corner of Rose Street.
13. Letter of Eliza Bell to Sarah Fuller, 26 September 1873; AGB to Mabel Hubbard, 1 August 1876.
14. *BBR*, XV, p40
15. Bruce, p80; *BBR*, II, pp58–9
16. Ibid.
17. James J. Trotter, *The Royal High School of Edinburgh* (London, 1911), p66; William C.A. Ross, *The Royal High School* (Edinburgh, 1949), pp63–76; Walter S. Dalgleish, *Memorials of the High School of Edinburgh* (Edinburgh, 1857), p37.
18. *BBR*, IX, p206
19. Dalgleish, op. cit., p37; prize lists in the *Edinburgh Evening Courant*, 21 July 1858, 26 July 1860 and 25 July 1862.
20. *BBR*, II, pp73–5

2. Out in the World, 1862–70

1. Trade cards and advertisements of Alexander Bell, 1849–50
2. George Bernard Shaw, Preface to *Pygmalion, a Professor of Phonetics* (London, 1913)
3. This was apparently not AGB's first absence

from home. He was away when the 1861 Census was taken, and his whereabouts at that precise time are not known.

4. *BBR*, II, pp73, 76-7
5. Ibid., pp68-70
6. George Bernard Shaw, *Sixteen Self Sketches* (London, 1949)
7. *London Morning Star*, 31 August 1864
8. *Elgin Courant*, 1 December 1865
9. AGB to Mrs Anna Acklone, 7 September 1916
10. *Every Saturday*, II, pp25-8 (14 July 1866)
11. AGB, Scribbler's Diary, 17 May 1867
12. Kendal parish registers. Adah Ruthven was the eldest child of George Ruthven, and bore James Murray six sons and five daughters. See also Murray's entry in *Dictionary of National Biography*.
13. Henry Bradley, 'Memoir of Sir James Murray', in *Proceedings of the British Academy*, VIII (1917-18)
14. Adam Scott to AGB, 12 October 1903
15. Adam Scott to Mabel Bell, 26 March 1918
16. See Frederick James Furnivall, *A Volume of Personal Record* (1911)
17. St Pancras, London, parish registers
18. AGB to AMB, 5 October 1868
19. Bruce, p62
20. Wigan parish registers show that she was baptised on 6 August 1847.
21. Eliza Bell to AMB, 14 November 1868
22. Adam Scott to Fred DeLand, 7 September 1926

3. Teaching the Deaf, 1870–73
1. AGB to AMB, 3 and 10 October 1870
2. AGB to AMB, 28 October 1870
3. *Silent World*, 15 June 1872
4. AGB to Sarah Fuller, 10 July 1872

4. The Musical Telegraph, 1872–74
1. Paisley parish registers show that George Coats was born on 25 June 1846, the son of Peter Coats, partner in the thread firm of J. & P. Coats.
2. Mabel Bell's manuscript notes, c1890-95
3. Mabel to her mother, Gertrude Hubbard, 19 November 1873
4. Mabel to her mother, 3 February 1874
5. AGB to AMB, 9 April 1874
6. AGB to AMB, 6 December 1873
7. Post Office Archives, London, Post 30/259C (E5153/1874)
8. AGB to parents, 8 March 1874
9. Clarence J. Blake, in *Telephone Topics*, IX, p350 (13 March 1916)
10. *American Annals of the Deaf and Dumb*, vol. 19 (1894), pp179–80

5. The Birth of the Telephone, 1874–75
1. *Report of the Eighth Annual Convention of American Instructors of the Deaf and Dumb*, 15-20 July 1874

2. See *People's Telephone, Complainants in Reply*, p121
3. AGB to parents, 23 November 1874
4. Thomas A. Watson, *Exploring Life* (New York, 1926), p55, hereafter referred to as Watson
5. The gist of these encounters with Orton was given in a letter to AMB, 22 March 1875

6. The Transmission of Speech, 1875–76
1. Gardiner Hubbard to AGB, 19 June 1875
2. AGB to parents, 30 June 1875
3. AGB *Journal*, 27 June 1875
4. AGB to parents, 30 June 1875, op. cit.
5. Mabel to Gertrude Hubbard, about 2 August 1875
6. AGB *Journal*, 4 August 1875
7. AGB to Mr and Mrs Gardiner Hubbard, 5 August 1875
8. AGB *Journal*, 6 August 1875
9. AGB to Mabel, 8 August 1875
10. AGB *Journal*, 9 August 1875
11. AGB to Mabel, 10 August 1875
12. Mabel to AGB, 15 August 1875
13. AGB *Journal*, 17 August 1875
14. AGB to Eliza Bell, 18 August 1875
15. Eliza Bell to AGB, 30 August 1875
16. AGB to AMB, 31 August 1875
17. AGB to Mr and Mrs Gardiner Hubbard, 24 August 1875
18. Gertrude Hubbard to AGB, 25 August 1875
19. AGB *Journal*, 26 August 1875
20. AGB to Mabel, 12 September 1875
21. See J.C. Dent, *Canadian Portrait Gallery* (Toronto, 1880); Alexander Mackenzie, *Life of George Brown* (Toronto, 1885)
22. AGB to George Brown, 4 October 1875
23. Gardiner Hubbard to AGB, 29 October 1875
24. AGB to Mabel, 5 November 1875
25. Mabel to Mary True, undated but written in early December 1875
26. AMB to Mabel, 6 December 1875
27. *People's Telephone*: Evidence before Swan, pp1679-81 (1883)
28. AGB to Mabel, 17 January 1876
29. Mabel to Mrs J. Penman, 30 October 1922
30. American Telephone and Telegraph Company: *The Bell Telephone* (New York, 1908), p83
31. AGB to Mabel, 7 January 1876
32. Gordon Brown to AGB, 27 February 1876
33. Mabel to AGB, undated but written on 16 February 1876
34. AGB to Mabel, 17 February 1876
35. AGB to AMB, 29 February 1876
36. Dowd case, Proofs II, pp718-19
37. Mabel to AGB, 5 March 1876
38. Mabel to AGB, 1 March 1876
39. Bernard S. Finn, 'Alexander Graham Bell's Experiments with the Variable-Resistance Transmitter', *Smithsonian Journal of History* (1966), I, p12
40. Watson, p78

41. Finn, op. cit., entry for 10 March 1876

7. Philadelphia, 1876
1. AGB, *Experiments*, Vol. 1, entry for 13 March 1876
2. AGB to Mabel, 2 April 1876
3. Ibid.
4. AMB to AGB, 16 April 1876
5. Gardiner Hubbard to AGB, 16 April 1876
6. AGB to AMB, 30 April 1876
7. *Nature*, 5 December 1878
8. AGB to Mabel, 21 June 1876
9. AGB to AMB, 27 June 1876
10. Testimony of Elisha Gray, 5 April 1879, in Proofs II, p446
11. Gertrude Hubbard to Gardiner Hubbard, 14 July 1876
12. AGB to Mabel, 16 July 1876

8. Practical Developments, 1876–77
1. AGB to Mabel, 5 August 1876
2. AGB to Mabel, 11 August 1876
3. Mabel to Eliza Bell, 11 September 1876
4. Watson, p104
5. AGB to Mabel, 6 December 1876
6. AGB to Mabel, undated but written about 23 December 1876
7. AGB to Sarah Fuller, 10 November 1876 discusses this agreement
8. AMB to AGB, 8 February 1876
9. AMB to Mabel, 13 February 1876
10. Mabel Bell, June 1922, recommending that it be kept in a safe at the Smithsonian Institution
11. *The Bell Telephone*, p168
12. *Providence Morning Star* and *Providence Journal*, both 8 May 1877
13. For Eckert's complicity in the assassination of Abraham Lincoln see my book *Allan Pinkerton* (Edinburgh, 1996), pp180–2
14. Diary of Sir William Preece, in British Telecom Archives
15. Watson, p107
16. Letters of AGB to Mabel, 17 and 19 January 1876; Mabel to AGB, 18 January 1876
17. AGB to Mabel, 6 December 1876
18. AGB to Sarah Fuller, 25 June 1877
19. Mabel to Caroline McCurdy, 3 July 1877
20. Mabel to Mrs J. Penman, 15 October 1922
21. Watson, p113
22. Gardiner Hubbard to Anthony Pollok, 4 July 1877

9. Europe, 1877–78
1. Later, Napoleon had this marriage annulled so that he could marry Jerome to Princess Catherine of Wurttemberg. Mrs Bonaparte went to Camberwell, London, where she gave birth to a son, Jerome, in 1805. He and his mother later returned to Baltimore where he died in 1847. He had no contact with his cousin Lucien with whom the Bells were on good terms in London.

2. Mabel to Gertrude Hubbard, 20 July 1877
3. Mabel to Eliza Bell, 30 July 1877
4. Mabel to Gertrude Hubbard, 4 and 10 September 1877
5. Mabel to Gertrude Hubbard, 24 September 1877
6. Mabel to Eliza Bell, 27 September 1877
7. Mabel to Gertrude Hubbard, 1 October 1877
8. Mabel to Eliza Bell, 7 July 1878
9. Mabel to AGB, 17 August 1878
10. Mabel to Gertrude Hubbard, 23 September 1877
11. Mabel to Gertrude Hubbard, 26 December 1877
12. Mabel to Gertrude Hubbard, 20 August 1877
13. E.C. Baker, *Sir William Preece: Engineer Extraordinary* (London, 1976)
14. British Telecom Archives, London, Box 71, Bell papers
15. Mabel to AGB, 27 February 1878
16. AGB, *To the Capitalists of the Electric Telephone Company*, 25 March 1878, Bell Canada, Montreal
17. Catherine MacKenzie, *Alexander Graham Bell* (Boston, 1928), p200
18. *The Times*, 26 April 1879
19. AGB to Mabel, 21 August 1878
20. Mabel to Gertrude Hubbard, 1 October 1877
21. Greenock School for the Deaf papers in Greenock public library
22. Watson, p152

10. Patent Battles, 1878–96
1. Amos Dolbear to A. Winchell, 20 March 1877
2. James Storrow to AGB, 18 May 1883
3. See entries on Elisha Gray in *Encyclopaedia Britannica* and the *Dictionary of American Biography*
4. AGB to G. Maynard, 11 March 1901

11. After the Telephone, 1878–86
1. Watson, pp173–9
2. Mabel to AGB, 20 March 1879
3. AGB to Mabel, 23 December 1891
4. AGB to W. Forbes, 29 March 1879
5. The incident was described by Eliza Bell in a letter to her husband, 5 April 1880
6. AGB to Mabel, 14 October 1889
7. Mabel's diary, 14 March 1880
8. AGB to Mabel, 26 July 1881
9. *Boston Herald*, 1 August 1881
10. AGB, *Upon the Electrical Experiments to Determine the Location of the Bullet in the Body of the Late President Garfield; and upon a Successful Form of Induction Balance for the Painless Detection of Metallic Masses in the Human Body* (Washington, 1882)
11. Mabel to AGB, 26 August 1882
12. Mabel to AGB, 22 July 1883
13. *The Times*, 27 August 1881
14. Mabel's diary, 3 February 1884
15. Mabel to AGB, 25 January 1885

16. Mabel to AGB, 22 July 1885
17. Testimony of C.S. Tainter in American graphophone v. Edison Phonograph, May 1896
18. Lab Notes, 18 November 1885

12. Washington and Beinn Bhreagh, 1887–1900
1. Charles F. Thompson, *Reminiscences* (1923)
2. *Aurora Herald*, 12 March 1889
3. Bruce, p299, quoting from notes in folder 'Washington Addresses of Alexander Graham Bell'
4. Mabel's diary, 17 September 1885
5. Mabel to Gardiner Hubbard, 5 January 1895
6. Thompson, op. cit.
7. AGB to Mabel, 5 May 1890
8. Mabel to AGB, 18 June 1888
9. Mabel to AGB, 18 May 1893
10. Mabel to AGB, 3 December 1889
11. Mabel to AGB, 28 May 1894
12. Mabel to AGB, 1 May 1895
13. AGB to Mabel, 20 May 1895
14. AGB to Mabel, 14 June 1885
15. For a complete list of his published papers see the detailed bibliography in Harold S. Osborne, 'Biographical Memoir of Alexander Graham Bell, 1847-1922' in *Biographical Memories* (National Academy of Sciences), XXIII
16. AGB to Dr Edwin A. Grosvenor, 19 February 1899, reproduced in *National Geographic Magazine*, October 1966
17. Ibid., p461
18. Mabel to AGB, 3 May 1900
19. Gilbert Grosvenor, *National Geographic Society and its Magazine* (Washington, 1957), pp32-3

13. The Deaf Shall Speak
1. Edward Gallaudet, *Report to the Board of Directors of the National College* (Washington, 1867), quoted in *Encyclopaedia Britannica*, IXth edition (1875), VII, p9
2. AGB to Gallaudet, 21 February 1887
3. AGB to Mabel, 18 March 1891
4. Report in *The Companion*, Faribault, Minnesota, 7 March 1891
5. *Greenock Advertiser*, 29 May 1882
6. Fred DeLand, *Dumb No Longer* (Washington, 1908), p149
7. AGB to Mabel, 19 October 1896
8. AGB to Mabel, March 1893
9. Helen Keller, *The Story of My Life* (New York, 1905), pp18-19
10. Quoted by Nella Braddy in *Anne Sullivan Macy* (New York, 1955), pp166-7
11. AGB to Mabel, 10 March 1892
12. Keller, p278
13. Van Wyck Brookes, *Helen Keller: Sketch for a Portrait* (New York, 1956), p32
14. Another film based on the life of Helen Keller was made in 1962 under the title *The Miracle Worker*, earning Oscars for Anne Bancroft and Patty Duke as Annie and Helen.

14. Heredity and Eugenics
1. This surname, in its various forms, seems to have been peculiar to the parish of St Andrew's and St Leonard's. Despite vague stories of an ancestor from Holland, c1730, mentioned in some standard reference works (notably the *Encyclopaedia Britannica*), the biographers of Thomas Alva Edison could not trace his ancestry further back than his great-grandfather John Edison who fled from New Jersey to Canada with the United Empire Loyalists after the War of Independence.
2. Bruce, p412
3. AGB to C. Wright, 16 May 1895. Also undated copy of formal protest headed 'Census' in Bell papers, National Geographic Society, Washington
4. AGB to Fred DeLand, 11 August 1915
5. MacKenzie, p13
6. David Fairchild, *The World Was My Garden* (New York, 1939), p288

15. Conquest of the Air
1. Thompson, *Reminiscences*
2. *McClure's Magazine*, vol. I, p39
3. *New York World*, 17 May 1896
4. Lord Kelvin to Mabel Bell, 20 April 1898
5. AGB to Mabel, 12 May 1898
6. AGB to Mabel, 9 May 1899
7. *New York World*, 2 February 1906
8. AGB to National Academy of Sciences, about January 1906. Original not traced, but quoted by AGB in his article 'Aerial Locomotion', *National Geographic Magazine*, XVIII (1907), p6
9. Mabel to Gertrude Hubbard, undated but written in 1904
10. AGB to Mabel, 2 April 1909

16. Active to the End
1. Mary Blatchford to Grace Bell, 24 September 1911
2. AGB to Gilbert Grosvenor, 2 December 1914
3. Home Notes, 16 October 1906, 11 November 1906
4. Mabel to Elsie Grosvenor, 3 April 1911
5. AGB to Mabel, 28 March 1901
6. Home Notes, 16 October 1915
7. AGB to H. Jenkins, 22 March 1916
8. MacKenzie, pp348-9
9. Mabel to Mr and Mrs Gilbert Grosvenor, 21 August 1910
10. AGB to George Sanders, 14 August 1911
11. *The Northern Scot* 27 November 1920; MacKenzie, pp357-9
12. *The Scotsman*, 1 December 1920. Royal High School magazine, *Schola Regia* (Christmas 1920), pp15-16
13. *New York World*, 19 December 1920
14. *American Magazine*, December 1921
15. J.H. Parkin, *Bell and Baldwin* (Toronto, 1964), p440

Select Bibliography

American Telephone and Telegraph Company, *The Bell Telephone* (New York, 1908)

Appleyard, Rollo, *Principles of Electric Communication* (London, 1930)

Baker, Edward C., *Sir William Preece: Engineer Extraordinary* (London, 1976)

Bell, Alexander Graham, *Beinn Bhreagh Recorder* (Baddeck, 1909–23)

────── *The Mechanics of Speech* (New York, 1916)

Bell, Alexander, *The Tongue: A Poem in Two Parts* (Edinburgh, 1846)

Bell, Alexander Melville, *Visible Speech: The Science of Universal Alphabetics* (London, 1867)

────── and Bell, David Charles, *The Standard Elocutionist* (various editions, from 1877)

Bruce, Robert V., *Alexander Graham Bell and the Conquest of Solitude* (London, 1973)

DeLand, Fred, *Dumb No Longer* (Wasington, 1908)

Fairchild, David, *The World Was My Garden* (New York, 1939)

Field, Kate, *The History of Bell's Telephone* (London, 1878)

Gray, Elisha, *Telegraphy and Telephony* (Chicago, 1878)

Grosvenor, Gilbert, *The National Geographic Society and its Magazine* (Washington, 1957)

Hitz, John D., *Alexander Melville Bell* (Washington, 1906)

Josephson, Matthew, *Edison* (New York, 1959)

MacKenzie, Catherine, *Alexander Graham Bell* (Boston, 1928)

Parkin, J.H., *Bell and Baldwin* (Toronto, 1964)

Pier, Arthur S., *Forbes: Telephone Pioneer* (New York, 1953)

Prescott, George B., *Bell's Electric Speaking Telephone* (New York, 1884)

Rhodes, Frederick L., *Beginnings of Telephony* (New York, 1919)

Simonds, William Adams, *Edison: His Life, his Work, his Genius* (London, 1935)

Waite, Helen E., *Make a Joyful Sound* (Philadelphia, 1961)

Watson, Thomas A., *Exploring Life* (New York, 1916)

Index